WATER FROM DRAGON'S WELL

MCGILL-QUEEN'S STUDIES IN THE HISTORY OF RELIGION
*Volumes in this series have been supported by the Jackman
Foundation of Toronto.*

SERIES ONE: G.A. RAWLYK, EDITOR

1 Small Differences
Irish Catholics and Irish Protestants,
1815–1922
An International Perspective
Donald Harman Akenson

2 Two Worlds
The Protestant Culture of
Nineteenth-Century Ontario
William Westfall

3 An Evangelical Mind
Nathanael Burwash and the
Methodist Tradition in Canada,
1839–1918
Marguerite Van Die

4 The Dévotes
Women and Church in
Seventeenth-Century France
Elizabeth Rapley

5 The Evangelical Century
College and Creed in English Canada
from the Great Revival to the Great
Depression
Michael Gauvreau

6 The German Peasants' War and
Anabaptist Community of Goods
James M. Stayer

7 A World Mission
Canadian Protestantism and the Quest
for a New International Order,
1918–1939
Robert Wright

8 Serving the Present Age
Revivalism, Progressivism, and
the Methodist Tradition in Canada
Phyllis D. Airhart

9 A Sensitive Independence
Canadian Methodist Women
Missionaries in Canada and the Orient,
1881–1925
Rosemary R. Gagan

10 God's Peoples
Covenant and Land in South
Africa, Israel, and Ulster
Donald Harman Akenson

11 Creed and Culture
The Place of English-Speaking Catholics
in Canadian Society, 1750–1930
*Edited by Terrence Murphy
and Gerald Stortz*

12 Piety and Nationalism
Lay Voluntary Associations and
the Creation of an Irish-Catholic
Community in Toronto, 1850–1895
Brian P. Clarke

13 Amazing Grace
Studies in Evangelicalism in Australia,
Britain, Canada, and the United States
*Edited by George Rawlyk
and Mark A. Noll*

14 Children of Peace
W. John McIntyre

15 A Solitary Pillar
Montreal's Anglican Church
and the Quiet Revolution
Joan Marshall

16 Padres in No Man's Land
Canadian Chaplains and the Great War
Duff Crerar

17 Christian Ethics and Political Economy
in North America
A Critical Analysis
P. Travis Kroeker

18 Pilgrims in Lotus Land
Conservative Protestantism in
British Columbia, 1917–1981
Robert K. Burkinshaw

19 Through Sunshine and Shadow
The Woman's Christian
Temperance Union, Evangelicalism,
and Reform in Ontario, 1874–1930
Sharon Cook

20 Church, College, and Clergy
A History of Theological
Education at Knox College,
Toronto, 1844–1994
Brian J. Fraser

21 The Lord's Dominion
The History of Canadian Methodism
Neil Semple

22 A Full-Orbed Christianity
The Protestant Churches and Social
Welfare in Canada, 1900–1940
Nancy Christie and Michael Gauvreau

23 Evangelism and Apostasy
The Evolution and Impact
of Evangelicals in Modern Mexico
Kurt Bowen

24 The Chignecto Covenanters
A Regional History of Reformed
Presbyterianism in New Brunswick
and Nova Scotia, 1827–1905
Eldon Hay

25 Methodists and Women's
Education in Ontario, 1836–1925
Johanne Selles

26 Puritanism and Historical
Controversy
William Lamont

SERIES TWO: IN MEMORY OF GEORGE RAWLYK
DONALD HARMAN AKENSON, EDITOR

1 Marguerite Bourgeoys and Montreal,
1640–1665
Patricia Simpson

2 Aspects of the Canadian
Evangelical Experience
Edited by G.A. Rawlyk

3 Infinity, Faith, and Time
Christian Humanism and
Renaissance Literature
John Spencer Hill

4 The Contribution of Presbyterianism
to the Maritime Provinces of Canada
*Edited by Charles H.H. Scobie
and G.A. Rawlyk*

5 Labour, Love, and Prayer
Female Piety in Ulster Religious
Literature, 1850–1914
Andrea Ebel Brozyna

6 The Waning of the Green
Catholics, the Irish, and Identity
in Toronto, 1887–1922
Mark G. McGowan

7 Religion and Nationality
in Western Ukraine
The Greek Catholic Church
and the Ruthenian National
Movement in Galicia, 1867–1900
John-Paul Himka

8 Good Citizens
British Missionaries and Imperial States,
1870–1918
*James G. Greenlee and
Charles M. Johnston*

9 The Theology of the Oral Torah
Revealing the Justice of God
Jacob Neusner

10 Gentle Eminence
A Life of Cardinal Flahiff
P. Wallace Platt

11 Culture, Religion, and Demographic
Behaviour
Catholics and Lutherans in Alsace,
1750–1870
Kevin McQuillan

12 Between Damnation and Starvation
Priests and Merchants
in Newfoundland Politics,
1745–1855
John P. Greene

13 Martin Luther, German Saviour
German Evangelical Theological
Factions and the Interpretation
of Luther, 1917–1933
James M. Stayer

14 Modernity and the Dilemma
of North American Anglican
Identities, 1880–1950
William H. Katerberg

15 The Methodist Church on
the Prairies, 1896–1914
George Emery

16 Christian Attitudes towards
the State of Israel
Paul Charles Merkley

17 A Social History of the Cloister
Daily Life in the Teaching
Monasteries of the Old Regime
Elizabeth Rapley

18 Households of Faith
Family, Gender, and Community
in Canada, 1760–1969
Edited by Nancy Christie

19 Blood Ground
Colonialism, Missions, and the Contest
for Christianity in the Cape Colony
and Britain, 1799–1853
Elizabeth Elbourne

20 A History of Canadian Catholics
Gallicanism, Romanism, and
Canadianism
Terence J. Fay

21 The View from Rome
Archbishop Stagni's 1915
Reports on the Ontario Bilingual
Schools Question
*Edited and translated by
John Zucchi*

22 The Founding Moment
Church, Society, and the
Construction of Trinity College
William Westfall

23 The Holocaust, Israel, and
Canadian Protestant Churches
Haim Genizi

24 Governing Charities
Church and State in Toronto's
Catholic Archdiocese, 1850–1950
Paula Maurutto

25 Anglicans and the Atlantic World
High Churchmen, Evangelicals,
and the Quebec Connection
Richard W. Vaudry

26 Evangelicals and the
Continental Divide
The Conservative Protestant Subculture
in Canada and the United States
Sam Reimer

27 Christians in a Secular World
The Canadian Experience
Kurt Bowen

28 Anatomy of a Seance
A History of Spirit Communication
in Central Canada
Stan McMullin

29 With Skilful Hand
The Story of King David
David T. Barnard

30 Faithful Intellect
Samuel S. Nelles and
Victoria University
Neil Semple

31 W. Stanford Reid
An Evangelical Calvinist
in the Academy
Donald MacLeod

32 A Long Eclipse
The Liberal Protestant
Establishment and the Canadian
University, 1920–1970
Catherine Gidney

33 Forkhill Protestants and Forkhill
Catholics, 1787–1858
Kyla Madden

34 For Canada's Sake
Public Religion, Centennial
Celebrations, and the Re-making
of Canada in the 1960s
Gary R. Miedema

35 Revival in the City
The Impact of American
Evangelists in Canada, 1884–1914
Eric R. Crouse

36 The Lord for the Body
Religion, Medicine, and
Protestant Faith Healing in
Canada, 1880–1930
James Opp

37 Six Hundred Years of Reform
Bishops and the French Church,
1190–1789
*J. Michael Hayden and
Malcolm R. Greenshields*

38 The Missionary Oblate Sisters
Vision and Mission
Rosa Bruno-Jofré

39 Religion, Family, and Community
in Victorian Canada
The Colbys of Carrollcroft
Marguerite Van Die

40 Michael Power
The Struggle to Build the Catholic
Church on the Canadian Frontier
Mark G. McGowan

41 The Catholic Origins of Quebec's
Quiet Revolution, 1931–1970
Michael Gauvreau

42 Marguerite Bourgeoys and the
Congregation of Notre Dame,
1665–1700
Patricia Simpson

43 To Heal a Fractured World
The Ethics of Responsibility
Jonathan Sacks

44 Revivalists
Marketing the Gospel in
English Canada, 1884–1957
Kevin Kee

45 The Churches and Social Order
in Nineteenth- and Twentieth-
Century Canada
*Edited by Michael Gauvreau
and Ollivier Hubert*

46 Political Ecumenism
Catholics, Jews, and Protestants in
De Gaulle's Free France, 1940–1945
Geoffrey Adams

47 From Quaker to Upper Canadian
Faith and Community among Yonge
Street Friends, 1801–1850
Robynne Rogers Healey

48 The Congrégation de Notre-Dame,
Superiors, and the Paradox of Power,
1693–1796
Colleen Gray

49 Canadian Pentecostalism
Transition and Transformation
Edited by Michael Wilkinson

50 A War with a Silver Lining
Canadian Protestant Churches
and the South African War,
1899–1902
Gordon L. Heath

51 In the Aftermath of Catastrophe
Founding Judaism, 70 to 640
Jacob Neusner

52 Imagining Holiness
Classic Hasidic Tales in Modern Times
Justin Jaron Lewis

53 Shouting, Embracing,
and Dancing with Ecstasy
The Growth of Methodism
in Newfoundland, 1774–1874
Calvin Hollett

54 Into Deep Waters
Evangelical Spirituality and
Maritime Calvinist Baptist
Ministers, 1790–1855
Daniel C. Goodwin

55 Vanguard of the New Age
The Toronto Theosophical
Society, 1891–1945
Gillian McCann

56 A Commerce of Taste
Church Architecture
in Canada, 1867–1914
Barry Magrill

57 The Big Picture
The Antigonish Movement
of Eastern Nova Scotia
Santo Dodaro and Leonard Pluta

58 My Heart's Best Wishes for You
A Biography of Archbishop
John Walsh
John P. Comiskey

59 The Covenanters in Canada
Reformed Presbyterianism
from 1820 to 2012
Eldon Hay

60 The Guardianship of Best Interests
Institutional Care for the Children
of the Poor in Halifax, 1850–1960
Renée N. Lafferty

61 In Defence of the Faith
Joaquim Marques de Araújo,
a Brazilian Comissário in the
Age of Inquisitional Decline
James E. Wadsworth

62 Contesting the Moral High Ground
Popular Moralists in
Mid-Twentieth-Century Britain
Paul T. Phillips

63 The Catholicisms of Coutances
Varieties of Religion in Early
Modern France, 1350–1789
J. Michael Hayden

64 After Evangelicalism
The Sixties and the United
Church of Canada
Kevin N. Flatt

65 The Return of Ancestral Gods
Modern Ukrainian Paganism
as an Alternative Vision
for a Nation
Mariya Lesiv

66 Transatlantic Methodists
British Wesleyanism and
the Formation of an Evangelical
Culture in Nineteenth-Century
Ontario and Quebec
Todd Webb

67 A Church with the Soul of a Nation
Making and Remaking the United
Church of Canada
Phyllis D. Airhart

68 Fighting over God
A Legal and Political History
of Religious Freedom in Canada
Janet Epp Buckingham

69 From India to Israel
Identity, Immigration, and the Struggle
for Religious Equality
Joseph Hodes

70 Becoming Holy in Early Canada
Timothy G. Pearson

71 The Cistercian Arts
From the 12th to the 21st Century
*Edited by Terryl N. Kinder
and Roberto Cassanelli*

72 The Canny Scot
Archbishop James Morrison
of Antigonish
Peter Ludlow

73 Religion and Greater Ireland
Christianity and Irish Global
Networks, 1750–1950
*Edited by Colin Barr and
Hilary M. Carey*

74 The Invisible Irish
Finding Protestants in the Nineteenth-
Century Migrations to America
Rankin Sherling

75 Beating against the Wind
Popular Opposition to Bishop Feild
and Tractarianism in Newfoundland
and Labrador, 1844–1876
Calvin Hollett

76 The Body or the Soul?
Religion and Culture in a Quebec
Parish, 1736–1901
Frank A. Abbott

77 Saving Germany
North American Protestants and
Christian Mission to West Germany,
1945–1974
James C. Enns

78 The Imperial Irish
Canada's Irish Catholics Fight
the Great War, 1914–1918
Mark G. McGowan

79 Into Silence and Servitude
How American Girls Became Nuns,
1945–1965
Brian Titley

80 Boundless Dominion
Providence, Politics, and the Early
Canadian Presbyterian Worldview
Denis McKim

81 Faithful Encounters
Authorities and American Missionaries
in the Ottoman Empire
Emrah Şahin

82 Beyond the Noise of Solemn Assemblies
The Protestant Ethic and the Quest
for Social Justice in Canada
Richard Allen

83 Not Quite Us
Anti-Catholic Thought in English
Canada since 1900
Kevin P. Anderson

84 Scandal in the Parish
Priests and Parishioners Behaving Badly
in Eighteenth-Century France
Karen E. Carter

85 Ordinary Saints
Women, Work, and Faith
in Newfoundland
Bonnie Morgan

86 Patriot and Priest
Jean-Baptiste Volfius and
the Constitutional Church in the
Côte-d'Or
Annette Chapman-Adisho

87 A.B. Simpson and the Making
of Modern Evangelicalism
Daryn Henry

88 The Uncomfortable Pew
Christianity and the New Left
in Toronto
Bruce Douville

89 Berruyer's Bible
Public Opinion and the Politics of
Enlightenment Catholicism in France
Daniel J. Watkins

90 Communities of the Soul
A Short History of Religion
in Puerto Rico
José E. Igartua

91 Callings and Consequences
The Making of Catholic Vocational
Culture in Early Modern France
Christopher J. Lane

92 Religion, Ethnonationalism,
and Antisemitism in the Era
of the Two World Wars
*Edited by Kevin P. Spicer
and Rebecca Carter-Chand*

93 Water from Dragon's Well
The History of a Korean-Canadian
Church Relationship
David Kim-Cragg

Water from Dragon's Well

The History of a Korean-Canadian Church Relationship

DAVID KIM-CRAGG

McGill-Queen's University Press
Montreal & Kingston • London • Chicago

© McGill-Queen's University Press 2022

ISBN 978-0-2280-1084-5 (cloth)
ISBN 978-0-2280-1085-2 (paper)
ISBN 978-0-2280-1302-0 (ePDF)
ISBN 978-0-2280-1303-7 (ePUB)

Legal deposit second quarter 2022
Bibliothèque nationale du Québec

Printed in Canada on acid-free paper that is 100% ancient forest free (100% post-consumer recycled), processed chlorine free

We acknowledge the support of the Canada Council for the Arts.

Nous remercions le Conseil des arts du Canada de son soutien.

Library and Archives Canada Cataloguing in Publication

Title: Water from Dragon's Well: the history of a Korean-Canadian church relationship / David Kim-Cragg.

Names: Kim-Cragg, David, author.

Series: McGill-Queen's studies in the history of religion. Series two; 93.

Description: Series statement: McGill-Queen's studies in the history of religion. Series two; 93. | Includes bibliographical references and index.

Identifiers: Canadiana (print) 20220133204 | Canadiana (ebook) 20220134758 | ISBN 9780228010845 (hardcover) | ISBN 9780228010852 (softcover) | ISBN 9780228013020 (PDF) | ISBN 9780228013037 (ePUB)

Subjects: LCSH: United Church of Canada—Missions—Korea (South) | LCSH: Missions, Canadian—Korea (South)—History. | LCSH: United Church of Canada—Relations—Korea (South) | LCSH: Christianity—Korea (South) | LCSH: Christianity and politics—Korea (South)—History—20th century. | LCSH: Koreans—Religion. | LCSH: United Church of Canada—Social aspects. | LCSH: Race relations—Religious aspects—United Church of Canada. | CSH: Korean Canadians—Religion.

Classification: LCC BV3460 .K56 2022 | DDC 266/.7925195—dc23

This book was typeset by Marquis Interscript in 10.5/13 Sabon.

I dedicate this book to my first Korean teacher, Professor Kim Kyeongjae. For his generosity, wisdom, and friendship I will always be grateful.

Contents

Acknowledgments xiii

Abbreviations xv

Introduction 3

PART ONE NATIONALIST MISSIONS AND MIGRATING
CHRISTIANS: THE BEGINNING OF A KOREAN-CANADIAN
CHURCH RELATIONSHIP, 1898 TO 1959

1 A Land in between "Our Ancestors" and "Our North-West": The
Beginning of a Korean-Canadian Church Relationship in Kando,
Manchuria, 1898 to 1942 31

2 "The Struggle to Express Their Own Identity": The Advent of the
PROK and the Emerging Identity of the Canadian Mission, 1907
to 1957 56

PART TWO DEMOCRATIZATION AND DECOLONIZATION:
HOW THE KOREAN CHURCH CHANGED THE UCC KOREA
MISSION AND TRANSFORMED THE LIVES OF CANADIAN
MISSIONARIES, 1960 TO 1979

3 Sinners, Partners, or Friends: Discursive Tensions on the Korean
Mission Field in the 1950s and 1960s 83

4 "Taking Hold of Its Own Domain": The Ending of the UCC
Mission Enterprise in Korea, 1970 to 1974 104

xii Contents

5 Minjung in the Mission House: A New Articulation of Mission from within the Shell of the Canadian Mission, 1970s and 1980s   128

6 "A Tremendous Source of Strength and Witness": The Gendered Third Space and the South Korean Democratization Movement, 1976   154

PART THREE   MISSION FROM THE EAST: KOREAN CHRISTIANS ENGAGE CANADIAN SOCIETY AND THE UNITED CHURCH OF CANADA, 1965 TO 1998

7 Seonguja: Pioneering Korean Christians in the United Church of Canada Wilderness, 1965 to 1988   179

8 "Struggling to Understand Ourselves as 'Receivers' as Well as 'Givers'": The United Church of Canada Responds to Korean Christians, 1976 to 1998   208

Conclusion   233

Notes   241

Index   291

Acknowledgments

The river of this book had many tributaries. I am especially grateful to Kyung Jae Kim, my first Korean professor. Rev. Dr Hyung Mook Choi has also been my teacher and has introduced me to many wonderful Korean scholars of the South Korean Democracy Movement. St Andrew's College in Saskatoon was the channel through which I was able to re-enter academic studies, and a springboard for the studies that led to this book. I would like to thank modern Korea scholars Namhee Lee, Paul Y. Chang, Andre Schmid, Sung-Deuk Oak, and Charles Kim for their generous help, time, and advice. Archivists, Sanghun Cho (UCLA Archival Collection on Democracy and Unification in Korea, Elizabeth Mathew (United Church Archives, Toronto) and Julia Chun (Cheng Yu Tung East Asian Library) were exceedingly friendly and considerate. Those who agreed to be interviewed by me for this dissertation are owed a special thanks. A special thanks, too, to Rev. Jung Hae-bin and the congregation of Alpha Korean United Church, whose spiritual support and enthusiastic endorsement have made all the difference. The Alumni of Hanshin University in Canada have generously encouraged me, especially my friends the Rev. Mun Eun-seong for his moral support, and Rev. Dr Kim Yun-jeong for her help in the library. I would like to thank the UCC missionaries who spoke with me about their experiences in Korea, particularly Marion Pope and Mary Collins. Thanks is owed to the family of Willa Kernen, especially her sister Jewel Reid who met and shared with me some things from Willa's time in Korea. A big thank you also goes to Elsie Livingston who shared pictures of her Victory Shawl. This work was mentored by professors Keith Carlson and Mirela David, my PhD co-supervisors. I am deeply appreciative of the entire history department of the University of Saskatchewan for creating a vibrant and supportive environment for scholarship. The history I have presented here would not have been possible without the help of all those mentioned above and more besides. All mistakes and shortcomings of this work, however, are mine and mine alone.

Abbreviations

BOM	Board of Overseas Missions of the United Church of Canada
BWM	Board of World Mission of the United Church of Canada
DMC	Division of Mission in Canada of the United Church of Canada
DWO	Division of World Outreach of the United Church of Canada
EMC	Ethnic Ministries Council of the United Church of Canada
KCIA	Korean Central Intelligence Agency
MEC	Mission and Education Centre of the Presbyterian Church in the Republic of Korea
PCK	Presbyterian Church in Korea
PROK	Presbyterian Church in the Republic of Korea
PRP	People's Revolutionary Party [a fabricated entity used by the Park Chung Hee regime to accuse and intimidate political dissidents]
TKUC	Toronto Korean United Church
UCC	United Church of Canada
UCW	United Church Women
UIM	Urban Industrial Mission
USAMGIK	United States Army Military Government in Korea
WCC	World Council of Churches
WMS	Woman's Missionary Society of the United Church of Canada
YWCA	Young Women's Christian Association

Yun Dongju (top right) and Moon Ik Hwan (top centre) were both students at the Eunjin Middle School run by Canadian missionaries in Yongjeong, a city in the Kando district of Manchuria whose name means Dragon's Well. Yun Dongju became a celebrated poet of the Korean Independence Movement. Moon Ik Hwan became a central figure in the South Korean Democratization Movement. Both were strongly influenced by the Korean Protestant Christianity that they encountered growing up. Used with the permission of the Moon Ik Hwan Memorial Foundation.

Moon Chai Rin and Kim Shin Mook, moved with their families to Kando, Manchuria, under the guidance of Silhak leader Kim Yakyeon. Their childhood memories of Kando, their commitment to their Christian faith, and their involvement in movements for Korean independence have given them a unique perspective on Korean events and the history of the Korean church. Used with the permission of the Moon Ik Hwan Memorial Foundation.

Canadian missionary William Scott (centre) served in Korea for five decades. An individual of considerable academic skill, he taught in seminary, translated Bible commentaries into Korean, and completed his career by compiling a detailed history of the Canadian mission to Korea. Here he is pictured with Yongjeong community leader Kim Yakyeon (right) and Rev. Yi Tae-jun (left), circa 1941. From the author's collection.

The church at Myeongdong, the village established by Kim Yakyeon and his followers, circa early 1900s. Moon Chai Rin and Kim Shin Mook were introduced to Christianity and baptized in Myeongdong, and attended this church and the Christian school connected to it. Myeongdong was a centre for expats in the Korean independence movement. Used with the permission of the Kim Ik Hwan Memorial Foundation.

Kim Yakyeon (front row, second from the left) is pictured here in traditional white Korean garb and black glasses. Canadian missionary George Bruce (front row, far right) was the principal of Eunjin School run by the UCC Korea Mission. Behind Bruce (back row, far right) is Kim Chai Choon, who taught at Eunjin for a year before serving as an early faculty member of Joseon Seminary. From the author's collection.

The Canadian Mission Compound in Yongjeong (Dragon's Well). A flagpole can be discerned in the centre of the frame. The Union Jack was hoisted here during the 1 March (3.1) Independence Movement of 1919 to signal British protection and ward off Japanese soldiers looking to retaliate against demonstrators. Dr Florence Murray reports that eventually the city of Yongjeong grew up around the compound, an urban hub where British and Japanese consulates were located and where Japanese schools and hospitals competed with similar facilities run by Western missionaries. Four large missionary residences can be seen on the top of the hill. Used with the permission of the United Church of Canada Archives (UCCA, 2000.017P/5654N, Foreign Missions Photograph Collection).

Eunjin School in Yongjeong, Kando, Manchuria, circa 1930. Korean independence poet Yun Dongju, along with Minjung theologians Moon Ik Hwan, Moon Dong Hwan, and Ahn Byung Mu, attended this mission school run by the United Church of Canada. The founder of the Presbyterian Church in the Republic of Korea, Kim Chai Choon, taught here. Rt Rev. Sang Chul Lee and many of his congregants at Toronto Korean United Church were likewise connected with the school. From the author's collection.

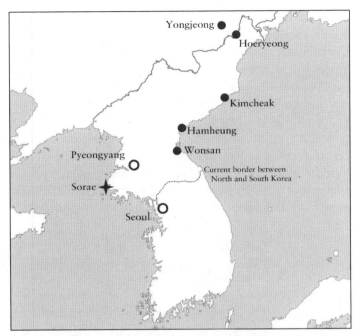

Map of Canadian Mission Stations in Korea and Kando, Manchuria. Base map provided by https://www.freeworldmaps.net/island/korean-peninsula, and modified by the author.

Principal George Bruce addressing a graduation assembly at the Eunjin mission school (circa 1936–37). Kim Yakyeon wearing traditional Korean clothing seated at the right of the picture. Eunjin (은진/恩眞) means grace and truth. Used with the permission of the United Church of Canada Archives (UCCA, 2000.017p/5655, Foreign Missions Photograph Collection.)

The inauguration of the Korean Presbyterian church in the city of Pyeongyang circa 1907. Used with the permission of the United Church of Canada Archives (UCCA, 2000.017p/4857, Foreign Missions Photograph Collection.)

Kim Chai Choon delivers a sermon following the creation of Presbyterian Church in the Republic of Korea (prok). The congregation cannot be contained in the church building but spills out onto the churchyard and street. Kim's pulpit is on the threshold of the church entrance, a fitting symbol for the beginning of a church that would be equally engaged with spiritual matters and social/political realities. Used with the permission of the Kim Chai Choon Memorial Foundation.

Unidentified man strolling on the new Hanguk Theological Seminary campus, circa 1950s. The United Church of Canada contributed $100,000 to the construction of the main seminary building pictured in the background. Kim Chai Choon would praise the Canadian church for this contribution that was made with "no string attached," leaving the Korean faculty free to teach the theology that made most sense for them. Used with the permission of the Kim Chai Choon Memorial Foundation.

Wilna Thomas pays a visit to Saekwan high school on her visit to Korea as the UCC's first woman in the role of executive secretary of overseas missions, circa 1961. Thomas' view of Korea was coloured by her Canadian upbringing and also by her time serving as a missionary in Japan with a colonial bias. But her notes from her travels around the world demonstrate a high level of openness to and engagement with the people she met. Used with the permission of the United Church of Canada Archives (UCCA, 2000.017p/4570, Foreign Missions Photograph Collection.)

Missionary doctor Florence Murray unloads relief supplies from an army jeep, circa 1950s. Murray was among the first Canadian missionaries to return to Korea following the Pacific War and Korean War. The missionaries' close association with the American and Canadian military in Korea gave them particular influence in Korean society. This influence rubbed off on the Korean church. From the author's collection.

Seodaemun house, circa 2015. This palatial missionary home was built by Canadian missionary doctor T.D. Mansfield, who had a reputation for building large houses, in 1921. When this house was turned over to the Presbyterian Church in the Republic of Korea, its living room had enough space to comfortably seat eighty students. The house serves to this day as the Mission and Education Centre, a storied institution with roots in the South Korean Democratization Movement. Photograph taken by the author.

Willa Kernen with unnamed Methodist minister, circa 1970s. Gendered spaces where women could safely interact were an important dynamic in the history of Korean Christianity. But during the South Korean Democratization Movement, it was the Western missionary women who found themselves most transformed by this space. Used with the permission of the United Church of Canada Archives (UCCA, 2008.011p/8999n, United Church of Canada. Division of Communication, Berkeley Studio, Wolf Kutnahorsky, 1983.)

Lee Oo Chung was the leader of South Korea's second wave feminist movement and an important contributor to the Christian wing of the South Korean Democratization Movement. Her engagement with women missionaries such as Willa Kernen, Marion Current, and Marion Pope both strengthened her contribution to these movements and transformed the lives of her Canadian friends. Used with the permission of the United Church of Canada Archives (UCCA, 2008.011p/8991n–8992n, United Church of Canada. Division of Communication, Berkeley Studio, Wolf Kutnahorsky, 1983.)

Sang Chul Lee with Songsuk Chong and other university students in Korea, 1961. Lee made many important relationships while ministering in Korea, relationships that continued with many who, like Lee, immigrated to Canada. From the author's collection.

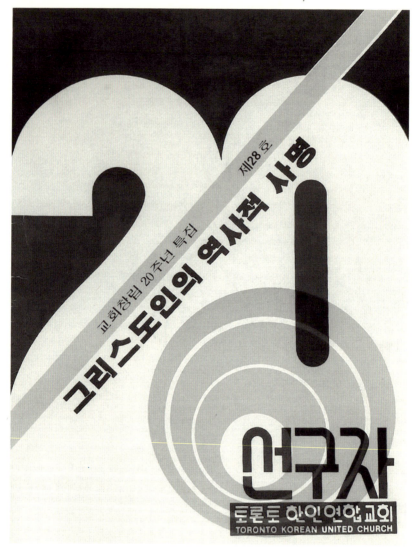

Front page of the twentieth anniversary edition of Seonguja magazine. Artist Kye Kim provided the beautiful artwork for the cover of this magazine for the duration of its publication. The magazine is a treasure trove of Korean immigrant experiences and reflections. Shared with the permission of the Alpha Korean United Church.

Victory Shawl with its owner Elsie Livingston. The shawl, and the story behind it, taught Livingston about how to conduct effective social justice campaigns. Korean women martialed intercultural symbolism to connect their plight to the lives of women around the world. The "V"-shaped pattern, the purple colour, and the four crocheted stitches were imbued with symbolism for the recovery of democracy in South Korea. Used with the permission of Elsie Livingston.

Gravestone of Beulah Bournes, whose service as a UCC missionary to Korea spanned the pre- and post-division history of the peninsula and the UCC Korea Mission. Like other missionaries to Korea, such was her connection to the land and the people that Bournes chose to be buried in the place where she had lived and worked. Her grave lies in the missionary cemetery in Seoul. Many Canadian missionary graves remain in North Korea. Photograph taken by the author.

Gravestone of the Rt Rev. Sang Chul Lee in York Cemetery, section 11, lot 487. Lee reflected on the meaning of burial in Canada with his congregation of Korean immigrants during his ministry at TKUC. For him, the burial of Koreans in Canada symbolized the growth of new roots in a new home. Photograph taken by the author.

WATER FROM DRAGON'S WELL

Introduction

Skirting the foot of a mountain on the edge of a field I go alone to find
a forsaken well and quietly bow to peer in.
In the water the moon is bright and the clouds drift and heaven opens
and a fresh wind blows it is autumn.
And a young man is there.
Somehow I begin to resent that young man and turn to leave.
Having turned away I pause and begin to pity that young man.
I return to where I was and bow to look in and the young man is there
as before.
Again I begin to resent that young man and leave.
Having turned to leave I pause and begin to miss that young man.
In the well the moon is bright and the clouds drift and heaven opens and
a fresh wind blows it is autumn and like a cherished memory that young
man is there.

September 1939
"Self-Portrait," Yun Dongju[1]

The poem "Self-Portrait" by Korean resistance poet Yun Dongju is
a lament for the Korean nation. Though coloured by personal and
national feelings of shame regarding Japan's occupation of Korea,
the poem is nonetheless forgivingly framed against the clear heavens
and hopefully inspired by a fresh autumn wind that breathes new
hope into the dream of a Korea that will once again be free. Yun
attended Eun-jin Boys Middle School, founded by Canadian missionaries in 1912 and run with their support until 1942.[2] The school was
located adjacent to the Canadian Mission compound on a hill in the
city of Yongjeong, Manchuria, a name that means "Dragon's Well."[3]
It is likely that this hill and this well was in Yun's mind when he

composed "Self-Portrait." Though the poem is constructed as a comment on the state of his country, the close association of Yun's life with the Canadian mission in Yongjeong allows it also to serve as an apt comment on the Canadian Missionary Enterprise. Canadian missionaries, like Yun, were sometimes helpless witnesses to and sometimes active participants in the East Asian history of conquest, revolution, and resistance. Some memories cause shame. Others affirm something lovely, an enduring relationship marked by sincerity and resilience. Peering into the bottom of distant Dragon's Well, the image of that encounter between Korean and Canadian Christians is still reflected in the deep waters of the relationship that was formed there.

The people Canadian missionaries associated with and the history they participated in through their Korea mission changed them, changed their church in Canada, and continues to shape that church in some surprising ways. Like Yun staring at this reflection in the water in Dragon's Well, this present study seeks to decern the identity of the Canadian church as it developed through an encounter with the Christians of Korea. In 1996, Young-Sik Yoo published a dissertation entitled "The Impact of Canadian Missionaries in Korea: A Historical Survey of Early Canadian Mission Work, 1888–1898," one of the first scholarly efforts assessing the significance of the work of Canadian missionaries in Korea.[4] The present volume turns the tables and aims to be the first sustained study of the impact of Koreans on the Canadian missionaries and the Canadian church that supported them.

In *Saving China,* mission historian Alvyn Austin asserted that "there are many areas of the missionary movement that need further research on both sides of the Pacific."[5] Thankfully, two relatively recent publications, one from each side of the Pacific divide, have made available the firsthand accounts of the earliest missions in Korea: Kim Shin Mook and Moon Chai Rin's memories *Giringabiwa Gomannye-ui Kkum (The Dream of Giraffe and No More Daughters)*[6] published in 2006 and Grieg McMillan's revised and expanded publication of missionary William Scott's *Canadians in Korea*[7] published in 2009. The present book depends a great deal on these two sources and is an attempt to bring them into closer conversation.

A sense of urgency motivated the writing of this history. Partly this derived from the fact that the number of eyewitnesses to some of the most compelling events of Canada's mission history in Korea is quickly dwindling and an effort is needed to preserve their stories. A feeling of urgency also came from the fact that most people in Canada, even those with a strong connection to Christian congregations, do not know very much about Canada's Missionary Enterprise, much less what resulted from that enterprise after Canadian missionaries removed from the mission fields. If they think of it at all, they likely imagine that the end of the Missionary Enterprise was a voluntary withdrawal on the part of the church, self-enlightened by its own reflections, experiences, and evolving theology. It is possible they may conversely be aware of anger on the part of Indigenous peoples (in Canada and abroad) that erupted in a demand for the end of missions in the period following the Second World War and forced the church to bring the Mission Enterprise to an end. But is it very unlikely that they would think of a relationship that was painstakingly negotiated by different parties in conversation with one another, in a variety of places and over the course of many decades.

Unaware of the ongoing historical nature of the trans-national and intercultural relationships initiated by the Missionary Enterprise, many in postcolonial Canada assume that there is nothing other to take away from past missionary engagements than a feeling of guilt, shame, and/or injury. The great tragedy is that though painful mistakes were made, and difficult lessons learned, as this story of the Korean-Canadian church relationship has shown, there are also examples of tremendous shared accomplishments that might serve as helpful clues for solving contemporary social problems in a multi-cultural and postcolonial society. This includes lessons for the troubled relationship in Canada between the Canadian state, churches, and Indigenous peoples.

This is a book about a transformative relationship between people of very different geographic origins, cultures, and histories. What bound them together was a religion and a historical context. These realities were very much intertwined. Both groups were passionate adherents to the Protestant Christian faith and both lived in an age of migration and of nation building. Special attention in this work is given to the engagement of Korean Christians with Canadian missionaries and on their impact on those missionaries, their mission institutions in Korea and their church in Canada. It is a story that begins at the end of the nineteenth century in Manchuria and northeastern Korea and follows the migration of Koreans Protestants associated with Canadian missions in those places down across the thirty-eighth parallel following the Pacific War and then over the Pacific Ocean to Canada starting in the late 1960s. The bonds forged between individuals and church institutions were resilient and had a demonstrable (and often laudable) impact upon Korean history, a fact of which most Canadians are unaware. But perhaps even more surprising to readers of this book will be the fact that the relationship also had an impact on Canada and particularly upon the institutions and culture of its largest Protestant church. White Canadians have learned to think of themselves as acting on other people rather than the other way around. While the contributions of Canadian missionaries to Korea's dramatic modern history have been recorded and recounted in other places and in various ways, this book will endeavour to tell the story about the effect of Korea Christians upon Canada's religious culture and institutions through the United Church of Canada (ucc) with which many of the first Korean immigrants were associated and within which an important minority group still resides.

At this point we should mention what will not be covered in this book. In a book about Canadian missionary history in Korea, one might expect to find a treatment of such famous (in Korea) missionaries as James Scarth Gale (1863–1937), Frank Schofield (1889–1970) and Oliver R. Avison (1860–1959). Gale was a remarkable scholar who mastered the Korean language and compiled a seminal Korean-English dictionary. He helped translate the Bible and a number of Western literary works into Korean and also translated important Korean works into English.[8] Schofield was a veterinarian who participated in the March 1 (3.1) Independence Movement of 1919. He was reputed the (unofficial) thirty-fourth signatory of the Declaration of Independence and is buried in the Patriots Section of the National Cemetery of South Korea, a unique honour for a non-Korean.[9] A statue of him was erected in the Toronto Zoo by the Korean community in Canada. Avison was personal physician to the Korean King. He started Severance Hospital in Seoul and the medical school that gave birth to Yonsei University. Severance Hospital and Yonsei University became very important institutions in Korea and remain so to this day.[10] The main reason these three remarkable individuals are not covered here is that they were not closely associated with the Canadian mission stations in Korea. Both Gale and Avison were largely supported by American churches. Schofield and Avison worked out of Seoul, far from the Canadian Mission centres in the northeast of the peninsula and Manchuria. Gale spent much of his time in Wonsan, the southernmost limit of Canadian mission territory but was not greatly involved in that mission. I have chosen to focus on the Canadian Mission and the Koreans associated with it because this was where institutional and national identities were most evidently worked out between Koreans and Canadians, a major interest of this study.

A big part of this book is about the UCC Korea Mission and the Koreans associated with it. However, the relationship between Korean and Canadian Christians both preceded and outlasted the Canadian Mission in Korea and continues to impact the Canadian church and society today. When the first Canadian missionaries were sent by congregations in Canada to Korea it was at the request of Korean Christians. They arrived to find a church already established and growing without missionary help. The Koreans who in fact invited them and welcomed them into their lives took the first step in creating a strong bond between Korea and Canada that would last for more than a century. While marked by real warmth and deep mutual respect it was also a relationship fraught with tension. At the heart of this tension were juxtaposed experiences of and attitudes towards colonialism and nation building and the relationship of these to the Christian faith. That tension is one of the central axes around which this study revolves.

The beginning of Canada's first modern missionary undertakings coincides with the birth of Canada. The first modern Canadian missionary of renown, John Geddie, left Nova Scotia in 1846 for New Hebrides (present-day Vanuatu)[11] just five years after the united province of Canada was formed. Canadian Protestants were committed to the creation of a Canada in their own (Anglo Protestant) image even as they were committed to converting people around the world to their version of the Christian faith. Some of them were fanatical. The Orange Lodge in Canada, for example – the political base of politician and Confederation father George Brown – were violently opposed to religious and cultural difference within Canada. When the French-speaking Catholic Métis of Manitoba forced the newly minted Canadian government to acknowledge their rights within Canada, hundreds of Orange Lodge members volunteered to be part of the militia that was sent to Manitoba in a shameful effort to violently eliminate those rights.[12] Not all Canadian Protestants were as brutal or closed minded as the Orange Lodge. Indeed, some sought to contribute to building Canada through understanding and partnership. Missionaries such as the Reverend George MacDougall, who played a key role in the negotiation of numbered treaties 6 and 7 in the Canadian West,[13] is an example of those who worked to bridge the cultural divide between Indigenous communities and build the foundation of Canada's future on the tradition of mutual agreement and good faith.[14] But even though these might be deemed respectful and constructive contributions, the Protestant religion they espoused was nevertheless indelibly stained with systemic bias. The desire to help in the construction of a nation (as well as competition with Catholics for Indigenous souls) led Canadian Protestant churches to participate in the sadly misguided and criminally culpable project of establishing and running Indian residential schools.[15] Temperance activists, social gospelers, and suffragettes, people such as Nellie McClung and J.S. Woodsworth, saw Anglo-Protestant values as the uniquely legitimate guiding ethical force behind Canada as a nation. When the UCC was constituted by an act of parliament in 1925, many of its founders envisioned the church as the "soul of the nation," offering a strong Anglo-Protestant counterbalance to a "national" French Catholic church in Quebec.[16] Protestants in Canada understood their religion to be the cultural and spiritual foundation of the country, almost always to the exclusion of other religious and spiritual perspectives.

The Koreans who received Canadian missionaries into their country likely had little knowledge of the specific activities of Canadian missionaries in other parts of the world or of the Canadian Protestant church's role in the colonization of Canada, but they were not unaware of attitudes that clearly conflicted with their own anti-colonial aspirations. Christianity was a mixed bag for Koreans. Many found the missionaries who promoted it a welcome support in a time when their country was isolated and their national pride crushed by Japan's Machiavellian annexation of their homeland. The missionaries did not look like or speak like the Japanese and were not explicitly aligned with the Japanese Empire and so offered a modicum of emotional and political refuge. Many missionaries, Canadians notable among them, were appalled by Japanese injustices and supported Korean protests and demands for more freedom. And yet at the same time it was clear to Koreans that very few missionaries were able and willing to offer unconditional support for their aspirations of national independence. Many, indeed, harboured feelings of admiration for a colonial Japanese government that they viewed as more desirable than and superior to Indigenous Korean rule. Western attitudes of cultural superiority and their overbearing material culture marked by cars, huge houses, and Korean servants were also troubling to Koreans – as was their autocratic approach to mission institutions and their oppressive wielding of spiritual authority. The relative success of the communist

Introduction

compared to the Christian movement beginning in the 1920s was a sign of Korean unhappiness with the missionaries. Most of the time, tensions between Korean Christians and the Canadian missionaries they worked with simmered beneath the surface but from time-to-time disagreements would erupt publicly and even result in violence.

As the Japanese invasion of China picked up steam and the Pacific War erupted, tensions with missionaries took a back seat to the much more pressing issues of war and survival. In 1941 the Japanese Imperial government sent Western missionaries packing, the last Canadian missionaries to leave were exchanged for Japanese nationals in a swap off the coast of Africa in 1942. With the end of the war and the division of Korea, Canadian missionaries were permitted to return to South Korea where they met thousands of refugees from their former mission field in the northeast of the peninsula. But the existential threat to Korean society remained utmost on everybody's mind as the Korean War broke out and Missionary and Korean Christian alike were forced to scramble to find safety and then to begin to rebuild their lives out of the ashes. Korean Christians had not been inactive, however. In addition to valiant efforts to support one another through these periods of crisis, danger, and depravation, some began to assert their independence from missionary institutions and ideas even as they struggled to take stock of the divided political reality of their nation. Meanwhile, back in Canada the UCC and other church denominations were enjoying a heyday of growth and influence in Canadian society. But cracks were beginning to show in Canadian Protestant assumptions about the centrality of their religion for Canada as a whole.

By the 1960s, the underpinnings of the UCC vision of itself as the soul of the Canadian nation were being thoroughly shaken. Anticolonial movements around the world were displacing Western colonial governments and making way for new religious and cultural perspectives. This was the case in South Korea where the Democratization Movement was starting to push back against insidious neocolonial forces. In 1965, the Pearson government introduced the point system for immigration, which opened the door to thousands of new (non-White) migrants, including Koreans. These new immigrants did not share a belief in the superiority of Anglo Protestant values and spirituality and did not feel compelled to conform. At the same time, Black and Indigenous voices across North American were beginning to make themselves heard regarding the injustices of racism and the legacy of colonialism in Canada and the US.

From Canada, the Korean diaspora kept a close eye on events in South Korea and the struggle for democracy in which their friends and family were deeply embroiled. As Koreans struggled against American hegemony embodied in their authoritarian president, the Presbyterian Church in the Republic of Korea (PROK) was at logger-heads with the UCC and its missionaries over an approach to overseas church work that they regarded as demeaning and oppressive. They confronted the UCC over its unilateral approach to decisions concerning their church. They negotiated the end of the UCC Korea Mission as such and the transfer of all UCC property to the PROK. They further developed a new Korean theology and urged Western Christians to join them in calling for an end to Western support of Korean dictators. At the same time, the Korean Christian diaspora in Canada found itself struggling with Anglo congregations and church structures stuck in a colonial paradigm of missions and failing to acknowledge the unique experiences and gifts Koreans brought to the Canadian church context – experiences and gifts that were in fact transforming the UCC despite itself.

A PERSONAL JOURNEY

As a White Anglo Canadian, I was first drawn to the story of the Korean-Canadian church relationship thanks to a period of study in South Korea. In 1997, I was sent as an exchange student from Emmanuel College of Victoria University in the University of Toronto to Hanshin Theological Seminary of Hanshin University in Seoul, South Korea (previously Joseon Theological College, and Hanguk Theological College). I was on hand the next year when the UCC and the PROK celebrated one hundred years since the establishment of a Canadian mission in Korea. When I first arrived in Korea, I was taken by stories I learned from Koreans about Canadian missionaries, particularly their role in the South Korean Democratization Movement. South Korea had only one decade earlier reinstituted democratic elections. The memories of the sacrifices that led to the replacement of the military government with a civilian one were still fresh, and the prospect of reunification with the north was being recharged with hope thanks to the election of former democratization activist Kim Dae Jung. Support that Korean Christian activists had received from some of the Canadian missionaries was still fresh on people's mind and it was remembered gratefully. The stories I heard at that time

Introduction

were stories I had not heard before despite my close association with the UCC since birth. I wondered why I had not been aware of these things in Canada. After all, the stories were overwhelmingly positive and I could think of no reason why they were not being shouted from the rooftops back home. In fact, despite a long and very involved history of missions in Korea, little if anything was being spoken about it in the congregations back home.

In time I came to know Canadian missionaries who had worked in Korea and began to fill out the picture some more. Though I longed to know more about their experiences during the Democratization Movement, I found little willingness to talk about themselves but rather an insistence that I learn more about the Koreans who had led the movement. The missionaries often emphasized how they had learned not to impose their own cultural perspectives but to appreciate the ways of Koreans, for whom they had enormous respect – especially given the acts of courage and sacrifice they had witnessed during the recent struggle for democracy. Failing to appreciate these experiences, I found myself feeling somewhat bewildered by what seemed to me an exaggerated posture of humility and attitude of deference. I was not unaware of criticism of criticism missionaries back in Canada, that their activities abroad were examples of cultural chauvinism from which the church wanted to distance itself. And I also learned, though Koreans were not quick to share such stories, that the relationship with Canadian missionaries had not always been easy. But the commonly held and readily shared story in Korea was overwhelmingly positive, and I was anxious to hear more about it.

Upon returning to Canada my circle of Korean friends expanded, and I began to see how hard many of them were working to make a go of life in Canada. Most of those I befriended worked in the church, as I did. I could see the efforts they were making to fit in and I would hear stories about their struggles to be accepted and, in moments of unguarded openness, also about their experiences of racism. I began to wonder what had brought them to Canada and why they seemed so committed to contributing something to the Canadian church despite the hard work and painful experiences. Slowly, I began to see the history of the Canadian mission to Korea in a new and complicated light. When I re-entered university in a bid to further deepen my understanding of the history of the Korean-Canadian church relationship, more tools became available to help me get at this history and I was further encouraged to explore things from a different point of view. How to put the different pieces of this puzzle together? How could I reconcile the praise for missionaries and the Canadian church I had heard from Koreans on the one hand and the silence about this history in Canada on the other? Why were stories of incredible drama and sacrifice not better known in Canadian church circles? And how could I reconcile this history with the experiences of Koreans in Canada who were struggling to fit into the Canadian church?

TELLING THE STORY IN A NEW WAY

My own personal journey reflects some of the ways the story about missions has been told in academia and Canadian society more broadly and how that story has changed over time. At the height of the Missionary Enterprise most of what was written about non-Western churches and peoples focused on missionaries and their accomplishments. For example, the first history of the beginning of the Canadian mission to Korea, *A Corn of Wheat* written by Elizabeth McCully in 1903, provided an account of one of the first Canadian missionaries to travel to Korea.[17] Written by another Canadian missionary, this hagiography emphasized the sacrifices of the missionary and their successes in bringing Koreans to Christ. This approach was replicated in church publications and distributed widely in Canada among Anglo-Protestant churchgoers. Such stories came not only from Korea but from many other places around the globe as well as from missions in Canada to Indigenous people, and new non-Anglo-Saxon immigrants. These stories served, among other things, to reinforce the notion that Canadian Protestants were contributing to the enlightenment and civilization of inferior peoples and cultures everywhere. Among the different places that were covered by these publications China garnered the most attention, but there were also many stories of missions in India, Japan, Africa, and the West Indies as well as the South Pacific in addition to the missions at home. The Missionary Enterprise in Canada reached its peak size in the 1930s.[18] But by then some contradictions in the movement were already starting to raise doubts about the viability of the enterprise. In North America the debate between a more liberal approach to biblical interpretation and a fundamentalist one was beginning to create a rift in the Protestant churches and among the missionaries they sent to work overseas. At the same time, people around the world were responding to the Wilsonian call for self-determination and beginning to reject missionaries as agents of colonialism. In Korea for example, the 1920s and 1930s saw many abandon the church in favour of the communist movement which they saw at the time as better able to deliver on their political aspirations.

The Second World War interrupted Western Protestant missions around the globe. When missionaries returned to their fields it was in smaller numbers and facing very different political conditions. Led by India and China, many former colonies and victims of Western exploitation were beginning to throw off their oppressors as well as the missionaries connected to them. In 1950, encouraged by political tensions associated with the Korean War, communist China expelled most of the missionaries in the country, rejecting what they saw as their religious agenda of cultural imperialism. By the 1960s, missionaries were being asked to leave Africa as well and their welcome in many other places including Korea was also under debate. In Canada, the attitude towards missionaries was changing quickly. Once regarded as heroes of the faith and champions of civilization they were now being silently and swiftly discarded as an embarrassment.[19] This was particularly true of missionaries working in Canada among Indigenous people. Residential schools had been recognized as a failure and were on the out. In 1984, Canadian historian John Webster Grant summed up the change in the attitude towards missionaries by saying that instead of Indigenous people it was now the missionary who needs to be explained.[20]

At the time attitudes towards missionaries were shifting, the Canadian Protestant church itself was undergoing a tremendous change. This change has been characterized by religious historians as "a catastrophic exodus" from institutional religion[21] and described as a "sudden," "broad based," "massive in scale," and "seismic"[22] event for the religious character of Canada. Post-1960s, the new social reality of Canada forced the Protestant Church, which had once been a dominant player in Canadian politics and culture, to accept its marginal place as one religion among many within an increasingly secular and multicultural Canada. It also occasioned the search for new heroes.[23] The UCC was forced to abandon its dream to be Canada's national soul along with its missionary ideals.

With this shift in the culture, stories about missionaries and their exploits in Canada and overseas began to focus on the negative implications of missions for non-Western nations and peoples. This "negative" approach was spearheaded by American literary critic Edward Said who offered one of the earliest and most influential postcolonial critiques of the missionary enterprise. Said argued that Christian mission societies, who sought to "save" the Orient, essentially contributed to a discourse that championed the expansion of Europe.[24] He also elevated the notion of "cultural imperialism" in the discussion of missionary collusion with imperialist agendas.[25] Though Canadian academics did not spend much time examining the history of Canadian missions in this light, many in the UK and US were focussed on how the missionary enterprise helped create the conditions whereby the domination of non-Europeans was justified, the humanity of the colonized was concealed and differences that existed across colonized cultures were masked. Canadian Mission historian Ruth Compton Brouwer has noted that scholars working in this vein felt embarrassment for even talking about missionaries lest they should appear to be an apologist for their activities. She found a "widespread assumption" that missionaries were "men and women incapable of change, too rigid or obtuse to learn from new circumstances."[26]

The irony here is that by the 1960s many missionaries had effectively absorbed the criticism of indigenous Christians overseas with whom they worked and were actually on the leading edge of this attitudinal change. What is more, they were qualified from years of close work with non-Westerners to offer guidance to the rest of the Canadian church and society as it began to navigate its way into a new postcolonial context. In her essay entitled "When Missions Became Development" (2010), Compton Brouwer alludes to this irony when she asserts that while overseas missionaries had changed, the attitude in Canada was such that their postcolonial insights had little impact on the culture of the churches that had supported their mission.[27] This observation is backed up by one church leader who, commenting in 1971, complained that the understanding of UCC parishioners regarding the church's missions overseas belonged in the nineteenth century.[28] Missionaries were among the first Canadians to understand postcolonial change because they were the ones who had been confronted most forcefully and consistently with the increasingly critical views of indigenous Christians at home and abroad. But just at a time when their expertise was most needed their influence and standing with the church at home was diminishing dramatically.

To the degree that missionary experiences were not communicated to churches in Canada, immigrants from these mission fields who landed in Canada were faced with the necessity of rearticulating their objections to Western colonial attitudes within the Canadian church.

Canadian religious scholar Greer Anne Wenh-In Ng shows that their efforts made a difference to the church in Canada just as they had made a difference in changing missionary attitudes overseas.[29] In the early 1970s the first wave of South Korean immigrants began to arrive in Canada, simultaneously pushed by the political and economic situation at home and drawn by the new, more open immigration policy of the Canadian government. The influx of immigrants into UCC pews and erstwhile ethnically homogenous Canadian neighbourhoods, an influx of which the Korean diaspora was a significant part, led to pressure on the UCC to change its approach to ethnic minority congregations in the 1990s.

Several things made the history of missionaries in Korea and the influx of Koreans into Canada particularly important to the Canadian church. For one, the Canadian mission in Korea had outlasted the missions in places like China and India, which had expelled Western colonial powers. In addition, the Korean church was the strongest among its Asian neighbours and the presence of missionaries was more easily tolerated. This fact also meant that as Koreans immigrated to Canada, a large number formed Christian congregations; many of these were connected to Canadian denominations, meaning that Koreans became a significant minority within established Canadian churches. By the 1980s Koreans were the largest ethnic minority within the UCC. By 1988, based on church names, there appeared to be ten Korean congregations within the UCC, followed by eight Japanese and seven Chinese distinct ethnic congregations.[30] Within these Korean UCC congregations were a number of prominent Christian dissidents fleeing the political violence and economic hardship in South Korea in the 1960s, 70s, and 80s. These would come to play an important role not only as expat leaders in the Korean Democratization Movement but also as leaders in the Canadian church, challenging received attitudes and structures. These Koreans were leaders of other Koreans in the UCC and also provided leadership to the church as a whole, participating with other minority groups in a push to try to change the church. UCC theologian Loraine Mackenzie-Shepherd says the arrival of migrants led to a shift in UCC policy from assimilation and integration to pluralism vis-à-vis ethnic minorities.[31] Korean church leadership was an important impetus for this change.

Time has come for a new telling of the story of the Korean-Canadian church relationship. This new telling must do more than critically chart a course between the extremes of hero worship and demonization of

Canadian missionaries. Rather, the story needs first to account for the agency of Korean Christians in the relationship and how they impacted not only the missionaries working among them and their mission institutions but also the church in Canada that had sent them to Korea. The present context demands such a retelling, not only because neither extreme offers a satisfying picture of the past but also because the perspectives from which the story can be told have multiplied. In the postcolonial context, non-Western points of view are critical for understanding the histories of Western cultures and institutions. Non-Western agency, furthermore, can no longer be ignored in the historical account of how Western institutions have changed over time. In the case of the Canadian mission to Korea, Korean perspectives cultivated over a long period of time through a strong and ongoing relationship with the Canadian church promise new and helpful ways of understanding Canadian missions, Canadian religion, and Canada itself.

This study approaches its subject matter with a postcolonial lens. This means that it is interested in non-Western perspectives from places that were often the site of exploitation and oppression due to colonial occupation up until the Second World War and impacted by neo-colonial hegemonies since. These perspectives highlight the agency of the colonized and explore themes of race, identity, and culture. Two postcolonial thinkers that are particularly influential for the present work are Homi Bhabha and Mary Louis Pratt. Bhabha's ideas about the fluidity of culture captured in concepts such as liminality, hybridity, and third space provide a language to talk about the ways that people from Western and non-Western places came together, found common ground and were transformed in that encounter.[32] Pratt provided the notion of a contact zone, which also helps to explain the encounter between the colonizer and the colonized in terms of a dynamic and transformative space. Within the contact zone Pratt found evidence, contrary to the typical Western narrative, that Indigenous actors effectively challenged the fixed binary categories of Western thinking and exerted influence on the Westerners that they met and also upon their societies across the ocean.[33] These kinds of insights are reflected in this undertaking which understands the whole length of the relationship between Canadians and Koreans through the Christian church as a kind of contact zone that extends across a century and bridges the Pacific Ocean.

While focussing largely on events that involved Canadian missionaries in Korea, this book will resist the inclination to be about the significance of those events for the Korean church and society. Rather, its novelty will be to emphasize the leadership of Korean Christians and show how encounters in the mission contact zone shaped Canadians and had consequences for the culture and institution of the UCC, the Canadian denomination with by far the largest investment of finances and personnel in the peninsula. Analyzing the change that occurred within the institutions and culture of Canada's largest Protestant denomination, it will offer an account of changes within the UCC Korea Mission and within the UCC itself that were precipitated largely by Koreans. In the late nineteenth century, many Koreans embraced Christianity on their own terms and in a manner that gave expression to a form of the faith that was uniquely their own and often flew in the face of what missionaries felt was the proper and true form of religion. By the time pro-democracy activists took to the streets of Seoul in the 1960s, Korean Christians associated with Canadian missionaries and the UCC church had begun to actively and systematically oppose missionary practices and Western church policies, which they saw as oppressive. As they started to immigrate to Canada in large numbers beginning in 1965, these Koreans also took their fight directly to the Canadian church. In the process of this engagement, Christianity was reshaped in both Korea and Canada. By 1987, mass popular demonstrations succeeded in re-establishing a democratically elected civilian government and the numbers of Korean immigrants in the UCC reached its apex. In 1988 the UCC elected a South Korean immigrant and political activist named Sang Chul Lee as its spiritual leader.

WHAT FOLLOWS

The main objective of this book is to present the history of Korean Christians' engagement with the United Church of Canada and its Presbyterian tributary, and the changes in both Korean and Canadian Christianity that were the result. This book will provide a narrative of Korean engagement with the Canadian mission to Korea from its beginning until its official conclusion in 1974 and extend the narrative to describe how that engagement continued afterwards with repercussions for the UCC into the 1980s and beyond. The argument put forward contends that a politically active tradition of Korean Christianity contested and transformed the United Church of Canada's approach to missions by opposing its colonial underpinnings and affirming their own cultural and spiritual identity in Korea and within the Canadian church. The record of Korean Christian engagement with the UCC sheds light on this previously overlooked historical process. It locates Canadian Protestantism within a postcolonial context. It reveals the agency of Korean Christians in challenging Canadian colonial attitudes and institutions. On the Canadian side it tells the story of how Anglo-Canadian attitudes and institutions resisted change and how they adapted under duress. The UCC response to the emerging postcolonial context post–1960 helps to contextualize and explain both the decline of a tradition of Canadian Protestantism and the emergence of a new expression of the same.

These arguments shall be made in three parts and over the course of eight chapters. Part I will focus on the advent of Korean Christianity in Korea and Manchuria. It will describe Korean Christians' earliest interactions with Canadian missionaries and follow developments in this relationship in the lead up to the formation of a separate and independently minded Presbyterian denomination in South Korea. The year 1898 represents the official beginning of the Canadian mission to Korea. The Canadian mission field centred on the northeast of the peninsula but extended north of the Korean border where Korean exiles were seeking to survive Japanese colonialism and restore their nation's independence. Many of these same Koreans were forced to flee south across the thirty-eighth parallel in the lead up to the Korean war. By 1957, a distinct Christian religio-political approach had coalesced around a new seminary and a new Presbyterian church denomination. The events that occurred between 1898 and 1957 challenged Canadian missionaries to clarify their allegiances vis-à-vis Western hegemony in Korea and positioned elements of the Korean church to make a contribution to the political direction of the South Korean state.

Chapter 1 will tell the story of the establishment of a community of politically minded Christians north of the Korean border in Yongjeong, Manchuria and their reception of Canadian missionaries at the turn of the century. Most of these Koreans saw Christianity as a vehicle for national liberation and not, as the missionaries might like to have imagined, as a means to align with Western colonial values and learn from missionary examples. Embracing the new religion as a way to counter Japanese incursions into their territory and usurpation of their sovereignty, these Koreans invited the assistance of foreign missionaries who were not closely aligned with their Japanese oppressors. Missionary attitudes toward Japan, however, were ambiguous.

Canadian missionaries, in particular, arrived on the scene with attitudes shaped by participation in the colonial agenda of the Dominion of Canada. With Canadian Church Union in 1925 the Canadian mission to Koreans came under the banner of the United Church of Canada, which continued to press its Canadian Protestant version of internationalism even as it began to respond to Korean demands on the mission field. This chapter explores the dynamics of the early Canadian-Korean mission relationship.

Chapter 2 relates how the eviction of Western missionaries by the Japanese created a moment which Korean Christians used to consolidate their own leadership in the Korean Christian community by establishing their own seminary independent of missionary influence. Towards the middle of the twentieth century, some Korean Christian academics supported by successful Korean business leaders began to dream of developing an indigenous and independent theological perspective for the churches in Korea. The education of early Korean Christian leadership up to this point had been monopolized by American missionaries with the ambivalent support from Canadians who themselves sometimes chaffed under American leadership. The closing of the missionary-run Pyeongyang Seminary due to controversy over the Japanese colonial government's requirement of Shinto obeyance and the expulsion of the missionaries with the outbreak of the Pacific War created space for these Koreans to establish the independent Joseon seminary in the Korean capital, Seoul. Under the leadership of professors like Kim Chai Choon, the seminary both embraced Western scholarship and asserted a more progressive and independent Korean theological agenda. When the American Presbyterian missionaries returned following the war and discovered they no longer had control of the theological training of ministers, the stage was set for a showdown over the control of theological education for the Korean Presbyterian church. The expulsion of Kim Chai Choon, who had associated closely with the Canadian mission, from the Presbyterian Church of Korea (PCK) forced Canadian missionaries and the UCC to reposition themselves vis-à-vis the Korean church and Presbyterian missionary colleagues. The excommunication of Kim and his followers from the US missionary-influenced PCK and the subsequent creation of the Presbyterian Church in the Republic of Korea (PROK) represented a moment of decision for Canadian missionaries and their church back home and ended up aligning the UCC with a theologically and politically progressive group of church leaders in Korea.

Part two covers the rise of the Christian Democratization Movement in South Korea and the simultaneous push from Korean church leaders for a new church-to-church relationship with the UCC and its missionaries. This section of the book illuminates the links between the political events in South Korea and developments in Korean church culture. It further shows how these links had consequences for UCC individuals and institutions in Korea. The section begins with the general uprising of 19 April 1960 that toppled the Rhee Syng Man regime and concludes roughly with the death of the dictator Park Chung Hee in 1979, a moment that coincides with the zenith of Christian influence on the Democratization Movement. This section will develop chronologically with the exception of chapter 6, which will zoom in on two critical events in 1976 that illuminate the special role that women played in the Democratization Movement and the unique ways female UCC missionaries were involved and impacted.

Chapter 3 tells the story of the attempt by the UCC to impose a new missiology of partnership on their relationship with the Presbyterian Church in the Republic of Korea (PROK). It explores the reasons for the ambiguity of the UCC approach vis-à-vis their colonial past and the expressions by Korean Christians of the simple desire for just and genuine relationship with Canadian missionaries. During the 1960s, indigenous churches on the various UCC mission fields around the globe were pushing back against decades of Canadian missionary paternalism and leadership in the UCC was trying to get out ahead of the changes by developing a new missiology of mutuality and by reprioritizing funding commitments. Koreans, however, took issue with the changes that were proposed and the way they were unilaterally developed and introduced. The simple desire for friendship across cultural divides and an end to the UCC missionaries' wielding of spiritual authority over them was an important motivating of the PROK membership at this time. "The Decision" of the PROK in 1960 to no longer request funding from the UCC began a conversation with the UCC regarding these desires and grievances. The UCC sent Wilna Thomas, the UCC's first female chair of overseas mission, to explain its new approach to the relationship. Her visit, however, served to underline entrenched colonial habits of the UCC and its personnel. The PROK continued to press for change in its relationship with the UCC against the backdrop of a dramatic national movement for political autonomy.

Chapter 4 focuses on the culmination of PROK demands that brought about a dramatic change to the material and institutional culture of UCC Korea Mission. Concentrating on the events between 1970 and 1974, this chapter will seek to explain how PROK leaders succeeded in negotiating this change. The push of the PROK to radically transform their relationship with the UCC came as South Korean society sought ever more passionately to assert its democratic sovereignty, a fact that helps to contextualize these developments. The joint statement signed by the PROK and UCC in 1974 represented a significant achievement for the Korean church. The joint statement had consequences for Canadian missionaries in Korea and effectively ended the Canadian Missionary Enterprise on the peninsula.

Chapter 5 covers the wider events surrounding the agreement between the PROK and UCC that contributed to the development of Minjung theology. It will provide the historical context to help understand Minjung theology as a response to the missionary tradition and the neocolonial context of South Korea. In the wake of the agreement reached between the Korean and Canadian churches in March 1974, steps were taken to transfer a large red brick Edwardian missionary house and adjacent buildings in the heart of Seoul to the PROK. As the missionaries vacated their grand home, a symbol of a colonial past in which they occupied an elevated status in the Korean church and society, the Korean Christians symbolically and literally became *maître chez eux* with a new indigenous-led educational, political, and cultural vision for their church and nation. The newly established sovereignty of the activist wing of the Korean church was made manifest in the emergence of a new theology. Responding to the exploitation and oppression of people by the American-sponsored dictatorship of Park Chung Hee on the one hand and the impact of the state-sponsored Billy Graham Crusade on the other, Minjung theology drew its inspiration from the Democratization Movement, which was forced for a brief moment to lean on the Christian community to keep the torch lit during its darkest moments. Minjung theology was discussed in UCC circles and challenged the church in Canada to acknowledge a form of Christianity that was not grounded on Western culture or philosophical first principles but on the Korean Democratization Movement itself.

The mediation of relationships between Korean Christian women activists and Canadian female missionaries during the Democratization Movement by a gendered third space is the subject of chapter 6. For early Canadian female missionaries, the women's quarters of traditional Korean houses were important as a place where they could be alone with Korean women to discuss matters of faith. This was a space where converts were made and from which the missionary agenda could be introduced to families and communities. Postwar Korea saw the replacement of traditional homes with modern apartment complexes, but gendered spaces survived for female missionaries and their Korean hosts. Korean women continued to grant female missionaries special access to personal gendered spaces well into the postwar period. In a surprising twist, however, the history of the Democratization Movement reveals that the transformational impact of these spaces was not on Korean women and society but rather on the Canadian women. This chapter focuses primarily on two pivotal events in early 1976, which highlight the power of this space: the destruction of the Imun Dong squatter village on 9 February of 1976, and the Declaration for National Salvation of 1 March 1976. This chapter will offer a description of the impact of gendered spaces on female Canadian missionaries, and their repercussions for the UCC.

Part III shifts geographical location and attends to the immigration of Korean Christians and their influence upon the Church in Canada between 1965 to 1998. During this period, the balance of the impact of the Korean-Canadian church relationship shifted from Korea to Canada. By the 1980s there were more Koreans serving UCC congregations than there were UCC missionaries serving churches and institutions in Korea and far more Korean immigrants participating in the life of Canadian congregations than vice versa. The nature of the Korean-Canadian church relationship in Canada had similarities and differences to the one in Korea. As in Korea, Koreans had to struggle against colonial attitudes that denied their existence and failed to acknowledge their gifts of leadership. Unlike in Korea, however, UCC institutions and attitudes were much slower to change despite some notable achievements by Korean church leaders and the influence of a number of gifted Korean ministers working in predominantly White UCC congregations. This section will present the two experiences of the Korean and non-Korean UCC side by side over a more-or-less identical period of time. It will compare these experiences and try to evaluate what the impact of Korean Christians upon the UCC in Canada was during this time.

Chapter 7 describes the advent of mass Korean immigration and the entry of many Korean Christians into the UCC as leaders and as congregations. It covers the period from 1965, marked by the introduction of Canada's point system for immigration, to 1988, which

Introduction

saw the election of a Korean to the position of spiritual leader of the UCC. The chapter argues that from the moment Korea Christians began to immigrate *en masse* to Canada they simultaneously struggled to survive the bitter winds of the UCC's colonial tendencies as they endeavoured to plant a new kind of non-Western Christianity in North America. The difficulty that White members of the UCC had relating to Korean Christian immigrants highlights the inability of the institutional church to effectively respond to global migration and the religious perspectives of non-Western Christians as they made a home within the UCC. Regardless, Koreans and other non-Western migrants successfully established themselves as part of the UCC. They represented a change in perspective, a change in theology and a change in worship practice for the Canadian denomination. This is an important moment that signals a challenge to entrenched Protestant nationalist assumptions of the UCC from within. The church magazine of the Toronto Korean United Church (TKUC) entitled *Seonguja* (meaning "Pioneer") offers an intimate glimpse into the experiences of Korean Christians within a UCC congregation. But equally important are interviews with Korean church leaders and congregation members, which provide a nuanced appreciation of the experiences in the Korean Christian community in Canada and a link to the UCC's missionary past.

Chapter 8 shifts its focus from Korean immigrants to the mainly White church members and UCC institutions that received them. Also beginning in 1965 this chapter will follow events up until 1998, the 100th anniversary of the arrival in Korea of Canadian missionaries sent by the Canadian church, and beyond. The ambiguous response to Korean Christians by UCC leaders and lay members demonstrates that, as a whole, the Canadian church was struggling to respond to the new postcolonial Canadian context. On the one hand, the branches of church governance in charge of relationships with overseas Christians were proactive in developing strategies for combating racism and promoting an open stance to immigration within Canada. On the other hand, the branches of the UCC concerned with church work in Canada were slow to see the significance of anti-racism policies for Canada and its own church. Canadian-born Christians began to interact with the Koreans in new ways and learned important lessons. A key example of this is the UCC first female moderator, Lois Wilson, who visited Korea in 1981 and came away with a transformed vision of the place of non-Western Christianity in Canada and around the world. But others in the UCC were slow to appreciate these experiences and insights. Nevertheless, partly thanks to Korean efforts, the UCC established an Ethnic Ministry Council in the 1990s, a watershed moment for the church. The chapter will conclude with reflections on how the Canadian mainline Protestant church had been impacted by the Korean church one hundred years after it had established a mission in Korea.

SOURCES

In addition to the two monographs mentioned at the beginning of this introduction, archived, written records of events of the Korean-Canadian mission relationship between 1898 and 1998 were important in developing the history here outlined. These can be found in different places. The United Church of Canada Archives in Toronto contains missionary correspondence, missionary reports, church committee reports, and a variety of other documents that can be used to reconstruct a history of the Korea-Canadian church partnership and of Korean immigration and involvement in the Canadian church. The University of Toronto Special Collection on Democracy and Human Rights in Korea held at the Cheng Yu Tung East Asian Library contains documents from the 1970s, 1980s, and 1990s curated by UCC missionary Fred Bayliss and focusses on the events of the South Korean Democratization Movement mostly in Korea but also in Canada. The UCLA Archival Collection on Democracy and Unification in Korea located in Los Angeles contains the minutes of meetings and correspondence of expat Koreans as well as documents related to Canadian and American missionaries' work to promote human rights and a transition to democratic government in South Korea. Other church archives in Canada and private or university archives in Korea supplement material from these three main archival sources.

There are large gaps in these archival source bases, however. Much of what there is still to learn about the history of Koreans associated with the Canadian mission to Korea and the Canadian church resides in the living memory of Korean church members. While church bureaucracies and mission committees left significant records of events and missionaries themselves recorded many aspects of their lives and interactions with Koreans, church and archival records contain precious few Korean perspectives. Collections of material relative to Korean migration to Canada are only just starting to be created. Those people who were involved with Canadian missionaries and the establishment of Korean congregations in Canada are now quickly passing away, a fact that lends urgency to the project. Semi-structured interviews with these actors will form an important historical database for this study. This constitutes a second and very important source of historical information. Oral histories are nuanced and complex, often locations where official histories are contested, as Ruth Sanz Sabido has beautifully shown in *Memories of the Spanish Civil War*.[34] My interviewees were sometimes themselves consciously reinforcing or contesting official histories. Their testimony was likely also shaped to varying degrees by my social location as the interviewer. I have tried to take my social location as a White male connected to the UCC into account. Any bias my identity may have caused in the oral testimonies, however, does not diminish the importance of the information that these interviews were able to provide. Ethnographic sources used in the book provide new insights into the development of the Korean-Canadian church relationship which are unavailable in documentary sources.

Finally, sources exist in missionary and Korean Christian writings of the period or later personal reflections on it. Some Korean church leaders published important works of theology during or immediately following the 1970s. Others wrote memoirs or biographies in the decades since. This intellectual and biographical material provides important data for this project as well. Collections of worship materials from the period including liturgies, sermons, prayers, and hymns offer another important source of ethnohistorical data for understanding the intercultural influences within the Korean and Canadian churches and on the mission field. Such material is to be found in the personal libraries of some surviving church leaders, in congregational libraries, and in seminary collections.

PARAMETERS

The approach taken in this study need not have limited itself to church relationships, missionary activity, and Christian migration between Korea and Canada, or focussed exclusively on the partnership between the UCC and PROK. This book's parameters, however, make possible a detailed account of a history and events specific to Canada's largest Protestant denomination and a significant overseas church. The UCC played an important role both in Canada's Missionary Enterprise and in the shaping of a Canadian Protestant nationalism. Its mission to Korea was neither its oldest nor its biggest, but it was particularly dynamic and offers compelling examples of indigenous church agency in relationship to Canadian missionaries and mission policy. Unlike the China Mission, for example, which was brought to an abrupt halt following the communist takeover and the outbreak of the Korean War, the UCC Korea Mission was able to wind down gradually and left time for missionaries and Korean Christians to work through the ambivalent legacy of the Missionary Enterprise in Korea together.

TRANSLATION OF KOREAN

I do not use a single system for translating Korean names into English. Rather, I use the translation that was common when the person in question first became known to an English-speaking audience, using the spelling by which English speakers would have come to know of them or which they would have used themselves when signing off of English documents. In the case of Sang Chul Lee, for example, even the order of his name is reversed to correspond with the name by which he was known to in English Canada. Where a person was not previously known to an English audience I employ the Revised Romanization of Korean (RR) system adopted by the South Korean Ministry of Culture in 2000 for transcribing sounds. The same is true where transliteration of Korean material is concerned. As Sebastian Kim and Kirsteen Kim point out, the alternative McCune-Reischauer system is more commonly used in academic scholarship but is less accessible to those who are not familiar with the Korean language. The new system is frequently employed by new scholars. It is more accessible to those unfamiliar with the Korean language and therefore more appropriate to a study which seeks to reach an audience familiar with the Canadian church and history as much as the Korean one. It is also more common on the internet since it is not easy to enter diacritical marks such as those used in the McCune-Reischauer system into search engines.[35]

LAST WORD BEFORE WE BEGIN

Born on the kitchen floor in a peasant's home near Vladivostok, Russia, Sang Chul Lee, the son of Korean refugees, was destined to live a migrant's life. In his English autobiography, entitled *The Wanderer*,[36] Lee shares the story of his family's flight from Siberia to Manchuria when he was a child, then his flight from Manchuria to South Korea at the conclusion of the Pacific War, and finally his voluntary migration

Introduction   27

across the Pacific to Canada. Though he liked to style himself after the wandering poet Kim Sat-gat, Lee nevertheless had two constants in his adult life that anchored his sense of self. The first was a sense of nationalism as it applied not only to the Korean community into which he had been born but also in a more broad sense of a commitment to the wellbeing of the community in which he found himself, a commitment that often meant opposition to larger transnational forces such as colonialism and international Cold War hegemonies that threatened these communities. The second constant since the time Lee was a teenager attending a UCC-run mission school in Manchuria was a devotion to the Christian faith. Christianity, as he understood it, not only unlocked deep springs of spiritual power but also encouraged a sense of national commitment. Lee's arrival in Canada, then, was marked by the sense that he had something to contribute to his new nation and church. In 1988, the Right Reverend Lee was voted moderator of the United Church of Canada, the first person of Asian heritage to be elected spiritual leader of Canada's largest Protestant denomination. Even as he accepted the honour, Lee had the sense that his culture was not being properly valued in the Canadian church. "I felt then as I do now, that the Christian church needs to develop a new missiology which recognizes the value of indigenous cultures and traditions," he wrote twenty years later.[37]

This book is ultimately about immigrants in a century marked by migration. It is also about the challenge migrants pose to colonial patterns of nationalism and neocolonial hegemonies. Sang Chul Lee's life like that of his daughter Irene Chungwa Lee quoted at the head of chapter 8, reflects the lives of thousands upon thousands of Koreans who were often forced to migrate north and south across the peninsula and east and west across the globe in wave after wave throughout the twentieth century as they sought new and stable homes. In some small but important way it also reflected a kind of migration by the missionaries themselves as they crossed cultural boundaries and were often forced to move from place to place or back to the country they had left decades earlier by forces outside their control. This postcolonial pattern of migration continues for tens or even hundreds of millions of people in the twenty-first century. Though this book focusses on one small group of migrants and their impact on one section of Canadian society, it seeks to draw attention to the impact of migrants more broadly, and to their contributions to the places through which they pass and into which they settle.

Lee attended the same Canadian Mission-run school in Manchuria that Yun Dongju did. With Lee and Yun, this book invites us to look down Dragon's Well together and draw insight from the water of this experience. As in the well of Yun's poem, we will see reflections of resentment and shame. We will also see reflections of forgiveness, hope, and love. In short we are invited to drink from the well of wisdom of a long relationship, its past, and its meaning for the future of Canada, Korea, their religions, and their peoples.

PART ONE

Nationalist Missions and Migrating Christians

The Beginning of a Korean-Canadian Church Relationship, 1898 to 1959

1

A Land in between "Our Ancestors" and "Our North-West"

The Beginning of a Korean-Canadian Church Relationship in Kando, Manchuria, 1898 to 1942

In the beginning when God created the heavens and the earth, the earth was a formless void and darkness covered the face of the deep, while a wind from God swept over the face of the waters.

Genesis 1.1–2[1]

The start of the Christian Bible is set in a dark space of swirling disorder and amazing creative potential. Its first chapter culminates with the advent of human beings, imbued with the same potential for chaos and creativity as their new world. Such is the biblical story of the beginning of humankind, a story that sought to affirm the human identity of those who first told it. Stories of beginnings were no less important for the Korean Christians and Canadian missionaries who first arrived on in the Kando region[2] of Manchuria at the turn of the twentieth century. Manchuria itself, like the world of the Bible, was a place imbued with both troubling chaos and limitless potential. It was a stateless nowhere land and the centre of numerous nationalist imaginings, a place where great powers collided and where humble peasants sought to make safer homes and plant gardens to sustain themselves. As people from all over the world were pulled into the power vacuum left by a retreating Qing dynasty and were propelled by their dreams into the emerging possibilities of Manchuria, they were telling themselves stories about who they were and where they fit into this new world.

This chapter is about beginnings. It is about the arrival of the first Korean migrants and the first Canadian missionaries into the Kando region of China on the border with Korea. For the former, the journey to Manchuria represented the return to an ancient homeland, a place from which to plan resistance against invading forces threatening to annihilate their nation. For the latter, it was an opportunity to convert a new group of people to a religio-political project that was an extension of the one being rolled out across the dominion from which they came. These were the stories each group told themselves. To some degree both groups achieved the objectives articulated in their stories. The Korean migrants recreated a community in Kando and successfully prepared a new generation to contribute to the independence of a renewed Korean nation. The Canadians missionaries, for their part, oversaw the rapid growth of Protestant Christianity and imparted modern religious and scientific knowledge as well as technical know-how to a responsive Korean following. But that is not the whole story.

The Kando environment also presented some unexpected challenges that required negotiation and compromise. The conversion to the Christian religion, for example, was not an anticipated outcome for the Koreans who migrated to Manchuria. Neither was the brutality of modern Empire foreseen by the Canadian missionaries. And there was another unexpected event as well: the beginning of a transnational relationship that would endure countless crises over more than a century. As they were not expecting this beginning, neither group told stories about (and we do not have a genesis narrative against which to assess) the successes and failures of the venture. This book is an attempt to tell the story of that unexpected event and particularly of what it has meant for Canadian missionaries and their church in North America. This chapter is the story of its beginning.

THE LAND IN BETWEEN

During the Qing dynasty, Kando, a name that means "island in between,"[3] was part of an area set apart as the sacred homeland of the Manchus, the society of horse-riding warriors who had overrun the ailing Ming dynasty and established themselves as rulers of China in 1644 CE. Off limits to any and all immigration from the beginning of this period to near the end of the nineteenth century, Manchuria in the last half of the nineteenth and first part of the twentieth centuries was the site of enormous movement and change. In the dying years of the Manchu reign, Manchuria received more immigrants than any other place on earth. Millions of peasants were drawn by the prospect

A Land in between "Our Ancestors" and "Our North-West"   33

of inexpensive, fertile land. Pushed by population pressures to the south and pulled by the allure of high value crops like opium, the population of Han Chinese increased from zero to more that 3.8 million between 1850 and 1907 in the newly created province of Jilin alone.[4] For wealthy capitalists, too, whether European or Japanese, it was a land ripe for exploitation and colonial expansion.[5] Russians settled there in the lead up to the Russo-Japanese war, building railroads, establishing the city of Harbin and asserting Russian influence in the area. New rail lines brought new economic growth and industrial development and the rate of immigration only continued to increase into the twentieth century as the new republican government of China doubled down on the policy of migrant in a bid to re-establish control of the area by further increasing the Han population.[6]

Nor did the rate of migration slow in the 1920s as the Japanese continued to pour resources into developing the region.[7] As Japan leveraged the economic rights that it had acquired through military victories against China and Russia, it further expanded rail, industrial, and financial infrastructure. Dairen (Dalian), the terminus of the railway system, was a seaport that came to approach Shanghai in capacity and helped to move the products of a booming agricultural sector, particularly soya beans, which constituted about 80 per cent of Manchuria's farming output in the early 1900s. Exports grew at 11 per cent per year from 1907 to 1929. Japanese further encouraged the migration of Koreans and then of its own people to Manchuria, an effort that continued with the creation of the new state of Manchukuo as it sought to grow and strengthen its empire.[8] A census conducted in Harbin by the new Manchukuo government in 1933 revealed the presence of Han Chinese, Taiwanese, Soviets, [White] Russians, Japanese, Koreans, Brits, Americans, Germans, French, Italians, Poles, Jews, Greeks, Dutch, Turks, Austrians, Hungarians, Danes, Latvians, Portuguese, Czechs, Armenians, Belgians, Serbs, Swedes, Latins, Romanians, Swiss, and East Indians.[9] Indigenous populations of Manchu, Mongol, and Tungic peoples, though left out of the census, further added to the diversity of the place.

Koreans had, with the Chinese, been some of the earliest settlers to move into this sparsely populated region in the mid-nineteenth century despite intimidating restrictions designed to keep them out. The Qing dynasty had made immigration from anywhere difficult and had policed the border with the Joseon dynasty carefully.[10] The Manchu Emperor had strictly limited immigration to Manchuria as a way of preserving a distinction between the ruling Manchu people and the ruled Han and for the sake of guarding a preserve of Manchu culture.[11] The Qing policy of "seal and prohibit" (fengjin) led to the creation of the Willow Palisade, an enormous earthwork planted with yellow willows that acted as a kind of symbolic line across which immigrants from northern China were not allowed to cross.[12] The same restrictions had been placed on Koreans using the natural boundaries of the Yalu and Tumen rivers. When the Qing realized that they were going to have to assert their sovereignty in Manchuria against foreign colonial powers such as Russia and Japan, they began to relax their restrictions against migration, particularly for Han Chinese, leading to hundreds of thousands of immigrants, which opened the gates to Koreans as well.

Particularly in the Kando region, just north of the Korean border with China, Koreans and Chinese lived in close competition with one another. Han Chinese were by far the most numerous in Manchuria as a whole and were, by and large, peasants. As Chinese nationals, however, they occupied a privileged space vis-à-vis the Koreans, who they often viewed as invaders. Only Chinese were allowed to hold legal title to land.[13] Among them were wealthy landlords who took advantage and taxed Korean peasants heavily. Ethnic prejudice coloured social relations. Koreans for their part took a lowly view of the Chinese. They were strange people, portrayed by Korean parents to their children as dangerous.[14] They were competitors who used their status to make life difficult for Koreans. Sometimes they were violent oppressors, easily manipulated to attack unarmed Koreans.[15] But in Kando, the little corner of Manchuria abutting the Yalu and Tumen rivers north of Korea, Koreans had the numerical and economic edge by the 1930s, forcing their Chinese neighbours into more marginal positions.[16]

The Japanese, the other conspicuous Asian nationality in Manchuria, were the dominant colonial power following the Russo-Japanese war of 1905. They were soon positioned as landlords with vast land holdings and part of a modern and awesomely powerful military machine.[17] They were oppressors but on occasion also projected a persona of educated benevolence.[18] The Japanese shared this colonial position with European powers (and by extension the Canadian missionaries who carried British passports and had access to British consulates in the area). Both Japan and Britain, for example, had secured extraterritorial rights from China in the aftermath of the Boxer rebellion. British extraterritorial rights extended to the Canadian missionaries and to their mission compounds as citizens of the empire.

Following the Japanese annexation of Korea in 1910, Japan used the Korean presence in Kando as an excuse to establish a consulate in the city of Yongjeong alongside the British one on the pretext of protecting their Korean-Japanese citizens. They stationed a garrison in the city as well and had a school and medical clinic which rivaled the Canadian mission schools and hospital.[19] Japan also vied with Britain in the opium trade. As Japan gained the upper hand in the area, it introduced laws that on the surface seemed to control opium consumption but were in reality aimed at edging out its European competitors.[20]

Just as Japan straddled both the ethnic Asian and colonial positions in Manchuria, Russians occupied both privileged and powerless social locations. Russian expats of aristocratic and peasant birth had settled in Manchuria when the Russian empire expanded into the area and had become refugees there following the communist revolution. Many were detained by Japanese authorities in Korea, held in horrible conditions, and then released to fend for themselves. Some were of high birth. There were also Russian peasants who made use of the Canadian mission hospital from time to time. These Europeans were regarded with particular sympathy by the Canadians and with a degree of pity even by the Koreans and Chinese as they had suffered a great deal. They were stateless and had been, in some cases, reduced to utter poverty.[21]

In the prefecture of Kando, Koreans numbered half a million by the early twentieth century. Most came from the northeastern Hamkyeong provinces of Korea that had had the closest historical ties to the area; their dialect remains prevalent among the Joseon-Chinese of this region today.[22] Anti-Japanese sentiment was particularly strong among Koreans in Manchuria and northeastern Korea, which had a long tradition of harbouring political exiles. Initially, as Japan tightened its grip on Korea proper, Manchuria became a haven for the *Uibyeong*[23] and others who had been marked as political opponents to the new colonial government. Interviewee Chun Sunyeong tells of growing up in Kando, having migrated with her family in the early 1900s. Her grandfather had been arrested and executed in Korea for military actions against the Japanese occupation, staining her family's reputation and fixing their names to a blacklist with the Japanese authorities.[24] Kando was a haven for many with similar family histories. The political and cultural environment of Kando and northeastern Korea shaped the Korean spirit of political independence. Kando was a place where groups representing various political interests, colonial agendas, and anti-colonial convictions converged.

Outside of the direct control of the Japanese empire, it offered more freedom of expression for Koreans than Korea proper and a space for militants and political opponents to organize and mobilize.[25]

By a clever use of propaganda the Japanese military used the Russian revolution to brand the Korean nationalists north of the border as Bolsheviks, garnering support from other imperial powers for their brutal suppression in the area.[26] Though this was not the case early on, by the mid-1920s most Koreans involved in armed struggle were in fact participating under the banner of Communism, and laying the groundwork for the origin myth of the future North Korean state.[27] A young Korean fighter named Kim Seong-ju had migrated to Manchuria by 1919 and joined the Chinese Communist Party in 1931. From Manchuria, Kim was an important player in the anti-Japanese armed resistance.[28] Korean folklore made Manchuria the stage for cultural heroes of resistance such as Nokdu and Kim Il-seong, formidable (magical) warriors of the popular imagination. Kim Seong-ju later changed his name to Kim Il-seong (Kim Il Sung) and, accruing the name of the mythical fighter, re-entered Korea installed by the Russians as leader of Korean communist forces.[29] Working as an officer in the Japanese Imperial army, Manchuria was also the location where Park Chung Hee – future South Korean President and military dictator – began his rise as an important figure in Korean history serving as a soldier in the Japanese Imperial Army.

There was an uneasy relationship between Christianity and communism when the later arrived on the scene in the 1920s. Generally speaking, the two groups were like oil and water and kept their distance both intellectually and geographically.[30] Unarmed Christians often suffered the most. Communist forces would harass Christians and generally viewed them with suspicion. The Japanese, for their part, saw no difference between Christians and Communists, correctly regarding both as being behind resistance to their occupation of Korea and ambitions in China. In 1920, the Japanese military undertook a punitive expedition sending 15,000 troops to Kando. According to missionary reports, 3,128 Koreans were killed in that operation. In addition, 2,404 Christian homes, 31 Christian schools, and 10 churches were burned.[31] Koreans relayed a particularly harrowing story of 50 to 60 people in a village called Norubao who were burned alive in their church.[32] Similar scenes were repeated in 1932, when Japan again undertook an antiguerrilla campaign in the area.[33] Christians were often caught in the crossfire with communists. Canadian Missionaries,

A Land in between "Our Ancestors" and "Our North-West"   37

helpless observers to the carnage, report that Christian villages were collateral damage in these operations, church leaders were terrorized, and several communities were "completely wiped out."[34] Korean school children and their parents were made to watch the beheading of other whole families by Japanese soldiers in their schools.[35] Few Koreans were left untouched by the violence.

The Canadian missionaries were not the only missionary or religious influence in the area. Foreign missionaries, Protestant and Catholic, serving Korean and Chinese populations were in evidence throughout the region. The Chinese living in Kando were under care of Scotch Irish Presbyterians who maintained contact with them from their centre of activity in Harbin. Methodists working with Koreans had withdrawn from the region to make room for the Canadians but had left behind a number of churches and schools that remained affiliated with them.[36] The Catholic church had a strong and loyal following as well.[37] Confucian influences were ubiquitous. Animist traditions were also common, as evidenced by the prevalence of stone mounds and carved poles that missionaries called "devil posts."[38]

Kando was truly an island in between, in between tradition and modernity, indigeneity and colonialism, diversity and intolerance, promise and poverty, new hope and violent suppression. It was in Kando that Koreans adopted and began to develop a unique approach to Christianity that would have an impact on their country for decades to come. It was in Kando that Canadian missionaries saw the most striking parallels between the geography, economics, and politics of their Canadian homeland and Korean mission field. As Canadian historian Diana Lary has noted, "The development of the two vast regions [Manchuria and the Canadian prairies] was based on similar concerns: sovereignty, migration, railway building, and urban development."[39] It was in Kando that Canadian missionaries were confronted with some of the most glaring contradictions of their missionary religion. Within this context both Korean and Canadian groups were tested and confronted with life and death decisions. In this context they also came to know one another.

IN THE LAND OF THEIR ANCESTORS: KOREAN PROTESTANTS IN KANDO

On the eve of the twentieth century two Korean children, Kim Shin Mook and Moon Chai Rin, crossed the Tumen Riven into Manchuria from northeastern Korea with their respective families and in the company of a whole village that had undertaken the migration together.[40] Kim remembers, "These people [of my village] were worried about the situation of Korea that worsened by the day. Heading off for Manchuria they embraced the great purpose of raising a new generation to be workers for the nation."[41] Recorded in *Kiringabiwa komannye-eui Kkum: Moon Chai Rin – Kim Shin Mook Hoegorok*, the published memories of this couple constitute a unique eyewitness account of the beginnings of the Korean migration to Kando.[42] This memoir was conceived by Moon in the 1980s,[43] and with his children's and grandchildren's support was completed in 2006 in a volume that included his wife's contribution as well.[44] From the beginning, Moon's reflections were specifically focused on the Korean independence movement and nationalism, interests that remained close to his heart until his death in January 1986.[45] Kim shared her spouse's political commitments and was even more involved in the independence movement in Manchuria since, in contrast to Moon who spent periods of time studying abroad, she was never absent from the geographic space where the nationalist struggle was most dramatically engaged. As prominent leaders in the Korean church, the focus of their memoir speaks to the central place of nationalist concerns in the Christian community. What they saw and remembered was also shaped by this perspective and produced a view of history that is not always substantiated by the scholarship.

Arriving as children in 1899, both Kim and Moon remembered their families' sense of amazement as they laid eyes on the fertile expanse of Manchuria. Together they had immigrated with a whole village from North Hamkyeong Province.[46] This was not an uncommon phenomenon as people tended to immigrate in communities rather than as individuals or as individual families.[47] The village had left its old location near Hoeryeong on the northern Korean boundary line and transplanted itself across the border. Their leaders were reform-minded Confucian scholars disillusioned with the Yi dynasty. They had encouraged the migration preaching a three-fold purpose:

1 To reclaim the land of their ancestors.
2 To construct an ideal, more just village.
3 To find a place where they could educate themselves as a vital step towards restoring their deteriorating nation.[48]

Moon and Kim describe the leaders of their community as scholars of the Silhak School.[49] This, they said, meant that they were committed

A Land in between "Our Ancestors" and "Our North-West" 39

followers of a line of Confucianism inspired by Mencius.[50] But it is clear they were open to new ideas from other cultural sources as well. They had participated in the Donghak Movement,[51] an uprising of Korean peasants inspired by a hybrid indigenous Korean religion that drew on Catholic Christian teachings as well as traditional Korean religion and philosophy. This Korean nationalist movement precipitated the Sino-Japanese confrontation of 1895 and was brutally suppressed by the Japanese forces whose presence on the peninsula the movement had strenuously opposed.[52]

The Silhak leaders of Kim and Moon's community were convinced that the land into which they were moving was part of their Korean inheritance. They pointed to ancient Koguryeo, one of the three original Korean kingdoms that had occupied the northern part of the peninsula and a large part of Manchuria before it had been subsumed within the unified Shilla Dynasty in 668 CE. They found evidence of older generations of Koreans who had lived there before their arrival, leaving no doubt in their minds that this had been Korean land.[53] They were impressed, too, by what seemed to be the fact that Chinese inhabitants of the area regarded Dangun, the mythical progenitor of Koreans, as their progenitor as well. The teacher at the Chinese school marked Dangun's birthday with a holiday on 3 October each year, they said, and the Han inhabitants also followed other customs similar to Koreans, such as marking the day by putting peppers on the roof. [54] Scholar's debate the historical veracity of Korean connections to this land and it is possible that the new community and their leaders' observations were shaped by their nationalist aspirations.[55] Nevertheless, this was what Moon and Kim remember and what they believed.

The Silhak scholars who led Kim and Moon's village were shaped by their experience in the Donghak Movement and as a result had a different approach than the typical Korean scholar. Confucian teachers, for example, generally claimed a high social status, wore white clothes, and shunned manual labour. Silhak scholars, by contrast, identified with the common people, generally wore black and were not above putting their shoulder to the plow. Moon and Kim both recall how Silhak leaders would return home late from a long day threshing crops or covered in mud from a day of work in the fields.[56] Though they engaged in hard manual labour, education was the great passion of the Silhak scholars of Kim and Moon's community, particularly education with a view to restoring the Korean nation. When they moved to Manchuria, each brought enough books to fill their own personal studies.[57] Upon settling in their new location, they immediately proceeded to open *seodang*,[58] Confucian schools where boys beginning at the age of seven learned the Chinese written characters and began to read the classics.[59] Kim Yakyeon was the most famous and well respected of the Silhak leaders in Moon and Kim's community. Following his nickname "the president of Kando," his school and teachings gained a reputation in Manchuria and Korea even among the Chinese and Japanese.[60]

The reputation of the Silhak leaders of Kim and Moon's community attracted other teachers passionate about restoring Korean independence. These new arrivals who were fleeing Japanese persecution nevertheless brought with them a modern approach to education learned in Japanese- and mission-run schools in the south. Demonstrating once again their practical approach and cultural flexibility, the Silhak leaders made way for the new ideas. They closed their seodang in favour of combining the students from various communities into a new and bigger elementary school with a modernized curriculum. On 27 April 1908, the new school was opened in Kim and Moon's village and students began to attend classes led by exiled patriots. The school was named Myeongdong,[61] "Light of the East," a reference to the restoration of Korea. Before long, it gained a reputation in the area such that the village became known by that name as well.[62] The new school for boys was soon twinned with a school for girls.[63]

The next year the community sought to hire a permanent principal for the school. They approached a man named Jeong Byeong-tae.[64] Jeong was willing to come to Myeongdong, but he was a Christian, and his religion was an unnegotiable pillar of his educational philosophy. He told the Silhak leaders he would come only if they allowed him to include worship in the curriculum of the school. After some discussion they agreed. Upon his arrival in 1909, Moon reports, "all the students became Christian."[65] A year later, Jeong threatened to quit if the adults didn't join the students in church. Neither Moon nor Kim comment on the meaning of this experience for the students and their parents at the time. Elsewhere, UCC Moderator Sang Chul Lee recalls that he had absolutely no idea what was happening to him when he was baptized at a Methodist school in a different village nearby.[66] Some, disturbed by the change and the teachings of the new religion, ended in rejecting the faith imposed upon them in this way and left the village.[67] But for people like Lee, Moon, and Kim, the faith eventually took hold and became an integral part of their lives.

It is clear from the leadership of others from this community that their experience was not unique.[68]

Regardless of whether the initial conversion to Christianity was of personal significance for the Myeongdong villagers at the time, Moon surmises that what was at stake for Jeong was not a zeal for the salvation of individual souls through the new Western religion, but rather a program of national salvation. Jeong was convinced that church and school together were an essential combination. It was not enough to merely educate and baptize children. It was important that the adults be involved in the transformation of their communities as well. Multigenerational education and conversion were essential to the mobilization of the community in the movement. The goal was ultimately the restoration of a sovereign Korea and Jeong saw a multigenerational Christian population as essential to achieving this objective.[69] Former resident of Myeongdong, Ahn Byung Mu, says about his experience that "Church was truly a formidable place, for it was there that my national consciousness, killed by the Japanese education at the elementary school, was revived. The dawn prayer meetings always included prayers for Korean independence, and interpretations of the Bible were guided by a yearning for the independence of our country and the awakening of a national consciousness."[70] Scriptures spoke with double meaning. The question of the disciples to Jesus in the opening chapter of Acts, for example, "Lord, is this the time when you will restore the kingdom of Israel?" was understood to be a question about the restoration of Korea to Koreans.[71] Upon reflection, Ahn realized that at the time he was part of a "church-based national movement."[72]

The connection of the school to the independence movement was never in question under Jeong and even its more militant aspects do not seem to have been tempered by the adoption of Chrisitanity as a religion. The school was used as a training ground for resistance fighters including An Jung-geun who is famous for the 1909 assassination in Manchuria of Prince Itō Hirobumi, a former Japanese Resident-General of Korea.[73] Kim Shin Mook reports that women in the church were a "force for independence"[74] and raised money to support independence fighters.[75] The road from Hoeryeong to Yongjeong, the major city of North Kando, passed right by Myeongdong school but Japanese authorities passing through were afraid to go near it because of its reputation. It is even reported that men sheltered in the school on their way to buy weapons in Vladivostok.[76] Whether Jeong was directly involved in armed struggle is unclear, but he was arrested at least once for his involvement in independence movement.[77]

The close connection between Christianity and nationalism was not unique to Koreans in Manchuria. However, the advent of Christianity in the Kando region had a major influence on this association. In 1873, John Ross and John MacIntyre, missionaries from the Presbyterian Church in Scotland, had set up base in Shenyang, Manchuria and made the acquaintance of a Korean merchant named Seo Sang-yun.[78] Seo undertook to teach them the Korean language and, in collaboration with another Korean, Yi Ung-chan, Ross translated the New Testament into Korean.[79] Ross and MacIntyre subsequently retired from the Korean field, but Seo Sang-yun took printed copies of the translated New Testament and began to distribute them throughout the border region. Soon the faith was spreading simply on the strength of these printed materials. By 1884, hundreds of Korean-speaking Christians could be found along the Manchurian border in places never visited by a missionary.[80]

The linguistic medium through which the religious message was communicated was as significant as the message itself for the spread of Christianity among Koreans. Ross and Yi had translated the Bible into the common phonetic Korean script, *hangeul*.[81] This was a script that had been developed centuries earlier by the fourth king of the Yi Dynasty. But court nobles at the time frowned on the use of a native Korean writing form that was accessible to the masses, preferring the complex ideograms commonly in use throughout the region, the medium of elite East Asian literati. The hangeul script, nevertheless, was kept alive and served the common people. As early as 1592, its use to rally the population against a Japanese invasion contributed to the beginnings of modern national consciousness.[82] It was into the common hangeul, rather than the ancient East Asian ideograms of the educated Confucian nobility, that the Christian Bible was translated for the first Korean Protestants.[83]

The average Korean took political inspiration simply from the fact that their common language was being used.[84] Christianity retained its symbolic connection to the Korean language, and therefore to nationalist aspirations as well, late into the colonial period. Christian worship services were one of the last places where Japanese authorities permitted Korean to be spoken publicly.[85] Minjung theologian Kim Yong Bok sums up the significance of the use of the hangeul script in the translation of the Bible this way: "Besides the general

A Land in between "Our Ancestors" and "Our North-West"   43

significance of the rehabilitation of the Korean script, the main significance of the translation of the Bible was the fact that it created a major
language-event, introducing a messianic language to the common people
of Korea, who were oppressed and exploited, and were suffering under
social chaos and foreign threat. This translation of the Bible into the
Korean vernacular became one of the most significant events in modern
history, which went beyond its religious significance for the Christian
church."[86] According to Kim, the translation of the Bible into hangeul
gave the Korean population a vocabulary that transcended class divisions and gave voice to their religio-political aspirations.[87] The compelling nature of that translation is witnessed by the fact that many
were converted simply upon receiving the printed text without having
seen a missionary.

These affinities between the new Protestant Christian religion and
Korean nationalism notwithstanding, the transition to Christianity
from a basically Confucian position was not easy for everybody in
Kim Shin Mook and Moon Chai Rin's village. The decision to bring
Jeong had required some careful discernment of religio-political loy-
alties. Above all the community was committed to the nationalism
inspired in the new Christian religion. The Silhak leadership also
resonated with many Christian ethical values, including the ideal that
educated religious leaders should not regard themselves above manual
labour.[88] However, Christianity also demanded the rejection of social
norms and cherished traditions. The practice of taking a second wife
or concubine was frowned upon, as was drinking. In some cases, the
new social norms were experienced as liberating, especially for women.[89]
One of the most difficult practices to let go of, however, was the
practice of *jesa*,[90] a ritual honouring the ancestors. This demonstration
of filial piety was a central pillar of Confucian ethics and practice and
jesa was a rite central to the community. It is no surprise that many
found the Christian proscription of it troubling.[91]

In addition to the fact that it was a cherished tradition that embodied
values that the communities continued to espouse, the jesa ritual had
deep political undertones. In 1645, the Catholic Church's Sacred
Congregation for the Propagation of the Faith condemned the practice
over the objections of Jesuit missionaries. The Jesuits shared the view
of Mateo Ricci, an early and highly regarded missionary to China,
that jesa did not contradict Christian doctrine. Two later papal injunc-
tions against the practice, however, led to the suppression of Catholicism
in China starting in the early eighteenth century and the martyrdom

of thousands of Korea's first Catholic converts in the late eighteenth and mid-nineteenth centuries.[92] At the time, the Korean court interpreted the rejection of jesa by Korea's first Catholics as an attack on the foundations of the kingdom itself. These historical considerations likely also gave the Silhak scholars of Myeongdong village pause and explains part of the conflict they felt regarding Jeong's demands that the community convert to Christianity. Eventually, however, all but one family in the village converted. But Kim Yakyeon, the principal Silhak leader, did not entirely give up the Confucian custom. He continued to perform the jesa rite, not on the birth and death anniversaries of his deceased parents as in the past, but on Christmas and Good Friday, thus combining Christian and Confucian traditions.[93] He was not the only one who continued the practise. Church Elder Yun Ha-hyeon also insisted that it continue to be practiced with as much fervour as the Christian holidays.[94] Moon Chai Rin, later as a minister in Yongjeong, made efforts to reconcile the two practices theologically for his congregations.[95] As we will see in future chapters, jesa remained an important rite in Christian communities and not only survived the conversion to Christianity for many Koreans but also the migration to Canada where it was translated with effect into the context of the Anglo-Canadian church (see chapter 7).

Successive exploratory and itinerating trips by Canadian missionaries into Manchuria and Siberia starting in 1903 raised the awareness of Korean Christians to the presence of missionaries working in the area and of their potential benefit to the community.[96] Kim Yakyeon put his name on a petition with others on 4 November 1912 to beseech Canadian missionaries to come and set up a station near their village.[97] Kim remained closely associated with missionaries from this time on as interviewees Chun Sunyeong and Kim Ikseon attest.[98] Photographs from the period present Kim Yakyeon as an important person in the Christian community and in Missionary circles.

The earliest expressions of Korean Christianity involved a message of social transformation and communal salvation connected to the political aspirations of Korean independence. In Myeongdong, the Silhak leaders' call for national restoration had been fully incorporated into the Christian gospel preached at church. This was not a religion of apolitical, personal salvation such as that preached by many Western missionaries, Canadians included, and later adopted by large numbers of South Korean Christians in the postwar period.[99] Rather, Christianity was viewed as a vehicle of communal redemption; its message was a call to liberate the community (and nation) as a whole and to raise it to a better place.[100] The Christian message, therefore, entailed political struggle. "Apart from this perspective," says Ahn Byung Mu, "we would never have an accurate understanding of Korean Christianity."[101] During the years of military dictatorship between 1962 and 1987, when anti-communist ideology reached its apex and a conservative theology was used to pacify Korean Christians, a contrarian understanding of the faith with roots in the Kando region of Manchuria continued to be an important religio-political force in South Korea in opposition to the dictatorships.

The unique tensions and contradictions of the region are clear in the expression of Christianity developed by Kando Christians. Their approach identified the Christian message of salvation with a cultural collective (Koreans), but not with the political institutions that claimed to represent the nation. As such their collective boundaries were ambiguous and defied strict definitions imposed by those in power. Christianity was, therefore, able to bridge several social divisions such as those between noble and peasant, and even, on occasion, between communists and capitalists. Kando native and founder of Minjung theology Ahn Byung Mu (see chapter 5) maintained that the Korean version of Christian nationalism stressed the needs of the "oppressed" and gave rise to a strain of Korean Christianity that did not shy away from confronting oppressive forms of government or religion. His experiences in Kando, he said, laid the foundation for his involvement in the Democratization Movement and the Minjung theology which he developed. [102] It was this tradition of Korean Christianity which Canadian missionaries encountered upon their entrance into the Korean mission field.

OUR NORTH-WEST ALL OVER AGAIN: CANADIAN MISSIONARIES IN KANDO

Canadian missionaries first began to arrive in Korea in 1888 under the auspices of ecumenical organizations or American churches.[103] These first Canadian missionaries travelled separately and worked independently of one another in locations scattered across the peninsula. In 1893, a self-supported missionary from Cape Breton, Nova Scotia named William McKenzie travelled to Korea and settled in a village in the northwestern part of the peninsula named Sorae.[104] Canadian mission work in Korea had started a little bit later than the work in Japan and parts of China. George Lesley Mackay, for example, had established himself in a village of northern Formosa (Taiwan) by 1872.[105] But in time, and partly thanks to MacKenzie, the Korean mission field would come to rival these other missions in the minds of churchgoers back home.

McKenzie's ministry made such an impression on the people of Sorae that when he died suddenly in 1895 of a self-inflicted gunshot wound suffered in a delirium of typhoid fever, the community wrote a letter to the Presbyterian church in the Maritimes (McKenzie's home church) asking that more missionaries be sent to them.[106] In 1898, after a dramatic series of events,[107] the Eastern (Maritime) Division of Mission of the Presbyterian church finally responded by dispatching five Canadians, two couples and a single male, the official beginning of the Canadian church-sponsored mission to Korea. This was followed by nine more over the next ten years, and then another stream sent by the Western (Ontario and Quebec) Division of the Canadian Presbyterian Church beginning in 1910.[108]

When they arrived in Korea, the Canadians had to confer with the mission boards from other nations and denominations that had preceded them in Korea. At question was the area in which they would undertake their mission activities. Concerned to avoid wasteful competition and conflict, missionaries in Korea had decided to divide the peninsula into separate areas, assigning each area to a specific mission of a specific country and religious affiliation.[109] After some deliberation, the Americans and Australians of Methodist and Presbyterian alignment, who were already active in much of the country, volunteered to withdraw from either the southeast or the northeast of the peninsula so that the Canadian Presbyterians could have a region of their own to focus on. The story is told by Koreans who worked with the Canadian missionaries that the northeastern region of the country was the coldest and least hospitable part of the peninsula and that the Canadians were the only ones willing to work there.[110] Missionary William Scott, however, recorded that the Canadians chose the northeastern provinces of North and South Hamkyeong for their mission field, in part at least, because it was closer to where their forerunner, McKenzie, had worked and died.[111]

The area of Korea for which the Canadian missionaries came to have exclusive responsibility was a huge and sparsely populated region extending 800 kilometres north from Wonsan (a city about midway between northern and southern extremities of the Korean peninsula along its eastern coast) to Hoeryeong/Kimchaek in the northeast corner of the country bordering Russia and China. From the East Sea it extended approximately eighty kilometres inland.[112] The Canadians quickly realized that they had landed in an area of the country that was historically, culturally, and geographically distinct from the rest of Korea. The northeast was a particularly mountainous region with a long history of rule by Manchurian-Koreans or Manchurians based north of the Tumen and Yalu rivers. The inhabitants of the northeastern provinces continued to look north, rather than south, for support in times of trouble, and were always on the margins of the Korean political economy whose metropole was Seoul.[113] As the Canadian missionaries became familiar with their surroundings, they realized that there were also many Koreans across the border in Siberia and Manchuria. A good number were already Christian and welcomed or even beseeched the Canadian missionaries for support.[114] The Canadians were stretched thin with one of the smallest mission contingents on the largest mission field. Nevertheless, in 1903, an exploratory expedition visited Kando and an area in Russia surrounding Vladivostok.[115] On their trip the missionaries met thousands of Koreans moving north.[116] Numbers crossing the northern border continued to surge in the ensuing years.[117] As a result, the Canadian Mission decided to establish one of its first three stations in the city of Yongjeong in Kando,[118] about 80 kilometres on the other side of the Tumen river, the northern limit of Korea proper.[119] The other two mission stations were in Hoeryeong, on the Korean side of the Tumen River bordering Manchuria, and Hamheung, further south along the coast. These initial three stations were later joined by two more in Kimchaek (Seongjin) and Wonsan.[120] But Yongjeong captured the Canadians' imagination in a particular way.[121] Pressing for the construction of a mission compound, missionary T.D. Mansfield wrote, "In all our territory we have no work so insistent, so promising, so white to the harvest, as this Yong Jung [sic] field."[122] The Canadian mission began to buy up land in the city and build on it soon after Mansfield's letter arrived in Canada. Yongjeong was, by the turn of the century, a hub of the rapidly growing Korean population in Manchuria.[123] As the town grew, the mission compound, which had been constructed on the outskirts of town, was quickly engulfed by the growing city and ended up occupying a place at its heart.[124] The Canadian missionaries ran Eun-jin Middle School for boys, a girls' school, a hospital, a nurses' training school and a Bible school for training church volunteers. These all clustered around a mission compound with three missionary houses.[125]

As if to their own reflection in a well, Canadian missionaries were drawn to the vast fertile plains and frigid winter temperatures, that they found in Kando, not to mention the signs of a burgeoning modern nation-state ripe for the civilizing work of Christian missionaries. Kando, the area into which a large number of Koreans had migrated in the early 1900s, was "surrounded by a splendid farming country" and, with railroad construction underway, it reminded missionary A.H. Barker "most forcibly" of the prairies.[126] Missionary J.M. Scott, reported back to the Canadian church that the Kando region "relates itself to Korea as Alberta and Saskatchewan have done to older Canada."[127] Noting the construction of railroad by the Japanese, Pioneer Canadian missionary Robert Grierson summed it up most eloquently: "It is so appropriate that [the Presbyterian Church in Canada] has taken up this work for Kando is our North-West all over again, including it's [sic] fertility. Not Mountainous like Korea proper, but like the foot-hill country [of Alberta], with soil black with loam. A goodly heritage for the coming settler, and the coming Missionary."[128] In relating his experience of itinerating beyond the Tumen river, Grierson drew a strong parallel between the Canadian northwest and Manchuria. With twelve years' experience as a missionary to Korea already under his belt, he had witnessed the Japanese takeover of the peninsula and the impact of its colonial policies on Koreans. He sympathized with the Korean point of view. In Manchuria, he and others could see that the Japanese would be using railway expansion to project economic and military power. Be that as it may, Kando also provided missionaries with a good environment to win Koreans over to the Christian religion in a territory that bore a marked resemblance to the young Dominion of Canada, which was at the very same time being crisscrossed in railway lines, colonized, and Christianized.

It had only been a generation earlier that Metis uprisings in Manitoba had spurred a surge of Protestant interest in the North-West. That interest had notably taken the form of armed Orange Lodge militias sent to oppress Metis communities and claw back the recognition of their distinct culture that they had just managed to negotiate with the Canadian government.[129] A much kinder, similarly motivated campaign was waged by missionaries who, confronted with indigenous populations and then a great wave of non-Anglo European "foreigners" following confederation, were convinced that Christianization must go hand in hand with a program of "Canadianization," a word that meant indoctrination into a unitary English-speaking state defined by Great Britain's traditions of government and allegiance to its language, religion, culture, and Empire.[130] This was an approach shared by both Presbyterians and Methodists, two founding denominations of the UCC.[131]

Religious leaders in Canada expressed their enthusiasm for this new "Dominion," which contained half the wealth of a continent and was "the peer of any power on earth."[132] Both immigrants and Indigenous people were subject to efforts at religious conversion and national assimilation. Tellingly, "Indian missions" in the Canadian Presbyterian church as well and the missions to the Ruthenians (Ukrainians), Chinese, and Japanese in Canada came under the responsibility of the committee overseeing missions overseas. In other words, the approach of the Presbyterian church in Canada was decided by the racial and ethnic identity of those they ministered to rather than by geographical location.[133] Fear of another Metis rebellion or similar uprising from foreign elements was an important impetus of missionary initiatives within Canada. The churches saw this as a reason to accelerate the assimilation process, which also contributed to the horrors of the residential school system.[134]

In the months before Grierson penned his letter to the mission committee in Canada describing Kando as "our North-West all over again," the church in Canada had been abuzz with the results of a national gathering of clergy, laymen, and missionaries that had convened to discuss the philosophy and practice of missions overseas and at home. Canada's Missionary Congress, which was held in Toronto between 31 March and 4 April 1909, had brought together close to two thousand men representing the Canadian Protestant church from coast to coast.[135] It was the first event of its kind in North America and prefigured the international gathering of missionaries in Edinburgh the following year. The Congress was focussed mainly upon the work of missionaries overseas but there was also discussion of the situation in Canada's western provinces. Canada's Indigenous population had been almost entirely overlooked but the "problem" of foreign immigrants had been the focus of one or two speakers who also compared it to the "Negro problem" in the United States, highlighting the anxiety of the gathering of White English-speaking men at the prospect of a nation made up of racially diverse people.[136]

Addressing the Congress on the first day, Chairman of the Canadian council of the Layman's Missionary Movement Mr N.W. Rowell, asserted that "Religion has ever been the most potent factor in individual and national life." It is religion, he went on to explain, that has been the main reason for the development of different political systems and cultures around the world: "nature worship has given the world Africa, agnosticism represented in Confucianism has given the world China, pantheism has given to the world India, and Christianity has given the world Europe and America."[137] Later that day, the Rev. S.M. Zwemer, stated "Christianity and non-Christian religions are two distinct conceptions. Their real relation, therefore, when they come into contact is that of impact, and not of compromise."[138] While there was an undeniable and persistent impulse among the speakers of the Congress to rise above racism and nationalism, the language of the convention prominently featured words such as "aggressive," "muscular," "control," and "conquest" to describe the missionary project. As keynote speaker, the American missionary to Korea Robert Speer framed it: "If I have a sword, and a man disputes the sharpness of my sword's edge, I will not convince him by handing him a treatise on the mechanics of sharp edges; I will cut him with it. If we have a Gospel that was meant of God to subdue the world, the best way in which we can convince the world that that Gospel has a right to be propagated everywhere and to conquer the world is by using it for its predestined end." This vocabulary, though never deployed in Grierson's correspondence, gives a sense of the kind of lens missionaries like him were applying to mission fields around the world and in Kando. Grierson notes the building of railroads. He also understood the power of the British Empire that stood behind him as he had once had gunboats dispatched to rescue him.[139] It is likely these factors, every bit as much as the geography, reminded Grierson of Canada's northwest.

Canadian missionary accounts of Korea such as Grierson's were not only a result of Canadian attitudes but were, conversely, helping to construct and reinforce them at the same time,[140] heroic tales to contribute to the "glorious history" of "Church and country."[141] By the 1920s Canada had more missionaries in the field on a per-capita basis than any other country in the world.[142] Hundreds of thousands of dollars were spent by Canadians to support them. "In return," writes mission historian Ruth Compton Brouwer, "missionaries and missionary literature broadened the horizons of ordinary Canadians, providing them with the materials for a world view whose optimism and idealism would for long mask its less attractive aspects."[143] Missionaries and their reports also helped to shape their supporters into "Canadians." They encoded the ideals of Anglo-Protestant nationalism, which were to be the foundations of the fledgling dominion and legitimated the process of colonization that was taking place on the Canadian prairies.

When the early Canadian missionaries to Korea remarked on the similarities between Manchuria and the Canadian prairies, they did so without awareness of the fact that the colonial commitments of the Mission Enterprise on display in Canada's northwest ran directly counter to the political aspirations of the Koreans to whom they professed to minister. In the early years of the mission, they showed no consciousness that their work aligned with global imperial or colonial designs in direct contradiction to the Christianity of the Koreans with whom they worked. But Canadians, in time, became more aware of the internal contradictions of their mission and despite their colonial/imperial leanings, missionaries in Kando came to feel a great deal of sympathy for Koreans and their desire to be free of their Japanese overlords. Interviewee Kim Ikseon is unequivocal that Canadian missionaries were committed to shielding Korean activists from Japanese reprisals when possible. He recalls that one missionary, William Scott, often hid political fugitives in the mission compound.[144] Scott was not the only one. Canadian missionaries generally gained a reputation for defending Koreans against Japanese aggression.[145]

Despite their sympathy for Koreans as the violence and oppression of the Japanese authorities intensified, overall Canadian missionaries still tended to side with imperial rule as a source of stable modern government.[146] When Canadian missionaries did criticize the Japanese government, they often leveraged their position as subjects of the British crown.[147] A famous example of this occurred following the independence demonstrations of March 1919 when missionaries Rev. A.H. Barker and Dr Stanley Martin raised the Union Jack over the Canadian compound and used the extraterritorial rights of the British Empire to shelter Koreans fleeing Japanese reprisals.[148] Persecution of Koreans notwithstanding, Canadian missionaries preferred the steady policies of Japanese colonial rule to what they regarded as the inevitable and unwelcome chaos of an untested Korean government. The position of the Canadian mission, as expressed by the chair of the Foreign Board of Missions in Canada, was that missionaries approved of Japanese government, but not its methods in dealing with Korean opposition.[149] The contradictions between the Canadians' own innate alignment with imperialist ideology and the nationalist commitments of their Korean Christian friends did eventually, slowly, occur to the missionaries as they worked in Kando and northeastern Korea. But it took many years.

A number of events highlight the growing tension between Canadian missionaries and the Korean Christians along the fault line of colonialism. The first is the difficulty they encountered in the rise of communism. One high-profile case was the renunciation of the Christian faith by a prominent Korean Christian leader, Yi Dong-hui. Yi worked closely with Grierson on the Canadian mission field and was admired by many as a great preacher and church leader. But Yi eventually became convinced that Christianity was not going to lead Korea to its desired independence from Japan, and he gave up the faith in favour of socialism. Many missionaries at the time attributed the stiff competition they were experiencing from the communist movement to the fact that they had been ineffective in addressing Korean national aspirations and ignoring the injustices of Japanese colonialism.[150] Another example is the conflict with students at the Canadian mission school in Hamheung. Angered that missionaries were not allocating funds to improve the educational standards of the school so as to match those of public schools run by the Japanese colonial government, students torched their school building in protest.[151] Indigenous students and parents in Canada had similar complaints about their mission-run schools and cases of residential schools being torched were not unheard of. A further example of Korean displeasure with the Canadian missionaries and the Canadian church comes from students travelling to Canada for graduate studies. These students were shocked to find overwhelming support for Japanese colonial expansion in the people they met. Studying in Canada in 1928, Moon Chai Rin, for example, voiced his displeasure when he learned that his Canadian theological colleagues and professors all supported Japanese Imperial aspirations in Korea.[152] Indeed a positive attitude towards Japanese expansionism was promoted by Canadian Protestant churches generally.[153] Even aggressive Japanese incursion into Manchuria and China was viewed with sympathy (and sometimes approval) by UCC missionaries in Japan.[154]

As clearly as these examples show a striking incongruence between the Korean and Canadian attitudes regarding colonialism, the most revealing example is perhaps the fate of the Church Union movement

A Land in between "Our Ancestors" and "Our North-West"   53

in Korea. At Canada's Missionary Congress in 1909, much progress had already been made towards institutional unity between Methodists, Presbyterians, and other Protestant denominations in Canada. Rowell remarked with pride that

> The Canadian colonies led the way in federation ... Canada led the way in the union of the various branches of the Presbyterian and Methodist Churches. Canada has led the way in the negotiations of a larger and more comprehensive Church union. The Christian men of Canada are the first to gather together in a great National Congress to consider their missionary privileges and responsibilities. As the Roman was called to teach the world law; the Greek to teach the world art; the Hebrew to teach the world religion; so we in Canada, if true to our opportunities, may be called to lead the world in the work of world-wide evangelization.[155]

This quote suggests a connection between Church Union, Canadian nationalism, and missionary enterprise. Indeed, the creation of the UCC was motivated by the conviction that church and government should have a close partnership, an idea with historical roots in the history of Christendom.[156] The new united Christian body sought to be the "national" church for the Dominion of Canada, and also free up resources for the missionary effort. Some who opposed the idea worried that the move was a grab at worldly power and pointed to a similar Protestant union that had taken place in Prussia one hundred years earlier.[157] Tellingly, the UCC's idea of the "national soul" seemed not even to include the diversity of the co-founding French people within that nation, let alone indigenous peoples and languages – a fact that speaks to the racial and cultural arrogance inherent in the project.[158] Indeed, the idea of a united Protestant church was strengthened by the belief that such a church could in tandem with the Canadian government play a central role in the construction of Canada as an Anglo Protestant civilization. By 1925 however, when Church Union was finally and formally achieved in Canada by an act of the Canadian Parliament, the Church Union movement on the Korean mission field had become problematic. The Japanese imperial government was beginning to take a positive view of church union, for reasons that demonstrate the affinity of the idea with colonial statecraft; rather than a means of promoting Christian influence upon the government, the creation of a single Christian denomination made it easier for the state to exercise influence over the church. Indeed, a unified governing structure was eventually forced on churches throughout the Japanese Empire in 1942.[159] Kim Kwan Sik was made head of that organization in Korea, a person closely associated with the Canadian mission, and the first Korean, in fact, to receive a scholarship from the mission to study in Canada. Kim was committed to church union on the grounds that it was good for the church and not out of desire to support the Japanese policy and consideration was given to keeping the structure going after liberation.[160] However, the association in Korea of church union with the Japanese colonial government ensured that the idea would be completely abandoned.

CONCLUSION

Kando, at the turn of the twentieth century, was a place of beginnings. The Island-in-Between was a unique environment where foreign colonial forces and indigenous independence movements coexisted, told stories, and supported and challenged one another in a liminal geography rife with both chaos and the potential of new life. Koreans who migrated to Kando claimed it as the land of their ancestors. But they also saw it as a place where their ancient nation could make a new start and repel modern powers that were pushing it down. Political and religious movements converged in this region, giving birth to a Korean Protestant Christianity that was closely linked to nationalist aspirations for a free and sovereign Korea. Christianity provided a new form of political organization and education that was essential for meeting the threat of colonization and the challenges of modernity. It also strengthened aspects of Korean culture, notably through the translation of the Bible into common Korean script. In the process of adopting the new religion, however, compromises had to be made vis-à-vis traditional Confucian practices and beliefs. But the conviction that Koreans were a sovereign people with a culture worth preserving was never in doubt.

Canadian missionaries were invited into this space by Korean Christians who saw them as a source of support for their movement. These missionaries, though sensitive to Korean aspirations, did not see Kando as a fount of Korean nationalism but rather as a mirror of the Northwest Territories of the new Dominion of Canada. These missionaries came out of a movement that was politically aligned with Imperial forces. The contradictions of the mission began to dawn on the Canadians as they witnessed and tried to protect Koreans from Japanese colonial violence, but they were slow learners. The Korean Christians themselves also noticed these contradictions. Some of them made their disapproval known by leaving the faith and joining the socialist movement which they felt better represented and more effectively progressed toward their desire for an independent nation. Others protested, sometimes violently, the Canadian missionaries' control of and priorities for the mission.

From the dissonance and harmony of the Kando region and northeast Korea was born a relationship between Korean Christians and Canadian missionaries. This relationship, like the Manchurian environment and the creation story in the Bible, was a dance between opposing forces of chaos and creativity, convergence and divergence, danger and promise. Like a good story, the relationship had enough depth and complexity to sustain itself over multiple generations. In the following chapter, we will explore how the Canadian mission to Korea responded to pressure from its Korean Christian colleagues and the interruption of its mission by the Pacific and Korean Wars. We will also see how an independently minded tradition of Korean Christianity, connected to the Canadian mission field, was the source of a distinct Korean Christian vision on the peninsula. That vision was manifested in a new seminary and a new Presbyterian denomination, the PROK. These two new institutions would force Canadian missionaries and the nascent United Church of Canada to distinguish itself theologically and politically from their American Presbyterian counterparts. The roots of that development can be traced to Kando.

2

"The Struggle to Express
Their Own Identity"

*The Advent of the PROK and the Emerging
Identity of the Canadian Mission, 1907 to 1957*

Is there a true "history" of the past 50 years of the Korean church? This question still remains unanswered. There are a series of records, of course, but the collection of records does not necessarily constitute a "history." A true history indicates the record of a unique and crucial event that provoked independent and creative changes in reality, which people would never forget. So the question is whether there is any event in the past 50 years of Korean church history that showed Koreans' subjectivity and spirit in both idea and substance.

Kim Chai Choon
Address to the General Assembly of the PROK, 1956[1]

When Kim Chai Choon spoke to the General Assembly of the fledgling Presbyterian Church in the Republic of Korea (PROK) on 25 May 1956, he sought to impress upon his audience that they stood in a tradition of Korean Christians who thought and acted for themselves, independent of the foreign missionaries who had for many years exerted a strong and controlling influence over the Korean church. The PROK was a new and relatively small Presbyterian church body created after Kim and a number of his students had been expelled from the larger PCK. The reasons for their expulsion were ostensibly a matter of Christian doctrine but behind the scenes the manipulating hands of a group of American missionaries worked to regain control of what they once commanded: the Korean Presbyterian church, its educational institutions, and its theology.

Even independent thinkers such as Kim acknowledged that missionaries had played an important role in the growth of the Protestant religion on the peninsula, but Kim argued that growth alone didn't say much about what made Korean Christianity "Korean." The spirit of Korean Protestantism, he told his listeners, lay rather in the animating desire for the wellbeing and freedom of the Korean people, it was a spirit of freedom and independence that sought to lift the entire community, not just "saved" individuals, and preserve what was good about Korean culture and history. This vision, he argued, was the mantle that the PROK had been chosen by God to carry, the mantle of *Korean* Christianity. Such, he sermonized, was God's way of choosing "what is weak in the world to shame the strong."[2]

The articulation of a uniquely Korean vision for the Korean church during the first half-century of its life had been a struggle. Not only were overt expressions of a distinct national identity strictly forbidden by the Japanese colonial authorities, but the foreign missionaries who worked with Koreans also often discouraged Koreans from thinking for themselves. Kim did not deny that foreign Protestant countries, especially the United States, contributed to the growth of the Korean Protestant church. However, he asserted, the church they engendered had "too little of the Korean 'spirit.'" Under their shadow, he said, "Koreans were not allowed to criticize any 'Christian thoughts' but just to 'memorize' and 'follow.'"[3] But Kim and others had long desired to give voice to an expression of their faith that was distinctly Korean. This did not mean a retreat into ancient traditions of a pre-modern Korea. On the contrary, it meant a theology that was based on the thoughts and aspirations of Korean people free to explore ideas, young and old, and express them for themselves and for their emerging context. There are other examples of Christians seeking independence from missionaries in Korean Church history, but of the postwar Presbyterian refugees from the north, Kim is the most well known of those who sought an independent Korean church. Following the liberation of Korea, Kim was finally free from Japanese censorship and able to begin to assert a distinctively Korean vision. But he was frustrated by resistance from missionaries returning to Korea.

Within the context of a liberated Korea, a vision of an independent Korean Church carried consequences for the missionaries who worked alongside it. Used to exerting considerable control over the shape and direction of the Korean church, missionaries were now being urged by some to take more of a backseat. Kim Chai Choon and the group of Presbyterian Christian leaders who eventually formed the PROK were especially insistent. The creation of the PROK not only splintered the Korean Presbyterian church, it also splintered the missionary community. The United Church of Canada (UCC) and its missionary organization chose to align itself with the PROK against the wishes of their American counterparts. That decision was based on a decades-old and evolving relationship with Koreans from the northeastern prefectures and Kando. Taking the decision meant that the UCC was now uniquely related with a politically active and independently minded Korean Christian leadership inclined to challenge missionary policies and Western political hegemony. Association with the PROK, therefore, reinforced emerging democratic and anti-colonial tendencies of the Canadian mission. It did not fully eliminate colonial chauvinism inherent in the enterprise, but it did set the stage for the UCC Korea Mission to address its colonial structure more fully in the post war period. This chapter will trace both the emergence of an independent Korean Christian voice and its consequences for the identity of the Canadian mission during the first fifty years of the Korean Presbyterian church.

THE PYEONGYANG SEMINARY AND THE BIRTH OF THE KOREAN PRESBYTERIAN CHURCH

During the early years of missionary activity in Korea, the greatest increase in Christian converts occurred in the northern half of the peninsula. The initial introduction of Protestant Christianity to Korea came from Koreans themselves. Korean colporteurs and preachers had made many converts on both sides of the Manchurian-Korean border before the arrival of missionaries (see chapter 1). Northern Korea, especially the northwest area around Pyeongyang, would act as the centre of Korean Protestant Christianity through the period of Japanese colonization and remain so until the division of the peninsula into communist north and capitalist south. Because of the partitioning of the Korean peninsula among the different national and denominational missions (see chapter 1), the city of Pyeongyang and the northwest of Korea where the largest number Korean Christians were concentrated came under the influence of the mission of the Northern Presbyterian Church of the USA.[4]

The remarkable success of Protestant Christianity among Koreans in the north meant that missionaries had more converts than they could effectively minister to on their own. As a result they identified the training of indigenous leaders as their most pressing need. In the year 1901, the Presbyterian seminary in Pyeongyang was established with the help of funds from Mrs McCormick, a wealthy American philanthropist associated with McCormick Seminary in Chicago and the Northern Presbyterian Church of the USA.[5] This further contributed to the influence of the Northern Presbyterian Mission on the Korean Presbyterian church in particular and the Korean Protestant church in general. The Canadian mission, however, contributed to the founding of the seminary as well and had some influence in its development. Pioneer Canadian missionary Dr Robert Grierson M.D. taught the first class of students who graduated in 1907.[6] Another pioneer Canadian missionary Rev. William Rufus Foote took over from Grierson and taught on a permanent basis until his death in 1929. Foote was in turn succeeded by Rev. Alec F. Robb who taught there until he passed away in 1935.[7] Both Foote and Robb taught Church History, and therefore stayed clear of the more sensitive issues of theology and biblical interpretation that eventually became matters of contention.[8]

As a professor at the Pyeongyang Seminary in 1907, Grierson was teacher to the first group of Korean ministers to be ordained by the Korean Presbyterian church. Until 1907, the "Presbyterian Council" of missions in Korea, which included the Canadian mission along with the Northern and Southern Presbyterian Missions from the US and the Presbyterian Mission from Australia, had effectively served as a governing body for the nascent Korean Presbyterian church.[9] There had been even broader cooperation with Methodist missions on the peninsula and talk of forming a single unified non-denominational Korean Protestant church. Missionaries gratefully acknowledged that the theological and ecclesial groundwork for the unified Korean church had been provided by church union efforts in Canada.[10] But the decision of the Presbyterian Council to establish a Korean Presbyterian church that year effectively foreclosed the possibility. The Presbyterians were impatient to establish a self-governing Korean church and setting up a Presbyterian denomination would take less time than negotiating a new church structure with other denominations.[11]

Missionaries in Korea had adopted a method for missionizing developed by Chinese missionary John L. Nevius. The Nevius method, as this method was later dubbed, promoted a "self sacrificing, self reliant, self respecting" church. Early on, American missionary W.D. Reynolds had articulated seven principles to guide the mission work towards a self-sustaining and self-governing Korean church that focussed on the kind of training Korean church leadership should be given. Future Korean pastors should know the basic tenets of the Christian faith but little more than that at first, he said. Rather, their education should focus on matters of the "Holy Ghost" and how to be a good "Christian soldier," implying an emphasis of spiritual experience and practical action rather than advanced academic learning.[12]

Furthermore, Reynolds explicitly stated that Koreans should not be sent abroad for an education. Robert E. Speer, a leader in the American missionary enterprise and keynote speaker at the Canada's Mission Congress in 1909 (see chapter 1) further claimed "there is little demand from the native [Korean] Christians as yet for higher education."[13] This attitude was partly born of practical necessity. The urgent need for locally trained Korean leaders meant that a crash course in the basic tenets of Christianity for a population that had little previous exposure to the new faith and rapid deployment of these leaders was an effective approach. According to Canadian missionary William Scott, the reason American missionaries discouraged advanced training overseas for Korean leadership was their concern that such leaders would be absent too long while they were urgently needed in their home communities.[14] But it was also an approach that seriously downplayed the Korean desire for higher learning and was patronizing in its assumptions about what Koreans were ready to learn.

What missionaries said they wanted to avoid was a Korean church that was directed from outside and lacked an identity and coherence of its own. Reynolds was emphatic: "no namby pamby half organised, mercenary ministry for an invertebrate mass of jellyfish Christian!"[15] Reynolds' exclamation, however, was both ironic and self-serving, if not downright dishonest. The policies against advanced training for Koreans meant that indigenous leaders would not be exposed to broader trends of theological thought that ran counter to the often-narrow conservative positions of the American missionaries who worked with them. While Protestant missionaries in Korea claimed that they wanted an indigenous Korean church that was independent and self-directed, the reality was that especially in the area of education their policies were designed to keep Korean leadership ignorant and under their control.

Reynold's policy for training Korean church workers and Speers' claim that advanced education was not desired by Korean Christians were contested by a number of Korean church leaders. Writing in 1929, Korean church historian Lak-Geoon Paik criticized this missionary approach: "The whole policy seems to us not to have been based upon far sighted vision. Self-respect and self-reliance are most to be looked for among educated leaders, and these Korean leaders were to be successors to the service that missionaries themselves had rendered to the Korean church. The intellectual training and cultural character of Korean ministers should have been elevated to a high plane in order to avoid an invidious comparison and wide chasm between him [sic] and the foreign missionary. It is strange, moreover, that the missionaries should have minimized the intellectual standard of the Korean minister."[16] In this period, young men and women in China and Korea of all religions and professional disciplines were clamoring for the opportunity to study in Europe, North America, and Japan. Holding back young Korean Christians from such an opportunity seemed strange indeed and hobbled the Christian leadership in its efforts to be taken seriously in Korean society which held education, and foreign education especially, in high regard.[17]

THE EVOLVING IDENTITY OF
THE CANADIAN MISSION

Regarding the missionary policy to limit the education of Korean leaders, Canadian missionaries were different than their American counterparts. Moon Chai Rin, who attended Pyeongyang seminary in 1923[18] attested that Canadian missionaries had a different approach to educating Korea church leaders. Aware of this fact, he suggests, American missionaries tried to limit their influence as faculty.[19] Indeed, Canadian missionaries, skirting rules set by their American counterparts, had from time-to-time offered classes in secret on subjects that were forbidden by school policy. Robert Grierson, for example, aware of his students' interest in science, offered clandestine classes on scientific subjects using the encyclopedia from the office of American missionary and seminary principal W.L. Swallen, who was at the time away on furlough.[20] William Scott, with a number of Korean leaders (including Song Chang-geun, who we will meet shortly), helped translate the Abington Bible Commentary, a landmark theological publication in Europe and North America that referenced current historical and literary criticism. Scott had done so against the will of his American colleagues and was censured by the staff at Pyeongyang Seminary for his efforts.[21] Canadians also differed from their American colleagues in their determination to send Korean leaders outside the country for a high-level education and funded many students to study abroad in Canada and elsewhere.[22] Moon himself was supported by the Canadian mission to study in Canada in 1928.[23]

William Scott attributes the difference in the Canadian approach to sociological factors. The United States missions had many wealthy backers, a fact that tended to develop paternalistic patterns of relationship on the mission field, he said. Canadians, on the other hand, tended to fund scholarships through a combination of church grants and individual donations. In the matter of funding buildings and intuitions these funds were combined with money raised in the Korean church.[24] The impression is that the process was more collaborative and less top-down. The Canadian mission also made the decision in 1926, immediately following Church Union in Canada, to devolve its control of the mission field by including Koreans on boards and in the decision-making process.[25] Moon Chai Rin observed a less paternalistic and more cooperative approach on the part of Canadian missionaries in matters related to polity. Canadian missionaries, he says, did not believe they should be making arbitrary decisions for Koreans. For this reason, they created committees made up of an equal number of Koreans and Canadians to decide on mission business. Moon points out that it took other missions many years to follow their lead.[26] Some of these policies came after dramatic protests on the part of Koreans such as the burning of a mission school in Hamheung,[27] but Canadians seemed to be learning nevertheless – and, if slowly, at least faster in comparison to others.

The American Presbyterians often resented the Canadians for their different approach. They distrusted what they viewed as their propensity for "liberal" theology, and were appalled when the Canadian Presbyterian mission came under the purview of the new United Church of Canada, a denomination they believed was tainted with heresy.[28] American missionary W.L. Swallen, principal of Pyeongyang Seminary whose encyclopedias had been used to educate Korean seminarians behind his back, wrote to ask the Canadian missionaries who voted for union to withdraw from the field since they had been granted the area to work in by the American Presbyterian mission based on the fact that they were Presbyterian. This was a false and disingenuous claim. Swallen further objected that the Korean Presbyterians in the area had not been given a choice of whether they wanted missionaries that were not Presbyterian working with them, despite the fact that they had not had the choice of which denomination of missionary came in the first place. Swallen also worried that the new "United" brand of missionary might lead to a split in the Korean church.[29] In hindsight, on this last point at least Swallen may well have had reason to worry. The group of Presbyterians connected to the UCC mission were eventually expelled from the Korean Presbyterian body influenced by the American missionaries. The distinct expression of Christianity articulated by these Koreans, however, likely came more from their own convictions than from the influence of the Canadian mission. What is more, important differences in the Canadian mission, whether due to the Koreans with whom they associated or because of their distinctive Canadian context or both, was evident prior to Church Union.

Canadians were often conscious of the differences between themselves and their American missionary colleagues. Writing in response to the negative reaction of American missionary colleagues to the formation of the UCC, William Scott asserted that the Canadian approach to missions was more democratic than the American approach: "Some of us feel, further, that we [as a] British mission have a decided contribution to make towards the mission enterprise here in Korea. We may come from an imperialistic nation, but our sympathies and our mission policies are the most democratic in Korea. And our religious outlook is more sanely liberal-conservative [i.e., balanced] than most American missions [which tend to lean strongly conservative]."[30] This reflection shows that by the 1920s, Scott was thinking critically about the Canadian mission's connection to a history of colonialism. No doubt this awareness was in no small part due to Korean Christians who publicly raised the "tarnished image of the so-called Christian West, with its militarism, its capitalism, and its imperialism." Scott had been confronted at a meeting in 1924 where a speaker demanded of the missionaries in attendance, "Release India and the Philippines; then pray for us."[31] With these encounters in mind and despite its historical ties to British Imperialism and association with the American Presbyterians, the Canadian mission had, in Scott's mind, distanced itself from both.

KIM CHAI CHOON

Among the Korean Christian leaders who, like Moon Chai Rin, would come to evaluate the Canadian approach to missions positively in comparison to the American one was Kim Chai Choon. Kim was born in 1901 in a little village in the North Hamkyeong province in northeastern Korea. Although this was an area where Canadian missionaries worked, Kim would have no direct involvement with them until he was a young adult.[32] His upbringing was rural and his family's religion and approach to education was Confucian. Kim had positive memories of both these aspects of his childhood.[33] Neither he nor his family were particularly engaged in the pro-independence movement that erupted in 1919 with the March 1 Declaration of Independence.[34] However, a friend who came to have a tremendous influence on the course of Kim's life, Song Chang-geun, was a Christian with close connections to both the independence movement and the Canadian mission. Song encouraged Kim to get more politically involved.[35] Kim took the advice to heart and left home to get an education in Seoul where he entered high school and was eventually converted to Christianity.[36] He reports being greatly affected by readings of by Saint Francis, Tolstoy, and the contemporary Japanese Christian Kagawa Doyohito in these days.[37]

In 1925, having recently been married, Kim made the difficult decision to leave home and pursue his theological education in Japan at Aoyama College.[38] Kim's education was largely self-funded and he struggled to survive on a very tight budget.[39] During his time in Japan his interests ranged beyond theology to literature and philosophy. A commitment to freedom of thought began to form in him in this period.[40] Returning to Korea, his friend Song wrote from the USA to tell him he had secured a scholarship for him in Princeton Theological Seminary. Receiving money from a wealthy church elder and a contribution from his family, Kim scraped enough together to travel to America in steerage to continue his theological education,[41] completing one year at Princeton followed by three years at Western Seminary in Pittsburgh.[42]

Kim felt, when he arrived back home in 1932, that the Christian message in Korea seemed stale and could really benefit from the things he had learned overseas.[43] After spending the winter in his hometown, Kim took a job teaching at a commercial school in Seungjin, one of the larger cities in the northeast province of North Hamkyeong where the UCC had a mission station. While a teacher, he received his license to preach and then in 1937 was ordained as a minister of the Korean Presbyterian church. He resigned as teacher in 1938, in protest against compulsory Shinto shrine observances (more on this below) and accepted an invitation to become a Bible teacher at the Canadian-Mission-run

Eunjin School in Yongjeong, Manchuria (see page xxii).[44] This was his first opportunity to work directly with Canadian missionaries such as William Scott. His time as a teacher in Kando was brief, lasting barely a year, but during this time he developed a relationship with a number of Koreans with whom he would have an important association for many years, including Moon Chai Rin and Kim Shin Mook (see chapter 1), their sons Moon Ik Hwan and Moon Dong Hwan (see chapter 6), and student Ahn Byung Mu (see chapter 5).

Kim was a gifted scholar who in addition to the Korean language was fluent in Chinese ideograms, Japanese and English, not to mention biblical Hebrew and Greek. He was a good speaker and was known to keep audiences spellbound for hours as he laid out various arguments and explained them clearly and engagingly. While soft spoken in person, his pen could be sharp and his attacks on paper pointed. In Kando, Kim published a monthly magazine which tackled issues such as the use of historical and literary criticism to interpret the Bible, the translation of the Abington Bible Commentary into Korean and the right of women to have a leadership role in the church. His positions were not welcome by all in the Korean Christian or missionary community.[45]

THE SHINTO CONTROVERSY AND THE CLOSURE OF PYEONGYANG SEMINARY

As mentioned above, the issue of Shinto rituals in schools was a factor in Kim Chai Choon's move from Seungjin to Yongjeong in 1939. The Christian community in Korea was alerted in 1925 to the Japanese authorities' first moves to use Shinto rituals as a tool of colonial control. In this year, the colonial government erected a Shinto shrine on Namsan (South Mountain) in the Korean capital, Seoul.[46] Koreans were expected to attend Shinto rituals at this site to mark important events on the calendar of the Japanese empire, a fact that Korean Christians, in particular, felt was an infringement upon their religious liberty. Japanese officials attempted to ease Christian objections by telling them that Shinto rites were civil and not religious in nature. Their assurance, however, did not do much to allay concerns. The matter got worse in 1933 when the escalation of Japanese military actions in China led to a desire on the part of the authorities to see their Korean subjects demonstrate more enthusiasm for the Japanese empire which was stoking feelings of nationalism at home and throughout its colonies. One of the consequences was that schools were now required to participate in Shinto rites at local shrines.[47]

The situation intensified further following the 1937 Marco Polo bridge incident that precipitated the all-out Japanese invasion of China. From this point on, Koreans were required to use the Japanese language exclusively outside the house (except in worship)[48] and to adopt Japanese names.[49] They were also scrutinized for their relationship with Westerners, including missionaries.[50] Those Christians who had been able to avoid a head-on collision with the government over Shinto shrine obeyance for many years found there was now no getting around the issue. The Japanese authorities insisted that Shinto rituals be observed in mission schools, and Christians were forced to examine their consciences to decide whether they could accept the official Japanese assurances that they were not religious rituals and keep the schools open or not.

According to William Scott, Korean Christians and missionaries generally fell into four groups when it came to deciding what to do about the schools under their care:

1 Those who adamantly opposed the Japanese and suffered imprisonment, torture, and death[;][51]
2 Those who left church leadership in order not to compromise their faith[;]
3 Those who tried to bend as much as possible without breaking in order to continue to serve their flocks, "not too readily consenting, not too strongly antagonizing"[;]
4 Those that collaborated with the Japanese[.][52]

At stake was not only the conscience and personal safety of believers but also the educational institutions that many Koreans depended on. Missionary-run schools were an important source of education for a significant number of people. Their closure would mean leaving students without a place to learn in some cases, or forcing them to travel away from home in others. It also had implications for the ongoing viability of the church itself. In the case of the seminary in Pyeongyang, the closure meant that no more Korean ministers could be graduated to provide leadership for the Korean Presbyterian church. Nonetheless, the board of the Pyeongyang Seminary decided they could not abide the Japanese demand in good faith. In 1938 they closed the theological seminary along with the primary, middle, and

"The Struggle to Express Their Own Identity" 67

high schools they operated throughout the peninsula. Many American missionaries also began to leave the peninsula at this time.[53]

The Canadian mission was divided in their opinion about what should be done but ended by deciding, contrary to the Northern Presbyterian Mission of the USA, that they would comply with mandatory Shinto rituals in order to keep their schools open in northeast Korea.[54] This decision meant that they could remain active in the community and maintain a presence that they felt was of real value to Koreans and, therefore, justified their decision despite their deep discomfort with the Shinto rituals. Scott explains the rational as follows:

> We find there is still scope for Christian witness. Worship and Bible study are conducted much as formally. Christian teachers are still able to make their influence felt. The committee on religious work of the student society finds opportunity for Christian service. The presence of a missionary is a constant reminder of the larger affiliations of the Christian Church. We regret the division in mission ranks, but we believe and pray that God, in his wisdom, may use both policies to his glory, blessing alike the witness of the closed door and the witness of the continued service.[55]

The position of the Canadian mission was not a capitulation or betrayal of Christian principles, as Scott saw it. Canadian missionaries based their decision on the quality of their relationships with Koreans, relationships that were effective for sustaining faith and hope. The importance of relationships as a consideration alongside theological principles would continue to shape the Canadian mission in the years to come. There were missionaries and Koreans on both sides of the debate and the Shinto obeyance issue continued to divide the Korean church for decades. But there were Koreans who, like the Canadian missionaries, judged that they could comply with the Shinto observances and remain true to their Christian principles. The Canadians were supported by Koreans in their decision.[56]

THE OPENING OF JOSEON SEMINARY

The opening of Joseon[57] Theological Seminary in Seoul followed closely on the decision of the American missionaries to close the Presbyterian seminary in Pyeongyang. Both William Scott and Kim Chai Choon suggest that this move came as a response to the vacuum left by the closing of the Pyeongyang Seminary.[58] Others insist that the idea for the school had been in the works for almost a decade and that the opening of the school following the closure of the seminary in Pyeongyang was pure coincidence.[59] All agree, however, that the idea for a new seminary was born of a concern for an independent Korean voice in the education of Korean Christians. Despite the clash between American missionaries and the Japanese government over the Shinto rituals, some felt that the conservative theology they espoused seemed to be more aligned in with Japanese colonialism than more liberal theological stances. But the principles of the new school were not based on a commitment to liberal theology per se but rather on the principle of freedom of theological thought.[60]

Money for the school had come from exclusively Korean sources. Kim Dae-hyun, a wealthy Korean elder in the Presbyterian church, had provided most of the funds for the new theological venture.[61] After less than a year in Kando at the Canadian mission school, Kim Chai Choon was invited to join the new theological seminary by his friend Song Chang-geun. Kim accepted and joined a small full-time faculty who shared his conviction that the Korean church needed more independence to think for itself.[62] This independent approach shaped the general philosophy of the new school. Joseon seminary would strive not just to give students the ability to proclaim the gospel but to raise their scholarship and thought to a higher level. The four-fold aims were articulated as follows:

1 To lead in spreading the gospel of freedom and to promote free research[;]
2 Without repressing students' own thoughts, to introduce the original foundations of theological thought and the principles of Calvin's theology accurately[;]
3 To introduce a critical approach to the study of the Bible, in preparation for the development of theology[;]
4 Constructive theology, Active theology to avoid the vices that will lead to the destruction of the church.[63]

The emphasis at Joseon seminary was to be on scholarship first and piety second, the reverse of the priorities of the Pyeongyang seminary, an order of emphasis carved onto the stele eventually erected on the campus of its successor, Hanguk Theological Seminary.[64] Along with the promotion of independent scholarship was the conviction that

"The Struggle to Express Their Own Identity" 69

the Korean church should be in direct relationship with churches in other countries through ecumenical organizations rather than isolated in its own practices and faith and limited in its association with others through missionaries.[65] From the beginning it was concerned to reform the Korean church in accordance to the best that Koreans had learned outside Korea as well as from within.[66]

Kim and the others involved in the establishment of the new seminary were convinced that they had entered a new era of Christianity in Korea. The missionaries were being forced to leave and the age of missionary leadership, like it or not, was over. It was time for the Korean church to step up.[67] Freedom of thought involved a re-evaluation of the distinction between Christian and non-Christian knowledge and culture. Kim was critical of missionaries for not taking time to learn or making it a priority to learn Eastern culture, literature, and religion[68] He developed a Korean theology that drew at times on Confucian principals and remained open to wisdom from Eastern religious traditions.[69] Perhaps the best example of this kind of theology is found in his development of the idea of a "community of cosmic love," for which he drew on the Confucian concept of benevolence "仁." Benevolence, like the Christian concept of love, is not something that can be legislated but comes from the human heart and must be cultivated. Here Kim connects the Christian church to Confucian "study," which is not about an accumulation of knowledge but the cultivation of virtue.[70] Independence of thought also involved a bolder engagement with political concerns. The historical critical approach introduced by Kim, for example, opened the minds of students to the circumstances of biblical times and introduced the possibility of making critical judgments regarding historically bound social-political realities. Students were taught to be aware of social injustices and to be socially engaged as religious leaders.[71]

OUTBREAK OF WAR AND RENDEZVOUS OF KOREAN CHRISTIANS AND MISSIONARIES IN THE SOUTH

Not long after the opening of Joseon seminary, the last of the missionaries were forced from Korea. The complete evacuation of American missionaries began in the autumn of 1940 and the Canadians began an official withdrawal soon thereafter.[72] The departure of the missionaries marked enormous changes for the Korean church as well. By the time the last Canadian missionaries had been repatriated in 1942, all of their schools were government run.[73] In an interview, Chun Sukyeong, who grew up in Kando, shared that following the departure of the Canadian missionaries, mission schools in Yongjeong were amalgamated with others. In addition, the sports that had been a highlight of the mission schools were discontinued and, in their place, hard labour was instituted to support the Japanese war effort. The use of Korean was forbidden.[74] Meanwhile the grand missionary houses were claimed by the Japanese soldiers.[75]

As the Pacific war progressed Christians and those who had benefited from education in the West or who had been associated with missionaries, were viewed with increasing suspicion by the Japanese authorities. In the final days of Japanese colonial rule, Moon Chai Rin was arrested because of his connection to the Canadians. He was taken from his home in Kando across the border into Korea and though marked for execution he was eventually released at the close of the war and made his way back to Yongjeong as communist forces were beginning to assert control of the area.[76] He was arrested twice more. North Korean communists picked him up and put him on death row again. But Moon had former students in the Chinese communist army who respected and liked their former teacher and managed to convince his jailers to release him after three months. Moon was picked up a third time by Russian soldiers at the behest of the North Koreans who had been angered that he had been let go. Again, Moon came a hair's breadth from being executed before he was released a third time for unknown reasons.[77] Aware of the danger the communists posed to Christians, especially those like himself who had worked with Westerners and lived in the West, many were fleeing south. Moon had not wanted to abandon his home in Manchuria. In addition to the memories it held for him and his family, there was also the matter of his congregation, many of whom had no choice but to remain.[78] His third brush with death, however, changed Moon's mind.[79] Not long after his release from Russian detention he made the decision to flee.[80] On 28 May 1946 he slipped out of his house alone at night with plans to rendezvous with his family in Wonsan, a city on the east coast of the peninsula close to the 38th parallel. The family successfully regrouped and continued their journey south, arriving in Seoul on 16 June. They went immediately to find Kim Chai Choon at the Joseon theological school. There they also met David Chung (see chapter 7), son of the first principal of the Myeongdong school,

Jeong Byeong-tae (see chapter 1), who was also at the Joseon Seminary. They stayed in Kim's home for some time, a testament to the close relationships that had been formed in Yongjeong.[81]

Joseon Seminary was still managing to hold classes and had added a women's college to the campus.[82] Although most of the first class of forty male ministry students had been pressed into military service,[83] with the help of its Japanese staff and friends in the Japanese Christian community, the seminary had been able to get permission for classes to be drafted into military work collectively.[84] This allowed them to resume classes together as a unit when they were released, which in turn helped to continue the educational program through the Pacific War period. Because it managed to stay open, Joseon Seminary was in a unique position to respond to the immediate and overwhelming demand for theological education when the war ended. In 1946, between three and four hundred students enrolled.[85] Not long after Moon and his family arrived in Seoul, his two sons, Ik Hwan and Dong Hwan, began their studies at Joseon Seminary as well.[86]

In 1946, former students of the Pyeongyang Seminary seeking to finish their degree also had no choice but to attend the Joseon Seminary for theological education. The different approach was a jolt to some of them. Upset by lessons taught by Kim Chai Choon, a group of students wrote a letter in protest of the new exegetical methods he introduced, methods they felt contradicted the teachings they had received in Pyeongyang.[87] The different missions (American Presbyterian and Methodist, Australian Presbyterian, etc.), newly returned to Korea and now jumbled together in the south, soon got involved in the controversy. A request from the Joseon Seminary board of directors for missionary assistance went out and was met by acceptance from the Canadians but not by the others. The UCC Mission welcomed the invitation and quickly assigned Canadian missionaries, including William Scott, to serve as lecturers.[88] The Northern Presbyterian church of the USA, however, pointedly refused to send teaching staff and instead sent a letter saying that that it objected to the teaching of historical criticism of the Bible and to the presence of Kim Chai Choon on the faculty, accusing him of heresy and undermining biblical author-ity.[89] Kim's intellectual commitments and his effectiveness as a teacher made him a flag bearer for an independent Korean theological tradition and a target for those who opposed it.[90] The Korean Presbyterian church formed a committee to look into these allegations, and it eventually exonerated Kim.[91] Meanwhile, however, Kim fought back, accusing his Korean opponents of unseemly politicking and charging US missionaries with missionary colonialism.[92]

The outbreak of the Korean War in 1950 caused a brief pause in the dispute. Kim Chai Choon and his friend Song Chang-geun, like many others, initially elected to remain in Seoul after the outbreak of war. Kim kept a low profile in a former student's house during the North Korean People's Army's first occupation of the city. However, the North Korean authorities soon decided to round up Christian leaders they suspected of being too close to the West.[93] Kim's friend Song Chang-geun was taken into custody and never seen or heard from again.[94] Consequently, Kim decided that he was in danger if he stayed and, when an opportunity presented itself, made his way to the southeastern tip of the peninsula to the city of Busan, which was firmly within a perimeter controlled by UN forces.[95] By March 1951, enough students and staff of the Joseon Seminary had been able to regroup within the Busan perimeter to make it possible to resume studies. They found a location on the side of a hill overlooking the sea and erected tent classrooms.[96] They renamed their seminary Hanguk[97] Theological Seminary. The name change likely reflects the fact that Joseon had become the name used by the communists for the newly liberated Korea and was therefore anathema for those aligned with Western forces. Hanguk, therefore, was the new politically correct way to say "Korea" in the south.

While operating the school in Busan, the Missions Board of the UCC approached Kim Chai Choon to ask how it could help. Kim reported that educated leaders were more important than desks and writing materials.[98] The UCC, therefore, provided scholarship money and Kim chose two students to travel to Canada to study out of harm's way during the remainder of the war. One of these was Kang Won Yong, a student from the Canadian mission school in Kando who would make an important contribution to Korean Christianity and the Christian Democratization Movement as director of the Christian Academy in Seoul. The other was Lee Oo Chung, who became one of South Korea's leading feminists and also played a key role in the Democratization Movement (see chapter 6).[99] In this way, the tradition of UCC Korea Mission support for the education of Korean leaders continued through the Korean War.

In the same way Kim and his students were able to find their way south to the oceanside tent classrooms of the Hanguk Seminary, the conflict within the Korean Presbyterian church likewise followed the exiled seminary to Busan. The General Assembly of the Korean Presbyterian church that met in 1951, under the pretense of making a fresh start and seeking a compromise between warring factions, ordered Hanguk seminary to disband so that a single new seminary could be created. It was soon learned, however, that plans for the new seminary did not include any of Hanguk's faculty or Canadian missionaries.[100] Hanguk Seminary refused to comply with the order. In 1952, the Korean Presbyterian church resumed the debate over control of theological education. Influenced by the wealthy and socially privileged US Presbyterian missionaries and a large and influential faction of Church leadership exiled from the northeast part of Korea,[101] the General Assembly passed resolutions to, first, annul the qualifications of students who had graduated from Joseon Seminary, second, call for the annulment of Kim Chai Choon's ordination and his expulsion from the Presbyterian church and, third, demand an investigation into whether William Scott, who was remembered and rued for his role in translating the Abington Bible Commentary and associated with the Hanguk Seminary through his recent role as faculty, was also guilty of heresy.[102]

The motions violated established rules of procedure and local churches were split between the two camps. Kim Chai Choon let his objections be known in sharp terms: "We regret the anachronistic mentality of [our American missionaries.] And even more we deeply regret the slave disposition and stupidity of our brothers [in the Korean Presbyterian church.]"[103] There was no backing down on either side. With a number of Hanguk graduates already serving churches and suddenly lacking official recognition as Presbyterian ministers, the supporters of Hanguk Seminary decided to proceed as a separate church body. As a result, on 6 June 1953 there were two General Assemblies of the Korean Presbyterian church who marked their beginning from the first Korean Presbyterian church established in 1907.[104] The much larger and more conservative group retained the historic name of the Presbyterian Church in Korea (PCK) and the other much smaller group adopted a new moniker, the Presbyterian Church in the Republic of Korea (PROK).

Both denominations came under the strong influence of Koreans from north of the 38th parallel but for the PCK they were refugees from the northwest associated with the American Presbyterian missionaries while the PROK refugee leaders were from the northeast and connected

74 Water from Dragon's Well

to the Canadian mission.[105] The PCK and PROK became known in Korea as the "Yejang" and "Gijang" traditions of Presbyterianism respectively, stemming from the Korean names of each denomination, the *Yesugyo Jangnohoe* and the *Gidokgyo Jangnohoe*. Translated into English the two names mean "The Jesus Presbyterian Assembly" and "The Christian Presbyterian Assembly." But English speakers came to speak of them as the "Jesus Presbyterians" and the "Christ Presbyterians." The Jesus Presbyterians, of which the PCK were the central representatives, but which included other splinter denominations who were more closely aligned theologically, were reputed to be conservative. The Christ Presbyterians, on the other hand, were understood to be liberal in outlook and more likely to be politically involved.[106] Later, in the heat of the Democratization Movement, it was said in some circles that Yejang Christians believed in Jesus and expected to go to heaven whereas Gijang Christians believed in Jesus and expected to go to prison. Indeed, from the first meetings of the separate bodies two distinct agendas were plain to see. The PCK, meeting in Daegu, moved that William Scott be excommunicated with Kim Chai Choon.[107] For their part the PROK made the following declaration:

a   The General Assembly [of the PROK] opposes any form of Phariseeism in ourselves or in others; We stand firm in the freedom of the gospel safeguarding the freedom of conscience of all believers.
b   While the General Assembly stands firm in the autonomy and independence of the Korean church, we oppose all narrow isolationism and cooperate faithfully in the ecumenical movement.[108]

UCC KOREA MISSION'S EMERGING IDENTITY

Though implicated, Scott says that during the heat of the debate he refrained from taking sides.[109] But the division of the Korean Presbyterian church created a dilemma for the Canadian mission which they could not ignore. Since the PCK retained the official title of the original Korean Presbyterian church, the mission was still officially affiliated with it. The smaller and isolated PROK requested the Canadian mission transfer their official support but the UCC missionaries thought a neutral response was best. The PCK, however, made this difficult. They declared that all who wished to continue to be associated with the PCK declare their belief in the infallibility of scripture, disassociate with Hanguk Theological Seminary and repudiate of the World Council of Churches, the largest recognized ecumenical organization in the world of which the UCC was a member.[110]

Finally, the Canadian missionaries realized that a decision needed to be made. They asked the UCC Board of Overseas Missions to send a delegation to investigate.[111] The delegation arrived in Korea on 24 March 1955 and remained for five days, interviewing members of the PROK, PCK, and other Christian organizations with which the UCC missionaries worked.[112] Their report attempted to be diplomatic but concluded that UCC missionaries should officially align with the PROK whom they judged to be both "needy and sincere." The basis of this decision, as with the decision to keep schools running by complying with the demand to participate in Shinto rituals, was explained in terms of the quality of the relationship with the Koreans with whom the mission associated rather than on the merits of a theological position. As Scott put it, "the value of cooperative Christian fellowship and service is not gauged by strict doctrinal conformity or financial support but by the mutual sharing of deep and rich Christian experience."[113] The new relationship between PROK and UCC took effect 1 July 1955.[114] Of all the overseas missions in Korea only the Canadian mission officially aligned itself with the PROK.[115]

Moon Chai Rin observes that "just as people were divided into north and south by the 38th parallel, the [Korean Presbyterian] church was divided by the 38th General Assembly [that created the PROK and PCK.]"[116] Though tragic, the division of the Korean Presbyterian church also began to define distinct visions, both for Korean Christianity and for Canadian missions. For the determined minority of Korean Presbyterians associated with the Joseon-turned-Hanguk Theological Seminary, the division allowed them to boldly articulate a vision for a Korean Christianity that was independent and free to explore Korean tradition and international scholarship as sources of religious expression and thought. These Christians also began to highlight what they saw as different in the approach of the UCC Korea Mission vis-à-vis the American Presbyterian Missions. PROK observers noted, for example, that subsequent UCC grants to the PROK came with "no strings attached."[117] The PROK also highlighted the historical support Canadian missionaries had shown for Korean independence,[118] their willingness to seek the best educational opportunities for Koreans, and a theology that was open to the influences of other religions and aspects of Korean traditional culture.[119] These, they identified, as the defining characteristics of the Canadian mission. Another aspect of the UCC Korea Mission that was raised in the PROK literature was the role that Canadian missionaries had in the cultivation of Korean Christian leaders, people who not only shaped the PROK but also the Korean Christian Democratization Movement in the 1960s, 70s, and 80s.[120]

While the PROK Christians identified Canadian missionaries with some positive anti-colonial tendencies, the general mood about the missionary legacy in Canada at this time was somber. The upheavals of the Second World War and its aftermath caused a real heart searching among the UCC missionaries who had served around the world, including in Korea. The dislocation of Canadian missionaries from their East Asian mission fields, representing two-thirds of the UCC missionary personnel at the time, represented a particularly big shock to the church back home and to the missionaries themselves.[121] The exile of missionaries represented a tremendous blow to the Missionary Enterprise of the UCC but more significant still, it called into question the Canadian denomination's belief that its Protestant spiritual ideals could bring the world closer to peace.[122]

Former missionaries to China were especially affected by this disruption and came to articulate a radically different understanding of missions in the postwar period. A surge of nationalist outrage against the West in China had turned even close associates against the Canadian missionaries there. Many of these missionaries had, in historian Robert Wright's words, "underestimated both the nationalist element in the Chinese revolt and their own complicity in the circumstances surrounding it."[123] Katharine Hockin, a missionary to China, was traumatized by the forced evacuation from the country in which her missionary parents had raised her[124] and turned her experience into a radical critique of the Missionary Enterprise. She was not alone. James Endicott, also a former missionary to China, emerged as a famous critic of American conduct during the Korean War and, accused of being a communist, was forced to resign from the ministry of the UCC.[125] Donald Faris was another missionary to China changed by his exile. In a letter to his son he wrote, "The exodus from China and growing sentiment in all countries of the world ... make the older concept of mission a complete impossibility."[126] This missionary experience would shape the final decades of the UCC's missionary presence in Asia, Africa, and Latin America. Faris would focus his energies on

"The Struggle to Express Their Own Identity"   77

developing the Canadian University Service Overseas (CUSO), part of a movement dubbed the NGOization of missions.[127] Hockin would go on to train the new missionaries, eventually renamed "mission personnel," leaving Canada for these fields, indoctrinating them in the dangers of cultural imperialism.[128] Among her students were included future missionaries to Korea, Marion Pope, Marion Current, and Willa Kernen (see chapter 6).

Unlike their Chinese counterparts, the Canadian missionaries in Korea, despite having lost much because of the Cold War divide, were able to continue their work in Korea and among Koreans who appreciated their contributions to the church and nation. But although UCC missionaries in Korea experienced their exile differently, with a less absolute dislocation, relationships with Korean colleagues and friends were nonetheless changed. Postwar realities had challenged old assumptions about the relative social positions of missionary and Korean and brought into critical relief lingering colonial attitudes. This was true of all missions in Korea, but the UCC's alignment with the PROK meant that they were associated with a group that was more sensitive to the change in mood. The PROK had set the bar high. Praising their anticolonial approach, they likewise did not hesitate to criticize the Canadian missionaries when they didn't live up to expectations.

With regard to the Canadian Missionary Enterprise as a whole, historian Robert Wright has noted that the Canadian missionaries' engagement with other races, cultures, and religions, "did not spell the immediate end of racism or cultural/religious chauvinism but it did contribute to creating a space and an attitude where these defects in the Canadian mind and culture could be addressed."[129] Wrights' turn of phrase is ambiguous about who was addressing the problems in the Canadian approach. It is clear, however, that the indigenous Christians with whom Canadian missionaries engaged were the ones who raised these issues, rather than the Canadians themselves. Korean Christians committed to intellectual and political independence from the northeast of the peninsula were particularly sharp when it came to missionary meddling in Korean affairs, thereby giving the Canadian missionaries an especially good chance to "address their defects."

These defects were not only obvious on the mission field but were also plain to see in Canadian immigration policies. Koreans, for example, would have had a very difficult time immigrating to Canada before the mid-1960s due to rules against the entry of non-White people. While Canada admitted more than 100,000 refugees from

Europe following the Second World War, refugees from Asia were less welcome.[130] The millions of Koreans internally displaced by the Korean War would have little recourse to refugee status in Canada. Despite participating in the drafting of the 1951 Convention Relating to the Status of Refugees at the United Nations, Canada declined to sign it until the 1970s out of concerns that were racial in nature.[131]

CONCLUSION

In 1956, the same year that Kim Chai Choon addressed the PROK General Assembly on the topic of the history of the Korean church, Morley and Anne Hawley embarked on a program of Korean language learning in preparation for their deployment as UCC missionaries. They arrived on the peninsula in 1957 to begin work in Busan. Over the course of the next twenty-two years, Morley Hawley was guided by the story of the creation of the PROK in his work. In a short written reflection, he summarized that history for me:

> In the early 1950s a debate had erupted in the Korean Church about the interpretation of the Scriptures. Influential American missionaries claimed they had the right to interpret the Scriptures for the Korean Church. A group of Korean scholars, led by Kim Chae Jun [sic], argued that Koreans should be free to interpret the Scriptures for themselves. The Canadian missionaries supported Dr Kim's argument wholeheartedly. Dr Kim was expelled from the Korean Presbyterian Church on the charge of heresy. It was with reluctance that he established a new denomination, the PROK. Over the years, Dr Kim Chae Jun [sic] has been a real hero for me. When the UCC, following the example of the missionaries, chose to become the Sister Church of the PROK, it strengthened the new denomination in its struggle for Korean independence. Perhaps it is an example of the ancient wisdom to put new wine into new wineskins.[132]

It is clear that Hawley came to identify with the history of the PROK and that it shaped the sense of who he was specifically as a *Canadian* missionary. In response to my question regarding the South Korean Democratization Movement, Hawley opined that the UCC missionaries' "main contribution has been their ability to identify with Korean people as they struggle to express their own identity." The quality of relationship between missionary and Korean Christian was, indeed, the touchstone for two of the most defining decisions of the UCC Korean mission as we have seen. Canadians were clearly supportive of Korean Christians' "struggle to express they own identity" as Hawley asserts, but it is important to note that that struggle and their ability to identify with it also shaped the identity of Canadian Missionaries in return.

In his 1956 address to the PROK, Kim Chai Choon declared that missionary history in Korea had little to do with the "subjectivity and spirit" of the Korean church.[133] This chapter has endeavoured to show, however, that the subjectivity and spirit of the Korean church did shape the history of the Canadian mission in Korea. In effect, the Korean church helped to determine the character of the Canadian mission by crystalizing issues of missionary colonialism and forcing it to make a clear and public choice about where it stood on those issues. In the beginning, Canadians had not been unaware of contradictions between the colonial alignments of the Missionary Enterprise and their own stated ideals for that enterprise. Their philosophical stance regarding the education of Korean Christian leaders, however, had differentiated them from the Northern Presbyterian Mission of the USA and began to help them to understand some of the issues at stake. Their decision to continue to operate schools when Shinto rituals were imposed based on the effectiveness of relationships to sustain hope also differentiated them from their American counterparts. After liberation, it became especially clear that trusting these relationships with the Koreans from their mission field was leading them along a path that further diverged from the approach of their American missionary colleagues. The decision of Kim Chai Choon and other independent-minded Korea Christians to stand up for the freedom of the Korean church to make up its own mind in matters of theology culminated in the most defining moment to date for the Canadian mission in Korea. This was an important step in the evolution of the UCC Korea Mission with consequences that would reverberate for Canadian missionaries like the Hawleys and for their church back home into the next decades and beyond.

PART TWO

Democratization and Decolonization

How the Korean Church Changed the UCC
Korea Mission and Transformed the Lives
of Canadian Missionaries, 1960 to 1979

3

Sinners, Partners, or Friends

Discursive Tensions on the Korean Mission Field in the 1950s and 1960s

Therefore you have no excuse, whoever you are, when you judge others; for in passing judgement on another you condemn yourself, because you, the judge, are doing the very same things.

Romans 2:1

For we have become partners of Christ, if only we hold our first confidence firm to the end.

Hebrews 3:14

Through the 1950s and 60s, the United Church of Canada Korea Mission continued to work to separate itself from its colonial legacy and embrace a direction for missions urged by the Koreans it worked with. At the same time, UCC missionaries in other parts of the world were getting the same message for the need for change and UCC members back in Canada were experiencing shifting attitudes vis-à-vis colonial and missionary history. *The Report of the Commission on World Mission* reported to the UCC General Council in 1966. At the core of the report was a central question with regard to its missions at home and overseas: "How can mutual respect be achieved."[1] It was clear that leadership in the UCC was taking the complicity of Canadian missions in colonial history seriously. A significant movement in the UCC was now talking about "partnership," "mutuality," and "Mission to Six Continents" (i.e., mission that included Europe and North America) rather than "winning souls" and "foreign missions to the heathen." Substantive change, however, was being held back by

84 Water from Dragon's Well

ingrained colonial attitudes and practices. A study of missionary correspondence from Korea during this period of political upheaval provides insight into the ways Koreans continued to push back against paternalistic patterns of UCC mission work and the contradictions that existed within the UCC as it tried to come to terms with the new postcolonial context.

In the 1960s, a heated exchange took place between the UCC Korea Mission and the PROK. The PROK-UCC relationship was unique among UCC mission relationships, which included, at this time, stations in Japan, Angola, Trinidad, and India. The UCC had come to refer to the PROK as their "daughter church" because of the close association of the UCC Korea Mission with the beginning of that denomination.[2] But while many in the PROK appreciated the fact that the UCC alone among foreign missions in Korea had supported them at the time of the schism with the PCK and that they had shown great generosity and respect (see chapter 2), by the 1960s the PROK was already feeling that their "mother church" was a little overbearing. They complained that Canadian missionaries were often contrarian and quick to use their spiritual authority. When it came to joint projects, Koreans continued to feel that the Canadians held a tight grip on the purse strings. As in Canada, the Korean church's growing awareness of the problems in the missionary legacy was connected to developments in national and global politics. The 1950s and 1960s proved to be important decades in the evolving discourse on mission.

A DISPUTE RESUMES

In the years following the creation of the PROK, UCC missionary William Scott saw much that told him the new PROK denomination was poised to make a positive impact on the Christian scene in Korea. A new journal of Korean theology entitled *Christian Thought*[3] was launched, taking advantage of the breadth of theological knowledge and imagination of a great number of Korean Christians returning from studies abroad. The new magazine was a testament to the spirit of Hanguk Theological Seminary and the PROK, and to Kim Chai Choon who had stood fast in his vision for a free voice for Korean theology.[4] The Canadian missionaries, says Scott, were "humbly proud" of their contributions to the new Korean denomination and its school. A number of the professors at Hanguk Seminary had been trained in Canada, and the principal Kim Chai Choon was well known in

Canadian circles. But not all was going smoothly in the relationship. Along with the many refugees from the former Canadian mission field in the northeast of Korea and Kando in Manchuria, the new denomination was populated by a large number of members from the southern part of the peninsula who had never worked with the Canadian missionaries before. Scott blamed relationships of distrust between these southern Christians and the missionaries they used to work with for tensions in the relationship with UCC missionaries.[5] However, there were a number of colonial patterns in the Canadian mission that survived the wars and continued to wreak havoc on the relationship.

One of the first things to happen following the official decision of the UCC to align its mission with the PROK was the resurrection of a democratic practice from the northeastern mission field, that is the creation of a Joint Board for making decisions about Canadian mission expenditures and priorities. An equal number of members of Koreans and missionaries would be represented on this board but the UCC missionaries still held the power to decide how much funding of the total from the UCC to Korea would be allotted to the PROK and how much would go to other organizations. The fact that the UCC Korea Mission could unilaterally choose to support hospitals, Christian publishers, and social service organizations at the expense of PROK support upset some members of the PROK who had different priorities. Missionaries on the Joint Board, however, felt that PROK requests for funds were "astronomical." Sorting out the differences of opinion, says Scott, "took time and patience on the part of both Korean and missionary members [of the Joint Board]."[6]

Missionary relations were not the only thing on the people's mind at this time. The path from division and war to political stability and prosperity was fraught with many difficulties for South Korea. One of the big problems was the nature of the government of the new Republic. Rhee, the first President of South Korea, had been all but directly installed by the United States Army Military Government in Korea (USAMGIK) that had taken control of the Korean peninsula south of the 38th parallel following the capitulation of Japan at the end of the Pacific War.[7] There had been a delay of some months between the surrender of Japan and the moment when US forces were able to arrive. In the brief interlude, local Korean councils had effectively managed the business of running the country and expected to be given lead roles in a liberated Korea. While not communist or aligned with Russian forces, these councils often had socialist leanings, something that made the new American military government uncomfortable. Though promising democracy, Lieutenant General John R. Hodge, the military governor of South Korea, called an election under conditions that divided the country and that Rhee won handily despite a deficit of popular support and organizational capacity.[8] Although most Christians, who benefitted under the USAMGIK and the subsequent Rhee government did not complain much, some Christians and many non-Christians who had had confidence in local Korean community councils to transition the country to a unified and independent government shared Ahn Byung Mu's (see chapter 5) despair: "To the bitter end we are a nation that is trampled down!"[9]

From the start, Rhee's methods were authoritarian. A group of right-wing paramilitary young adults under Rhee's influence called the Northwest Youth terrorized neighbourhoods where there were known to be socialists and communist sympathizers.[10] The Korean military, aided and abetted by US advisors, carried out massacres and atrocities in the lead up to and following elections.[11] As Rhee's government lost any semblance of virtue and abandoned all pretence of democracy the population grew rapidly more disillusioned. Larger and larger student-led rallies against government violence, corruption and election meddling culminated on 19 April 1960 with police opening fire on a large demonstration in Seoul. Nearly two hundred protesters lost their lives and Rhee, by this time an embarrassment to the US, stepped down under pressure. The events were memorialized in South Korean history with the numerals 4.19, marking the day of sacrifice (19 April) which was pivotal for the ending of the Rhee regime.

In the wake of the student uprising there was concern in Canada for the safety of Canadian missionaries in Korea. For missionary supporters in Canada, the events of 4.19 evoked memories of the Boxer Uprisings in China two generations earlier that had had serious consequences for many UCC missionaries working there at the time.[12] Canadian missionaries in Korea were concerned for their safety as well. "One or two of our missionaries packed bags in case of evacuation, I suspect the majority of us did so mentally," wrote Canadian missionary Romona Underwood to the chair of the Woman's Missionary Society.[13] Overlooking the unrest in Busan, the missionaries Morley and Anne Hawley watched police hide in the bushes near their stations and realized "law and order was breaking down."[14] Although the missionaries themselves were never in danger,[15] they knew that students were paying a terrible price. Canadian missionary doctor

Ian Robb had been to prisons to attend to student prisoners and had seen corpses with "grotesquely elongated" necks.[16]

In her letter back home, Underwood felt it important to mention the fact that the missionaries had been brave and continued to exemplify Christian behavior. "Some of the missionaries donated blood at Severance Hospital," she wrote, "and actually set the example which was followed by some of the Koreans."[17] This account of the missionaries' commendable act of citizenship which, she noted significantly, they performed on the grounds of the hospital founded by Canadian missionary Oliver R. Avison[18] was a well-used trope in the Missionary Movement. It had been used to justify the Missionary Enterprise with the idea that missionaries the world over were teaching others how to be model modern nationals. In 1960, on the cusp of a global shift in the politics of former colonies, this was still a message UCC missionaries were uncritically repeating to themselves.

Although some church leaders in Canada feared the consequences of Korean political dissent for the safety of their missionaries, Underwood showed understanding of the political significance of events and empathized with the protestors. Underwood was clearly in solidarity with the students in what they had accomplished. "At first, in spite of my concern and sympathy for the students who lost their lives and their families," wrote Underwood, "my personal reaction was one of resurgence of hope for the welfare of this country. I must admit I have been very discouraged during the past year and particularly at the time of the 15 March election. The students have been the great heroes of the crusade against corruption."[19] Students of the 4.19 uprising gave voice to a general desire among Koreans south of the thirty-eighth parallel for greater sovereignty in the decisions of the nation. Underwood understood and sympathized despite the colonial tradition of the UCC Korea Mission in which she found herself.

Tensions and contradictions existed in Korean society as well. The student demands stressed the need not only for democracy in the south, but also reunification with the north. Ironically, it was student action to organize a meeting with North Korean student counterparts at Panmunjom, the village straddling the dividing line between North and South Korea, that scuppered their movement. The plans provided South Korean General Park Chung Hee with the pretext for the military overthrow of the democratically elected government that had been the crowning achievement of their 4.19 uprising.[20] Dismissing the barely-one-year-old government as weak, Park led a successful coup on 16 May

1961 (5.16). In the years following that coup he would impose a disciplined, militaristic, ideologically anti-communist, and gendered program of modernization that would survive his death in 1979 and continues to shape South Korean society up to the present day.[21]

As the forty-sixth General Assembly of the PROK gathered in 1961, days after the 5.16 coup, political developments would no doubt have been on the minds of its members. Kim Chai Choon was swift in his condemnation of the military action.[22] Others like him were genuinely distraught by the blow to Korean democracy. As urgent and dramatic as national politics were at that moment however, it is a surprising fact that Canadian missionaries were the hottest issue. When the question of UCC Korean Mission attitudes towards the Korean church came up for discussion, emotions erupted. At issue was the lack of trust and respect missionaries were showing to their Korean partners. Missionaries, it was charged, hovered over their Korean colleagues accusing them of the misuse of funds and wielding the charge of "sin."[23] Koreans took exception to this treatment.[24] An angry motion was passed that the Korean church would no longer request funds from the UCC.[25]

This was the first such open conflict between Korean Christians and the UCC Korea Mission since the 1920s, when students had set fire to a Mission-run school to protest the missionaries' funding priorities, a move that had given birth to the first Joint Board.[26] This 1960s outcry might well be understood as the resumption of a contentious debate that had been interrupted by the Pacific and Korean Wars. That debate had focussed on the sharing of decision-making responsibilities in mission institutions.[27] Koreans wanted more say. In 1926, the Canadian missionaries responded with an attempt to "devolve" power and include Koreans in equal numbers on school and hospital boards. The motion, some thirty-five years later, to reject UCC funding can be seen as part of an ongoing discussion about the proper balance between missionary and Korean control of the church agenda, underlining the fact that despite the UCC's support of the PROK there were still serious issues of missionary colonialism for Canadians to resolve. The events at the PROK General Assembly in 1961 were of such significance that the resolution to not request funds came to be known as "the Decision" for many years. Discontinuance by the PROK of the only major source of overseas funding had huge consequences for the young Korean Presbyterian denomination. The new church was financially fragile. The UCC was the only overseas church offering them significant financial support. For Canadians, the breakdown in the relationship with the PROK called into question their whole mission in Korea. "The Decision" inevitably, therefore, precipitated earnest efforts at reconciliation on both sides. A lively debate ensued over the course of which a new missiology began to be articulated.

The 4.19 uprising and "the Decision" were part of a decolonizing moment for the Korean nation and church. It is possible the Canadians of the UCC Korea Mission were partly aware of the local and global significance of events that were occurring around them.[28] At UCC headquarters in Toronto the church bureaucracy was starting to come to grips with a sea-change in their foreign missions around the world. A year later in 1962, the Woman's Missionary Society (WMS) and its Board of Overseas Missions (BOM) were amalgamated into the Board of World Mission (BWM). The omission of the final "s" in "Mission" was a nod to a missiology that acknowledged that there was only one mission, God's, and that mission work should be regarded as directed towards every place, not just from the West to the rest.[29] In the same year the Commission on World Mission was struck by the UCC General Council to do a comprehensive re-thinking of the history and direction of missionary activity. Fundamental to these moves was a new awareness that whereas the UCC had once considered others to be exclusively in need of the gospel, the Canadian and other Western churches were now regarded as definitely in need of some evangelization as well. To Korean theology student Lee Young Min (see chapter 4) who was studying in Canada on a UCC scholarship at the time, these changes in UCC missiology felt like "a big switch in the right direction."[30]

The UCC bureaucracy was also getting a new face to go with its new approach to mission. In 1960, Wilna Thomas became the Executive Secretary of Overseas Missions and, in 1962, the Associate Secretary of the new BWM with responsibilities for East Asia. Thomas was born on 6 March 1917 in Ogema, Saskatchewan.[31] The only student in her class at her rural school to advance to university, she graduated with great distinction with a BA in mathematics and economics from the University of Saskatchewan.[32] Soon after, she enrolled at the United Church Training Centre to begin a career in church work. While studying there, a request came to the United Church for a theologically trained female to provide spiritual support to the Canadian Women's Army Corps. When she graduated from her theological program in 1941, Thomas was recommended for the work of military chaplain.[33] She began her service with a rank of Lieutenant at the Advanced Training Centre in Ste Anne de Bellevue,[34] one of the two first women padres in the Canadian army.[35]

After being decommissioned from the military in 1946, Thomas applied for a position with the WMS serving in Japan and was sent overseas in 1947. Unlike her groundbreaking role as one of the army's first female chaplains, as a single female missionary Thomas was part of a long tradition of women who had gone before her. By the 1940s, the missionary vocation had been offering women unique opportunities for personal and professional development for over a century. Single female missionaries, not usually from elite backgrounds, often managed to achieve a kind of elite status in Canadian society and abroad[36] and the work offered unmarried women attractive careers in places others could only dream of going. Meanwhile missionary societies appreciated the fact that these women worked for a lot less than their male counterparts.[37] While helping their "heathen sisters," missionary women had also been both helping themselves and proving to women back home that they were more than capable of doing work that had once been considered the exclusive domain of men.[38] From its beginnings in the mid-1800s the tradition of single female missionaries had been a significant contribution on the Canadian mission field. Combined with that of missionary wives, the numbers of female missionaries easily exceeded those of their male colleagues. In 1960, the UCC Korea Mission, for example, employed thirteen male and twenty-one female missionaries, nine of the latter single.[39] In some places, however, the number of single women exceeded those of all male colleagues on their own.[40] Serving as a single female missionary was nothing new and came with colonial baggage, but the tradition was also one of women pioneering new roles for women.

After serving in Japan for more than a decade, Thomas returned to Canada in 1960 to take an executive position in the church structure. With this move Thomas was once again trailblazing for women by breaking through a glass ceiling for female leadership in the UCC: the first woman to serve in an executive position with responsibility for male missionaries as well as female. Thomas has not been remembered in the UCC for her two pioneering roles, forgotten between the landmark accomplishments of Lydia Gruchy's ordination as the first female UCC minister in 1936 and Lois Wilson's ordination as the first married woman minister in the UCC in 1965 and later first female moderator in 1980. In 1960, however, Thomas' was another important achievement for women and a sign of the times for women in Canada who in the sixties saw Indigenous women win the vote, Quebec married women receive the same rights as their husbands, freedom from discrimination based on gender enshrined in the Ontario Human Rights Code, and the advent of the Royal Commission on the Status of Women.

It is to be wondered what impression this sign of the times made on those with whom Thomas came into contact as she visited UCC mission fields around the world. Interviews with members of the church in Canada (see chapters 7 and 8) suggests that gender issues were an important obstacle to Korean-Canadian relationships. Korean patriarchy proved an extremely painful barrier for Korean women in leadership both in Korea and Canada. Thomas' notes, however, contain no hint of whether there had been a reaction to her as a woman, good or bad. Canadian Missions scholar Ruth Compton Brouwer surmises that though the situation would certainly have "called for an all around wariness," it would not preclude the ability to work together on a project that was clearly important.[41] Also, the fact that Thomas had received the position with the support of her male colleagues would certainly have carried weight with the Koreans she had met.[42]

Regardless of Koreans' reaction to her, it is clear that by the time of her appointment to the BWM, Thomas had herself already formed an idea of Koreans. In 1957, Thomas had been asked to be part of an ecumenical mission to visit Korea and meet with students to discuss the theme of "Revolution and Reconciliation." The wounds of Japanese colonialism in Korea were still fresh, and it was impossible for a Japanese citizen to get a visa to visit Korea. As a Canadian missionary in Japan, therefore, Thomas was asked to stand in and represent the Japanese church.[43] Her delegation met three thousand Korean students in fifteen different universities and discussed various inter- and intra-Korean controversies. Notably, the disagreement that led to the creation of the PROK was talked about and Thomas was left with the impression that the split was due to nothing more than an internal Korean power struggle. "One group is definitely fundamentalist; the other group is called liberal, but is so conservative I could scarcely tell the difference," she wrote in her report following the visit. She further mused, "Perhaps a greater reason for the split has been the clash of personalities, and the desire for power on the part of certain leaders."[44] This assessment would have been quite surprizing to UCC missionary colleagues working for the UCC Korea Mission. Thomas had somehow failed to appreciate the meaning of the event for the Korean church and the UCC Korea Mission (see chapter 2).

The possible reasons for Thomas' cynical view of the Korean church split are worth considering. There is no doubt that the division had been the result of a power struggle and that the PROK had conservative members.[45] It is likely that Thomas was not briefed by a UCC Korea Mission colleague and therefore left in the dark about its circumstances. It is unlikely fellow UCC missionaries working in Korea would have been ignorant of the circumstances and significance of the creation of the PROK. The split had affected everyone in the mission and all the missionaries would have been well acquainted with its details. UCC leadership in Canada had been solidly behind the PROK and was clear that the PROK more closely reflected its own theological commitments and ethos.[46] Left to her own impressions, Thomas' judgement of the schism in the Korean church likely had another source: the colonial biases she picked up in Canada and Japan. Raised in a Canadian Protestant environment, Thomas would, like the missionaries that preceded her, have been inclined towards a view of the world that sided with colonial power rather than with the colonized (see chapter 1). The interwar church in Canada took a favorable view of Japan and its colonial expansion.[47] Further, having served in Japan for thirteen years she would have been exposed to the views of Japanese regarding their erstwhile colony. Mission historian Hamish Ion has noted that Canadian missionaries serving in Japan easily adopted Japanese colonial attitudes regarding Koreans and Taiwanese.[48] Thomas' dismissal of Korean divisions as nothing but a crass power struggle would have represented a dominant Japanese stereotype of Koreans.[49]

The issue that most interested Thomas on her first trip to Korea in 1957 was Korean-Japanese relations. There were clearly strong opinions in Korea against doing things together with the Japanese church. In her reflections on the visit, she shows some sympathy for the Koreans and their experience of colonization: "I think we can understand why the Korean people think and feel as they do," reported Thomas regarding the distrust and resentment she encountered among Korean Christians for Japanese people. "For thirty-six years they were under Japanese rule. They couldn't use their own language. They had to change their names. No Korean could advance to a position of leadership." The legacy of bitterness and dysfunction for Thomas, however, was more the responsibility of the Koreans than of the Japanese, "Children were taught that to lie and to deceive the Japanese authorities was good. Now those children are the leaders. They have no training for it. Deceit and distrust are evident in every area of life. Even Church leaders deal in the black market." [50]

These views seem to have carried over into Thomas' visits as executive secretary in the 1960s. Her notes from the 1961 visit demonstrate an interest in reconciliation between Japanese and Koreans but put the onus on Koreans. She felt it was incumbent upon Korean Christian students as Christians to forgive their Japanese counterparts for the colonial history they had endured.[51] Their failure to do so disturbed her. She felt it was an example of human "sinfulness."[52] There is nowhere in her discussion of the trip to Japan that she speaks of the need for repentance on the part of the Japanese. In subsequent visits to Korea, Thomas reiterates the idea that the Korean church was riddled with corruption.[53]

The notes from Thomas' visits to Korea and other mission fields as Mission Secretary in the early 1960s, however, were not completely coloured by her bias and indeed reflect an evolution towards a more positive assessment of Koreans. She concluded her 1964 visit in Korea by saying that although the Korean Church was "fraught by all the sins of institutionalism that are part of the weakness of the Church everywhere" she nonetheless "left Korea more conscious of the opportunities confronting the Church than in its weaknesses in meeting them."[54] Thomas' notes paint a complex and multidimensional picture of change both personal and institutional.

Canadian mission historian Rosemary Gagan has noted that Canadian women in mission often sincerely believed in "the ideal of a universal sisterhood transcending race and class" even if this was not always achieved.[55] Brouwer has further noted that the changing attitudes towards race and the increasing level of education in non-Western countries would have made mutuality in relationships between missionaries and indigenous Christians more easy to attain as time went on.[56] There is no doubt that Thomas tried hard to listen to, and to respect, the people she met while visiting other countries. Her notes' unique attention to the voices of the Christians she encountered overseas distinguishes them from the records kept by her male predecessors and are a special example of attentiveness and openness to the voices of those she encountered in Korea and elsewhere.[57] But in addition to betraying a colonial bias against Koreans, she seems not to have been able to escape the pattern of the Canadian church's history of paternalism. After all, Thomas had not come to Korea to listen only.

She was there to make decisions about the dispersal of funds. And Thomas was determined to combine this fiscal power with a lesson to enlighten Koreans about the nature of missions going forward.

Thomas' notebooks from 1961 and 1964 trips to Korea outline the main points she sought to make as she met with local leaders. In her talks at PROK presbyteries around the peninsula Thomas introduced the UCC's new approach, one that had been developed in consultations at ecumenical institutions such as the World Council of Churches (WCC), but not directly with the local Korean churches or with other indigenous church members in other parts of the world – or even with Canadian church members for that matter. This was a position that stressed social service rather than making converts as a focus of mission work. The "new" approach was actually not new. As early as the 1890s the Social Gospel movement, which also emphasized social change over individual conversion, had been a prominent feature of the Canadian Protestant church and others around the world.[58] But the exclusion of concern for evangelism marked an important shift.

Some might have said that Thomas was a harbinger of the avalanche of secularization sweeping the Canadian church and society.[59] The leadership in Canada preferred to think of it as winning souls through "service for Christ's sake,"[60] but there is no doubt the emphasis had changed. In Canada these two aspects of Christianity, which had been tied together in a tight knot since Church Union were coming loose and even unravelling all together. The idea of a liberal evangelical had come to seem oxymoronic.[61] This is not to say that the church did not understand its work in terms of making new Christians, or that those focussed on social justice were in fact abandoning evangelical commitments. However, in the religious psyche of the UCC leadership it was becoming very difficult in the 1960s to hold the two concepts together and give them equal weight. Social justice language was used more enthusiastically than the language of evangelism. It is doubtful that congregation members of the UCC back in Canada who supported overseas missions with their financial offerings were on board with the new emphasis.[62] Neither was it clear that Korean Christians would feel comfortable with this approach.

Though clearly evangelical, the social dimension had also been an important concern of the Korean church since its inception (see chapter 1). From its beginnings, Korean Christianity contained a strong communal dimension and understood salvation in terms that were national as well as individual.[63] There continued to be a strong positive response to church sponsored social programs through the 1960s. The Urban Industrial Mission (UIM), for example, which sought to address social injustices and promote the formation of unions in Korean factories, became a strong movement in this decade and the UCC was gratefully acknowledged as the first foreign church body to financially support this initiative.[64] But the goal of conversion and the experience of individual salvation continued to be important for the Korean church.

Based on Thomas' notes, many in Korea resisted the idea of abandoning the element of conversion in Christian missions. PROK Christians that Thomas met asked the UCC to renew its commitment to evangelism. For some this situation had urgent political dimensions. "South Korea must become Christian quickly [in order to fend off the] communists next door,"[65] one person told her. Even before the division of the peninsula, there had arisen serious tension between Christians and socialists over questions of how to deal with the Japanese occupation, and what was the most effective path to modernization. To these ends, Christians and communists had been uneasy partners in prewar Korea. Generally, the two groups – though they shared central commitments – did not mix well, and tried to keep away from one another.[66] There were some who tried to combine both Christianity and Communism, but this was a rare position and hard to maintain.[67] By the 1930s, communists were confiscating Christian schools and churches.[68] As most Christians in South Korea were refugees from the north, their position regarding communism was more than ideological. With the Russian occupation and then the imposition of Kim Il Song's communist regime in the north, persecution of Christians had become severe. Association with a Western mission station could get one thrown in jail or executed.[69] The great number who managed to escape the north made up a large and powerful fraction if not the majority of the Christians in the south.[70] They had suffered great personal losses. Scarred by communism, many genuinely feared it and saw conversion of people to the faith as one way to combat it.

For others, the priority of making converts was simply a religious desire to bring the Christian message to the many Koreans who had yet to encounter it. Some complained that even with many missionaries on the field few unbelievers were being reached. Notes from the minutes of the United Work Committee (aka the Joint Board) indicate that the priority for the Korean church was planting more churches and increasing the number of Christians in Korea.[71] Koreans stressed to Thomas that they were very disturbed by the UCC mission move away from evangelism, which they could not understand.[72] But Thomas wished to correct the view of the centrality of proselytization to the Missionary Enterprise. She informed her Korean audiences that the UCC now had a new understanding.

Mission, Thomas insisted, is the essence of the church. However, as the UCC now understood it, mission was no longer about conversion but about service. Or at least, the church had a different understanding of what conversion and evangelism meant. Converting the social order was held in higher importance than leading individuals to profess the Christian faith. "The Church," she proclaimed, "must involve itself in all the problems of people: political, economic, educational, family, health."[73] It is ironic that Thomas should preach such a message to a church that, from its beginning, understood itself as a movement of national salvation. But Thomas was far removed from that history.

Equally ironic was Thomas' insistence that mission was not to be understood as the special domain of missionaries. "I dislike very much the fact that there is an organization called the Korea Mission of the United Church of Canada," Thomas declared, "This was true long ago – overseas churches as part of their mission to the world sent missionaries abroad and became related to these countries in the terms of these missions ... Now we realize that there will be developed effective ways of partnership between the overseas church and the church here for the mission of the whole church."[74] For this to be true, she proclaimed, "Your Assembly organization must be your own, supported by your own members so that it becomes your servant and is responsible to you. It seems to me that these days we are called to enter into a *partnership* of *equals* before God" (with "partnership" and "equals" underlined).[75] But this is exactly what the PROK leadership had been saying all along.

This discursive effort to emphasize equality between Canadian and Korean Christians and churches can be seen as having its roots in the origins of Christianity itself. From its beginnings, the tensions between peoples of different social, cultural, and gender positions had created real friction in the early church. Famously, the apostle Paul had declared "There is no longer Jew or Greek, there is no longer slave or free, there is no longer male and female; for all of you are one in Christ Jesus."[76] Missionaries, who took for granted the privilege of their status as representatives of colonial Empires in the 1800s and early 1900s, began to feel the contradictions between the message they were delivering and the reality they were embodying more keenly in the aftermath of the First World War, when assumptions of cultural and spiritual superiority were exposed as hollow. In the 1930s Canadians began to claim that their churches had moved beyond the view that the people in other countries and from cultures different from their own were in any sense inferior to themselves.[77] Thomas' claim that the understanding of missions was still changing underscored the reality that Western Christians were still well shy of the biblical ideal and that her authoritative tone was perhaps misplaced.

The position Thomas articulated sounded to her like a departure from the colonial era approach to missions. However, it is clear that there was a disconnect between the message that Thomas was delivering and the views of the Christian membership on the ground in Korea. The way in which the message was delivered from a privileged Westerner to a non-Western audience without opportunity for debate belied its progressive rhetoric. Despite its claim to be more mutually respectful in nature, even egalitarian, the top-down delivery reinforced the reality that it was coming from the powerful to the powerless. There was an element of self-interest concealed in the new policies as well. Shifting the focus from church support and growth to social programs and self-sufficiency could also justify the phasing out of financial transfers to indigenous churches.

Accompanying the new theology of partnership was a policy to accelerate the transition to self-funding, self-governing overseas churches. Liberal churches had been wounded by accusations against the missionary movement, that it essentially constituted a form of cultural imperialism.[78] If they got out of the business of making Christians in other countries, they could say they had changed their tune. And if defunding indigenous churches was a sign of repentance, it also conveniently helped address financial pressures back home. Even while withdrawing support, the UCC knew that overseas churches could not afford to maintain the institutions that missionaries had built.[79] Justifying the move by pointing to a new theology of partnership would perhaps have helped to ease their conscience. Contrary to its stated intention, the shift in approach from evangelism to social service and the defunding of the PROK risked deepening colonial attitudes and patterns. Compton Brouwer has, for one, concluded that "as liberal missionaries became increasingly involved in trying to improve here-and-now conditions for the missionized rather than 'saving' them for the hereafter, it was they, rather than more narrowly focused proselytizers, who were closer, in practice, to 'cultural imperialism.'"[80]

A DESIRE FOR TRUE FRIENDS

If Thomas was promoting a new vision of mission as partnership and chiding the Korean church to "get with it," the Rt Rev. Lee Nam Kyoo, former moderator of the PROK, had his own chiding to do vis-à-vis the attitude and approach of Thomas and the Canadian missionaries. At a meeting of the Study Committee tasked with looking into PROK-missionary relations following "the Decision," he complained that missionaries showed little acquaintance with the Korean Church situation and were not supportive of Korean projects, goals, or aspirations. What is more, he said, they were misusing their spiritual authority, accusing the PROK leadership of "*sin*" simply because they disagreed with or could not understand their priorities.[81] His report had underlined the word to emphasize the seriousness of the term. Tensions between missionaries and PROK leadership in Korea were indeed dangerously high, described by UCC sources as "strained to the point of breaking."[82] In September 1964, the General Assembly of the PROK met and, among other business, received the full report by the study committee. In line with many of Lee Nam Kyoo's observations, the study committee identified that the problems contributing to tensions between missionaries and PROK leadership were connected primarily to the role of missionaries within the governing structure of the PROK, that they wielded too much power and were out of touch with the needs of the Korean church. The aloof posture was surely exacerbated by their use of servants such as drivers, cooks, and nannies and by the large gated homes in which they lived.[83] The UCC missionary residence at Seodaemun (the Great West Gate) was a case in point, a huge red-brick structure of Edwardian vintage that "loomed" over Korean residence (see chapter 5).[84] Koreans may have felt the sting of this social inequality in the past, but in the 1960s they were now prepared to voice their objections in no uncertain terms. There were those in the Korean church who felt the report did not go far enough in criticizing the missionaries. Some desired to send the missionaries home.[85] Others felt kicking the missionaries out was too extreme, but nonetheless desired to see a radical shift in the relationship.

In a letter to the editor in the *Presbyterian News*, a denominational organ of the PROK, the Rev. Chung Yong Chul, who agreed with much of what Thomas was saying, argued that missionaries and their money should be entirely subject to the will of the General Assembly of the PROK.[86] The sovereignty and unity of the Korean church body was of the utmost importance for Chung. There should be no hierarchy or parallel structure for missionaries, he explained, and no special parameters placed on the spending of overseas funds besides those set by the Church in Korea. But beyond matters of policy and structure, Chung also touched on the question of attitude. "It is necessary for us to receive help from *friends* (emphasis added)," he said, but "we do not want money given as if it was to charity." "Charity" had come to represent for Chung and others who had been its recipients an attitude of condescension on the part of the Western church. It entailed a sense of shame for those who were receiving it. Koreans were keenly aware of the implications of receiving aid both for their feeling of independence and for their sense of self-worth. They did not want to be treated as children or as people of lesser ability. For Chung, the concept of friends foreclosed the possibility that one party in a relationship would feel inferior. In a friendship, if there was need, help would be given and received without implying a hierarchy of position and without negating anyone's autonomy. If we are dependent and humiliated, said Chung, "it is not good."[87] Lee Nam Kyoo had said something similar: "Missionaries must not continually travel about prying into our mistakes since this is very upsetting to us. They must try very hard to have an attitude of sympathy and understanding and so develop a *true friendship* between us."[88]

To what degree were relationships of mutual affection, understanding, and trust possible on the uneven social terrain of the mission field? It is hard to say. But we do know that Chung and Lee were not alone among indigenous Christians globally in lamenting the absence of qualities of friendship in their relations with foreign missionaries.[89] Wilna Thomas had heard as much in other places.[90] In honest moments of reflection Canadian missionaries would also admit that they had failed at being friends. In 1975, missionary William Scott concluded his extensive reflections on the Canadian Korea mission with the following:

Our missionary mode of life tended to isolate us from close contact with Korean people. We lived, for the most part, in Canadian-style homes, wore Canadian-style clothes, ate North American foods (imported or home grown), and formed a neighbourhood of our own – a community apart. It is true that in our work, in church, school, or hospital, in the city or the country village, we rubbed shoulders with Korean of all classes, but in our off-duty hours, in our homes and social contacts, we tended to keep to our own missionary group. In recreation, where familiarity is encouraged, we seldom mixed. Few missionaries learned the Korean form of tennis, with soft-ball and lighter racket. Fewer still could play their favourite games of ping-pong or soccer.[91]

Scott may have been too hard on himself and too harsh in his judgement of the mission as a whole. Historian of the Canadian mission in Korea Grieg McMullin argues that there were very good reasons for the decisions that set a cultural fence around Canadian missionaries in their personal and professional interactions.[92] These include the mental health and wellbeing of the missionaries for whom a total break with their own culture could be dangerous. W.J. MacKenzie, the self-funded missionary who had sparked the beginning of the Canadian mission to Korea was often pointed to as a case in point. He had lived as a Korean but had succumbed to disease early (see chapter 1). And it is not the case that meaningful friendships and mutual respect were absent from the mission field. Some in Korea vividly remembered the heartfelt farewell Scott delivered at his retirement in 1956, in which he recited classical Korean poetry from memory and stirred in the students feelings of courage and awareness of their inheritance and duty as Koreans.[93] Others remembered that he coached a boys soccer team.[94] Scott, himself, expressed feelings of deep abiding friendship with Koreans.[95] His tribute to Kim Chai Choon likewise demonstrates a deep respect, if not friendship.[96] It could be that his "confession" had more to do with indirectly calling out unhelpful attitudes or negative tendencies he had observed in some or most of his colleagues, Canadian or otherwise.

Nevertheless, there was undeniable truth to the confession. Language remained an important symbol of the relationship as well. There were examples of Canadian missionaries who had achieved a high proficiency in the Korean language. James Scarth Gale, for example, was a gifted translator of texts and has left his mark on Korean history through his work creating a Korean-English dictionary and translating the Bible and also *Pilgrim's Progress* into Korean. Interviewee Kim Ikseon remembers that some (though not all) missionaries stationed in Manchuria were quite comfortable interacting in Korean.[97] In the 1960s, however, UCC missionaries as a group felt that they had failed to achieve a proficiency that would allow them to work with their Korean colleagues in their own linguistic territory.[98] For Lee Nam Kyoo and Chung Yong Chul, friendship would only be possible if the missionaries gave up their position of power and privilege within the PROK body. To some degree, this was the vision that Thomas, despite her own colonial baggage, was also articulating. But to what degree could she or others from the UCC truly overcome paternalistic attitudes and neo-colonial structures?

Mission historian Dana Roberts has underlined the importance of the twentieth-century discourse on friendship for the Missionary Enterprise. The appeals of PROK members to UCC missionaries in the 1960s echoed with the famous cry "Give us friends!" uttered at the World Missionary Conference in 1910. Roberts argues that Indian Christian V.S. Azariah's emotional speech before the missionaries at Edinburgh carried a prophetic note of hope. Missionaries sometimes did develop cross-cultural friendships on the mission field. Indeed, these friendships, where they were achieved, gave the Missionary Enterprise legitimacy and made it effective. But the discourse changed somewhat after the Second World War and shifted to the concept of "partnership." The shift had to do with danger to Christians in some postcolonial nations if they claimed "friendship" with Westerners as this would expose them to accusations of collusion with the oppressors. The idea of friendship was also unsuitable to the challenge of developing a more systematic approach to combating racism and economic inequality. The idea of partnership was more corporate and structural than personal, writes Roberts: "During the 1950s and 1960s older mainline denominations transferred assets and projects to their overseas 'partners.' The evolving meaning of partnership was also a source of dispute, as Western mission boards seemed to prefer the creation of global denominational fellowships as a framework for partnership, while a number of non-Western leaders preferred regional or national approaches over the denominational ... Colonial guilt and pressure for reparations turned ideals of partnership into development projects that often lacked the personal and faith commitments of the friendship ideal."[99] It seems that in the context of Korea, at least, the shift to the corporate and less personal did not sit well with everybody. Ironically, as we have already mentioned, there were aspects of the shift that felt downright colonial. Roberts similarly points out that there is something about the depersonalization of mission relationships in a world of widening economic divides that allows Western church to indulge in "a self-deluding rationalization that makes the wealthy feel good about their charitable activities."[100]

Thomas and the UCC Korea Mission continued to struggle with these issues through the 1960s. By 1969, UCC missionary Morley

Hammond insisted that the PROK already had much more say in and control over UCC mission funds and institutions than other Korean churches had in relation to overseas missionary churches. Yet this was clearly not enough. And Hammond admits in his year-end report that few concrete solutions had been achieved toward ending the acrimonious debate that had started with "the Decision" eight years earlier. Rather, he described progress in the "mood," sensing a deepening of mutual understanding that might serve as a springboard for material steps in the decade to come. There was, he said, "an atmosphere of mutual expectation for the future, accompanied by conviction and confidence that the shackles of old patterns must and can be broken for mission in the seventies. There remained, then, the business of transforming this mood into practical decision and action."[101]

CONCLUSION

The 1950s and 60s represent an important period in the history of Canadian missionary activity in Korea, when political movements, theological developments, economic realities, and postcolonial consciousnesses were challenging the tradition of Canadian missions. Following a popular uprising against an unpopular US-backed president, PROK Christians also sought to overthrow the old order of missionary relations. Lingering Korean unhappiness with foreign missionary policies, practices, and attitudes were aired, and conversations were initiated. Back home the UCC had begun to address some of these issues based on high level consultations in global ecumenical organizations but the work to translate these policies to people in the pews of their own church and the church in Korea seems not to have been done, leaving the impression of a top-down decision-making process. Indeed, the exercise betrayed the persistence of colonial patterns.

The correspondence of Wilna Thomas offers a valuable glimpse of the complicated and contradictory dynamics of the mission field. Thomas was a pioneer for women in the UCC, the first woman to serve as executive secretary for Foreign Missions. Her approach to her responsibilities for oversight of UCC missions in Korea and other countries was engaged and she left a number of notebooks recording her conversations with church leadership and ordinary church people, a testament to her openness and interest in others. But the colonial legacy of the UCC and Thomas' time in Japan, the former colonial master of Korea, seem to have prejudiced her against the Korean church.

What is more, the resistance she received from Korean leadership to the changes she proposed uncovered ongoing patterns of colonialism that lingered behind new UCC policies wrapped in progressive theological language.

"Partnership" was the new catch word meant to articulate a new egalitarian relationship on the mission field. Koreans, however, tended to express the change they desired in terms of a less jargony word: "friendship." Their use of the word "friend" did not undergird a policy agenda but was an echo of a desire found on mission fields the world over for genuine personal connection with the missionary. The fact that Koreans had to remind Canadian missionaries, as others had done at other times in other places, of the simple desire for respect, comradery, and a more equal social position was testimony to the fact that there were still things that had to be worked on in the relationship. The following decade would indeed see meaningful action to resolve the uneven relations between UCC missionaries and PROK Christians in Korea, but not without a crescendo in the debate and increased tensions between PROK leaders and UCC missionaries. The result would eventually be the dissolution of the UCC Korea Mission. The missionaries that remained would, as Chung Yong Chul had suggested, work directly for the Korean church. In addition, all UCC mission property would be transferred to the PROK. Indeed, the whole culture of the Canadian Missionary Enterprise was about to change. But these changes did not happen on their own. They were something for which Koreans Christians would have to continue to fight.

4

"Taking Hold of Its Own Domain"

The Ending of the UCC *Mission Enterprise in Korea, 1970 to 1974*

Basic Victim Positions ... are the same whether you are a victimized country, a victimized minority group or a victimized individual.
Position One: To deny the fact that you are a victim.
Position Two: To acknowledge the fact that you are a victim, but to explain this as an act of Fate, the Will of God ... or [using] any other large general powerful idea.
Position Three: To acknowledge the fact that you are a victim but to refuse to accept the assumption that the role is inevitable.
Position Four: To be a creative non-victim.

Margaret Atwood, *Survival* (1972)[1]

As the relationship between the Presbyterian Church in the Republic Korea and the United Church of Canada Korea Mission developed and stretched into the 1970s, Koreans continued to struggle to emerge from out of a history of colonial victimhood. They had suffered at the hands of Japanese imperialist government, from national division by Cold War superpowers, and now in the 1970s under the military dictatorship of Park Chung Hee. Perhaps more surprisingly, they had also suffered through the colonial attitudes and missionary privilege of the United Church of Canada. There were many in Korea who aspired for something better. This was certainly the case for PROK leadership as they negotiated with their UCC "partners" during the first part of the 1970s.

The UCC's response to PROK demands for more sovereignty were complex. While it agreed in principle that indigenous churches should have more control of their finances, there was also a desire to reduce their own expenditures. UCC membership and its budget in Canada were contracting. The UCC, therefore, was eager to reduce funding to the overseas churches, a move that would force these churches to become more independent of their erstwhile UCC benefactors. But PROK leadership was unhappy that the UCC was making major funding decisions without consulting them. At the same time, there were Canadian missionaries who were resisting the idea of giving up control of their own mission projects and were digging in their heels. The UCC seemed reluctant to respond to PROK suggestions at first, but eventually agreed to a consultation. The joint statement signed by the two churches in 1974 represented a significant achievement for the PROK and had major consequences for the material, political, and theological culture of the Canadian missionaries in Korea.

DIVISIONS AND INEQUALITY IN THE KOREAN MISSION CONTACT ZONE

South Koreans in the 1970s knew, as did others who had been exploited under a colonial system, what it meant in postcolonial theorist Homi Bhabha's words "to produce, to labor and to create, within a world-system whose major economic impulses and cultural investments are pointed in a direction away from you, your country or your people."[2] As the 1960s began to transition into the 1970s, South Koreans began to feel the pressures of those power structures with new intensity. Park Chung Hee's move to re-establish diplomatic and economic ties with Japan in 1965 had been forced through following pressure from the US and had the effect of bringing South Korea more securely within their former colonial master's sphere of economic influence.[3] Kim Chai Choon, founder of the PROK (see chapter 2), was among those activists and intellectuals in Korea who recognized and lamented the "neocolonial" status of the Republic of Korea and expressed their unhappiness with the status quo.[4]

The economic growth that occurred under the Park Chung Hee government has been celebrated in the West and in Korea and is the focus of many studies. Political economist Choi Jang-jip, however, has referred to the creation of a "success myth."[5] Within the span of Park's rule, the per capita income of South Korea rose from somewhere near the bottom of a group of comparable middle-income countries to somewhere near the top.[6] While the growth of GDP is not in doubt, what few people outside the country recognize is the degree to which that "success story" came at the expense of poorer Koreans, impoverished women in particular. Economist Martin Hart-Landsberg has shown that South Korea's economic growth and industrial transformation "was largely the result of highly centralized and effective state planning and direction of economic activity."[7] Its success, he argued, had a lot to do with its integration into the US-Japan hegemony in East Asia and the effective surrender of much of its political and economic independence.[8] In its patterns of exploitation, the structure of South Korea's economic growth was an evolution of (and not a break with) the political economy of its days as a colony of Japan.[9] What's more, under Park Chung Hee South Korea began to aggressively exploit other countries[10] and also benefitted by compensation received from the US in return for the deployment of 300,000 troops in support of the American war in Vietnam.[11] The essence of Hart-Landsberg's findings can be summed up as follows: "Japanese colonialism did more than create the conditions for a dominant state to arise in Korea, it also directly transmitted a development model based on military power, state direction of economic activity, production by large family-owned conglomerates, and extreme exploitation of workers, especially women."[12] Historian Seungsook Moon has also shown how thoroughly the militarized mobilization of South Korea's economy depended upon gender divisions and the exploitation of women by forcing them to forego education and enter the manufacturing sector en masse as unskilled labour.[13] Park's policies were equally harmful to farmers who were forced to contend with artificially low prices for their produce in order to support the government's export strategies.[14] Labourers, women, and farmers would go on to play a central role in protests against the Park dictatorship. The conditions these Koreans faced contributed as much to the motivations of the Democratization Movement as Park's attacks on democracy.

Korea historian Bruce Cumings has convincingly argued that economic and political developments in Korea and other East Asian countries at the time were connected intimately to changes in the US and North America.[15] It is worth considering the ways those changes were related to developments in Canada as well. During the time that Park Chung Hee was in power, Canada began to import many manufactured goods from South Korea including cars and electronics. But Canada's own industrial output likewise expanded largely because of an increase in car manufacturing.[16] Canada's immigration policy shifted in the 1960s to allow a far greater number of immigrants to arrive from non-Western countries. These immigrants would often fill the less desirable and less well-paying jobs. The typical Korean immigrant, for example, would run a small business such as a corner store. Women began to enter the workforce in greater numbers as well. This was a sign of emancipation as society began to encourage women's independence, but it was also a form of exploitation as wages for women never matched that of their male counterparts.

The economic growth of Korea may have contributed to changes in the church relationship as well. In the 1970s, the Korean economy was growing rapidly, something that was not lost on missionaries. It could be that those responsible for the mission expenditures of the Canadian church were beginning to feel that their Korean church partners should start to shoulder more of the financial burden. This dynamic certainly played out on a micro level in Canada between the Bloor St United church and Toronto Korean United Church in the 1980s and 90s. The Anglo congregation saw its budget shrink while the Korea church that rented its space seemed to be growing. This set off a fraught dialogue regarding the rent for the use of the church space (see chapter 8). If this was the thinking of the UCC regarding the PROK, however, it is not apparent in the correspondence. Indeed, there was still a significant financial gulf between the two churches in the 1970s.

Within the overarching sphere of the international political economy, the global Protestant church, through the Missionary Enterprise, had its own political economic order. Although in 1970 Christians were still a small minority in South Korea (Protestants comprised less than 10 per cent of the national population and Catholics less than 3 per cent),[17] their influence on the new nation was disproportionately strong. Beginning with the US occupational government below the 38th parallel, the small but educated Christian population provided important talent for running the country. The USAMGIK and the subsequent authoritarian regimes relied on missionaries for overseas funds and international public support. For this reason, churches in South Korea wielded more influence than their percentage of the Korean population would suggest. American missionaries and the churches they supported would have been particularly influential but Canadian-related churches and institutions would have been similarly significant.

In comparison to American supported Korean churches and missionary organizations, however, the PROK and the UCC Korea Mission were quite marginal. The PROK was the lesser of two churches that emerged from a fracture of the PCK. Outside of some 680 congregations, it had no property or institution other than a college for training ministers, the independent Hanguk Theological Seminary. In terms of membership, it was only a fraction of the PCK in size. In the context of other Korean denominations as well, the PROK was small and, according to interviewee Dong-Chun Seo, many dismissed it as quite unimportant.[18] Similarly, the UCC Korea Mission had also found itself greatly impoverished after the war. The signing of the armistice that ended hostilities between North and South Korea in 1953 had not restored their former mission stations in the northeast. Rather the indefinite continuation of the war posture between the two sides meant the UCC Korea Mission had effectively lost all its buildings, schools, and hospitals, save for a single house in Seoul, the only property that had been in their possession south of the 38th parallel. The rest had to be permanently abandoned in North Korea and Manchuria where their pre-war mission field had been located.

Although the PROK and UCC Korea mission were both significantly diminished in the postwar environment, their relationship was typical of political economies between Western missions and indigenous churches throughout the globe. The budgets of each highlight this unevenness. In 1971, the PROK General Assembly passed a program budget of 31,184,017 Won, an equivalent of CAD$82,622.27.[19] Better than two-thirds of this amount, 20,731,000 Won (CAD$57,586.11), was from the Cooperative Work Grant provided by the UCC. By contrast the UCC's annual budget for the same year was $33,088,773, almost four hundred times greater than its South Korean partner's.[20] The UCC Korea Mission was receiving more funds from the UCC for its own separate programs and operation than was being provided directly to the PROK. Reporting an operating budget of 24,420,000 Won (CAD$67,833.33) in 1971, the Mission's budget was greater than two-thirds of the budget for the whole PROK General Assembly, the denomination's governing body.[21] Missionaries could use these funds at their own discretion to maintain property, hire help, and cover expenses connected to their work in the field.[22] Another striking comparison can be made using the numbers of UCC and PROK congregations and educational institutions. In 1969, the PROK had 680 affiliated congregations.[23] The UCC yearbook for 1971 counts 4,525 congregations, more than six times as many. The PROK boasted a single post-secondary institution, Hanguk seminary. The UCC had thirteen.[24] These figures paint a striking picture of the relative status and power of each institution. In correspondence related to the 1971 PROK budget, Frank Carey, assistant secretary to the East Asia Desk of the Board of World Mission (BWM), stated that the Cooperative Working Grant funds sent from the UCC that year came "with no strings attached."[25] With such a lopsided financial and institutional position, however, it is hard to imagine that the PROK would not be extremely sensitive to UCC actions and attitudes regarding their work.

On the basis of compensation for leadership, the differences in salaries were also quite stark. Missionaries made a minimum full-time salary of 135 per cent of Canadian minister's minimum salary plus a housing allowance, about CAD$7,500.[26] The UCC pension fund was worth CAD$53 million.[27] Korean ministers had no minimum salary and no pension. Some UCC missionaries in Korea at the time were deeply aware of and embarrassed by the discrepancy between their financial position relative to the ordinary Koreans with whom they worked.[28] Their feelings were shared by UCC missionary colleagues serving in other parts of the world.[29] Into the 1970s, however, UCC missionaries in Korea still enjoyed the services of Korean drivers, cooks, and nannies, and lived in compounds consisting of grand western-style homes.[30] Cars were a particularly potent symbol of missionary privilege,[31] which missionaries in the UCC Korea Mission regarded as "essential."[32] Koreans in the PROK felt these material inequalities keenly and there were some in the PROK who truly resented the presence of the missionaries because of the social privilege they projected. They regarded it as a betrayal of the Christian gospel they purported to spread. Some thought this betrayal was grounds upon which to ask them to leave.[33]

BUDGET AND PROPERTY: AN ISSUE OF INDEPENDENCE

As it entered the 1970s UCC membership began to shrink, and the church experienced budgetary pressure to reduce its regular grants to overseas churches associated with its missions abroad. The BWM also began to speak of "disengagement." Where Korea was concerned, some on the board thought this could mean simply weaning the PROK off UCC funds by incremental cuts. In a letter to PROK General Secretary Lee Young Min in early 1971, associate secretary for the BWM, Frank Carey, tipped the Korean church off to the permanent nature of these looming budget cuts. He impressed upon Lee that the UCC was looking to cut funding to all its overseas missions. He suggested that cuts to PROK funding would be "gradual but increasing" so that within ten years it was expected that the indigenous churches in Korea would be operating independent of UCC money. "In other words," wrote Carey, "we would hope that the PROK will begin to make plans for the gradual phasing out of financial support."[34]

This letter lit a fire under the PROK leadership. The organization moved rapidly and proactively to suggest ways that it could phase out its dependence on the UCC while at the same time guarantee some financial security for its organization into the future. It quickly responded with four proposals for the UCC. The first was an endowment fund equivalent to five times its current annual funding (amounting to CAD $185,000) to which the UCC would contribute the whole and after which discontinue its regular grants entirely.[35] Carey responded to General Secretary Lee with some misgivings about the plan and countered with the suggestion that the BWM might provide half the requested amount (CAD $92,500) up front and continue annual grant funding at half the present amount for five years after which it would be entirely discontinued. He also suggested that the only way to secure the large amount of cash upfront would be through a sale of property held by the UCC Korea Mission in Korea.[36]

Carey arrived in Korea soon after as part of a planned tour of East Asia late in 1971 and sat down with PROK representatives and UCC missionaries to discuss the proposals from the Korean church. Present from the PROK were PROK General Secretary Lee Young Min, Moderator Cho Hyang Rock, former Canadian scholarship recipient Kang Won Yong, and seven others. Along with Carey, missionaries Fred Bayliss, Walter Beecham, Marion Current, and Willa Kernen were present. The discussion was recorded and translated.[37] After Moderator Cho Hyang Rock welcomed Carey and opened in prayer, the associate secretary of the BMW was invited to make some remarks. Carey addressed the "changed situation" that necessitated "changes in our relationship." The Korean church was hungry for more independence and the Canadian church was experiencing budget pressure. He reiterated what he had stated to Lee in his earlier letter, that the UCC was looking for ways to phaseout funding for the running of overseas churches. The goal was "mutuality" in mission, "to make World Mission a reality not just 'the West to the rest.'"[38] After Carey had been thanked for his "refreshing ideas," Kang Won Yong, a graduate of the UCC theological college in Manitoba, pointedly asked Carey to explain how budget decisions made unilaterally by the UCC could be described as "mutual." His discontent was echoed by the other Korean members who joined in asking for "a top-level consultation" before decisions were made.

Before the conversation ended, Moderator Cho raised the issue of missionary property reverting to PROK. This, he said, was a "matter of theology." There was no need for "Mission Compounds" anymore, he insisted, but the property could be "used for broader mission." By "Mission Compounds" Cho was referring to the properties on which missionaries had traditionally lived, usually in large houses with servant help. By stressing that the matter was theological in nature Cho, as the spiritual head of the PROK, appears to have been stressing how deeply this issue touched the membership of the Korean church and threw into question the spiritual integrity of the Canadian mission. Though the meeting had been convened to discuss future funding, it was clear that the issue of the material culture of the UCC Korea Mission vis-à-vis their Korean sisters and brothers was even more important.

By the 1970s the UCC owned properties in three places. The first was a "compound" in the neighbourhood of the Great Western Gate in Seoul, the one remaining property from the UCC Korea Mission's pre-war mission. The second was property acquired since the end of the Korean War near the town of Iri in the North Cholla province (roughly two hundred kilometres south of Seoul). This property had been purchased in the 1950s with the plan of creating an agricultural education and mission centre. The third place the UCC Korea Mission owned real estate was in the city of Wonju in Kangwon province (roughly one hundred kilometres east of Seoul), which had also recently been purchased with plans to start a hospital. Each of these three property clusters had a missionary residence, but the most conspicuous of these was the large house and collection of other buildings on the compound in the heart of Seoul near the historic site of the Great Western Gate. The big red brick house in the compound was on land that had been purchased in 1918. A stately home had been built upon it in 1921 by Dr T.D. Mansfield. Mansfield had arrived in Korea as a medical missionary of the Canadian Presbyterian mission in 1910, part of the first contingent of missionaries from the "Western" Presbyterian church in Quebec and Ontario.[39] He served in north-eastern Korea and Manchuria until 1917 and then moved down to Seoul to serve at Severance hospital.[40] This was not the first house Mansfield had built in Korea. In his first year in the northeast, he had also undertaken to construct a home for himself at the mission station in Seungjin. A church representative sent to inspect the work of the mission criticized Mansfield for making it too big and going over budget. In a defensive letter sent to church HQ in Canada Mansfield conceded "Our houses do loom up bigger than I thought they would."[41] He did not seem to take the criticism to heart, however. The home he built for himself in Seoul nine years later "loomed" over its neighbourhood as well.[42] Later converted into a Mission Training School and Seminary, the living and dining rooms alone had room for about eighty students. Another classroom for forty students, five study rooms, a library, and the director's office also all found room in Mansfield's converted residence.[43]

Following Church Union in 1925, Mansfield's Seoul dwelling became the property of the UCC Korea Mission. Dr Mansfield used it for one more year until his retirement in 1926. Subsequently, Dr Stanley Martin, who had served until then as a missionary doctor in Yongjeong, Manchuria, had moved in and lived there until the forced evacuation of missionaries from the peninsula in 1940.[44] During the war the house had been used as the private residence of an officer in the Japanese army. This officer had added new residential buildings to the back of the property. These new buildings along with the original residence reverted to the UCC Mission when the missionaries returned after the Pacific War in 1946.[45] Once again they took up residence on the property. During the Korean war, the house had been temporarily abandoned again and its cellar used briefly by the People's Army of North Korea as a prison. With the signing of the armistice Canadian missionary Rev. Milton MacDonald (Don) Irwin, Mrs Alice Irwin and their family occupied the large house. Missionaries Willa Kernen and Marion Pope lived in an adjacent building on the same property. The fact that their missionary colleagues had moved into such a grand property in downtown Seoul, and perhaps also the fact that the buildings were associated with Korea's colonial oppressors, did not sit well with PROK leadership. It was clearly something they felt was wrong. Sensing the urgency of this matter Carey had to agree: "We should do what we can immediately."[46]

But it was not only the material culture of the mission field that Koreans in the PROK were angry about. The political culture was also proving to be problematic. In this regard, the specific issue on the minds of those at the meeting with Carey had to do with the Iri Farm Project. Beginning right after the war, the UCC Korea Mission

Table 4.1
Iri lands held by the UCC Korea Mission, 1963

LAND

	Number	Land kind	Size (pyung)
Ma Dong, Iri	San 45–1	Forest	2670
	San 45–3	Forest	150
	165	Rice field	226
	165–1	Site	177
	165–3	Field	332
	165–4	Field	2373
	165–2	Field	918
	165–5	Field	40
	165–7	Rice field	1185
PyongWhaDong, Iri	39	Site	63
	40–9	Site	219

BUILDINGS

	Site number	Construction	Size (pyung)	Note
Ma Dong, Iri	San 45–1	Wood, grass roof	8	
	San 45–1	Wood, grass roof	8	
	San 45–1	Wood, grass roof	8	
	165–1	Wood, slate roof	21.5	
	165–1	Iron roof	6	
	40–1	Tile roof	42.36	Baker house
	40–1	Tile roof	0.84	Toilet
	40–1	Iron roof	6.3	Storage
	San 45–3	Cement block, tile roof	50.21	Findlay house
	165–1	Wood, iron	12	Garage
PyongWhaDong, Iri	39	Wood, tile roof	15	
	39	Wood, tile roof	10	
SunWhaDong, Taejon	340–1	Wood, slate roof	35.47	
	84–35	Wood, slate roof		

Water from Dragon's Well

Table 4.1 (*Continued*)

Site number	Construction	Size (pyung)	Note
84–54	Wood, slate roof		
84–54	Wood, iron roof	2.25	Garage
84–54	Cement block, tile roof	11	Servants' house

had begun to purchase tracts of land in the southwest of the peninsula near a town called Iri. By 1963 the UCC's juridical body in Korea had an extensive list of holdings in the area.[47]

The Iri Farm, as the project was called, used the land as a place where UCC missionaries worked with Korean farmers to introduce modern farming practices. In a letter to Carey that accompanied the 1970 UCC Korea Mission annual report, Canadian Missionary Morley Hammond had taken some time to update the BMW associate secretary about this ongoing project.[48]

The Iri Farm amounted to about half of all UCC Korea Mission land holdings in South Korea at the time. Due to an agreement reached in 1969, many UCC programs in Korea had already been or were in the process of being transferred to the direct supervision of the PROK.[49] The Iri Farm, however, was still being run by two UCC missionaries, lay agriculturalist Clare Findlay and evangelist the Rev. Russell Young. The two did not want to give up their control of the project. In response to pressure by the BWM to allow the farm project to transfer to the PROK, Findlay and Young began to lobby to be exempted from the policy. Their reports took pains to explain their program and argue that its transfer to the PROK would jeopardize its future.[50] Findlay and his wife, Irene, had arrived in Korea in 1959 and started work in Iri immediately. Part of a UCC's mission policy to appoint more lay people with practical skills rather than theological training, the couple from High River Alberta had experience in agriculture and rural life and were sent to share this expertise with Korean farmers. The Rev. Young and his wife Shirley were from central Canada – Ontario and Quebec, respectively – and trained in theology. Appointed in 1963, they, too, soon made their way to Iri to work with the Findlays on the farm project. By 1970 both couples and their young families had been in Korea for enough time to feel invested in their work and at home in their environment. Both Findlay and Young felt strongly about the program that they had developed with village farmers in the area.

The approach of Findlay and Young at Iri did not focus on religious conversion but was very much in line with the new thinking about mission that Wilna Thomas had insisted would be the focus of UCC missions when she had visited Korea in 1964 (see chapter 3), an approach that emphasized social development rather than religious conversion. "The essential characteristics of change and improvement must enter into all of life, industry and agriculture," Findlay and Young asserted in their 1970 report.[51] They pointed to economic, land-use, and demographic pressures affecting South Korea and rural communities as some of the specific problems they sought to address with a program they felt was a great assistance to rural Koreans. Their focus was on education, and they introduced a combination of pig farming and credit unions to willing farmers in three villages.[52]

When pushed to comply with the request to transfer control of the project to the Korean church, the two Canadians, along with their farm board made up of local farmers and Christians loosely associated with the PROK, decided they would rather hand the project off to a local organization called the Union Christian Service Centre (UCSC), which was not affiliated directly with the PROK. That arrangement, they explained, would safeguard the integrity of the program and their own role in it.[53] Findlay and Young were arguing that a firm missionary hand on the tiller meant better results for disadvantaged Koreans. These two missionaries were strong-willed and had a clear vision of what they wanted for their project, but their resistance to requests from the PROK to share more of the leadership seems also to have been motivated by complex factors. They did not trust the PROK leadership. They also had misgivings about the ability of Korean church leaders and their ethical integrity as Koreans. In a long letter to Carey, Findlay outlined some of his concerns. He complained, without giving examples, that Koreans' plans for the farm were "outlandish": "Everyone tries to get into the act, as the saying goes, and then often they bring in their family," he wrote, echoing Wilna Thomas' colonial prejudices about Koreans, "Nepotism is a very large and continuing problem of longstanding in the orient generally and in Korea in particular."[54] Addressing the move to transfer responsibility for programs to the indigenous church, he had the following to say: "All foreign missions working today in Korea are feeling the pressure of institutional take-over, or the wish for the transfer of mission properties to denominational holding committees or is it just the plain administrative rights over mission-run programs. Would it help to make sense out of all of this if we realized that the price per acre of land in Korea, at present, often exceeds that of the price of land in this Canada of ours [*sic*]."[55] Findlay was suggesting that PROK leadership had only dollar signs in their eyes rather than any genuine commitment to the work. Findlay's correspondence contains sweeping generalizations and reflects colonial attitudes that were common in Canada, that, for example, Indigenous people were not able to manage their own affairs.

As Carey corresponded with Findlay and Young trying to work through their concerns, he simultaneously maintained a dialogue with PROK General Secretary Lee about the farm. After a meeting with Lee in 1971 Carey had advised Findlay and Young that no moves to dispose of mission property should be made without consulting the PROK. Both Carey and Lee recognized that the two Canadian missionaries were planning to do just that, but they also agreed to give the matter some space to breathe rather than apply too much pressure at that time.[56] By the next spring, however, an incident involving Young at a meeting of the executive of the PROK General Assembly had forced Lee to confront Young directly. "Let me say frankly," he wrote in a letter, "that in connection with your work, there is a lack of communication, and a resultant distrust or fear on both sides. I personally feel that there should be love and mutual respect. This may perhaps be more important for a missionary than the work or enterprise he is undertaking, for it is through this that we can witness to the Christian gospel of love. What you said in your letter about the present and future of your work might be legitimate, but at the same time, it is most unfortunate that the farm has given the impression, as I have been told by a number of people from the Chun Puk area [North Jeolla Province where the Iri Farm was located], that yours is a situation 'extraterritorial,' and that your work lacks any support from the Church."[57]

These were the tensions that were stewing when Carey came to meet PROK leadership late in 1971. According to Lee Young Min it was, first, the issue of missionary compounds (i.e., the apparently grand lifestyle of UCC missionaries), and second, missionary attitudes vis-à-vis the PROK (i.e., their lack of respect for the Korean church and their unwillingness to relinquish control) that were at top of mind, and that these were even more important than the issue of funding. But the three were connected and Carey was clearly reluctant to commit to a high-level consultation to resolve these issues on the PROK's terms. Rather, he insisted, there was a need for more study and correspondence to clarify the issues. Lee, however, pressed for something sooner. The issues, he said, were urgent and needed to be settled by "sitting down together both here and in Canada, sharing our concerns and hopes, and thus coming to meaningful relationships as we work together."[58] Despite his urgings, the problems festered for another two years before they were addressed.

A year after Carey's visit, a meeting of the Iri Farm Board of Advisors was held with representation from the PROK executive, the Rev. Kwon Young Min. Present were Young, Findlay, Park Chong Muk, Chun Chang Il, Park In Kyu, and two women, a Ms Chung and UCC missionary Marion Pope. Young reported that he had visited Lee and said "there was a basic disagreement" about who was ultimately in a position of authority to make decisions about the future of the farm and its land. Concern was also raised that the PROK did not take its agricultural mission seriously. Pope asked Kwon, "Does the General Assembly and the PROK have any involvement in rural development programs and as it relates to agriculture?" Kwon had to admit the PROK executive did not, but that individual members within the PROK did and that the executive did support rural centres financially, including the one to whom Young and Findlay were trying to transfer the Iri Farm Project. But he quickly brought the discussion back to the relationship between the missionaries and the indigenous church. The heart of the issue was, for him, the matter of control and of respect. "Our General Assembly has had and still has a relationship with the UCC and because of this we cannot see how you can transfer the farm to another organization," insisted Kwon, "In the future, if the farm was transferred to another organization the PROK would feel bad."[59]

By the next year the tension had escalated still further. Despite numerous assurances that Young and Findlay would have an important role in the running of the farm under PROK leadership, neither were willing to accept the change. In a letter to Carey, Findlay again expressed his frustration that the new Division of World Outreach (DWO – successor of the BWM) was giving the PROK point of view "prime preference" and threatened that if the farm came under the control of the PROK, he would quit.[60] Once again he articulated his low view of the indigenous church leadership, a view partly informed by a perception of rural-urban differences. "If you care to know all the things that I know of PROK policies and dealings," he wrote, "I will write a very long epistle to you to clarify the situation." He objected that "the top 3 or 4 people that you are dealing with in Korea are not the PROK" and do not represent "the real PROK," driving home his point that the leadership was disconnected to the people in the pews. He argued that the PROK was in essence a rural church and that the needs of this rural constituency were neglected in favour of "the big urban churches which they feel are their show cases and their strength." On this point, Findlay's concerns ring true. The divide between rural and urban interests in church economies in Canada were also a problem. Korea at this time was undergoing an extremely rapid process of urbanization and rural communities were being marginalized. Findlay, coming from a rural background himself, would have empathized with this situation and it would be natural for him to want to defend fellow rural folk.

If Findlay's concerns for the rural Korean church were legitimate, however, prejudice also clearly poisoned his correspondence and undermined his argument. He blasted the PROK "hierarchy," which he pointed out depended on the funds they got from DWO and said they wished simply "to gather in as much capital as possible before you leave them to fend for themselves." "You must realize," he continued, "that the United Church of Canada has led a long and paternalistic relationship with the [PROK] and this has built up in the minds of all the major minister participants who have enjoyed its benefits, that this is the only role that you have to play."[61] Findlay's comments certainly went to the heart of the matter. Paternalism was at issue. But in dismissing the interests of members of the elected PROK leadership as self-serving, he was deflecting criticism of himself and Young for their own paternalistic approach to missionary work and their dismissal of both local and national Korean church input. Carey responded to Findlay's invective by defending the objectivity of the DWO and the legitimacy of the PROK executive leadership as a body elected by the whole PROK membership. He reminded Findlay that a lack of trust had resulted from his own farm board's tendency to ignore the PROK executive. He also announced plans for a consultation, which Lee Young Min and others had sought during his visit two years earlier, a consultation that he hoped would deal with the issue of the farm as well as the related issue of UCC Korea Mission property and future funding for the PROK.[62]

The long-awaited consultation took place on 13 and 14 March 1974 in Seoul. On the PROK side, Moderator Lee Joon Mook, General Secretary Lee Young Min, General Assembly Secretary Cho Duck Hyun, president of Hanguk Seminary Kim Chung Choon, and former moderator Cho Hyang Rock attended. All but one had studied at a United Church college in Canada.[63] On the UCC side, DWO secretary Roy Webster, DWO Assistant Secretary for East Asia Frank Carey, and the Rev. Clifford Elliott, a member of the DWO executive, had flown to Korea for the meeting. The agenda included three main topics: "1. A Self-Support Plan for the Present On-going Co-operative Work, 2. New Areas and Special Ministries for Co-operation in the Future, 3. Discussions on Needed Areas, Roles, Orientation and Problems of Missionaries."[64] The agenda was also left open to discuss other matters as they arose.

Under the first topic, the matter of the Iri Farm was to be discussed and matters related to the discontinuance of funding to the PROK General Assembly from the UCC. Under the second topic, however, some novel areas of discussion were proposed. Items under the heading of "Co-operation for Overseas scholarships and Overseas Missions" signalled an important shift in the mission relationship between the Canadian and the Korean church brought about by an influx of Korean migrants to Canada. One way that Koreans from the Korean church had traditionally made their way to Canada was as scholarship students. This was a long-established practice, the first student Kim Kwan Shik having travelled to Toronto (presumably to study in the Presbyterian seminary, Knox College) just prior to Church Union.[65] The second, Moon Chai Rin, went to Toronto in 1928, to study in the new United Church seminary, Emmanuel College.[66] The UCC mission had been an early proponent of sending students from Korea abroad. Many of them traveled to Canada and studied theology at a United Church seminary. Others were funded to study theology in the United States, Europe, or Japan. Still others received funding from the UCC to study a non-religious discipline, like medicine or nursing. By comparison, American missionaries were less inclined to send Koreans abroad (see chapter 2). But Koreans valued Western education.[67] Across Asia, the opportunity to study in the West was coveted as a way to modernize society and the nation. The UCC and its missionaries were happy to encourage this desire and continued to fund Koreans to study abroad into the 1980s. By the seventies, however, it was not only scholarship students who were travelling from Korea to Canada. Hundreds were arriving weekly as immigrants and many of these were Christians.

The agenda for the 1974 consultation introduced this paradigm shift in the relationship and recognized it as the advent of Koreans travelling as missionaries to evangelize and serve the Canadian church.

Nine years after the first PROK minister had travelled to Canada to serve a UCC congregation (see chapter 7),[68] both churches had become aware of this possible shift in their relationship. It is significant that this was acknowledged in the document. The shift was further formalized in 1989 when PROK minister Yi Gwang-il, was commissioned as a missionary from the PROK to serve the UCC.[69] A one-time political prisoner of the Park Chung Hee regime and student at the Mission and Education Center (see chapter 5), Yi was the first and last to serve in this capacity. But there were what might be regarded as many unofficial "missionaries" that started travelling from Korea to Canada in the 1960s, who became members of leaders of the church there and who, by 1974, numbered in the thousands. These were Koreans who had moved to Canada as a result of a new immigration agreement signed between the Pearson and Park governments. Hundreds of these immigrants ended up in the UCC and among them were dozens of Korean clergy who served in the UCC in both Korean- and English-speaking congregations. The 1974 consultation was the first time the PROK and DWO had addressed, at an institutional level, the migration of Koreans to Canada and their role in the church there.[70] This fact gives important transnational context to the church relationship, and points to the fact that the movement of ideas, people, and resources was no longer one way but two way – and, in fact, was starting to tip in favour of the flow from Korea to Canada.

Under the third topic the PROK idea for a lay training centre was mentioned. The significance of this would become clear immediately following the consultation when, as a result of the agreement reached, the big house in Seoul was transferred to the PROK and became the location of the Mission and Education Center (MEC), soon to be ground zero for much of the Christian resistance against the Park Chung Hee government and incubator for the uniquely Korean "Minjung theology." Minjung theology would contribute to the ideological development of the Democratization Movement in South Korea starting in the late 1970s and continuing into the 1990s. It also had an impact on the global theological discourse of the Christian church. These developments could not have been foreseen by the Canadians or the Koreans who proposed a lay training centre. However, the ingredients of Korean leadership, Canadian open-handedness, and political moment combined to create something truly remarkable. The MEC, located in Mansfield's huge missionary residence, represents a new moment in the Korean-Canadian church relationship (see chapter 5).

The statement that emerged from the consultation "charted a new and significant course" in the relationship between the UCC and the PROK.[71] It was hoped that the new agreement would "enhance mutual understanding and fellowship" and emphasize "solidarity" through human and financial participation and collaboration.[72] The delegates agreed that all remaining property held by the UCC Korea Mission would be transferred to the PROK, that all UCC missionaries would come under the direction of and be directly accountable to the PROK General Assembly staff, and that UCC funding for PROK church institutions would be discontinued. What emerged from the consultation was a fundamentally different relationship than had existed before. Essentially, it evened the social position between missionary and Korean and gave the Korean church considerably more agency and responsibility in the use of church funds. According to former General Secretary of the PROK, the Rev. Kim Sang-geun, the UCC was the first and only foreign mission to take this step in its relationship with a Korean church, folding its mission, putting missionaries under Korean church control, and giving over all its assets.[73]

The new arrangement affected both church organizations, but both the process leading to the agreement as well as the results were remembered differently by the PROK and the UCC. PROK memory credits its own leadership with forcing the hand of the UCC. The PROK records say that Lee Young Min was dismayed that PROK issues were being ignored at a DWO consultation with various global churches in 1973. As the consultation approached its close, Lee suddenly interjected in the course of the meeting. The Korean church had granted the UCC trial jurisdiction of land for the Iri Farm Project, but the missionaries were not consulting with the PROK, he said, "In the meantime, the work that these missionaries have been doing is our shared work and they came as partner missionaries to work with us. But changes to their thoughts and policies the general secretary of the denomination knows nothing about. I don't understand this."[74] It was this outburst, according to the PROK's account, that embarrassed the DWO and caused it to schedule the bilateral consultation.[75]

On the UCC side, the events are recorded much differently. Minutes state that, rather than having been invited to a "consultation" (a gathering that would imply the intention to shape policy) as the PROK account suggests, Lee had come to a regular meeting of the Executive Board of the DWO as a "fraternal delegate" along with three others, a Welsh missionary serving in Haiti, the Vice President of the Lesotho

Evangelical Church and Peter Wong of the Hong Kong Council of the Church of Christ.[76] The minutes record that after individual presentations in the morning, the panel discussion in the afternoon resulted in "lively discussion" but nothing was said of what that discussion was about or what came of it. Minutes from an earlier meeting also indicate that at a meeting with Lee in 1971, Carey had already been persuaded of the need for a consultation with the PROK to resolve the issues described above. One had been planned for the spring of 1973, but was postponed because of political developments connected to the Park regime's arrest of PROK church leaders.[77]

When it came to the results of the 1974 consultation, the PROK remembers it as one of the most significant moments in its institutional history. It viewed the meeting as decisive for the partnership with the UCC and praised the Canadian church for what it saw as a bold move to create a more just relationship. Lee Young Min summed up as follows:

> It was an epoch-making occasion for policies of both churches and for the self-support plan of the PROK. Discussions took place in an atmosphere of frankness and cordiality. Ways of discontinuing recurring budget from DWO were agreed upon. The PROK was to receive titles of property held by the DWO. The so-called "Canadian Mission in Korea" would cease to exist and the PROK would assume the responsibilities of placement of missionary workers, etc. At the same time, the UCC made a suggestion to actualize this kind of policy. It must be said that in those days, the UCC was the first in taking the lead in making suggestions and implementing such policies over other overseas church mission stations in Korea.[78]

Not only did the PROK receive all of the UCC property, they also became the effective directors, supervisors, and landlords of the UCC missionaries, who were henceforth to be called "overseas mission personnel." Of particular significance for Koreans was the transfer of missionary residences, which they felt brought them into a relationship of intimacy with those whom they previously resented for their apparent privilege. Seeing the Canadians vacate their former residences – such as the "looming" house on the Seodaemun compound – and being allowed to take ownership of and move into them, Koreans experienced a real sense of reconciliation. In fact, Koreans were both surprised and relieved to find that, despite appearances, Canadian missionaries lived humbly even in their imposing houses. Interviewee Chung Suk Ja, in fact, was moved to tears remembering the frugality of her missionary friend Willa Kernen.[79] This Korean account is given: "The especially exciting thing was that the house and furniture for DWO missionaries was shared as one family between the two churches with everything shared in common and we were shown a glimpse of the simple life that missionaries lived."[80] For Koreans, this transfer pulled the curtain back on the lives of the missionaries who had been living among them for years, addressed the inequality of UCC material culture, and relieved Koreans of the feeling that their Canadian missionary friends were lording it over them.

The event is remembered as politically significant and was credited with allowing the PROK to play a more effective role in the protests against Park's dictatorial regime. According to former general secretary of the PROK Kim Sang-geun, the UCC's approach to missions made it possible for the PROK to act independently as they saw the need. Other missionaries and sending churches[81] tended to require that assets and funds be used in a certain way and that the receiving church toe the line on theological or political issues. This was not the case with the UCC, according to Kim.[82] Kim's personal assessment is supported by Korean sociologist Kang In-cheol, who speculates that this autonomy was a big reason the PROK was an effective actor in the Democratization Movement. The organizational autonomy of the PROK, i.e., the ability to gather people, raise funds and direct activities towards its own goals, seems to have been quite high compared to others[83] and this gave them tools few other groups had to evade the tight grip of government control. But the PROK remembers that the move had important repercussions for the freedom of the UCC as well: "It meant that the PROK was able to demonstrate its own ability, establish its own identity, and take hold of its own domain in the area of missions even without the help or support from outside the nation. From the other side the result was that the UCC could, rather than seeing the PROK as an object of mission work, join with the PROK as a mission partner to work together with the Korean church as it laboured under its own growing mission responsibilities."[84]

The irony of this statement is that, though the PROK version of events, which celebrates the liberation that the UCC achieved for itself, is still preserved in the living memory of many in the PROK there was not a whisper of it in the Canadian church then and there is no memory of it now. The results of the consultation seem not to have been forgotten so much as to never have been shared at all. UCC membership had supported the UCC Korea Mission for generations, but there is no record that news of the end of that mission and its significance was communicated to congregants in Canada. The story did not make it into official reports that circulated widely in leadership circles connected to UCC missions. Neither was there any acknowledgment of the transfer of the property in church news. In a 1976 account of activities at the missionary house near the Great Western Gate and its transformation into a special training centre for political dissidents, the UCC yearbook reads as follows: "In 1975 the General Assembly approved the establishment of a Mission and Education Centre in Seoul ... *The United Church of Canada has offered its Sudaimoon* [*sic*] *missionary residential property for this Centre.*"[85] Significantly, the report speaks of the UCC offering "*its*" property with no reference to the 1974 consultation or account of the transfer of properties. Technically, the transfer of the Seoul house was delayed by a few years due to the difficulty in establishing UCC ownership (records having been abandoned in North Korea). But the omission is significant. Nowhere in any UCC yearbook or publication was the decision to transfer UCC Korea Mission property to the PROK or to dissolve the UCC Korea Mission mentioned. On some level it must have been difficult for the UCC to give up its property, not only because it meant the end of a kind of colonial privilege, but also because it had been the focus of generations of Canadian church member fundraising and interest. It is possible that the membership in Canada would not have understood this move, and possibly even resented it. It is also possible that the leadership just did not know how to frame the decision in a way that people in the pews could celebrate, let alone understand. One might have thought that the Korean church's praise and clear admiration for this decision and the reconciliation it achieved might have registered in some form back in Canada. But it did not.

Nevertheless, the transfer of property to the PROK marks an important milestone in the UCC-PROK relationship with significant creative consequences for the Korean and Canadian church. For the UCC, the change involved extracting itself from a financial commitment, but also, as the PROK stated, freeing itself to support the leadership of Korean Christians, particularly those involved in the Democratization Movement of the 1970s. For UCC missionaries in Korea, the changes had personal implications. The 1974 statement required a shift in attitude to the point that their Korean colleagues not only became

"Taking Hold of Its Own Domain" 125

their "boss," but also their landlord. It also entailed a much more intimate disclosure of assets to the point that their house and furniture became the property of others. In some cases, their Korean colleagues were touched by the glimpse they were afforded of the simple life that missionaries lived,[86] but it must have been a frightening step into the unknown all the same for a Western church institution with its colonial past to give up its power and position to such a degree and for missionaries, used to being providers and guardians, to put such basic aspects of their lives in the hands of the cultural "other."

Not all were willing to participate in that transformation. Rev. Russell Young and Clare Findlay quit their work on the Iri Farm Project following the decision of the consultation. Efforts by both PROK and UCC colleagues to convince them to stay and work within the new structure had no effect. In an article for a widely distributed UCC church magazine, Young took aim at the political involvement of the church in Korean Democratization Movement as a way of levelling a parting shot at both the UCC and PROK leadership who negotiated the transfer of the Iri Farm. He suggested that, as in the case of the Iri farm, they were out of touch with the people in the pews. "The vast majority of Koreans are content with the present situation," he said referring to the Park dictatorship, "Rightly or wrongly, this is what they want."[87] Young had been comfortable with the status quo and his article in the church magazine intuits the connection between changes occurring on the UCC Korean mission field and the postcolonial movement fighting for political change in Korea. His comment about the disconnect between church leadership and church membership may have been valid, but in the matter of decolonization and democracy he was clearly out of touch. Young was not alone in resisting changes that would see Western Christians relinquish control of programs and property to indigenous churches. But PROK voices had won the day 1974, voices that would now be more focussed on the problems facing their nation and communities than on the missionary legacy of the Canadian church.

Rev. Clifford Elliott, a member of the DWO delegation in 1974, tried to encourage his Canadian congregants to do the same. The Sunday following his return from the Korean consultation, he preached a sermon at Metropolitan United Church in Toronto on what he had seen and heard in Korea. Above all, he had been impressed by the way Korean Christians were refusing to be victimized by the authoritarianism of the Park Chung Hee regime, but rather had "come out fighting for the rights of the oppressed." Elliott likewise challenged his parishioners to think about their own Christian commitment: "We do not have to face open political oppression as the Koreans face. Nevertheless, we know that there are many subtle pressures which intimidate us when we try to be Christians in our world. Perhaps threat of imprisonment is not as great a threat as the temptation to conform in a secular society. Let us beware lest the pillows of apparent freedom silence us even more effectively than the chains of tyranny."[88] The Canadian church was at that moment under pressure from a dramatic exodus of people from the pews. But was this exodus the result of secularism, social change, and a comfortable Western life, as Elliott suggested? Or was it the failure of the church to articulate a new vision for itself in a postcolonial context? It is sad that Elliot did not mention the struggle of the PROK against the UCC Korea Mission and the brave gesture of reconciliation the UCC had made. At least then the news of this momentous event would have been shared with the Canadian church and the members of a UCC congregation would have heard the good news of how it is possible to reboot relationships undermined by years of colonialism.

CONCLUSION

The history of the PROK-UCC negotiations circa 1974 provide a clear example of the way Canadians missionaries participated in systems that privileged them at the expense of others on the global playing field. The story of the transfer of mission property to the indigenous church is not unique to Korea. Starting as early as the 1960s, it was the policy of the UCC to do this on other mission fields as well.[89] But how and when this unfolded in other places is a matter for future research. In the same way the story of the Korean transfer was ignored or hidden, these stories are not well known because they were never talked about or circulated in the church.

One reason these stories were not common knowledge is perhaps because mission work had dropped significantly from the radar in the Canadian church by the 1970s. Once a *raison d'être* for the Canadian denomination and a praiseworthy activity used to attract adherents to the faith, by the 1970s the Missionary Enterprise had become an embarrassment. It could be, too, that church leaders feared that the giving away of church property would draw criticism rather than praise from the UCC members who had supported the Korean mission to the tune of millions of dollars for three generations. It was a teaching moment that was lost on the Canadian church. But regardless of its non-impact in Canada, it did have a significant effect in Korea and has not been forgotten.

1974 marks the end of tensions in the relationship between the PROK and the UCC that had been demanding a lot of energy since 1961. From this point on, documentary evidence of major friction between the PROK and UCC personnel or policy completely disappears from the written record, proof that the new arrangement had healed a number of sores that had been festering since the beginning of the Missionary Enterprise. For another thing, the transfer of the property contributed significantly to the political freedom and activism of the PROK. Symbolically, too, it was important. The grand house by the site of the ancient Great Western Gate, symbol par excellence of UCC missionary elitism in South Korea, was immediately repopulated with Korean Christian dissidents and became the womb of an indigenous Minjung theology, which served to justify and inspire broad democratic resistance against political and economic hegemony. An indication of the new material and political culture that emerged from the 1974 agreement is that Lee and Carey began to address each other in correspondence using first names. They had, in effect, become friends. But this is not to say that the UCC and Korean Christians associated with it did not continue to labour at many levels under old colonial attitudes and patterns of behaviour, as will be made clear in following chapters.

The 1974 Joint Statement of the UCC and PROK is a unique case, the first and only such agreement in which a progressive decolonizing approach to the missionary relationship prevailed to such a degree in Korea.[90] It is clear that the leadership for that decision came largely from a core group of PROK members who were determined to be creative non-victims, not only of missionary attitudes, culture, and policies but also of foreign-backed military dictatorship. The impact on the Canadian mission was transformative, completely changing its material culture and political relationship to the Korean church. These changes not only helped to give voice to a unique Korean Christian perspective, they also led to life-changing experiences for individual UCC missionaries and hint at a new postcolonial identity for the Canadian Protestant church (see chapter 6). But in Canada, the meaning of these events would barely register. The history of the change in the relationship speaks to both the liminality of postcolonial possibilities and the intransigence of colonial worldviews and practices in Canadian society and religion.

5

Minjung in the Mission House

A New Articulation of Mission from within the Shell of the Canadian Mission, 1970s and 1980s

Now after John was arrested, Jesus came to Galilee, proclaiming the good news of God, and saying, "The time is fulfilled, and the kingdom of God has come near; repent, and believe in the good news."

Gospel of Mark 1:14–15

The transfer of all United Church of Canada Korea Mission property to the PROK included a big red-brick Edwardian home that looked like it might have been transported whole from a small town in southern Ontario. The structure, however, was located in a location symbolically central both to the pre-modern Korean history and the modern Korean struggle for independence and democracy. It was near the historic site of the Great Western Gate (Seodaemun) of the Yi Dynasty's capital city and in the heart of modern Seoul, a stone's throw from the notorious prison by the same name that was used by the Japanese colonial government, and later the South Korea authoritarian regimes, to detain, torture, and execute political dissidents. It represented an ostentatious missionary history. But with its transfer to the PROK, it was about to be transformed into a symbol of Korean Christian political activism, the beating heart of a new articulation of Christian belief, Minjung theology.

Minjung theology was a globally recognized phenomenon in the late 1970s and early 1980s. It was part of a Korean Christian tradition that struggled to articulate a message of salvation from within the double colonial context of Japanese Imperialism and the Western Missionary Enterprise. Minjung theology was a systematic articulation of a postcolonial Christianity in opposition to ongoing neocolonial realities. Its message came out of a political movement against the exploitation and oppression of people by the state and in reaction against a missionary legacy that was creating obstacles for the full realization of Korean sovereignty. Its structure was based not upon a Western ecclesiology or colonial hierarchy, but upon the South Korean Democratization Movement itself. Its language of liberation, therefore, had the potential to help the Canadian church articulate a new vision for its postcolonial context as well.

As we have seen in previous chapters and will continue to see in following chapters, the postwar Canadian Protestant church was undergoing considerable change in the second half of the twentieth century. Membership peaked in 1966 and then began a steady and precipitous decline. At that very moment the UCC's Commission of World Mission issued a report that would lead to the winding down and wrapping up of the Missionary Enterprise, an project that had been at the heart of the UCC's raison d'être since before Church Union. At the same time, a new approach to immigration by the Canadian state opened the doors to hundreds of thousands of new immigrants from non-White nations and non-Western cultures. These new immigrants began to decenter the white-Anglo norms of Canada through their presence and involvement in multiple aspects of Canadian society, including church. In the UCC the Korean population grew faster than other immigrant groups and struggled to assert itself within the predominantly Anglo culture. The apology for residential schools and the decision to allow sexual minorities to serve in leadership roles within the church were on the horizon. In the midst of this change, the appearance of a new theology developed within the shell of its Korea mission promised a positive new approach to issues facing the UCC in a postcolonial world. But did the church have eyes to see and ears to hear?

A THEOLOGICAL CRUX

In 1971, a close brush with electoral defeat spurred the Park Chung Hee regime to execute a "self-coup" and institute the Yushin Constitution, which had, in 1972, eliminated almost all pretense of democracy in South Korea. By this time a few Christian leaders were beginning to translate their alarm at the worsening political situation into action. Among their first significant protests was the 1973 Easter sunrise service on Nam San (South Mountain) in Seoul led by the

Reverend Park Hyung Gyu of Seoul First Church, a PROK congregation. At this Easter service, flyers were distributed and placards displayed that read "Politicians Repent," "The Resurrection of Democracy Is the Liberation of the People," and "Lord, Show Thy Mercy to the Ignorant King." The Rev. Park and others involved in the display were arrested and accused of plotting to overthrow the government.[1] The arrest of Rev. Park became widely known in Korean Protestant circles and spurred more Christians into action.[2] As yet, missionaries were not much engaged in political activism.

One of the spin-offs of Rev. Park's arrest was the formulation of a theological response to the political oppression of the Park Chung Hee dictatorship. A group of Korean theologians met in secret and came up with the "Theological Declaration of Korean Christians," which was issued on 20 May. The group remained anonymous for fear of the government backlash, but it is now known that Kim Chai Choon (see chapter 2) was one of their number. The declaration objected to the Park Chung Hee regime on the grounds that it was destroying the rule of law and governing by the threat of force alone. The theologians championed freedom of conscience, freedom of religious belief and the importance of a truth-telling, independent media. Over against the government's claim to authority, the declaration appealed to the authority of God over all governments. The document was smuggled out of the country, published in different languages[3] and even featured in the *New York Times* under the title "Manifesto of Korean Christians."[4]

The Theological Declaration was released just days into another religio-political event of tremendous importance for South Korea: The Korea 73 Billy Graham Crusade. The Billy Graham Crusade took place in two stages. First, between 16 and 27 May, members of Graham's team fanned out across South Korea to hold advance meetings. Second, on 30 May, Graham himself arrived for the crescendo event, leading a revival meeting in the huge Youido Plaza in Seoul.[5] The 1973 Seoul Crusade hosted the largest crowds of any Billy Graham Crusade that had previously been held. Graham preached to a gathering of 1.1 million. Lead-up and follow-through meetings across Korea had reached at least a million more.[6] Covering the event for the Billy Graham Crusade, Stephen Wirt told how the Graham team "kept busy night and day" visiting Korean army and navy installations as well as other social institutions such as prisons, factories, offices, schools, universities, seminaries, and churches.[7] Wirt was overwhelmed by what he regarded as a miracle wrought by the Spirit of God. It seemed to him almost as if he was observing scenes from the Bible transposed onto the topography of modern South Korea: "As people walked across the Han river bridge from Seoul, and across the Yongdungpo bridge from the south, it seemed to be a scene out of Hebrew history. Seeing the crowds of the eight-lane highway, now emptied of vehicular traffic, one could imagine the children of Israel crossing the Red sea (without bridges) in multiplied thousands on their journey from Egypt to Canaan."[8]

In addition to divine intervention, Wirt credited "the President of the Republic, the Prime Minister, the mayor of Seoul and government officials" who "gave warm cooperation" and to the missionaries who had come almost a century earlier and without whom "none of those miracles would have been possible." At the conclusion of his address in the Yoido Plaza, Graham had been picked up in a helicopter and whisked away as "hundreds of thousands of arms were lifted and waved in one of the most spectacular farewells of the age."[9]

The juxtaposition of biblical and modern Korean imagery in Wirt's account is striking. Here is an event of profound religious significance taking place within a nation that was rapidly embracing modernity, a throng of the faithful, hands raised to bid the modern-day Moses farewell as he is lifted heavenward in a marvel of aviation technology. While the secularization thesis predicts that religion will decline with the rise of modernity, Evangelical Christians such as Wirt generally did not see a conflict so long as historical-critical tools or scientific theories were not used to question their message of salvation. Lost on Wirt, however, were the deep indigenous roots of what he was witnessing.

Revivals were not unique to Korea, but the unparalleled energy of the South Korean revivals of the 1970s had its own unique source. In terms of numbers alone, the two-week-long South Korean revival had eclipsed Graham's five-week-long crusade of 1957 in Madison Square Gardens.[10] But revivalism in Korea should not be equated with, or simply measured against, Western experiences. Korean revival history was different; the source, in fact, of Korean Protestant Christianity itself; a distinct Christian tradition. Although Korean Protestant congregations and organizations bore denominational identifiers such as "Methodist" or "Presbyterian," which were adopted from the Western Missionaries and suggested continuity with these Western traditions, Koreans themselves saw a distinct underlying experience that was uniquely theirs and shared among all Korean

Christians regardless of denominational signifiers. "Some of you go back to John Calvin, and some of you to John Wesley," explained one Korean to a Western missionary colleague, "but we can go back no further than 1907 [the Korean Revival] when we first really knew the Lord Jesus Christ."[11] Korean church historian Lak-Geoon Baik expressed its significance as follows: "The religious experience of the people gave the Christian Church in Korea a character which is its own. Following the revival, the new religious experience was severely tested, but it has survived as a moral and spiritual force. Korean Christians of today [1929] look back on the movement as the source of their spiritual life."[12] The 1907 Revival was a paradigmatic event for Korean Protestantism.[13] It initiated many of its unique practices. For many it was the distinct Korean tradition of ecstatic prayer that had shaped their sense of Christianity. Sang Chul Lee, future moderator of the UCC, describes it thus:

> For people who have never witnessed a Korean prayer meeting, this may be hard to understand. Korean Christians pray fervently, loudly and at great length. In their prayers they pour out all the concerns that weigh heavily on their hearts, in full expectation that God will listen and respond. During a church service, if the minister asks the people to pray, the whole congregation will pray spontaneously and simultaneously, but not silently. They all voice their concerns in their own words, at the same time, out loud. In a large church such prayer can sound like the roar of ocean waves smashing against the shore during a storm. It can send shivers up and down your spine.[14]

This experience was not contained within one denominational tradition in Korea. Even those Christians deemed "liberal" because of their involvement in political activism identified with this practice. Christian dissident Lee Oo Chung described a prayer meeting for political activists with language such as "heaven piercing prayers" and "a feast for a people drunk with the Holy Spirit."[15]

The Revival of 1907 broke down barriers between Koreans and Western missionaries. It showed that Christianity was suited to Korea and could be called a Korean religion.[16] Missionaries came to identify more closely with the Koreans they worked among but also were humbled by the realization that Korean Christians often had something to teach them about the faith that they had not appreciated before.[17] Missionaries were moved to confess their own shortcomings to Koreans who in turn began to appreciate the humanity of those they had often regarded as of saintly nature superior to themselves.[18] This religious event permitted a glimpse of a new reality but did not by any means dispel or banish the political hegemony, unequal social positions, and paternalistic colonial patterns of the Missionary Enterprise in Korea. In this sense it, like the development of Minjung theology discussed below, was a liminal moment that continues to serve as a reference in an ongoing postcolonial struggle.

One commentator reflecting later on the Korea 73 Billy Graham Crusade in *The Third Day* – a progressive Korean theological journal published in Canada by the self-exiled Kim Chai Choon – questioned Graham's authenticity. The writer pointed out that Graham's stay in Korea had been noticeably short and would not have allowed him to understand the people, their lives, or their needs. Nor did Graham's history of choosing the side of government escape attention: "The government protected the Billy Graham Crusade because they felt it could create a good impression among the public in the United States." Having followed Graham's career in the US, the commentator also recognized that "Graham frowned on those who resisted the Vietnam war and was a supporter of Nixon. This is the kind of church minister [dictator] Park [Chung Hee] needs." By way of contrast, he pointed out, missionaries who had stood up to the Park regime had been thrown out of the country.[19] The liberty Park provided to Christians to conduct huge evangelistic events such as the 1973 Crusade did indeed win him the support of a number of influential Korean Christian leaders. Korean evangelist Billy Kim, director of the Korean Campus Crusade for Christ, lobbied informally for the Park regime in the States saying, "In no other country in the world, including the United States, is there more freedom to talk about Jesus Christ than in South Korea."[20]

The revivalist tradition in Korea offers an important historical lens through which to appreciate the relationship between Korean Christianity and the Democratization Movement. The Revival of 1907 coincided with moves by Japan towards the annexation of Korea including the dissolution of its army, an event of tremendous political drama. Many missionaries at the time, fearful of the latent political potential of the feelings generated by the revival, had been careful to guide Koreans towards the spiritual otherworldly realm of religion and away from the political earthly one. This, however, could not expunge the reality that many of their new converts had turned to Christianity seeking a salvation that was, at least in part, national.[21] In later years, as Korean Christians began to feel that missionaries did not share their aspirations for an independent country, the growth of the Christian church sputtered and many began to turn to communism instead.[22] Missionaries and Korean Christian leaders had had to take this into account and adjusted their approach as a result. They embraced the idea of Korean independence, though not the revolutionary means to attain it. They also became stronger advocates for those Koreans who had suffered persecution and violence as a result of their call for the end of Japanese colonialism.

By the 1970s, however, the nuanced position of Korean Christianity vis-à-vis politics generally, and communism specifically, had shifted. Differences between Christians and communists during and following Japanese colonization had sown deep seeds of distrust and mutual hatred between the two camps. The perceived incommensurability on both sides made it difficult to recognize shared political interests[23] – the eradication of economic inequality, the elimination of class distinction, the modernization of Korean society, and the achievement of national independence being four of the most obvious of those interests. The experiences of the war and the tales of persecution and atrocities against Christians at the hands of the communists had convinced many that an anti-communist stance was not political, but simply a logical extension of the Christian faith. The missionary aversion to politics in the early days had also successfully instilled within Korean Protestantism a tendency towards pietism and a sense that religion was more about the hereafter than the here and now.[24]

Graham, as many missionaries had done before him, reinforced the "a-political" stance of Christianity. Denying that they were anti-communist, Graham's team claimed that only the communists were intolerant. Wirt, for example, reported that Radio Pyeongyang, the voice of communism in North Korea, was casting aspersions on the Graham revival meeting. In contrast, he wrote, the crusade was holding special "prayer services of love" for North Korea.[25] There can be no doubt, however, that an underlying theme of the crusade was a desire for the end of the North Korean regime and the expulsion of communism from Korea. This played into the hands of Park Chung Hee who, though a nominal Buddhist himself, had used the Christian suspicion of communism to attract the active support of Christian organizations. Five major denominations representing 22.9 per cent of Korean Protestants at the time had taken the bate and aligned with Park who also garnered support from organizations such as the International Council of Christian Churches in Korea (ICCCK), Korean Campus Crusade for Christ (KCCC) and the Korean Evangelical Federation (KEF).[26]

For this significant cross-denominational group of Christians, supporting Park was not a political act but simply a Christian duty. Park's government was protecting them from the North. And after all, had the Apostle Paul in chapter 13 of his letter to the Romans not instructed Christians to submit to the God-appointed ruler of the land? These views were strikingly similar to those the Protestant missionaries had espoused in attempting a politically "neutral" stance in the face of Japanese colonization.[27] It did not occur to Park's Christian supporters that the programs they ran, such as the National Prayer Breakfast for the President, might be construed as political or indeed that the freedom to be non-political had effectively been removed by Park's strategy to crush dissent.[28] On the contrary, they were persuaded that "when church and government are harmonious through assistance and cooperation, the church will be holy and the state will prosper."[29]

The divisions within the Christian community regarding the appropriateness of political protest were serious and did not strictly follow denominational lines. Even the PROK, the denomination most engaged in anti-Park activism, was rent by serious differences.[30] The overwhelming success of the Billy Graham Crusade and other revival movements through the 1970s put Christians in the Democratization Movement on the defensive. They came under attack by those who accused them of being foolhardy or of looking for martyrdom.[31] And the Park regime, armed with the backing and rhetoric of its Christian supporters, was eager to join the critical voices. Park's prime minister, Kim Chong Pil, who was not a Christian, publicly derided Christians taking a stand against the government and threatened to expel missionaries who supported them, citing Romans chapter 13 and the threat of divine judgement.[32] The passage reads in part as follows: "Let every person be subject to the governing authorities; for there is no authority except from God, and those authorities that exist have been instituted by God. Therefore, whoever resists authority resists what God has appointed, and those who resist will incur judgement. For rulers are not a terror to good conduct, but to bad."[33]

One wonders if the Prime Minister knew that Japanese police had quoted the same Bible passage at Christians and their missionary supporters seeking independence for the country prior to the liberation of Korea.[34] In the 1970s, however, his rhetorical attacks, supported now by a number of conservative missionaries and influential Christian leaders who disapproved of the Democratization Movement, succeeded in dividing both indigenous Christians and missionaries in South Korea.

In response to criticism for their support of political activists, twenty-four missionaries representing at least eight denominations or orders of the Protestant and Catholic churches in North America, Europe, and Australia sought to articulate the reasons for their overtly political stance.[35] UCC missionary Ian Robb penned a letter on their behalf that sought "to clarify to ourselves and to others the reasons, both personal and theological, on which we base our actions."[36] They addressed the interpretation of Romans 13 by stating that although Christians were called to respect the ruling authorities they should also expect those authorities, Christian or not, to abide by notions of justice commensurate with God's law. And when a government claims to be democratic, as Park's was doing, it was surely legitimate to challenge them on those grounds. "In a democracy, the governing authorities are the people themselves," the pro-dissident missionaries reasoned, "and it is improper for any one person or group to assume absolute power."[37] Then they took aim at the tendency in mission and church circles to see evangelism and social activism as two separate things, finding them instead "to be common and inseparable concerns of Christ and the New Testament." "Christ healed, fed the hungry and ministered to the poor, and at the same time also directly challenged the authorities," they argued, "We frankly see no way to live in Korea as missionaries attempting to be true to Christ's example without sharing these concerns for the total life of men." How far, they asked, were missionaries of any stripe willing to allow the South Korean government to decide what was religious activity and what was political.[38] Indeed, added one missionary in a separate response, "The government by its attempt to control every facet of Korean society has politicized the entire society. There is no act that now does not have some political significance for one side or the other." [39]

Missionaries supporting the Democratization Movement faced real pressure from colleagues and the government to cease their collaboration. Two were deported for their activism in support of the political dissidents and labourers, one American Methodist and one American Catholic. Missionary visas were being extended for shorter periods of time, threatening those who did not refrain from political "meddling" with an early exit from the field.[40] While the pressure and consequences for Koreans themselves were much more severe, the personal risks taken by missionaries who chose to support them were also considerable. It was understandable, given the potential cost, that many should choose not to get involved. But for some, their connection with people negatively affected by government policies led them to believe that political protest was an inescapable consequence of their religious convictions. The same reasoning was at work for the Korean Christians involved in the movement. And as had occurred for pro-activist missionaries, pressure from the evangelical movement also forced them to give a theological rational for their own actions and sacrifices.[41] Much of that rational would be worked out in the space vacated by the Canadian missionaries.

MISSION HOUSE TRANSFORMED

In 1975, the General Assembly of the PROK passed a motion to create the "Mission and Education Centre" (MEC).[42] This was billed as "a new design for mission" and the directorship of this endeavour was given to Dr Ahn Byung Mu, a Yongjeong native and German-educated New Testament professor. Ahn was one of eleven Korean university professors who had recently lost their jobs because of pressure from the government.[43] Suh Nam Dong and Lee Oo Chung, professors of church history and New Testament Greek respectively who had been educated in Canada on UCC scholarships, had also been expelled from their universities. The brothers Moon Ik Hwan and Moon Dong Hwan, sons of Kim Shin Mook and Moon Chai Rin from Yongjeong, Manchuria and former students with Ahn at the UCC mission-run Eun-jin Middle School (see chapter 1), had been dismissed from their positions at Hanguk Seminary at the same time. Suh, Lee, and the Moon brothers were to join Ahn in teaching at the MEC. They would come to constitute a "who's who" of the new movement in Korean theology.[44]

At the close of the Pacific war legal documents referring to the Canadian Mission ownership remained in the communist-controlled north and permanently out of reach of the Canadian Mission.[45] As a result, legal transfer of the property agreed upon in 1974 between the PROK and UCC was complicated by the geopolitical reality and was not consummated until after 1976. Nevertheless, the UCC HQ in Canada had given permission for the PROK to use the Seodaemun property[46] and by the end of 1975, Canadian missionaries had vacated the premises.[47] A video produced for a Korean television history program provides a diagram and virtual tour of the structure, featuring an enormous kitchen and living room areas that were converted into classrooms.[48] The land and the buildings were an essential asset to the project. Extensive renovations were undertaken on the sizeable Edwardian house to turn it into a learning institution: "The living and dining rooms were changed into a lecture room for about eighty students. Two upstairs bedrooms were combined to make a classroom for about forty students. There are also five rooms for study groups and there is also a library. The upstairs sun-porch is being used as the director's office. There is a small dormitory for about thirty people, and dining facilities for the same number. The latter is a skillful rearrangement of the two-car garage."[49] The transformation of the space is symbolic of the transformation of the UCC's presence in Korea itself. Gone was the privilege of expensive properties and big houses that accompanied the Mission Enterprise. In its place a Korean run institution designed to educate and train Koreans in a struggle against political and religious hegemonies. The transformation was the result of Korean leadership filling space left by the supportive self-withdrawal of the Canadian church.[50]

Back in Canada, news of the "exciting new enterprise" in the Seodaemun house was shared in the annual missionary report from Korea.[51] The unexpected arrest of all five founding professors, Ahn, Lee, Suh, and the Moon brothers (see chapter 6), put the beginning of the program in doubt but did not stop it. The first classes were underway on 15 April 1976, and an opening worship service was held on 26 April 1976.[52] When Ahn Byung Mu was released from prison in 1977, the program picked up steam. By this time the goals and constituency of the MEC program had become more focussed. A program was designed for students who, like their professors, had been expelled from their schools, harassed, and forbidden from getting a degree or meaningful work. Some had served prison terms or had been forced into military training. Dong-Chun Seo's experience sheds light on the difficult situation many of these students found themselves in. Seo recalls being dogged by private detectives who did all kinds of "dirty tricks" to make it impossible for him to get work or find a place to stay.[53] Those who did not have family in the city found it very difficult to pay for room and board let alone school fees,[54] but the MEC was able to provide a number of these students each year with a chance to study, help them get work, house them, and support them. "It was a place where we could live/stay alive," remembers Gwon Jin-gwan.[55] Over the course of ten years, 123 students registered for courses and 49 students completed their degree.[56] Most of those who completed went on to become ministers in the PROK but others continued their studies in subjects like social welfare and went into different professions. Many of these ended up teaching in universities.[57]

Most students had already received a viscerally impactful education in political oppression and police brutality. Ahn Byung Mu's approach as director of the Centre was to make these lived experiences foundational. The program was also designed to help students overcome arbitrary social divisions. Lay and clergy students were mixed at the MEC, breaking down a professional/social boundary. The subject matter, too, crossed disciplinary lines. Theology was combined with politics, economics, sociology, and feminism. Fieldwork, in addition to classroom lectures, was a required component of the curriculum. Theology, social studies, and practical elements were taught in a 2:1:1 ratio but professors also allowed students to suggest foci for education according to their interests.[58] Though a centre for "mission," the pedagogy at the MEC was engaged with non-theological disciplines, critical of Western theological traditions and saw no significant divide between Christians and non-Christians when it came to working out their salvation.[59] It also clearly identified with Korean tradition and history, including non-Christian religions. Graduates from the MEC wore the traditional robes and hats of Confucian scholars.[60] This was a fitting nod to the Korean cultural inheritance that informed their theological education. One wonders whether Ahn and the Moon brothers associated the gowns with Kim Yakyeon, the Silhak scholar who had been a leader of the church community in Yongjeong, Manchuria (see chapter 1).

There were four sections in the program that the students could choose as a focus: 1. Urban Mission; 2. Rural Mission; 3. Mission to Youth and Students; and 4. Mission for Women.[61] The introduction of a course focussing on women was a novel development for a theology school in Korea at that time. Lee Oo Chung, lecturer at the school had been on the forefront of a number of important women's issues since 1970.[62] Her course, "Mission for Women," while unique in its focus on women's experiences, nonetheless gives a good example of the kind of pedagogy generally employed at the MEC. The first goal of Lee's course was "to grasp the reality and reasons for the oppression of women" using a process that combined study, field praxis, and special research assignments. There was a strong community component as well where the students lived together for a short period of two or three days and discussed problems related to faith, to life, and to the MEC itself.[63] It was a program of study that seamlessly combined Christian and secular ideas and engaged in a critique of Christianity and its institutions, a far cry from the days when Western missionaries controlled Christian education, insisted Korean Christians only be taught the Bible and demanded they toe the theological line (see chapter 2).

A NEW THEOLOGY

Ahn Byung Mu, who had conceived of the idea for the school, was well pleased. "We discussed in groups," Ahn recalled; "it was an entirely different way of learning. We gave lectures in the morning and discussed during the afternoon. We concentrated mainly on our situation and asked ourselves what imperialism, colonialism etc. was, where dictatorship came from, and so forth. It was a very important period for us as well as for the younger generation. Together we developed new thoughts."[64] The new thoughts that Ahn referred to were contributing to a new theology that drew its inspiration from the Korean idea of the *minjung*.[65] This concept was not new or unique to the teachers and students at the MEC. First used in political speeches addressing the peasants and their grievances against the ruling class in the late nineteenth century, the idea of the minjung was articulated later by Korea's first modern historian, Shin Chae-ho in the early twentieth century.[66] Shin was the first to write Korean history from the perspective of the minjok,[67] or nation, rather than from the perspective of the court elite, a history of the people rather than of a dynasty in the way Confucian literati had done in the past.[68] But later Shin became disillusioned with the state he had hoped would champion the aspirations of Koreans and adopted an anarchist stance. In his later thinking he deployed minjung to represent a group with a specific allegiance vis-à-vis Korean politics, the subjects of a new history that would displace Korea's old structures of intellectual, economic, and political domination as well as overthrow the Japanese colonial government.[69]

Whereas minjok was an East-Asian neologism associated with the rise of nationalism in East Asia and composed of two characters representing "people" (min) and "tribe" (jok),[70] the concept of minjung combined the character for "people" (min) and the character for "masses" (jung). It was a looser, less well-defined designation than minjok and sought, in opposition to the concept of minjok, to identify a disparate group of people united in their experiences of oppression and desire for a better government. The concept of minjung, then, sought to give definition to a group who were united both by an experience of oppression and aspiration to be emancipated. The definition could easily be applied to the first Korean Christians who converted to the new faith out of a sense of desperation at the plight of their country, but it was not conceived as a religious designation. Shin, for example, did not have a faith group in mind when he coined the term. Following this lead, theologians at the MEC included in the definition of minjung any group who by virtue of their lower status in the social hierarchy had developed a culture of resistance. Anthropologist Nancy Abelmann, working from the definition of the Minjung theologians, described the minjung as "not merely a stratum in a divided society or a legacy of oppositional activity," but as an "imagined horizontal community," "an indigenous cultural socialism – the grist of a particular historical gaze."[71] As the concept was born of the Korean context, it applied specifically to Koreans, but as it developed theologically, it became clear that it need not be limited to an ethnic group any more than it was limited to a religious group.

The concept found a very special niche in the 1970s and 1980s allowing activists to evoke certain political horizons while avoiding the polarized ideologies of the North's communism and the South's anti-communism. In the South, the Park regime had laid claim to minjok, a concept it interpreted as a people who owed allegiance to the gukka,[72] or state. North Korean communism, on the other hand, deployed the rhetoric of inmin,[73] literally "human people," to refer to the revolutionary proletariat of Marxist theory. Those in the South Korean Democratization Movement who did not wish to align themselves with Park's right-wing state or with Kim's communist proletariat began using minjung as a way to capture the notion of a people connected to a national identity, but oppressed by the powers above them. The concept gained currency in South Korea through the 1970s and, although "leftist" by Park Chung Hee's standards,[74] could credibly deny identification with the communist North. By the 1980s, the Democratization Movement had adopted the nomenclature. Referring now to a Minjung Movement, activists managed to gain the support of a wide swath of South Korean society of all religious and social backgrounds who rejected the binary categories of communist and anti-communist that had stood in the way of democratic progress.[75]

Minjung theology was an important variant of[76] and contributor to[77] Minjung ideology and the Minjung Movement. The first inklings of a Minjung theology came in the form of "The Declaration of Korean Christians" issued in the midst of the Korea 73 Billy Graham Crusade. This statement made use of the term minjung, but did not develop its implications. In 1975, two articles in the Korean Christian academic journal *Christian Thought*[78] (see chapter 2) by Suh Nam Dong and Ahn Byung Mu had started to distinguish the concept of minjung from minjok and to draw on Korean history and culture in an effort to carve a space for Christian political dissent in the context of the South Korean dictatorship. It was not until 1979, however, that Minjung theology received its official name. This came about as the result of a conference hosted by the Christian Conference of Asia (CCA). The papers produced at this conference were collected and published by the National Conference of Churches in Korea (NCCK) in an edited volume under the title *Minjunggwa Hanguksinhak* (*The Minjung and Korean Theology*).[79]

Minjung theology, like other liberation theologies of the period, was concerned with the structural evils of capitalism and authoritarian governments and sought to change the social realities in which people lived.[80] Where it differed from many other brands of liberation theology, however, was in its emphasis on the liberating function of culture.[81] Whereas Latin American liberation theology drew on a Marxist critique of religion,[82] Minjung theology embraced religious influences, including non-Christian ones, as examples of the minjung's expression of their own historical subjectivity and a means by which they subverted the ruling elite.[83] According to postcolonial biblical scholar R.S. Sugirtharajah, "minjung theology was different in that it was not only political but also an intensely cultural discourse."[84] It was hard to define exactly who the minjung were outside of the fact that, for minjung theologians, they were essentially "the subjects of history," people who through their cultural and political acts of resistance were capable of bringing about true liberation. In this, Black theologian James Cone who wrote the preface to the English publication of *Minjung Theology: People as the Subjects of History* found a close connection with the experience of Black Christians in the United States and their culture of resistance.[85] Minjung theologians embraced what they saw as the Korean Christian tradition of nationalism that understood true liberation from foreign and state powers to be found in a movement of the masses united by their culture of resistance to oppression.

Minjung theology also had something to say about the historic influence of missionaries. On the one hand, Minjung theologians regarded missionaries as having been a source of salvation to which "Koreans stretched out their hands ... for relief from bondage."[86] Contributions of the missionaries to the translation of the Bible into vernacular Korean script, which had empowered the common people, where recognized as particularly important.[87] At the same time, however, Minjung theologians noted that missionaries had often identified themselves with a higher class and were guilty of regarding their interpretations of the Bible as superior. Furthermore, they had pandered to the Korean aristocracy and Japanese imperial authority by discouraging or even forbidding Koreans from applying the Gospel politically.[88] Minjung theology saw similar patterns contributing to the present ills of Korea. In a lecture delivered in Canada shortly before his death, Suh Nam Dong pointed out the limits of the approach he had received at his Canadian alma mater, Emmanuel College in Toronto. "The language of conventional theology is that of logic, dialectics, and abstract concepts. Its approach is deductive, and its substance is a discourse on the existence of a transcendent God. Conventional theology starts either from the premise that a transcendent God exists or from the written Bible and/or doctrines that are derived from the tradition that has been handed down. Even liberal theology does no more than enhance brain language, and contemporary theology limits itself to reinterpreting existing doctrine."[89] For Suh, the culture of the common people and their experience of oppression was what rightly provided theological matter and conveyed spiritual authority. This authority, he argued, stood in opposition to Western theological concepts, which, rather than being truly liberating, had become an oppressive ideology dressed up in God language.[90]

The concept of "sin" was especially problematic. For Suh, the doctrine of sin was "heavily charged with the bias of the ruling class." Instead, he proposed the concept of han,[91] a character which he asserted had special significance in Korean culture.[92] Suh described han as a "sticky" experience of resentment and suffering born of a long history of accumulated oppression. "If one does not hear the sighs of the *han* of the minjung," Suh contended, "one cannot hear the voice of Christ knocking on our doors."[93] To experience liberation, then, it was important that Christians break out of western theological categories that divided the individual from society and Christians from non-Christians. "We Christians tend to think that Jesus Christ alone redeems people and that redemption is only a religious act," he said, "Yet, such acts of redemption have been performed throughout history in every corner of the earth. Redemption was originally a social issue, but was later transferred to the religious world."[94] Ahn Byung Mu used a biblical analogy to explain this approach: "We intended to contrast Galilee [where Jesus ministered among the poor and outcasts] with Jerusalem [the seat of religious power] which had monopolized the will of God exclusively for itself."[95]

Minjung theology developed a profoundly ecumenical consciousness. Christians in the movement organized protest events that pulled together a number of diverse interest groups.[96] Through the seventies Protestant and Catholic Christians started doing more things together. But their sense of solidary extended even beyond the Christian faith and indeed beyond religion. From the beginning they saw the democracy movement as something that was bigger than the Christian church and they had a healthy understanding of the place they occupied in the movement relative to the many others who were also leading the struggle and making sacrifices. MEC professor Lee Oo Chung expressed this reality as follows: "Denominations and even religions transcended [their differences] so that the ecumenical movement of solidarity was able to form ... When the church became conscious of its suffering neighbours it also began to follow the students getting involved in a number of different activities in order to live up to its responsibilities [as the church.] This consciousness made solidarity possible with Catholics and even progressive Buddhists. This kind of ecumenical movement did not start with conceptual or abstract theology. It came naturally from a posture of sober openness to the reality that surrounded us, from a place of solidary that formed the whole activity. That was its meaning."[97] So while Minjung theologians were articulating the reasons for their participation in the democracy movement in very Christian terms they were also able to see, affirm, and celebrate a spiritually unifying principle at work in the diverse groups of people with whom they shared the struggle.

For Minjung theologians, the solidarity with non-Christians was more than a marriage of convenience, it was a matter of faith. For Ahn, many of the experiences at the core of the new theology derived from his experiences in Kando. Acknowledging that Minjung theology had sprung from the experiences of oppression under Park Chung Hee's dictatorship, he asserted that his "heartfelt thoughts" about the minjung had their genesis in Kando. He recalled the misery of people like his mother trying to make a living, the vulnerability of the average person to poverty and the reprisals for the Japanese colonial government. Kando, "like Galilee during Jesus's time," said Ahn, "was a site of minjung's life, a land of gentiles.[98] Growing up in a multi-religious and multi-ethnic environment, Ahn knew that the "nationalist" dreams of Korean Christians should never fall victim to the arbitrary divisions along ethnic and religious lines that Europe had fallen victim to. "We must distinguish the word "min chung" [*sic*] from the German word "Volk" which was used during Hitler's time," he explained, "Although "min chung" [*sic*] is the substance of the nation, historically it has always been oppressed and exploited by the powerful and that in the name of the nation."[99] Ahn's understanding of the term was informed by his interpretation of the Bible. "In the Old Testament we also find the term 'Min Chung' [*sic*] alongside the term 'nation.' The prophets were their friends and the prophets fought for their rights. In the New Testament the term 'nation' has disappeared. Here we find only 'Min Chung.' Instead of the nation Israel there emerges the new 'crowd,' who, chosen as new bearers of the will of God, do not remain in exclusive nationalism but break through the boundary between nations and between ideologies and are entrusted with creating a new world history."[100] In working to support and defend the minjung, Ahn highlighted the need for people of different nations and different religions to work together.[101] The nationalist/post-nationalist tension in his understanding of the "oppressed" reflects the cultural, national, social, and religious realities found in the Canadian mission field in Manchuria and clearly demonstrate the formative influence that that time and place had on Ahn (see chapter 1).

Minjung theologians were suspicious of established structures, whether ecclesial or secular, nation states or church hierarchies. This reflects a socio-political reality in Korea in which no mediating institutions existed to express the will of the people to their government and in which only mass popular uprisings had the power to effect democratic change. Korean political scientist Choi Jang Jip, in *Democracy after Democratization*, asserts that whereas the bourgeois class and bourgeois institutions were the condition for democracy in Europe, the democracy movement itself was the condition for democracy in Korea. The reason for this was that after decades of Japanese colonization followed by autocratic leadership, power had been monopolized by the state. A grassroots movement was the only thing that could fill the power void and provide the foundation upon which Korean democracy would thrive.[102] Historical developments have seen the persistence of this reality in South Korea as the scholarship of sociologist Kim Sun-Chul has shown.[103] Social activism and mass protest have remained important vehicles by which South Koreans seek political change. This is witnessed by a number of recent events including the ousting of the 2016 South Korean President Park Geun Hye (the daughter of President Park Chung Hee) in the wake of "Candlelight Protests" that saw millions of Koreans take to the street in peaceful mass demonstrations.

Minjung theology was, therefore, a postcolonial expression of Christianity in its rejection of religious and political dichotomies. Its approach focussed on the experiences of people displaced and oppressed by the political economies of dominant power structures. It posed a direct challenge not only to the Park dictatorship, but also to the status quo of the UCC and other Western Christian churches and organizations. Interest in Minjung theology expanded through the eighties to the rest of Asia and to North America and Europe. Cone, mentioned above, clearly recognized that Minjung theology shared with other theologies of the poor a "rejection of European theology and their affirmation of their own cultural history as a primary source for doing of theology."[104] Cone also recognized Minjung theology's uniqueness and the centrality of the Korean story for understanding it.[105] But others raised objections. World renowned German theologian Jürgen Moltmann, for example, though supportive of many of its ideas, suspected that the minjung had displaced Christ in Minjung theology.[106] Others dismissed Minjung theology as being just another variety of liberation theology, whose methodology they discredited as Marxist.[107] It can be argued, however, that these objections simply showed that Western churches and theologians were not prepared to listen to a message critiquing its colonial past and its privileged place on top of the world religious order. Postcolonial feminist theologian Kwok Pui Lan has astutely noted that "the creation of a new narrative discourse of Christianity through the use of Asian idioms and stories" continues to challenge Western Christian circles that deem it acceptable only "if it does not self-consciously challenge imperialistic impulses."[108] This highlights the challenges members of the UCC and its missionaries might have had in coming to terms with this emerging Korean theology.

RECEPTION OF MINJUNG THEOLOGY
BY CANADIANS

In an address to Hanguk Seminary in 1978, Douglas Jay, member of the UCC's Commission on World Mission and a leading Canadian theologian, acknowledged that some in the West feared liberation theologies. He did not attempt to analyze or explain why this was so but stressed that all theologies were rightly conditioned by their contexts. "What is true or appropriate for Canada may not be fully translatable to the Korean context, and vice versa," he said, but "here is where we need each other ... it often takes others in the Christian family to help us see that our particular expression of the Christian faith is not absolute, not universally valid." Jay's insights reflect a postcolonial move towards the contextualization of knowledge, but he clearly felt challenged by, maybe even uncomfortable with, the new theology. As a Canadian theologian he was compelled to recognize that his own understanding of the Korean Christian faith and experience was limited, and that the Korean expression was no less valid than his own, but he didn't say that he understood or agreed with it.

Ecumenical dialogue, Jay professed, was "extremely important not only to help us find 'the truth' but also the truth about ourselves."[109] Many of the UCC's missionaries on the ground in Korea had found "the truth about themselves" over the course of their participation in the Democratization Movement and they were profoundly impacted by their close association with the Minjung theologians at the Seodaemun-missionary-compound-turned-MEC (see chapter 6). Their experiences helped them to see their own social context, not only in Korea but in Canada as well. Transformed by the Minjung Movement, these missionaries came to challenge colonial assumptions that had clearly shaped Canadian society and continued to disadvantage some to the benefit of others. Marion Current testified as follows: "Growing up in Northeastern Ontario, I was too naive to wonder why the English-speaking minority held the power even though French speaking Canadians were in the majority there. I grew up never knowing any aboriginal, native Canadians, although many lived in the area. In Korea, in retrospect, I realised that I had been completely brainwashed by the dominant culture. It never occurred to me to ask why the society was so skewed in favour of White Protestant Catholic English speakers. I was unaware of my prejudice, and it took quite a bit to change my attitude ... What finally woke me up was the conscientization I received at the hands of the Korean human rights activists."[110] It was unusual for missionaries to describe their work on the mission field in such terms. It speaks to the impact of the Democratization Movement and its articulation of a new political horizon in Minjung theology that someone like Marion Current could be affected in this way.

Rather than being tuned into the politically transformative aspects of the new theology, however, other UCC observers of the Korean church in the 1970s and 80s were more interested in superficial aspects of Korean Christianity that reinforced the nostalgia of the thriving Canadian church of yesteryear. In the latter part of 1983, UCC journalist Dean Salter travelled to South Korea to report back on the Korean church. He visited and worshipped with a number of congregations and reported two main points about this experience for UCC readers. First, he noticed how Western it was. He accounted for this by the fact that Korea was one of the most "missionized" countries in the world. Second, he reported an energy in worship that seemed to be missing in Canada. The pews, the pulpit, the choir, the communion table, the baptismal font many of the hymns, and the order of worship in Korean churches would be familiar to Canadian church people, he said. However, he asserted, there was a power, a joy, and a fiery spirit in Korean worship that was clearly unique to the people and very exciting to the visitor.[111] He did not make the connection, as Cone had done, to the liberatory dimension of Christianity for Black Christians in America and Africa whose worship was likewise noted for its energy.

For Salter, it was this "energy," an excitement about worship which was also translating into church growth, that was the defining character of what he dubbed "Christianity Korean-style."[112] Salter's apparent equation was: Western roots + Korean energy = vibrant church. It is not surprising that energy and growth would attract the Canadian gaze. The church back home was shrinking. Salter did speak to Suh Nam Dong about Minjung theology from which he came to understand that "Minjung theology is a distinctly Asian theology which connects people directly to their God … The rulers are not subjects of God's history; the people are."[113] And he did attend a number of churches that were less Western in form. These he described in some detail. Nevertheless, it was the energy and church growth that made the strongest impression. The sense that something radically new and critically relevant to the Canadian context was taking place in Korea seems to have been lost.

While there is no one who explicitly articulated the implications of Minjung theology for the Canadian church, a pamphlet created for American Christians named a twofold challenge. First of all, it asserted, "in the dominant American sub-culture of success," Minjung theology highlights "the theological perspective of the poor and oppressed," which is lacking in the American Church. Secondly, "the Korean Christianity of the suffering people presents us in the U.S.A. with a galling reminder. We realize how deeply implicated we are as a nation in the present sad state of affairs of South Korean civil and political liberties, because of our overwhelming military presence in that country for two generations."[114] While the claims of Minjung theology specifically on the Canadian church were nowhere published in such a clear way, there was a group of activist leaders in Canada that seems to have drawn similar conclusions as their American counter-parts when they created an organization entitled the Canada Asia Working Group (CAWG). This organization began publishing a flyer entitled *Canada Asia Currents* in 1979.[115] The CAWG took the systematic links between the Canadian political-economy and Korean political oppression seriously. One of the issues, for example, focussed attention on the incommensurability of then-Prime Minister Pierre Elliott Trudeau's stated commitment to human rights and his coddling of South Korean dictator Chun Doo Hwan in an effort to sell Cando Nuclear reactors. Starting in the late 1980s, the CAWG also began to present annual briefings to the Canadian Ambassador to the United Nations on the situation of human rights in East Asia.[116]

Notwithstanding the signs that some were taking notice, there is little evidence that theologians in Canada as a whole seriously engaged with Minjung theology. Of course, the majority of Korean pastors and theologians were not Minjung theologians either and many paid little to no attention to this new theology. As stated above, more than a quarter of Korean Protestants were affiliated with Christian denominations that strongly supported the Park Chung Hee regime. The majority of Christian denominations took a more neutral stand but likewise felt uncomfortable rocking the boat and were having success applying the more conservative approach to Christian theology in their congregations.[117] Why then should we expect Canadian churches and theologians to show more interest than they did in this novel articulation of Christian belief? Perhaps because, while Korean churches were still growing with state support, Canadian churches were facing an existential crisis connected to their association with colonialism and no longer enjoyed a central position in Canadian culture as it once had. In this sense, one might expect that more may have picked up on the potential of this postcolonial theology and its close association with the Canadian mission as a way to make sense of the current reality of the Canadian church.

Part of the problem may have been a disconnect between those who were in a position to learn about Minjung theology through church institutions and the average church member. Historians have noted that while the 1970s and 1980s were a period when the United Church leadership was particularly attuned to global issues of political and ecumenical justice and offered "radical support" to justice movements at home and around the world, there was little engagement with these issues by the general membership.[118] Ecumenical coalitions formed and liberation theologies were discussed, but this took place "at arm's length" from the congregations and were "largely unknown to the people in the pews."[119] At an institutional level there was an effort to come to terms with structural racism, especially with regards to indigenous people, but at a cultural level there is not much evidence the membership of the UCC connected with postcolonial movements or responded to their call for radical transformation.[120]

Another dynamic that seems to have contributed to preventing members of the Canadian church from learning from Minjung theology despite their close association with its development was that missionaries had become anathema in the Canadian church. Despite the lessons that Canadian missionaries such as Marion Current had clearly been learning in Korea through the Minjung Movement, it was precisely during the 1970s that missionaries were losing their ability to impact Canadian society. The association of the Missionary Enterprise with a colonial past was prompting many Canadians to shun missionaries and the stories of their work. Ironically, this was occurring at the very same time that many of these same missionaries were starting to be able to articulate what they had been learning from Christians in non-Western churches and how they were being dramatically changed by their experiences. As a result, those in Canada who pointed the finger as a way of absolving themselves from the sins of the church's missionary history were unable to benefit from missionary insights in the postcolonial era.

One case was found in which Minjung theology was part of a consequential decision in the UCC. It was deployed by a coalition of ethnic minority church leaders in 1994 who were seeking a stronger voice for ethnic minorities within the church. Proponents of a new

Ethnic Ministry Council (EMC) that could exercise real power within the structures of the UCC deployed the concept of han to articulate a shared experience of suffering shared by people marginalized within the church because of their minority ethnic status and identified these people as minjung.[121] How central a role minjung theology actually played in the rational for the new council or whether it affected the eventual decision of the UCC to create the Ethnic Ministry Council is an open question. In fact, there were voices from within the ethnic minority coalition who were not entirely comfortable with this theology.[122] It is telling, however, that in this one instance where there is an example of the theology being used to rationalize actions taken within the UCC, it was racialized voices that made use of it and that there is no sign of the dominant White institution deploying this vocabulary.

CONCLUSION

Though interest in Minjung theology continues today, contemporary biblical interpreter R.S. Sugirtharajah contends that the fire of the movement faded as the context of protest against the dictatorship disappeared.[123] Its lasting impact on the Korean church itself is up for debate. It was too countercultural, too challenging perhaps for most Koreans to hear. Under the economic leadership of Park Chung Hee the quality of life for many South Koreans improved and most Christians, privileged within the South Korean state from its beginnings, were reluctant to challenge the status quo. Minjung ideology and the language of the Minjung Movement grew through the 1980s as the injustices of the military government became harder to bear for an educated public. Pressure was also mounting on the South Korean government with the coming 1988 Olympics to show that the nation was on a par with other developed Western countries. But as more and more of the growing middle class joined the call for a return to democratic government the radical identification with the poor and dispossessed and the demands for a fundamentally reorganized economy associated with Minjung theology became unpalatable. With the return to democracy, the discourse soon shifted and reference was more often made to the Si-in (Citizen's) Movement. This discursive shift occurred in theology as well.[124] As is Canada, most were not ready to be transformed by the message of Minjung theology. However, the idea of a minjung and their lingering complaints did permeate

South Korean consciousness and remains real to this day, perhaps in the same way that the calls for "reconciliation" emanating from the Canadian Truth and Reconciliation Commission echo in the political and religious discourse of Canadian society.

On this note, the advent of Minjung theology and its connection to the Canadian mission in Korea raises questions about its relevance for the Canadian context. Contemporaneous issues connected to the colonial history of the church were emerging in the Canadian church as Minjung theology was coming to the fore in Korea. Minjung theology's close association with the Canadian missionary past would suggest that if any Western church would be inclined to learn from this new theology it would be the UCC. After all, had the Canadian church not made a bold move in relinquishing control of its properties in Korea and had this not resulted in real experiences of reconciliation and a creative outburst of Korean Christianity? But UCC observers seemed unable or unwilling to connect the dots and see the relevance of this Korean expression of Christianity for the Canadian context. It appears that within the Canadian church only missionaries serving overseas were truly impacted and transformed by the new theology as we shall see in the next chapter. Ironically, the Canadian church was no longer interested in what missionaries had to say.

EPILOGUE

In the last year of his life, Minjung theologian Suh Nam Dong was conferred an honorary doctorate at his alma mater, the UCC's Emmanuel College in Toronto, and was invited to take up a temporary teaching post there for a term. He travelled to Toronto to accept the degree, but felt that he should turn down the teaching position because his work at the MEC was too urgent. "As you know," Suh wrote to Asia Desk secretary of the UCC's Division of World Outreach, Frank Carey, "this is an underground activity, these students have no other place they can study and cannot secure employment; our Institute [the MEC] is the only place which offers them their education. If I'm absent for a semester, it will be very difficult to continue this course."[125]

Since 1982, the government had become aware of the program for theology students at the MEC and ordered it discontinued,[126] but Suh had managed to keep it going secretly with twenty seminarians still enrolled. Officially it had reverted to lay training programs and continuing education for clergy.[127] Suh died suddenly of liver cancer upon his return to Korea from his visit to Canada. He was sixty-six years old. The underground seminary managed to continue until 1985[128] and the MEC survives to this day in the same Edwardian building, a piece of Canadiana in the centre of Seoul.

Suh's death came at the high-water mark for Minjung theology with the Christian Council of Asia's 1983 English republication of the *Minjung Theology* and Jürgen Moltmann's 1984 edited volume in German *Minjung Theologie des Volkes Gottes in Sud-korea*,[129] stimulating discussion around the world. But the fleeting nature of this theological phenomenon belies the lingering relevance of the questions it raised about Western political hegemony in general and the colonial roots of the Canadian church in particular. "Christendom," Suh insisted, "had to collapse and enter the universal Oikoumene in the post-Christian era."[130] As the Canadian institutional church continued its rapid decline, these words had the ring of the prophetic.

6

"A Tremendous Source of Strength and Witness"

The Gendered Third Space and the South Korean Democratization Movement, 1976

The Bible women carried the Christian message into the homes of the women. They went from house to house and village to village, contacting women in their private quarters (*sarang*).[1] Initially, only women missionaries and Bible women could directly contact women – Korean custom did not permit males to contact women, except their immediate family: father, brothers or husband. Because of their isolation, families were not converted until the matriarch was converted. Most women in Korea, until the coming of the Christians, could not read or write.[2]

Early Canadian missionaries such as William Scott knew that gendered spaces were essential to the success of the Missionary Enterprise in Korea. Places where female missionaries could engage Korean women as women and present the missionary agenda of religion, health, and education were essential. In such a milieu, Korean women were able to safely discuss, collaborate, and make decisions for themselves and their community. Gendered spaces also created an environment where cross-cultural relationships were possible. Postwar Korea saw the replacement of traditional homes with modern apartment complexes, but the gendered space survived for female missionaries and their Korean hosts. Korean women continued to grant female missionaries special access to their lives well into the postwar period. This chapter will explore the ways that the time-tested tradition of women hosting women continued to be radically transformative in the 1970s and 1980s, drawing women into dramatic struggles for justice and teaching them lessons about themselves and the cultural other.

"A Tremendous Source of Strength and Witness"

This chapter is an interlude in what has been until this point a chronologically ordered account of the development of the Korean-Canadian church relationship. It will focus on an important time in the South Korean Democratization Movement. Focussing on a single pivotal moment, it offers a theoretical exploration of a postcolonial concept of the "third space." In the Korean context, the collaboration of Christian women in the Democratization Movement provides an important lens through which to view the history of missions in Korea. It further highlights a unique aspect of gendered cross-cultural encounters on the mission field that leveraged intercultural resources and transnational relationships to effect social and political change. Two interconnected incidents in the South Korean democracy movement illustrate the power of this space: the destruction of the Imun Dong squatter village on 9 February of 1976 and the Declaration for National Salvation of 1 March 1976. The documentary evidence of these events reveals the pivotal role women played in them even as it elucidates the pivotal importance of the gendered third space. While that importance for the Korean Democracy Movement is undeniable, in a surprising twist we discover that the impact extended well beyond Korean women and society, to Canadian missionary women and the church that sent them.

THE GENDERED THIRD SPACE

Dr Florence Murray,[3] a Canadian missionary, recounts in her memoir how late one night in 1942, while under house arrest by Japanese authorities, she was surprised by a Korean female colleague who let herself into the house and slipped under the bed covers with her.[4] This act was repeated in the nights to follow. As Japanese police were known to visit the homes of suspects at night, Murray's Korean colleague had joined her hoping that, should the police invade Murray's home, the presence of another person would offer some protection for the missionary doctor. The action of the Korean woman was a gesture of solidarity and concern for her friend. Had the police arrived to find her there, it would have cost her dearly. This act was a demonstration of tremendous courage and intimacy. It represented a remarkable shift in social positions for Murray, who was used to thinking of herself as someone who helped Koreans, not vice versa, and who usually commanded personal distance in her professional relationships. When she was reunited with her colleague in South Korea following the trauma of the Pacific and Korean wars, there was evidence of a different relationship between them than had existed before. The new relationship could be characterized as friendship. The change might have been the result of many things.[5] Nevertheless, intimate spaces shared by Korean women and missionaries were clearly part of the transformation of missionary relationships and the Korean political landscape.

Postcolonial theoretician Homi Bhabha describes a "third space" occupied by women in the British Miners' strike of 1984–85. According to Bhabha, this space was neither wholly defined by a feminist agenda, nor subsumed by their labour commitments, but was a "hybrid" position that sought to advance and negotiate both, while at the same time envisioning something more. "Here," wrote Bhabha, "the transformational value of change lies in the rearticulation, or translation, of elements that are neither the One (unitary working class) nor the Other (the politics of gender) but something else besides, which contests the terms and territories of both."[6] Bhabha's theory gives us a framework to understand the goals and activities of women as gendered subjects in pre- and postwar Korea. Lee Oo Chung, a Korean Christian activist, scholar, and second-wave feminist leader who features in the stories below, asserted that "the transformation of Korean society is the most important premise for achieving women's liberation." Thus, "the objective of the women's movement is to work for democratization and autonomy of Korean society and women's liberation."[7] Lee understood that women closely identified with the movement to restore democracy and reassert Korean sovereignty but also that there was a need to work "separately" such that the new national horizon would be shaped by women's own aspirations.[8]

A song sung by women in the South Korean Democratization Movement demonstrates women's commitment to democratization, including labour justice and Korean reunification, while at the same time claiming their own experiences and setting their own priorities:

Take your child on your back, shake off your grief and rise,
even though we can die we cannot fail.
Together with comrades in the bloody struggle, penetrate
the thorny path
Broken-back peninsula, divided land, you are our mother.
We will absolutely win and Minjung will dance, women's
liberation, worker's liberation.
With our hands we'll unify the nation, women workers,
Mansei!!![9]

For Christian women in the Democratization Movement, the extra dimension of their religious commitments further contributed to the complexity of the "third space." In terms of theology, there was very little published by or about women, but certain concepts developed by Minjung theologians became important. Christian women in the labour movement, for example, appreciated the association Minjung theologians made between "*han-* 恨," what they believed was a distinctly Korean experience of historical suffering and oppression, and Korean women's exploitation in modern factories. Through the Christian Council of Churches a group of women published a booklet in 1982 entitled "From the Womb of Han."[10] "The women workers movement is not a 'side issue,'" the booklet insisted, "but is the focal point of the democratic movement in South Korea." The experience of han understood through the Christian lens was, it further asserted, at the heart of their engagement with democratization and labour rights. These reflections on the concept of han notwithstanding, the best insights into the way women understood their Christian commitments in the context of the Korean Democratization Movement are found in the record of their activities. As mentioned above, some of these activities had their genesis in or around intimate personal spaces: homes, makeshift churches, and secret gatherings.

From their arrival in the late 1800s, Canadian missionaries had put an emphasis on the empowerment of their female converts. The Martha Wilson Bible Institute in Hamheung, the capital city of South Hamkyeong Province, had been a centre of women's education in the area. In addition, numerous girls' schools throughout the Canadian mission field had gained a positive reputation for the Canadian mission among Korean women and girls. In postwar Korea, too, Canadian missionary influence is acknowledged for its contribution to the development of key women's organizations and institutions in the Korean church. An officially endorsed history of the PROK credits Canadian missionaries for creating a culture in which, for the first time, the Korean church "was able to articulate a role for women based on the Bible that did not exclude them or force them into an extremely patriarchal structure."[11] Credit for the astounding leadership of Korean women in modern Korean history belongs to Korean women and not to missionaries. But the contributions of the Canadian Mission were noted and appreciated, and these contributions help us understand the historical context in which Canadian women missionaries in postwar Korea were invited by Korean women to participate in the gendered spaces of the Democratization Movement. The relationships that formed in these spaces not only contributed to the efficacy of Korean women in the struggle against the dictatorships of Park Chung Hee and Chun Doo Hwan; they also effected deep personal change in the Canadian missionaries and in church women in Canada.

The impact of Korean Christian women on the Democratization Movement is summed up in a report from a confidential meeting of the Unit on Faith and Witness of the World Council of Churches (WCC) convened in December 1975 for the sake of establishing a support network for Korean Christian activists. Those at the meeting recognized that women were occupying a unique place in the movement. The description captures characteristics of the gendered third space, at once quiet and effective, Christian and inclusive, local and international: "There is a group of women, particularly Christian women, who have been deeply involved in the struggle for human rights and social justice but have not received recognition for the quiet work they have been doing in the community all this time. These women have studied the political situation in the country, not simply from a secular point of view, but in the light of biblical teaching and through prayer. This way they have come to a new realization of the mission of the church. You've seen their involvement with members of the whole community, including women and families outside the institution of the church. The supportive role has been a tremendous source of strength and witness to the local community as well as to those of us who have had a chance to meet and talk with them."[12] Covering the Korean Democratization Movement for the *New York Times*, Andrew H. Malcolm noted that "Women, who are sometimes believed to hold a subservient position in Asian societies, are playing an increasingly prominent role in the struggle for human rights in South Korea" comparable to "the militant work of many women during the civil rights struggles of the 1960s in the American South."[13] The article made special mention of Lee Oo Chung, whose part in the March 1 Declaration of National Salvation discussed below landed her in jail. Malcolm noted that police interrogations of Lee Oo Chung and others "revealed a belief that the women had played a vital liaison role among the more closely monitored male dissidents." He also mentioned the religious services led by women "to pray for their men [in prison], to offer moral support to one another and to gather funds for the financially stricken families, whose main bread winners are in jail," as well as the knitting of purple "victory shawls," which raised awareness internationally for their cause.[14]

The work of Korean Christian women was a source of tremendous inspiration for Canadian women missionaries and women from the UCC visiting Korea. Willa Kernen, who worked closely with a number of women's organizations, reflected that the Korean church had challenged her to "grow as a person, as a woman, and as a Christian."[15] Marion Pope learned about justice issues and "protesting skills" in Korea, which she transferred to life in Canada when as a retired missionary she "joined others in front of our Ontario provincial legislature asking the provincial government to stop the war against the poor."[16] Marion Current's world view was changed and her eyes were opened to systemic injustices she had been blind to growing up in Canada (see chapter 5).[17] Lois Wilson's life was changed on a visit to Korea and her assumptions about the prerogative of Western church to share the Christian gospel with others was shattered[18] (see chapter 8). And Elsie Livingston, living in Saskatchewan, was taught an important lesson about social justice activism[19] (see chapter 8).

The impact of gendered third spaces were not unique to Korea, nor were they exclusively a postwar phenomenon. Gendered spaces were in fact an important reason for the prominence of women missionaries on the mission field and the new opportunities this afforded these women (see chapter 3). As missionary institutions began to understand the centrality of women in the places they were working and the influence they exerted on the family, education, and religion in their communities, they started to envision a pivotal role for female missionaries. In places like Korea where contact between men and women was limited, female missionaries would be in a unique position to approach and engage the matriarchs whose decisions would have significant impact on the spread of Christianity and the effectiveness of the missionary agenda in education and health. This fact, then opened the door to single females in Western nations to fill roles, from teachers and preachers to doctors and administrators, that had once been denied them and to travel and see things that married women in their own culture could only dream of.[20] These third spaces, therefore, had a significant impact on Western societies in the pre- and interwar period and this continued in new ways in the postwar period.

Were there comparable spaces for men in the context of postwar Korean missions? What is clear is that the documentary record is not the same. There were clearly male missionaries involved in an intimate way with Koreans in some very intense situations. Canadian missionary Walter Beecham, for example, worked with the Urban Industrial Mission (UIM). The UIM sent missionaries and Korean church leaders to work alongside workers in factories under very difficult conditions and often at risk of violence at the hands of management and state authorities. The goal was to raise the awareness of workers to their rights and to organize them to defend those rights. But no accounts of the relationships forged doing this work could be found similar to the accounts left by women and so it is hard to know to what extent the UIM depended on male gendered spaces and how men were affected by their interactions.[21] William Scott's tribute to Kim Chai Choon together with whom he suffered slander and ostracism from the Presbyterian Church in Korea for challenging theological norms (see chapter 2) suggests an important and formative friendship but to what degree this friendship depended on intimate male gendered spaces is an open question. Most of the documentation from and about men comes in the form of meeting minutes and public statements. Ian Robb's letter in defense of the position of a number of missionaries who chose to voice their opposition to South Korean authoritarianism is a case in point[22] (see chapter 5). This courageous statement must have been born of intimate personal discussions and interactions with Korean male colleagues, but we are not privy to the ways and contexts in which these occurred or if they were in some way a result of gendered male relationships.

In the case of female missionaries, however, a very strong record is left of gendered encounters in intimate spaces that lead to important personal transformations and significant social and political developments. My assessment of the qualitative difference between male and female gendered spaces in the Missionary-Korean Christian community is supported by observations made by Korean historian Koo Hagen who, commenting on the relationships between Korean labours and missionaries observed, "female workers, not male workers, developed a special relationship with church organizations."[23] This was in part because women workers were most severely exploited by the reality they found themselves in and therefore had more to gain and less to lose from such relationships. But another and more important reason he believes is that female workers were simply "more interested" in small-group activities organized by church leaders, activities that happened to be a central component of church programs. It was

"A Tremendous Source of Strength and Witness"   161

in these intimate spaces, he suggests, that women were able to get the psychological and emotional support they needed. Women also showed more curiosity and a desire to learn. Koo also cites observations that women "had fewer inhibitions about participating in unfamiliar social activities with strangers" and that they were less rigid and hierarchical than men.[24] These reasons may also help to explain the special quality of the gendered third space for female missionaries and Korean Christians in the Democratization Movement.

THE DESTRUCTION OF THE IMUN DONG NEIGHBOURHOOD

On January 30, 1975, a worship service was held to celebrate the establishment of the Sarangbang Church. In Korea the sarangbang is a detached living room used for entertaining guests. But this worship "room" had no walls. It was simply a gathering space among the slum dwellers' tents.[25]

The Sarangbang Church in the Imun Dong squatter village was central to one of the most important events of the South Korean Democratization Movement of the 1970s. Almost everything we know about this church in the archival records comes from the three female Canadian missionaries who are the focus of this chapter. This unique faith community was born in the context of South Korea's rapidly expanding urban squatter neighbourhoods of the 1970s. As a consequence of government policies aimed at rapid industrialization and development there was tremendous pressure on rural people to move to cities and take up low paying work in factories.[26] The gendered nature of South Korean development contributed to the especially difficult circumstances that women faced.[27] Young women and girls left the farm and travelled alone to the city to earn money to support their families, often ending their journey in sweat shops or prostitution.[28] In some cases pressures were such that people moved to the city despite the fact that there was no guarantee of even a low paying job. Those who could not find work often lived in makeshift buildings on land that they did not own and from which they faced eviction on a regular basis.[29]

Imun Dong was one such neighbourhood in southeastern Seoul. Having been served notice that they would soon be evicted, a number of residents decided to organize. They petitioned the city government, churches, and other institutions, but received little sympathy from these quarters. They did, however, find a gathering known as "Thursday Prayer Meetings" where people from the Christian community were eager to learn of their situation and did take an interest.[30] Regular Thursday gatherings of the Christian supporters of political prisoners had started in the summer of 1974 not far from Imun Dong.[31] Its young Protestant leaders had originally envisioned Thursday meetings as a gathering of church ministers concerned for the state of democracy and planned to hold them on Mondays, a typical "day off" for church leaders.[32] This reflected the specifically Christian context in which the meeting was first conceived. However, circumstances soon caused it to adapt.

At about the same time, a major government crackdown occurred. This crackdown was a pre-emptive move against a nation-wide protest planned for 3 April. The protest had been organized by an umbrella student organization, the Youth and Student Federation for Democratization of Korea.[33] Among the student organizations linked under this umbrella were university student unions and Christian student clubs such as the Korean Student Christian Federation (KSCF). These Christian clubs were ubiquitous, politically conscious, and effective organizers. To counter the threat of an effective nation-wide protest, the South Korean government concocted a story about a plot by a fictional North Korea-backed People's Revolutionary Party (PRP), which was said to have organized the protest as a prelude to a North Korean invasion of the South. Under this pretext, the army and police arrested thousands of students, imprisoned hundreds, and eventual executed eight men they falsely accused of being leaders of the fictional PRP. Hundreds of victimized families with loved ones in jail or facing the death penalty, some of them Christian, found the prayer meeting arranged by the young ministers welcoming and helpful.[34] Thursdays coincided with other activities connected to the plight of these families and students and so the prayer meeting was moved from Monday to Thursday to accommodate them.

The Thursday Prayer Meeting quickly gained momentum. It attracted the attention of many Protestant Christians who were concerned, not only for their imprisoned fellow co-religionists, but also with the increasingly harsh tactics of the Park regime and its impact on society broadly. The circle expanded further when a number of Catholics began to show up in support of an imprisoned bishop.[35] Others, often non-Christians, with family members in prison

"A Tremendous Source of Strength and Witness" 163

connected to various protests or breaches of the Yushin Constitution also began to frequent this gathering. Canadian missionaries Willa Kernen, Marian Pope, and Marion Current and some other missionaries came often, as well.[36]

The authorities did their best to shut down the Thursday Prayer Meeting, but it managed to survive by going underground, varying meeting times and locations. After the government promised to release some of its most prominent political prisoners the organizers agreed to stop the regular gatherings. However, when the promise was not kept, they started it up anew, once again in the open and this time with official support from a number of public and internationally recognized ecumenical Christian organizations. The support came from a broad representation of individuals, churches, and other organizations sympathetic and increasingly indignant at the government's intransigence. Numbers rapidly swelled so that by late 1975 their regular attendance numbered 250. For special services, 500 turned out.[37] These meetings had powerful spiritual significance, described by Lee Oo Chung as "a feast for a people drunk with the Holy Spirit."[38] They were politically significant as well, offering a point of contact for dissidents and affording an opportunity to exchange information and to organize. They reflect a special role that progressive Christians were playing in the movement. This was not a central role, but it was unique and essential. While student unions and labour activists without any religious affiliation were leading most of the protests and suffering most of the persecution up to this time, Christians, under the protection afforded the Christian religion by the Park dictatorship, were we able to keep the torch of protest burning when other organizations were hard pressed.[39]

A number of the women from Imun Dong also began to attend the Thursday Prayer Meeting. Perhaps moved by its spiritual component or impressed by the organizational efficiency of its Christian organizers, or both, they decided to start a church.[40] Kernen and Current made a connection with these women at the Thursday Prayer Meeting and came to the new church to visit. They participated in worship in a space among the makeshift homes and were sometimes joined by other prominent women leaders of the Korean Christian community.[41] Kernen was struck by the special music used at their services: "They are new Christians and don't know the hymns, nor do they have a hymn book, so they have written their own words to traditional Korean songs. They have a couple of beautiful indigenous 'hymns.'"[42]

Current was moved by their vulnerability and courage, the fact that their services were conducted between the tents in the slum, a "church without walls."[43] This was not a church that drew its power from impressive architecture, elegant stained-glass, or stately organ music. Rather, its focus was on a community of people and their needs.

"Sarangbang" was the name given this remarkable church. As noted above, the word sarangbang refers to the inner sanctum of a traditional (and relatively wealthy) Korean house. For a church of slum dwellers who had no permanent physical structures to call home this name had the ring of irony, but it carried a double meaning. In its traditional usage *sa-rang* denoted ideographs "舍" and "廊" which together mean a specific kind of room in a house. But the word *sarang* is also the common Korean word for "love." *Bang* simply means "a room" in common parlance. The name for the church could in this way be read as "Love Room" and, therefore, suggested a place of Christian empathy, caring, and solidarity. The nature of the space in which they worshipped was a reflection of their overall living conditions. Like the Minjung theology that would be inspired by it, it lacked a definitive boundary between sacred and secular.

The new Christian community at Imun Dong had a religious impact that went beyond the immediate slum community and eventually exceeded the Korean church itself. Marion Current witnessed the impression it made on Minjung theologian Suh Nam Dong who spent time listening to the members of the church describe their life in the slums. "Looking back, I can see how situations like this influenced Rev. Suh [*sic*]," she wrote, "The slum dwellers became his teachers."[44] Sarangbang Church and its connection to Christians with sympathies for political prisoners made an impression on the authorities, too.[45] After trying to discourage the budding relationship between Imun Dong residents and the Thursday Prayer Meeting, they took extreme measures and decided to demolish the shanty town along with its church.[46] Kernen reported that on 9 February 1976 "a group of wreckers from the local government offices, together with some fourteen police men, guarded by KCIA agents, helped by the Reserve Force Army (the location is next to their training ground)" bulldozed the worship space and the surrounding makeshift homes.[47] Thirty people including children were taken into detention, six women were sentenced to five days in prison, and four men to ten days, one child was injured, and the belongings and homes of the entire community were trashed.[48]

Current was left traumatized by what had transpired.[49] She attempted to document the aftermath with her camera, but in the emotion of the moment her hands were trembling so badly that most images came out blurry.[50] One photograph, however, was captured clearly: "It was of Rev. Moon Ik Hwan,[51] head bowed, holding a smashed white plywood cross on his shoulder. The cross had been trampled on, broken, and splattered with excrement."[52] The image vividly captured the drama and significance of what had taken place and was circulated widely.

There was a clear connection between the leadership of the Imun Dong women, Korean women church leaders and Canadian women missionaries. The events at Sarangbang Church are also linked to one of the most pivotal moments of the South Korean Democratization Movement, the March 1 Declaration for National Salvation.[53] Korean church leaders connected to the Sarangbang Church, including missionaries Kernen, Pope, and Current, played a central role in the March 1 Declaration less than a month later. "Of course," wrote Current, "the Sarang-Bang [sic] church tragedy was only one part of the story, but it is my belief that it was a major factor behind the March 1st Declaration."[54] In his testimony to the court for his role in this March 1 action, Suh Nam Dong corroborates Current's analysis, crediting his encounter with people in the slums for hardening his resolve to participate: "I had some relations with slum area people. I found out they are poor not because they are lazy but because of policy that makes them poor. Unless they fight to change the policy, they will not be able to get a better life. But the government will not change its policy. But if government does not change, then communists will infiltrate the slums. That endangers our country. So, I signed the declaration."[55] Moon Ik Hwan, who lifted the desecrated cross from the rubble of the church and later penned the March 1 Declaration, was also convinced by this incident he needed to do something more than just pray.[56]

The story of Sarangbang Church shows that a group of the most marginalized women in Korean society had a significant impact on the Democratization Movement by hosting other women and men from the Korean Christian and missionary community. It also gives an idea of the ways in which the missionaries who participated were personally impacted by events, a direct result of their willingness to share a gendered third space with Korean women. Finally, it adds a layer to the history of the March 1 Declaration that has not been appreciated to date.

THE 1 MARCH DECLARATION

> While ... [writing this letter], I'm enjoying the sunshine coming in the window beside me of our new southern exposed Apartment, as well as the panoramic view of a section of Seoul looking out of the 5th floor (the top one) of a building already set rather high on a hill. We can look beyond the small apartment building where Marion Current is to the overhead road to Sin Chon. Marion Pope and I are enjoying settling into this lovely new apartment. We hope we will be able to continue enjoying it together for a long time.[57]

Prior to December 1975, Willa Kernen and Marion Pope had lived in the UCC Korea Mission compound near Seodaemun. At times they had hosted Korean friends in their home, serving such dishes as Yorkshire pudding with the help of a Korean cook.[58] The 1974 agreement between the UCC and the PROK (see chapter 4) caused them to vacate the compound and move into a new residence provided them by the PROK. The old home was in the midst of becoming the Mission and Education Centre (MEC) (see chapter 5). The two women were now tenants of the Korean church rather than the matrons of a Mission-owned property with Korean staff. Though centrally located in a good neighbourhood of Seoul, the apartment did not communicate privilege or a raised social position in any way. There was nothing to distinguish Kernen and Pope's new residence from that of millions of South Koreans who had moved into the modern concrete structures rising like "forests"[59] out of the quickly modernizing urban landscape. It was a different position, but did not seem to create any discomfort or resentment. Indeed, judging from her letter cited above, Kernen seems to have been quite pleased with the new arrangement; she had a sunny room with a view, one close friend for an apartment-mate and another nearby.

Kernen and Pope would continue to host Koreans in their apartment. Some were friends. Some were strangers, fugitives who sought a safe house in which to hide from the authorities. The fact that Kernen and Pope were foreign nationals of a Western country did not always provide the desired protection for these internal refugees. It is hard to know whether the walls of the Seodaemun compound or the imposing structure of a large brick home might have provided more safety,

"A Tremendous Source of Strength and Witness" 167

but in their new apartment the police did not hesitate to visit them in the late hours of the night and demand they give up their guests. Reminiscent of the earlier story of Dr Murray's house arrest under Japanese colonial authorities, Kernen and Pope had, in February prior to the March 1 incident (described below), given shelter to a young woman who was wanted by the police for publishing a statement by the imprisoned Catholic poet Kim Chi Ha.[60] Unlike in Murray's case, however, the police did visit and little could be done to stop the woman from being taken away.[61]

Days later[62] on 29 February, less than a month after the destruction of the Sarangbang Church, Kernen "innocently" invited her friend Lee Oo Chung over after Sunday worship. Perhaps seeking to insert some normalcy into an extraordinarily turbulent time for the three missionaries and their Korean friends, Kernen and Current were planning a celebration of Pope's birthday (which was the next day on the first of March). Lee accepted, but after dinner surprised her hosts with a request to spend the night. Lee explained that she had in her possession a statement written by Moon Ik Hwan and signed by twelve prominent Christian leaders calling for President Park Chung Hee to resign. Such statements were strictly outlawed by Emergency Measures #9, which had recently been promulgated by the government and which prohibited criticism of the president or the regime in any form. Nevertheless, the signatories, Lee included, were determined to have it read out at a public worship service the next day. Aware that the Korean Central Intelligence Agency (KCIA) were on the lookout for any indication of political resistance, organizers of the protest surmised that women would be less of a target for authorities. Lee Oo Chung, the only woman among them, had therefore been charged to keep the document safe until the evening of the next day. Notwithstanding the fact that the missionaries' home had recently been visited by the police, Lee felt that she and the document would be safer there than anywhere else.[63]

The reading of the declaration was planned to take place during an evening mass at the Myeongdong Cathedral in the centre of the old capital. A special mass had been planned for members of the Catholic church who were currently in prison for their political views. In the end, hundreds of concerned Catholics and dozens of supportive Protestant leaders were present. The place was undoubtedly swarming with undercover police as well and Lee was worried that she might be intercepted on the way to the service. As a further precaution, therefore, they decided that she should give the document to one of the missionaries to smuggle in. As a signatory to the declaration, Lee Oo Chung was also aware that the action would likely result in her arrest. In anticipation of this eventuality the four of them developed a strategy to alert various Christians organizations overseas if this should occur. Plans were made to contact the WCC, Conference of Churches in Asia (CCA), American Council of Churches, and the Canadian Council of Churches, among others. The signal that Lee had been arrested was to be a phone call from Lee explaining that "she would be unable to meet with them for their appointment." [64]

When they arrived at the cathedral at 7 p.m. the next evening, Pope had the paper upon which the Declaration for National Salvation was inscribed safely stashed away in her purse. Once inside the sanctuary she gave it to Lee who took it to her fellow signatories. At this point Lee was informed that the police had indeed got wind that something was about to happen and detained the man who the group had originally decided should read the declaration. Lee was asked if she would read it to the gathering in his stead. It was no small request, and the other signatories were later upbraided by female leaders for asking Lee to take this risk. [65] Nevertheless, following mass she mounted the pulpit and delivered the statement "with a clear and ringing voice." [66] Lee's voice rang all over Korea and around the world. The declaration was to succeed beyond the organizers' wildest dreams.

Part of the power of the declaration came from the tremendous symbolic significance of the date and place. Fifty-seven years earlier to the day, on 1 March 1919, Koreans had risen up to demand independence from Japan. A massive and peaceful public demonstration had been timed to influence the post-First World War deliberations in Paris and put pressure on US President Woodrow Wilson to abide by his precept of "self-determination" for nations under foreign rule. The event prefigured the 5 May Movement in China. It was met with a bloody crackdown by the Japanese colonial police and soldiers and failed to secure Korean independence but 1 March galvanized a sense of national pride and purpose and was enshrined as a national holiday in the south. In addition to the symbolism of the date, the 1976 Declaration shared two other features with the 1919 event that are of interest. The first is that Canadian missionaries were intimately involved in both. In 1919, Frank Schofield was teaching veterinary medicine at Severance Hospital in Seoul and was taken into the confidence of the signatories of the declaration. He documented the ensuing protests with his camera and smuggled the pictures out with his own account of events to the international media. These acts got him deported but also earned him a place in history and a burial in the Patriot Section of the National Cemetery of the Republic of Korea, a singular honour for a non-Korean.[67] Another similarity was the ecumenical nature of these two events. In the case of the 1919 Declaration, the thirty-three signatories represented Christian, Cheondogyo (an indigenous Korean religion related to the Donghak Rebellion (see chapter 1) and Buddhist faiths, a significant example of interreligious cooperation before the advent of the Ecumenical Movement in Europe and North America. In the case of the 1976, only Protestant and Catholic Christianity was represented but this was also a significant act of interreligious collaboration at the time and began to bring the different religions together in the Democratization Movement.

The date for the 1976 Declaration for National Salvation was chosen precisely because it had the power to evoke the memory of a peaceful grassroots nationalist uprising in opposition to an oppressive ruling authority.[68] The location of the 1976 Declaration, Myeongdong Cathedral, was also important. The building was one of the oldest and most prominent Catholic churches in the nation. The event, therefore, marshalled powerful cultural symbolism which signalled a connection to the West, but also more than 200 years of Korean Christian leadership and martyrdom. Kim Dae Jung, the only Catholic signatory to the declaration and a well-known political opposition leader, was particularly conspicuous as a symbol of dissent. The event captured the imagination of Koreans and energized activists in the country.[69] Significantly, it also captured the attention of the international press and Christians overseas.

The 1976 March 1 Declaration was the first large act of political dissent following the promulgation of Emergency Measures #9. It was the moment when Christian activism took the lead in the Democratization Movement, all other groups including students and press having earlier been effectively silenced by the regime's heavy hand.[70] It also galvanized Catholic-Protestant ecumenical and political cooperation[71] and catapulted Korean Christianity into the spotlight. During the trial for his part in the 1976 March 1 Declaration, Kim Dae Jung, who would eventually be elected president of South Korea in 1998, made the following statement: "The March 1 Democratic

Declaration – not just because of this Declaration but because this has become a symbolic moment – has lifted the status of the Korean church so high that the world church cannot speak of the problems of the Christianity of a new generation without mentioning the Korean church."[72] Kim's boast was not without reason. The event had indeed captured the attention of the international community. The degree to which it had raised awareness for their cause came as a surprise, even to the Christian activists who had pulled it off.[73] This success was due in large part to the plan set in motion by Lee Oo Chung from within a gendered third space hosted by her missionary friends.

When the shrill ring of the telephone broke the silence of their apartment at midnight following the events at Myeongdong Cathedral, Lee Oo Chung's calm voice informed Kernen in English, "I'm sorry I won't be able to keep our lunch appointment tomorrow."[74] The police had arrived at her apartment to take her away and she had persuaded them to allow her the call by explaining it would give a bad impression of Koreans if she were to break a promise with foreigners without notice.[75] Following the plan devised the night before, Kernen and Pope then got on the phone to their friends around the world. A follow up call was made immediately to the *New York Times* which quickly published a notification.[76] Lee Oo Chung maintained that an article appeared in the *New York Times* about her arrest on 1 March as well as a translated copy of the declaration.[77] This is not possible as 12 midnight on 2 March, the time Lee called Kernen to alert her to her arrest, would already be 11 a.m. 1 March in New York. It is possible that there was a report in the 2 March edition of the *New York Times*, but one was not found in the archives. A 3 March article from the *Japan Times*, however, reads as follows:

> Miss Lee Oo Chung, 53, president of Korean Church Women United, was arrested Monday by Korean authorities in Seoul, the US National Council of Churches reported. Miss Lee, a human rights activist, was arrested after her participation in an ecumenical mass celebrating Korean Independence Day, the interdenominational church body here said. She recently resigned her position as professor of Christian ethics at Seoul Women's College, rather than capitulate to Ministry of Education pressures that she stop her work with Church Women United and her effort on behalf of detainees and their families. Miss Lee has been detained for questioning three times – for five, six and two days. This is the first

"A Tremendous Source of Strength and Witness"   171

time she has been arrested, however, the report said. The US council has consistently joined with the national council of churches in Korea in opposition to alleged violations of human rights there. Church officials here said they see Miss Lee's arrest as an example of a pattern of oppression in Korea.

The speed with which the news came out was significant. It shows how well the Democratization Movement participants were organized. It also speaks to the effectiveness of women's networks for getting information out.

The article mentions that Lee had previously been detained and held for days, but that this was her first arrest. On this occasion the police also used torture. Lee Oo Chung was subjected to sleep deprivation and kept awake for a whole week.[78] One thing the KCIA wanted to know was how the news of her arrest and the declaration had gotten out so fast.[79] People around the world had responded immediately. At Toronto Korean United Church (TKUC), leaders Kim Chai Choon (see chapter 2) and Moon Chai Rin (see chapter 1) who were self-exiled in Toronto, put on mourning clothes and went to the Korean consulate to hold a protest. American Church Women United started a writing campaign to petition for Lee Oo Chung's release. In America, the Netherlands, Sweden, Japan, and other places, women wrote letters and sent them to their governments to ask that they apply pressure to South Korean embassies and government agencies demanding freedom for the imprisoned, and to the prisoners to encourage them and inform them of their solidarity. The WCC and the Christian Council of Asia (CCA) weighed in as did the International Council of Judges.

The Korean Authorities were shocked by the forceful international response and wanted to know how it was started. They were unable to get anything out of Lee under interrogation, however, except a scolding: how, she demanded of her interrogators, could they treat her and others this way simply for telling the truth!?!80 At her trial, Lee was sentenced to three years in prison, which was suspended, and an additional three years suspension of civil rights.[81] This meant, among other things, that she was not entitled to vote or to leave the country. But in the United States she was given the Human Rights Award by *Christianity and Crisis*, a magazine out of Union Theological School in New York. While she was prevented by the government from travelling to receive it, the distinction further raised the stature of the Korean Democratization Movement and the Christian church's involvement.[82]

Korean church historian Wi Jo Kang has characterized the March 1 Declaration as "the most eventful and climactic demonstration of all Christian political dissent under the Park regime."[83] Korean historian Kenneth Wells has pointed out its significance in fusing Protestant and Catholics into a "Minjung Christianity."[84] Kang and Wells are not alone in their assessment that the March 1 Declaration was a pivotal event in the South Korean Democratization Movement and a defining moment for Christian participation in that movement.[85] Sociologist and Korea scholar Paul Y. Chang's argues that Christian activists had stepped up at a critical moment.[86]

The reading of the March 1 Declaration at a church service introduced to the wider Korean society the debate about the relationship between religion and politics. The declaration had called for the freedom to criticize the government and had been particularly strong in demanding Park Chung Hee take responsibility for the economic ills of the country including a burgeoning international debt. It also called for the reunification of the nation by democratic means.[87] The fact that these issues were raised in the context of a Catholic mass invited questions about the place of politics in religion and vice versa. This relationship was debated in the courts when Lee Oo Chung was sentenced.[88] Lee herself had tackled this topic in a prayer before her trial. Calling on God for support, Lee had stated that "so called political persons" had spoken out "based on their religious belief and conviction rather than political belief. They tried to build the Kingdom of God with their religious determination ... They had been arrested for calling right things right and wrong things wrong."[89] This was an important discursive challenge that Lee and other Christians were presenting to the state. The March 1 Declaration had brought it to the fore.[90]

Lee and the women whose husbands were arrested following the March 1 Declaration added a further dimension to the discursive battle with the government by using cultural symbols to make their case transnationally. Malcolm's December 1976 article in the *New York Times* entitled "Women Playing Important Role in Rights Struggle in South Korea" noted one such action that was garnering attention in the United States: The Victory Shawl project.[91] The act of crocheting shawls was an intriguing culturally hybrid move, involving Korean women in an activity which traditionally belonged to women of Western heritage. The art of crochet, the shawl as an item of clothing, the colour purple signifying suffering in Christian tradition and the "V" shape, which symbolized the English word "Victory,"[92] were all

Western cultural symbols used to imbue the project with meaning that could be understood by an international Christian community. In these respects, the shawls were a translation or representation of a Korean experience in a medium to which Western women could easily relate. But they contained important Korean meaning and symbolism as well. In a letter explaining the shawls to women in North America, the wives of the men imprisoned for their role in the March 1 Declaration explained that while purple is the Christian colour for suffering, it is also the colour of Korea's national flower, the Rose of Sharon, symbolizing the love of Korea. What's more, they explained, "for each 'V'-shaped pattern, four crocheted stitches are required. It takes four words in Korean to say The Recovery of Democracy – Min Chu Whay Bok.[93] As we crochet, instead of shedding tears for our husbands, we repeat the words, Min Chu Whay Bok." The letter tried to inspire support by underlining the fact that the completion of one Victory Shawl required a total of ten thousand stitches, which symbolized the need for ten thousand voices of support for each shawl. Therefore, "we need your voice saying to your government – the Recovery of Democracy in South Korea now." [94] These shawls were distributed around the world, including Canada through women in the UCC at women-only gatherings,[95] raising awareness for the struggle of democracy in South Korea and engaging a transnational network of Christian women in that struggle[96] (see chapter 8).

Two nights before Lee Oo Chung had arrived at the missionaries' apartment for Pope's birthday party, Marion Current had a dream that Lee was an important official in the government.[97] While many of her comrades in the Democratization Movement did eventually find positions in the Korean government when Kim Dae Jung was elected president, Lee was never inclined to get involved in this way. Nevertheless, the dream seems to have been a premonition of the central role she would play in the nation and the new possibilities her leadership would present. Scholars agree that the March 1 Declaration of National Salvation was a complex event with many contributing actors. They also agree that it played a pivotal role in the South Korean Democratization Movement. Furthermore, there is consensus that it defined the Christian contribution to that movement. However, the critical role of women in the March 1 Declaration of 1976 has been overlooked. Without the encounter in Kernen and Pope's lovely new apartment, new vistas may never have unfolded for the Democratization Movement or the UCC women who supported it.

CONCLUSION

The gendered third space shaped the contribution of Korean Christian women and Canadian female missionaries and empowered them to voice experiences, concerns, and goals that were both nationalist and feminist, and something more besides. In part, these spaces made it possible for women to resist South Korean military rule in an especially effective way. Speaking specifically of the Christian community, Kernen noticed that Korean women had, in the struggle for democracy and human rights, "come into their own." "Their success in many undertakings," she said, "has done much to enhance their self-image, as well as given them considerable respect from their male associates."[98] There is no question that this "third space" was transformative; it contributed to the Korean society and transformed the lives of individual Korean women as well. The testimonies of the UCC women to their own learnings explored elsewhere in this study underscore the fact that as foreign women they were also very much transformed by their involvement in this space.

The gendered third space created through the interactions between Korean and missionary women in the early years of the Missionary Enterprise, survived the interruptions and transformations of the missionary relationship wrought by war and modernization. This was an intimate space in which women hosted women, a space that was at once personal and political. Early on, Christian missionaries described this as a space where conversions were made and Korean women were empowered. However, in the case of later missionaries at least, gendered third spaces were especially transformative for them, as witnessed by the testimony of Kernen, Pope, and Current.

Mission encounters are by definition intercultural and encounters between women provide examples of female gendered interactions across cultural differences. As an environment that was intimate and secure, these encounters enabled an appreciation and exchange of cultural meanings that was different from what might have been possible in other environments. In the example of Sarangbang Church, Kernen was able to identify the value of Christian music derived, not from missionary hymn books, but from indigenous musical traditions in Korea. In the Victory Shawl project, Korean women were able to adopt a Western cultural practice to communicate the meaning of their experiences of oppression and also something of their own history and culture to a Western audience. There are many examples of such cultural exchanges, and the direction of those exchanges went both ways. The gendered third space has spotlighted the contribution of women to broader historical events. Without an appreciation of what occurred in this intimate, subversive, and caring space our knowledge of events such as the March 1 Declaration for National Salvation is incomplete.

PART THREE

Mission from the East

Korean Christians Engage Canadian Society
and the United Church of Canada,
1965 to 1998

7

Seonguja

Pioneering Korean Christians in the United Church of Canada Wilderness, 1965 to 1988

Since the 1970s I have participated in the multi-racial activities of the denomination [United Church of Canada]. I have been on many committees. Always I am told "you are the first ethnic minority to sit on this committee." But wrestling with White people is not always pleasant. Once or twice I have felt like discontinuing my engagement. But I have thought that this is the pioneering work that an ethnic minority has to do and so have continued the difficult struggle. And I have always found this struggle difficult.

Sang Chul Lee, "Sermon: Honest before God,"
Toronto Korean United Church, 25 January 1987[1]

In August 1988, the United Church of Canada elected the Rev. Sang Chul Lee as its thirty-second moderator, the first Asian (and second non-White person[2]) to hold the position of spiritual leader of Canada's largest Protestant denomination. According to Hugh McCullum reporting for the *Observer*, members of the church saw Lee's election as "further proof of the United Church's desire to continue inclusivity, justice and reconciliation."[3] At the time, interviewee Patti Talbot felt it was a brave move by the UCC.[4] It is likely, however, that few realized the courage required for Lee, himself, to get to this stage. Lee had been born to refugee parents in Siberia and was twice over a refugee himself. Neither had his immigration to Canada in 1965 been the end of his challenges. If members of the UCC were telling themselves that they had achieved something on the road to racial equality as they watched Lee's installation as moderator, they may have been unaware of the experience of racial minorities within the church and of how much further they had to go.

As for the Korean immigrants who took notice of Lee's installation, it was likely that they saw it more as a sign of the arduous path-breaking accomplishments of the community than of the generous accommodation of Canadian society and the UCC. Korean Christians in the UCC never forgot that their story was of one of exhausting pioneering efforts to plant themselves in often-rocky-and-unwelcoming soil, of survival in the wilderness of racism and of struggle against ongoing paternalistic patterns and attitudes. These stories were themselves closely connected to other stories about a historical missionary presence in their country of origin and a push and pull relationship within the context of colonialism and modernization. Overseas in Korea, the tides had turned; the missionary enterprise and the missionaries participating in it had been radically changed. But in Canada, there was still much work to do.

The story of Korean immigration is not only a story of struggle, however, but also one of transformation. The presence of Koreans and others immigrating to Canada from 1965 onward underlined that the UCC was not a church made up solely of White English-speakers and, in fact, never had been. This fact was harder to ignore with the growth of Korean congregations and the installation of Lee as moderator. Koreans and other non-Western migrants were themselves now more than ever a growing part of the Canadian Protestant church. Their voice from the 1960s on could no longer be dismissed as the voice of outsiders but now had to be acknowledged as the voice of the Canadian church itself. They represent a change in perspective, a change in theology, and a change in worship practice in the UCC. This is an important moment that signals the rise of challenges to entrenched Anglo-Protestant nationalist prejudices from within the UCC.

BEGINNING OF THE KOREAN MISSION
TO CANADA

A warm summer day at the Gimpo Airport in Seoul in the year 1965 marks an important turning point in the relationship between the Korean and Canadian churches. On that day a young Korean family boarded a plane bound for British Columbia. The father of the family was a young church minister ordained by the Presbyterian Church in the Republic of Korea (PROK) who was on his way to take up a new job at Steveston United Church in the city of Richmond, BC. This did not represent the first time a minister had been called from an overseas mission field to serve a congregation in Canada. Already by this time the UCC had brought a number of ministers from Japan and Hong Kong to serve congregations of their own "ethnic groups."[5] But Sang Chul Lee was the first Korean minister to move to Canada to serve an Anglo church and may represent the first non-White minister to be called to do so. In fact, Steveston United was not entirely White, but a congregation of English speakers near Vancouver that had, in a unique arrangement, merged with an established Japanese congregation. It was, in other words, a mixed inter-cultural congregation.

Steveston United had heard about Lee from his time studying as a UCC scholarship student at Union College in Vancouver between 1961 and 1964. Having been raised in colonial Manchuria under Japanese rule, Lee had been required, along with all the Korean children of his generation, to learn the colonizer's language. The congregation at Steveston needed someone who could preach and minister in both English and Japanese and, aware that Lee was fluent in both, sent a request across the Pacific that he return to Canada and be their minister. Lee reports having felt ambivalent about the call. His father-in-law, Kim Chai Choon (see chapter 2) encouraged him to accept the invitation, however, telling Lee that after so many years of missionaries coming to Korea, it was time for something different: it was Lee's turn to be "a Korean missionary to Canada."[6]

Coincidentally, Lee's return to Canada occurred just ahead of the first wave of Korean immigration into the country. In 1964, the year he had completed his studies and departed for Korea, there had been very few Koreans in Vancouver. Shortly after his return in 1965, however, a steady stream began to flow through the Vancouver airport.[7] As a result, in 1966, while still serving the English and Japanese congregations, Lee found himself responsible for an additional congregation of Koreans which met at the Union Theological Seminary (currently the Vancouver School of Theology) on the University of British Columbia campus.[8] Though many who arrived were not baptized, Lee's main objective was not to make new Christians. Lee was motivated, rather, by a need to provide a supportive community for the new immigrants. Koreans faced many challenges upon their arrival: from communicating in a new language, to learning new customs, to knowing what clothes to wear, to dealing with racist attitudes, to finding work in a society that did not recognize their expertise, to raising children in a new school system.[9] The church was one of the only places where Koreans could understand what was said, and be understood in return.[10] This sense of being understood had as much to do with shared experiences of migration as it had to do with language and cultural background. The fact that the church was an organization run by and for fellow Korean immigrants in the new land drew people in.

Lee's connection to the church back in Korea was strong. Not only was he married to the daughter of the man who was a founding professor of Hanguk Theological Seminary (formerly Joseon Theological Seminary), he was also a graduate of that seminary and former chaplain to students from the seminary and other universities. Prior to his graduate studies in Vancouver, Lee had worked as a campus leader organizing events and providing care for students in Seoul. Songsuk Chong and her husband James remember his ministry to them as university students. As we sat together in the basement of the building rented by Alpha Korean United Church (one of two congregations that once formed Toronto Korean United Church), they eagerly shared with me their positive memories of that time. Songsuk and James migrated to Canada in 1968. They had brought with them their relationship with Lee and the community connections and others from the PROK, including Canadian missionaries.[11] These kinds of connections were important in the seeding of new churches in Canada.

The influx of Korean immigrants to Canada was due to a major shift in Canadian immigration policy and a new immigration agreement between Canada and South Korea. In South Korea, a coup d'état in 1961 had brought to power an autocratic government with a strong agenda of economic development. In order to generate foreign capital, it had set out early in its rule to establish diplomatic relations with Canada and other countries that fought during the Korean War for the South under the United Nations flag. On 1 January 1963 Korean and Canadian embassies were established in their respective countries. The move corresponded with significant changes in Canadian immigration law. John Diefenbaker's government, in 1962, had begun to introduce legislation to eliminate racial prejudice from the immigration act. This was a response to pressure from Black immigration activists who leveraged the rapport with Diefenbaker that Black train porters had built up as they served him on his travels to and from his riding in Saskatchewan.[12] This initiative culminated in 1966 with the "points system" introduced by Lester Pearson's government, which was, on the surface at least, about erasing race as a factor from the immigrant selection process.[13] The government in Seoul headed by military-general-turned-President Park Chung Hee was eager to send Koreans abroad to earn foreign currency. It seized the opportunity presented by these changes to Canadian immigration policy and dispatched Trade Minister Jeon Taek-bo to work out an immigration agreement with the Canadian government. Jeon's assignment to this file may have had something to do with the fact that he had been a student in a UCC mission school and had known UCC missionaries in northeastern Korean and Manchuria prior to the war. Jeon successfully negotiated the Canadian-South Korean immigration agreement circa 1966[14] and was directly responsible for the first wave of Korean immigrants into Canada, many of them hand-picked from among the families Jeon had known through Christian circles connected to the UCC Korea Mission.[15]

The connection between the first Korean immigrants to Canada and the UCC Korea Mission was particularly apparent in Toronto at the church to which Sang Chul Lee was later called in 1969. This point was brought home to me in an interview with one of the earliest members of the Toronto congregation, Jeong Hak-pil. Jeong had come to Canada as a direct result of a personal connection with Jeon Taek-bo. Jeong had initially struggled hard to get his credentials recognized in Canada and had suffered underemployment for a number of years, an experience shared by many Asian immigrants like him.[16] Finally he landed a job at the University of Toronto under a man who was himself an immigrant from India and understood the situation Jeong was in as a racialized immigrant. As we sat down to talk over a Tim Hortons coffee, Jeong's eyes sparkled as he related with pride his roots in northern Korea. He explained to me that just about every member of the first Korean congregation in Toronto was from the northeastern provinces of Korea and across the border in Manchuria, the areas covered almost exclusively by Canadian missionaries from the UCC. Jeong had maintained a connection with North Korea, and through the 1970s, 1980s, and 1990s had returned there often to visit his hometown and family. This connection was important to him, and I got the impression that he relished the opportunity to challenge my White-Canadian assumptions about contemporary life and government in the North. For him, the connection with other Koreans from the northeast of the peninsula was an important aspect of life at TKUC.[17]

Jeong's feelings about the importance of the connection of TKUC with northeastern Korea were clearly shared by others. Richard Choe is another interviewee whose perspective, though different on account of his age and background, echoes Jeong's. Choe immigrated as a child and grew up in the Toronto congregation. Eventually he went on to be ordained in the UCC. He has had experience at all levels of church governance and, at the time of our interview, was serving a congregation north of Toronto. We met in a mall to conduct the interview. Choe was eager to share his experience with me and trusted me enough to share deeply personal feelings in the telling of his story. Indeed, vulnerability seemed to be a theme in his family's story of migration.

Choe was a youth when his family was forced to flee South Korea. His father had been a senior military officer under the Park regime and had fallen out with his superiors. He was not Christian, but he was well educated and originally from the northeast of Korea. It was this northeastern identity that drew him to TKUC. As in Vancouver, many non-Christians attended the Toronto church because it was a place to meet other Koreans; it was a community centre of all the new arrivals.[18] Likewise, a diversity of religious backgrounds characterized the congregation. But as later waves of South Koreans arrived in Toronto, a unifying identity marker of the TKUC congregation was that it continued to be a place where Koreans originally from North Korea and Manchuria felt at home. Koreans from the north shared an extra layer of experience with one another. They had all been internal refugees within South Korea following the war. And they were all easily distinguished from Koreans from the south of the peninsula by their accent.[19] In South Korea this meant they were often discriminated against. Korean refugees from the north also tended to share a political outlook distinct from that of their compatriots in South Korea, more open to socialist ideas despite having been displaced by communist rule. Those who found their way to TKUC were often well educated. The church was one of the only places where it was possible for them to engage in intellectual conversation about the world and politics. These were important facts that shaped the Toronto church community.[20]

When Moon Chai Rin and Kim Shin Mook (see chapter 1), arrived in Toronto in 1973, Moon said "it was like going to church in my hometown [in Kando]."[21] TKUC had strong ties to the communities in Myeongdong and Yongjeong. David Chung (Jeong Dae-ui), the son of the first Christian principal of the Myeongdong school, Jeong Byeong-tae (see chapter 1), served as TKUC's minister in 1968 before taking a job as professor of religion at Carlton University in Ottawa.[22] Sang Chul Lee, who would follow him, had been educated in the

Canadian run school in Yongjeong. Moon reported that many of the people at TKUC had come to Canada because of the connection to Canadian missionaries.[23] The connection of the congregation to the northeast of Korea and its status as a UCC congregation was fused and reinforced by a shared history of Canadian mission work.

TKUC, the first Korean church in Toronto, had been established in 1967, but quickly split into two congregations. The reasons for this split were complex, but Moon says that TKUC had a more "inter-denominational" approach while the splinter group was more committed to its Presbyterian roots.[24] The denominational affiliation had been debated by the first Koreans in Toronto from the moment the idea of a Korean church was discussed. Most of the early Korean Christian immigrants were from a Presbyterian church but not from the same Presbyterian denomination, PROK (Gijang) and PCK (Yejang) being two of many that existed in Korea by this time (see chapter 2). There was no equivalent of the UCC in Korea, however, although many from the PROK felt a connection to the UCC. Missionaries had tried to organize a single denomination for the Korean church in the early 1900s, but with no success. Koreans preferred to stick with the denominational diversity due in part to a sense of loyalty to the missionaries who worked with them and in part because a decentralized church was more effective in resisting the Japanese colonial government (see chapter 1).

As a Yongjeong native, Moon Chai Rin discovered when he arrived in Toronto that many of the UCC missionaries who had served in northeastern Korea and Manchuria were still alive and were serving the Korean immigrants in Canada.[25] The Rev. W.A. Burbidge, for example, who had worked for the UCC Korea Mission in northeastern Korea, had been active since his return to Canada supporting the few Korean immigrants living in Toronto and Hamilton. When the influx of Koreans arrived in 1966, the UCC Board of Home Missions responded quickly by forming the "Ad Hoc Committee to Consider Ministry to Korean Christians in Toronto and Hamilton Area," which included Burbidge and a few local Koreans.[26] A meeting of the wider Korean community was then called to discuss the beginning of a Korean congregation. Burbidge and Korean theology student Pak Jae-bong, who was in Toronto on a UCC scholarship at Emmanuel College, were assigned to lead the new church.[27] Its first worship service was held on 23 April 1967 in St Luke's United Church chapel. David Chung took over from Burbidge and Pak on 26 June 1968.[28] Following the departure of David Chung the congregation split and

TKUC reached out to Sang Chul Lee and asked him to come fill the position of minister hoping that he might bring some stability to their divided community.

The two Korean congregations and denominations quickly multiplied as more and more Koreans arrived in Canada. While there were eleven Korean congregations within the United Church by the 1980s, there were almost double that in the Presbyterian Church in Canada (PCC). Congregations that were officially related to neither UCC nor PCC numbered in the hundreds across Canada. Many of these, perhaps the majority, remained affiliated with denominations in Korea. The experience of the Korean church resembles that of the Taiwanese church whose first congregations also split numerous times due to internal and external pressures and different denominational allegiances.[29] Though the experiences of these various congregations would be diverse, the example of TKUC, the first Korean Congregation in Toronto and one that played a leadership role in both the UCC and wider Korean community, provides us with important insight into some of the foundational experiences of Korean Christians in the Canadian context.

THE PIONEER MAGAZINE – *SEONGUJA*

After four years of ministry in Vancouver, Sang Chul Lee accepted a call to serve the fledgling TKUC. TKUC at this time had started to rent the sanctuary of Bloor St United Church for their worship. Bloor St UC has a symbolic importance for the UCC as a whole. It was a church at the heart of the Church Union movement. Originally a Presbyterian congregation, its minister at the time, the Rev. George Pidgeon, was elected the first moderator of the newly minted UCC in 1925. In the same way, TKUC and its minister, Rev. Sang Chul Lee, would come to play an important historic and symbolic role in the UCC.

In his inaugural sermon on Sunday 3 August 1969 Lee opened with the recent news of the historic Apollo mission and Armstrong's first moonwalk. It was a new age, he told his parishioners, where new things were possible. What was needed was humility, courage, and hope to leave the old things behind, learn new things, and face the novel challenges that lay ahead.[30] He quickly introduced the congregation to his theological commitments. On the first Sunday of the very next month, he preached about the mission of the church, that it was not to extract people from society, but to permeate society with a sense of human empathy. Sometimes, he advised, this meant that the church needed to involve itself in politics and concern itself with economics. "As an immigrant church," he explained, "we have first-hand experience of certain social problems (racism, culture shock, conflict of values, family problems, problems of independence, and problems of participation in society) and as a church we are called to address them as part of our mission."[31]

Lee's approach went beyond words from the pulpit and included concrete acts of engagement with the wider UCC. It was not enough for him to be involved alone as the minister and leader of the congregation. In his mind, the congregation as a whole needed to take on that work. James and Songsuk Chong, to whom Lee had ministered as students in Korea, impressed upon me in our interview that the engagement of the congregation with the dominantly White church was something Lee felt very strongly about. One of the most compelling memories shared by Songsuk was of Sang Chul Lee approaching her one day to tell her that the regional church was looking for a representative to sit on the United Church Women (UCW) committee. Songsuk, who was unsure of her English and had had little interaction with members of the Anglo church, was reluctant. But Rev. Lee insisted! Likewise, James was tapped to serve as a representative to presbytery, a regional level of church government. Engagement with the White church was an important feature of their experience at TKUC. But the two also expressed great pride in how the congregation, under Lee's leadership, engaged the wider Korean community as well, listing a number of important Korean community organizations that had that had been started with leadership from the TKUC congregation. These included the Korean community choir, a seniors' organization called Samaritans, the Hope Broadcast (a Korean language program on the radio) and the Korean Business Association of Toronto.[32] These organizations were not meant as places where Koreans could withdraw from the dominant English society, but were platforms for asserting their place in the Canadian environment.

With this vision of the potential contribution of the Korean church to Canadian society and of the need for Koreans to engage with all levels of Canadian society, Lee set out to launch a monthly magazine to be published by the congregation touching on topics connected to immigrant life. He explained the reason for this move in his first editorial: "As we live life in this strange land, often experiencing loneliness, there is little that we are as grateful for as 'news.' In the midst of the problems of life we face day after day thinking of one another, the news we share is very precious. The reason is that this kind of news permits us to feel sympathy and encourages us to find a way to solve our problems together. Also from time to time the exchange of opposing opinions actually helps us to prosper."[33] Called *Seonguja*,[34] meaning "pioneer," the magazine ran for more than twenty years and offers a detailed glimpse into the experiences and thoughts of Canada's first Korean immigrants, touching on many aspects of their lives.

For Lee the idea for the title of the magazine may have been connected to his experience growing up in Siberia and Manchuria. Korean families had been pioneers there in much the same way early European migrants to Canada had been. Lee may have chosen this title to connect Korean experiences in Canada to iconic North American settlers and thus to help them to locate themselves within Canadian history in this way.[35] "The pioneers of any nation or group to the next generations are always much respected and the 'details of their lives' are collected as a model of all future generations," he explained, perhaps holding both the Manchurian and Canadian experiences in mind at the same time.[36] Explicitly, Lee focused on the importance for Korean immigrants to think of future generations, a consideration which constitutes "the character of a great pioneer." Koreans, he felt, should embrace the new land as their home and "lay a prudent and foundational life" for the generations to come.[37] For Lee, Canada was not a place where Koreans would simply sojourn and then return to the motherland, but a new home where they would have to break ground and sow their own future.

Most of the contributions for the magazine were solicited from members of the TKUC congregation. Sometimes material came from outside the Korean community, from UCC church leaders, government officials or experts on a given topic. This material was always translated into Korean. While the magazine had a readership beyond the congregation, beyond the province and even beyond the Christian community, it is unlikely that anyone outside the Korean community would have been able to read its contents, save the returned missionaries. This created a special space for Koreans to voice opinions, experiences, and thoughts that they may not have felt comfortable sharing with others. The magazine gives evidence of a strong critique of Canadian society, but there is little evidence to suggest that that critique was presented outside the Korean community in the same form and tone. However, there is clear evidence that leaders in the

Korean Christian community were finding other ways to raise their concerns with the Canadian church as they struggled to find a place for themselves and their congregants within its organization and culture. *Seonguja* was a place where those concerns could be aired and worked out among Koreans.

In the words of one of the magazine's first contributors, the job before the Korean community in Canada was akin to making "the dry land a land of plenty."[38] For all the opportunities that the new life in Canada offered them, there were certainly challenges. One theme that ran through the pages of *Seonguja* was the issue of racism. The second addition of *Seonguja* was dedicated to "Seeking a Korean-Canadian Identity" and tackled the problem of racism head on. Sang Chul Lee opened the issue by contrasting "melting pot" and "mosaic" approaches to immigrants taken by the USA and Canada respectively. "Sometimes there are assumptions in America that the descendants of the minority groups need to be 150% American," and that this would result in "ethnic minorities losing their identity and becoming marginal." On the other hand, the "Mosaic Society" idea was more positive, but more difficult. "It is not easy for one community to have many different peoples clearly asserting themselves," he said. The danger was that "it becomes a 'vertical mosaic' with some pieces affixed to the bottom and some to the top," he explained, referring to sociologist John Porter's seminal 1965 work that revealed the reality of racism below the veneer of the Canadian mosaic ideology.[39] "So we have to find our Korean identity within this land," Lee urged.[40]

In support of this idea, Lee solicited the contribution of a former UCC missionary, W.A. Burbidge. Burbidge encouraged his Korean audience by telling them he believed they had much to contribute to Canada and to Christianity in Canada by virtue of the unique cultural roots that shaped their culture and their faith.[41] He told them that their presence in Canada was not only good for them but good for Canada, too. But he warned, "In Canada you will have to overcome ethnic discrimination, nationalism, alcoholism and drug addiction, poverty and these may seem like giants to face. But I believe we can overcome them with our courage. Especially you need to contribute to the elimination of ethnic discrimination."[42]

Seonguja sought input from the Japanese community, too. The Japanese congregations had a longer history in Canada than the Koreans, but also one that was fraught with tensions. Japanese immigration to British Columbia had started in the early 1900s. A minister named Hwan Jim-mu[43] told of the influence of the Black community in shaping the Japanese-Canadian approach to racial discrimination. "It cannot be kept a secret that over the past number of years the white [*sic*] race has been forcing its culture on coloured races," he wrote, "White people always think that if you live in North America you must adapt to white [*sic*] ways for things to go well with you" and he pointed to the assumption in the White church that "Christianity is White culture and that anyone who wants to become Christian needs to adopt that culture." But he countered, prophetically, that if Japanese and Korean people could understand their culture correctly it would be a benefit, not only for them, but for North American society as well.[44]

Many who wrote for *Seonguja* found that racism was a reality that they could not avoid. It could make finding a job very difficult and negatively impact their self-confidence.[45] Some of them applied their considerable education and understanding of the historical context to analyze the situation. The most biting criticism of Canadian society came from two members of TKUC who attended a Heritage Ontario event called "Unity through Diversity" that took place in the Skyline Hotel between 2 and 4 June 1972.[46] Pak Eun-myeong reported that organizers of the event seemed to feel that since the British (and French) had come before other immigrants, they deserved a privileged place at the Unity through Diversity conference and in Canadian society generally. Faced with criticism about their presumed privilege, he noticed, these same people protested that they were just ordinary Canadians, the same as others, and disliked being labelled Anglo Saxon or WASP. "I don't know if the British people's claim to be the same was sincere," wrote Park sarcastically.[47]

Another TKUC member who attended the event was very critical of the Canadian Government's Multiculturalism Policy.[48] Jeon Jung-lim complained that the policy's vagueness benefitted the ruling class. "We can't forget how the indigenous people have suffered from the English colony," he cautioned; "English colonial rule was skillful. We have to acknowledge that in addition to economics and trade and military force and medicine they even used religion, specifically the Christian religion in their invasion policy. What they did is the same as the Japanese did to us. Their international policy is to separate tribe and nations from one another. Look at India that was under their rule for 400 years and now has been divided into three pieces with the shedding of much blood."[49] Jeon pointed out that minority communities were not the beneficiaries of the "enlightened" policies of the colonial state such as multiculturalism, but rather that they had earned their rights through political organizing. He offered as an example Quebec's achievement of language rights. Jeon urged solidarity among minority groups as a way of avoiding "the furnace" of the North American melting pot.[50]

While Pak and Jeon were venting their anger at the perceived hypocrisy of the Heritage Ontario event, nationally the UCC was taking initial steps in addressing global racism through a World Council of Churches (WCC) initiative called "The Program to Combat Racism." The stated goals of this initiative were to confront racism anywhere in the world. However, the issue as the UCC understood it was particularly framed by the anti-apartheid struggle in South Africa. Consequently, the focus tended to be directed outward, to the problems of other nations. A sign of this was the fact that the UCC's Division of World Outreach (DWO) was most involved in rolling out this program. The DWO was the branch of the UCC bureaucracy with oversight of missionaries and relations with overseas churches, meaning that domestic aspects of the church were little affected by the anti-racism initiative.[51] A timeline of UCC anti-racism initiatives published in 2021 reveals that most of what was considered "anti-racism" work of the church in in the 1950s through the 1970s consisted of the organization of different ethnic groups to preserve and promote their culture within the UCC.

In the 1960s the UCC officially acknowledged that the destruction of Africville in Nova Scotia was an example of racism, in 1974 it elected its first (and to date only) Black moderator and in 1977 began to review its relationship with Indigenous people. But serious recognition of systematic racism within its own institution did not begin to occur until 1985 when, at the November executive meeting of the General Council, Alberta Billy of the Native Ministries Council demanded that the church apologize to Indigenous peoples for its role in colonization. Even then, the evidence suggests that work in this area did not pick up until 2000 when the 36th General Council voted to implement an anti-racism policy entitled "That All May Be One."[52]

In the 1970s, there were, however, programs for UCC members to learn about racism. One of these was attended by TKUC member, Jo Seong-ju. This was a conference called "Multicultural Society and Racial Problems" offered by the Educational Committee of the UCC at the Cedar Glen Retreat Centre located to the north of Toronto

Table 7.1

Anti-racism and racial justice work in the United Church of Canada, 1943 to 1998: a snapshot

1943	The United Church's first National Japanese United Church Conference (Kyogikai) is held in New Denver, bc. Kyogikai later focuses on promoting fellowship and publishing and distributing culturally specific materials for Japanese United churches.
1960, 1964	The United Church acknowledges racism as a sin in response to the removal of members of the Black community and the destruction of the Africville neighbourhood in Halifax, ns.
1970	The Association of Chinese United Church Congregations is first convened formally in Vancouver. This group later focuses on sharing experiences as well as developing culturally specific prayers and liturgical resources.
1974	The 26th General Council elects the Very Rev. Dr Wilbur K. Howard as moderator, and he serves from 1974 to 1977. He is the first – and to date the only – Black person to serve in this role.
1977	The 27th General Council decides to review the United Church's work with Indigenous people.
1978	The first gathering of Korean Canadian congregations of the United Church takes place in Vancouver. The Korean Association of The United Church of Canada later focuses on sharing its Korean heritage with the younger generations, translating Christian educational resources from English into Korean, and supporting local ministries among the Korean United Church congregations in Canada.
1980	The first National Aboriginal Consultations are held (in June and October) and others follow every one to three years. The last one is held in July 2005.
1982	The Euro-Caribbean Group of United Churches is formed. In 1990, Taiwanese members join the group, and the diverse group is renamed the Coalition. The Coalition sought to maintain and nurture its members' heritages, and to provide a sense of belonging for ethnic minority congregations who felt isolated in their ethno-cultural identities in the church.
1984	The Dr Jessie Saulteaux Centre for Indigenous ministry training (a centre designed to train Indigenous ministers in a way that respects Indigenous spirituality) is formed.
1985	At the November meeting of the Executive of the General Council, Alberta Billy of the Native Ministries Council demands that the church apologize to Indigenous peoples for its role in colonization.
1986	The 31st General Council offers an Apology to Indigenous peoples for the church's role in colonization.

Table 7.1 (*Continued*)

1987	The Francis Sandy Centre for Indigenous ministry training is formed.
	The Division of Mission in Canada issues the worship and learning resource Moving Beyond Racism.
1988	The 32nd General Council elects the Very Rev. Sang Chul Lee as moderator, and he serves from 1988 to 1990. A Korean Canadian, he is the first – and to date the only – person of Asian descent to serve in this role.
	All Native Circle Conference is founded. At the 32nd General Council, it acknowledges the Apology, expressing its hope that the church will live into its words.
1992	The 34th General Council elects the Very Rev. Dr Stan McKay as moderator, and he serves from 1992 to 1994. He is the first – and to date the only – Indigenous person to serve in this role.
	General Council acknowledges the need for anti-racist initiatives, and calls for anti-racism resource materials for worship and education.
1993	The first Sounding the Bamboo conference is held for self-identified women who are Black, Indigenous, or people of colour. It focuses on the intersections of racism and sexism, and continues once every few years until the mid–2000s.
	The United Church of Canada makes a submission to the Royal Commission on Aboriginal Peoples.
1994	The United Church of Canada's Filipino Association is established. It plays a key role in welcoming new Filipino families to Canada, assisting newcomers to find new church homes, sharing mutual concerns, and supporting and encouraging Filipino people who feel isolated in the church.
	The United Church of Canada's Healing Fund (a fund created as a response to the needs of residential school survivors) is established.
1996	The Ethnic Ministries Council is officially inaugurated in June. Its work focuses on supporting ethno-cultural congregations and diverse racialized and language minority communities of faith.
1997	The first racial-ethnic minority youth conference is held concurrently with the inauguration of the Ethnic Ministries Council. Later, in 2009, a Consultation for Racialized Youth is held to gather recommendations for the church from youth who are Black, Indigenous, and people of colour.
	Twenty-seven former Alberni Indian Residential School students launch the "Blackwater" lawsuit against the United Church and Government of Canada, seeking compensation and damages for abuses committed by Arthur Plint, a dormitory supervisor. This is the first in thousands of claims that will lead to the Indian Residential Schools Settlement Agreement.

194   Water from Dragon's Well

Table 7.1 (*Continued*)

1997	St Andrew's United Church makes an apology to former students of Alberni Indian Residential School in May.
	The 36th General Council makes a Statement of Repentance regarding residential schools in August.
1998	The United Church offers an apology to former students of United Church-run residential schools, their families, and communities in October.
	The Executive of General Council establishes the Residential Schools Steering Committee and a dedicated staff position.
	The Ethnic Ministries Council conducts a United Church print media survey to identify areas of racial bias in images and words, and suggest solutions.

Source: 43rd General Council, Special Meeting, 24 October 2020.

from 25–26 August 1972.[53] If Jo's report in *Seonguja* about the event is anything to go by, however, there was little by way of real analysis of racism presented to participants. His report from the event was lacking in critical insight and included such advice as "individually we [Koreans] need to do our best to shine so that others form a positive impression of the 'Korean image'" and "we have to raise our kids well."[54] These were clearly not lessons that challenged the structural whiteness of the UCC or Canadian society. Rather, Jo's take away from the event was that it was best for Koreans to try to make a good impression so as to avoid drawing negative attention.

Notwithstanding the inadequacy of this approach which placed responsibility for the elimination of racism on the shoulders of immigrants, some in the Korean community embraced their own agency as individuals and as a minority group to promote a multicultural society by avoiding the temptation to retreat into a cultural ghetto. Ok Yeong-ju, for example, exhorted her community not to be discouraged because their skin colour is different. "US, Canada, Australia and even the UK are mixed nations," she said, and "whether we like it or not we have a heavy responsibility to develop this society." She even voiced disappointment that the Korean language newspaper was promoting the need to build a Korea Town in Toronto. "In a mixed society do we want to carve out an exclusively Korean space?" she asked.[55] Her minister, Sang Chul Lee, was unequivocal, "If we are not going to resign ourselves to life of simply eating and making money then we have to, as a people of one culture and tradition, find a way to make human connections with people of other cultures and also take an interest in this country's culture and social policies."[56]

Lee did not minimize the responsibility of White Canadians and UCC members for racial prejudices and policies. He and his family had had to face their fair share of racism.[57] But he did want to instill a sense of agency and responsibility in his flock. Lee and other Korean church leaders in Canada did their best to lead by example. Lee's approach contributed to the special ethos of the TKUC congregation and underscores the fact that Korean Christians within the UCC were making intentional efforts to engage with and shape UCC culture and politics. Their experiences engaging the UCC on Canadian soil are enlightening and speak to their determination and resilience in the face of intransigent colonial attitudes in UCC church pews and governing structures. Below, we turn our attention to three Korean church leaders and their experience working with and within UCC structures.

THREE KOREAN CHURCH LEADERS IN THE UCC:

SANG CHUL LEE

Sang Chul Lee came to play one of the most important roles of any leader in the UCC Korean community. Lee's earliest opportunity to work within the national UCC structure came in 1972, when he was asked to serve on the executive of the DWO, the unit in the UCC polity entrusted with, among other things, the deployment and oversight of missionaries outside Canada. The invitation was likely due in large part to critical developments regarding the UCC Korea Mission and political events in Korea (see chapters 3 through 6), events which were drawing UCC missionaries into the South Korean Democratization Movement. Lee had maintained many personal connections with Korean church leaders in the PROK who were taking an active role in the opposition to the Park dictatorship. As minister of TKUC, Lee was genuinely concerned about these developments and had kept them in front of his congregation despite objections from some members who voiced discomfort with their minister's mix of religion and politics.

Lee made sure that TKUC served as an important source of news about home for his congregants and offered a means for the expat community to comment on developments.[58] Throughout the 1970s and 1980s, TKUC members and leadership were kept engaged in the Democratization Movement in South Korea and participated in actions against the South Korean government and in support of activists. On 20 July 1974, in protest against the executions of eight men falsely accused by the KCIA of organizing a communist plot to overthrow the South Korean government (the PRP incident discussed in chapter 6), a number of members from the TKUC congregation went to Ottawa to protest in front of the South Korean Embassy.[59] Members were involved in protests in Toronto at various important moments such as in the aftermath of the March 1 Declaration for National Salvation in 1976 (see chapter 6) and the Kwangju Massacre (see chapter 8).[60] TKUC brought prominent leaders in the South Korean movement to Toronto and hosted speaking engagements for them. Ham Seok-heon, Yi Mun-yeong, Suh Nam Dong, Yi Hae-dong, Moon Dong Hwan, Lee Oo Chung, and Han Wan-sang were among those who spoke at the congregation.[61] Kim Dae Jung (who eventually became the president of South Korea in 1998) was also invited but was prevented by the South Korean government from travelling to Canada. Sang Chul Lee's father-in-law, Kim Chai Choon, fled Korea and moved to Toronto where he became a member of TKUC. Sang Chul Lee was able to go back and forth between Canada and Korea frequently and served as a bridge of information. This practice and the connections sustained with the Democratization Movement helped his congregants to feel a part of what was happening.[62]

In 1975, the DWO had tapped Lee and Kim Chai Choon to represent the UCC at a secret consultation hosted by the WCC. This consultation sought to explore ways that the global ecumenical organization could support Christian activists and turned out to be pivotal in the struggle for democracy and human rights in South Korea.[63] This role earned Lee respect in UCC circles and in that same year his contribution to the UCC was recognized by his election to President of Toronto Conference, an important regional governing body within the national UCC structure. In 1988, largely on the strength of these credentials, Lee would be elected moderator for the national church. Lee's leadership was tested as moderator. He had to provide spiritual guidance as the UCC experienced inner conflict and outside criticism for its decision to permit the ordination of gay and lesbian ministers. This was a controversial decision by the 1988 General Council that created great tension in the UCC, not least of all in its Korean congregations. Some complained that it was another example of White Christians forcing their own values on others. Korean criticism was often also motivated with a desire to maintain standing among peer ethnic congregations outside the UCC.[64] Lee proved himself equal to the task. Indigenous congregations of the UCC, who were also positively affected by his ministry recognized his accomplishments by honouring him with the title of "rainbow chief."[65]

From the beginning of his time in Canada, Lee was attuned to issues of cultural and national identity. His experience as minister at the Steveston United Church congregation in British Columbia drove home lessons he had learned growing up in Manchuria about the importance of culture and language.[66] The experience of working with both Japanese and Korean migrant communities instilled in him a deep appreciation for Canada's policy of bilingualism, and beyond that for the place of all language traditions practiced on Canadian soil, from indigenous languages to those of the newest immigrants. "When Prime Minister Trudeau first introduced multiculturalism as an official government policy," wrote Lee, "I thought I could teach him a lot about the subject."[67] Lee's interest in language rights highlights two significant failings of the Canadian church with which the UCC was just starting to come to terms in in the 1970s and 1980s, its marginalization of its French minority and its history of residential schools. From Church Union in 1925, francophone members of the United Church had been largely forgotten, their congregations ignored and their educational institutions left without support.[68] In the same way, the history of residential schools implicated the UCC in a project of cultural genocide, the erasure of Indigenous culture and language.[69] With the influx of ethnic minorities following the liberalization of immigration laws in the 1960s, the accommodation of language was one area in which the UCC was especially pressed. Its inability to embrace different linguistic traditions speaks to the Protestant nationalist vision of its Anglo founders. Lee worked to explain why this was a serious problem for the church.

Lee's early experiences with Canadian congregations and their attitudes towards overseas mission work had disturbed him as well. As a student in British Columbia in the 1960s, Lee had found that UCC congregations saw him as little as more than a poster boy for their Missionary Enterprise, using him to raise money for the cause. Requests by local churches to have him come and speak left him in a "very awkward position." Though Lee genuinely appreciated the positive things missionaries had done for Korea and for himself personally, he was not about to "sing their praises without qualification."[70] The sense that his culture was not being properly valued bothered him as did the assumption by Canadians that Koreans were little more than empty vessels into which they could pour their Western religion and values. As moderator from 1988 to 1990, Lee was still trying to explain to White UCC members why this was not a helpful way to look at things.

In a sermon entitled "Witnesses to the Gospel to the Ends of the Earth," Lee informed his Korean congregation that they had something to share when it came to their faith: "We are minorities who have come to North America. We are living in the land of the first people who brought us the gospel. Thanks to these people spreading the gospel we are Christian. When we moved here, we brought our faith … We have developed a Koreanized Christianity which we now reexport. This reexported Christianity and the local Christianity do not have to be the same or relate to one another without friction. In fact, sometimes they seem to be in collision."[71] Part of what Lee saw as the strength of Korean Christianity was its experience as a minority faith, rather than a religious norm with a privileged place guaranteed by society. At the 17th Annual Meeting of the Association of Korean Christian Scholars in North America in 1983, he presented a paper called "Unique Roles of the Korean Ethnic Church for the North American Host Church." "Christianity in Korea was originally introduced by Americans and Canadians," he said, "but as the Korean Christian community moved into America and Canada, there began a movement of reverse missionary work" based on their own experiences and insights as Christians. Korean Christians, "have learnt how to survive as a minority. They have also learnt how to become a creative minority." The church in Korea, after all had always been a minority religion. This had not stopped it from having a vibrant life or from making a contribution to Korean society. What's more, the Minjung theology, which was at this time gaining fame around the world (see chapter 5), was explaining how the Christian identity itself was malleable and, that in the present era, it could no longer profess to hold an exclusive view of religion or monopoly on salvation. These were things, Lee said, that the post-Christendom church in America and Canada now had to learn how to do.[72] This determination underscores the role Lee undertook for himself and others in the Korean Christian community, the role of missionaries to the Canadian Church bringing the Gospel of a new approach to the Christian faith, one that had loosed its bonds to colonial ways of thinking.

Lee did his best to raise a new generation of Korean leaders at TKUC. There were many young Koreans who were drawn to the congregation for various reasons. Some of them had come to church with their families where they found a special home among Koreans from the northern part of Korea and a springboard for activities in the broader Canadian society.[73] Others were grateful to find a comfortable ethnic niche from which to continue to serve the Korean church within Canadian society and even to participate in the struggles of Korean democratization from outside of Korea. Unique among these young people was a young man who, like Lee himself, had been a refugee twice in his life. Also like Lee, he was both animated by the ethos of the UCC and determined to change it. We turn now to his story.

DONG-CHUN SEO

Dong-Chun Seo (Seo Dong-cheon) has had a long career in the UCC. Ordained in 1987, he went on to serve congregations in Alberta and Ontario. At the time of our interview (2018), he was in his thirty-first year of ministry, serving a congregation in Toronto. Even before he was ordained, Seo had served the TKUC congregation and the wider UCC church with energy and determination. As we sat down together, he smiled readily and our conversation stretched on for close to two hours. Not only did Seo have information to share about events in the past, he had insights to share from time spent thinking deeply about the things he learned and experienced in the UCC. He was particularly interested in the place of "ethnic" groups and people within the Anglo-dominant institution.

Seo was born in northeastern Korea just prior to the Korean war. His grandfather had worked with the Canadian Presbyterian missionaries (before the creation of the UCC) in North Hamkyeong Province, the most north easterly province of Korea, before moving to Manchuria to escape Japanese rule. His father studied for the ministry in Pyeongyang and then moved his family back to North Hamkyeong Province, where they were when the Korean war broke out. Seo's family was one of the lucky families who found a place on American boats leaving the Heungnam port in a famous escape celebrated in South Korean stories of the war, but which also ended with the tragic abandonment and death of many. Growing up in South Korea, Lee attended Yonsei University and as a university student union leader was involved in demonstrations against the Park Chung Hee government and its implementation of the Yushin Constitution in 1972. On one particular day the authorities surrounded the campus, rounded up the student protestors, and took them away to the police station. Marked as a political troublemaker from that day on, Seo was dogged by plainclothes KCIA agents who, disguised as students, attended all his classes and harassed him at every turn, making it hard to work, study, or carry on a regular student life. By this time Seo's older brother and sister had moved to Canada and they invited Seo to come and join them. It was the only way Seo could escape the police harassment, so he accepted and moved to Toronto.[74]

Seo's brother was a member of the Korean Presbyterian Church that had broken away from the original TKUC congregation, but his sister was attending TKUC. Seo attended both. By this time, he was feeling the call to enter the ministry and was torn between whether to align himself with his brother's church or his sister's. One day he came across a book about the history of the United Church which tipped the scales in the UCC's favour. There was something about the national vision of the UCC that appealed to him, that it was a church created to fit the unique Canadian context. In his conversation with me he explained that he liked the UCC's "policy, direction and ethos," that it was "a new expression of faith for a new world." It was not easy to tell his brother who was looking for his help in the Presbyterian church or to break his family's Presbyterian tradition, but he did find support in TKUC for his goal to become a UCC minister. He began working for the church in 1974 and was eventually ordained into the ministry in 1987 after which he served both predominantly White and Korean churches in the Greater Toronto Area and Edmonton.[75]

Because of his leadership role in the congregation and vision for the UCC, Seo was asked to help lead a denominational study looking into the relationship between Anglo and non-Anglo congregations. Seo and a colleague from an Italian congregation interviewed members from the fifty or so "ethnic congregations"[76] in the UCC. Generally, immigrants from different countries who sought a home within the UCC did so as part of congregations that retained the use of their own languages and cultures in worship. While this created cultural enclaves within the UCC where people were free to worship and relate in ways that were familiar to them, it meant that a sense of distance was created between many immigrants and the dominant Anglo congregations of the UCC. But it was more than the choice of these different cultures to worship separately that was preventing a healthy interaction with Anglo-Christians. "When I interviewed the ethnic congregations in the 1970s ... what I discovered," said Seo, "was that ... [these] Congregations wanted to be part of the power structure and leadership opportunity [of the UCC]. But most Caucasian congregations were content to say, 'You do your own thing.'"[77] In the report he wrote for the UCC, Seo noted that the relationship between ethnic congregations within the UCC and its White congregations was "too superficial" to promote mutual understanding and that ethnic peoples "have more frequent and 'normal' relationship with their own people, and even other ethnic peoples, than with [White] Canadians."[78] In his opinion, too little was being done to overcome cultural barriers and bring people together in community.

Seo also noticed that Christian immigrants were not drawn to the UCC as a denominational home because there was no equivalent in their countries. Most ended up in other denominations. For those who did end up as part of the UCC, it took a lot of effort and time to try to educate them in the UCC ethos, which was different in its polity and theology than either Presbyterian or Methodist churches. The more "inclusive" reputation of the UCC on matters of theology and sexual diversity did not mean that it was necessarily more open or inclusive when it came to issues like race and ethnicity. After all, on the agenda of the UCC at its creation had been the assimilation of non-Anglo-Protestants into "civilized" Canadian society.[79] Seo noticed that there was no strategy on the part of the UCC for promoting the contribution of ethnic congregations to the leadership of the church and few resources were dedicated to ethnic congregations to encourage their participation. As a result, he observed, there was a serious deficit of trust. In Seo's judgement this was due in large part to the absence of any church structure to accommodate ethnic churches. "Maybe discrimination was [also] a factor," he confided. Seo's report called on the UCC to "share your power and share your leadership" and urged the White churches to "be involved with ethnic congregations 7 days a week." But he finds that even in the twenty-first century ethnic congregations still cry out for recognition within UCC structures.[80]

While Seo spent a lot of time and effort at the national and regional level of church government, valuable leadership was also being offered at the local level. Through the 1970s more and more Koreans were following Sang Chul Lee's lead and offering themselves as leaders in Anglo-congregations. They faced considerable obstacles to their leadership and had to work hard to carve out a place for themselves. In the process, they discovered they had unique and valuable gifts to offer members of the Anglo-community who were open to them. One of these Korean leaders, and the first female Korean minister of the UCC, will be the subject of our next section.

KAY CHO

For my interview with Kay Cho (Cho Kyong Ja) we met in her home in the community of Richmond Hill. The day saw one of the first snowfalls of the winter. We sat in her cozy living room looking out big windows at the large flakes of snow coming down. She served tea and we talked about people we knew in common before starting in on the interview. The contrast of the cold outdoors and the warm living room of Cho's house, upon reflection, mirrored the contrasting experiences of rejection and welcome that Cho was about to share with me.

We began the interview by talking about her origins and about her first encounters with Canadian missionaries. Cho was born in northwestern Korea near the Yalu River bridge on the border with Manchuria. Two years ahead of the Korean War her family crossed over to the south. As a young woman, she entered Ewha Women's University in Seoul, where she met her first missionaries, including two female UCC missionaries, Dorothy Hurd and Elda Struthers. These women were an important influence in her life and she credits them for giving her a broader vision of the world beyond Korea.[81] Years later, the recollection of their ability to move into and serve the Korean community encouraged Cho to believe she could do the same in Canada.[82] After graduating from university she was granted a World Council of Churches scholarship to study in San Francisco. Following two years of study, she returned to Korea with a Master's degree in theology.[83] After marriage, her husband was urged by his family to move to Canada. His sister had immigrated as a nurse and had brought her mother over to help when she had a baby. To leave Korea at that time was a big sacrifice for Cho. She had a good job as a chaplain at a hospital and lots of good friends and colleagues. But she was also pregnant and so consoled herself with the thought that at least she would have a baby to keep her busy in her new home. Not long after her arrival in Burlington, Ontario in 1971, her baby was delivered, but tragically died soon afterwards. It was an experience of deep grief and isolation for Cho who had no one outside of her family to reach out to for comfort or support.[84]

As a way of recovering from her grief Cho tried to find work to keep her mind busy. She took some typing and stenography courses and worked as a secretary. She eventually found a job at McMaster University and later at Scarborough College when her family moved to Toronto. But secretarial work was not something that demanded enough of her gifts and so she started to think about church leadership. By this time, she was attending a United Church congregation that happened to be near her house. Her choice of congregations reflects the fact that denominational identity was not strong for many Korean immigrants. For Dong-Chun Seo, the choice to attend a UCC congregation has been partly a matter of principle and partly due to the connection he had through his sister. But for others, it was often simply a question of which church was closest. Cho's example also offers a glimpse of the experience of those immigrants who chose to attend a non-immigrant church and relate to Anglo-Canadian congregations. Information about how many Koreans became part of the UCC in this way is unavailable but Cho's experience raises questions about how common this was and what the experience was like.

Cho would also visit TKUC on occasion and had the opportunity to meet with former UCC missionary Elda Struthers who had taught her at Ewha University and was now living in Toronto. Cho inquired about ways she could work for the church and began the process to become a minister. "There were so many requirements," she remembered, "although I had already received a lot of education [in Korea and San Francisco.]" She was sent to the Centre for Christians Studies and then to Emmanuel College. Finally, she was commissioned as a diaconal minister in 1979 and then ordained in 1984, the first Korean woman to serve in these roles in the UCC.[85]

For Cho, her unique accomplishment was "only a matter of survival," a way to cling to life in a "cold wilderness." It was about finding a purpose for herself in a place where she often felt "bewildered." If the road towards leadership in the White UCC had seemed daunting at first, she had been given some hope in 1974 when the UCC elected its first non-White moderator, Wilbur Howard, a Black man from Ottawa. "I thought, this is interesting," she recalls, and came to the conclusion that "this church is really open to everybody." But it wasn't going to be so easy and the reality of racism that she quickly encountered in the process was disillusioning. During a regional meeting of congregations, complaints were made about the three Koreans (including herself) that were seeking ordination under their supervision. "What do we do with these people?" someone asked referring to the Koreans.

"Congregations won't accept them [as their ministers once they are ordained.]"[86] It seems that White congregations were willing to allow Koreans to enter the process towards being ordained, but when it came to actually ordaining them, few could imagine that another congregation would be willing to accept them as their minister.

Cho's early experiences of work within the UCC were also a tremendous challenge. It was a very "cold" work environment. "You can't imagine how hard I had to work to prove myself," she said. There were no Asians in the congregations she served. On one occasion a couple refused to be married by her.[87] At the time, she remembers, racism was a fearful word and people were very reluctant to talk about it.[88] Cho must have struggled not to be discouraged in the face of these challenges. It seems that, despite years of relationship with the church in Korea through the missionary movement, congregations were just not equipped to work with or appreciate the gifts of ministry coming from that country.

Cho's challenges came from being female as well as from being Korean. Women seeking to lead churches in Korea were also facing challenges but making progress at this time. The first women elders ordained were ordained in the PROK soon after the denomination formed, in 1957.[89] The first female minister of the PROK, Yang Jeong-shin was ordained in 1973. The PROK was one of the first churches to ordain women, but women faced steep challenges in both church and society when it came to asserting their leadership. The conservative nature, already inherent within the Christian religion, tended to be reinforced by both neo-Confucian notions of gender and the gendered exploitation of women by Park Chung Hee's militarized state. Strong prejudice against women being ministers accompanied Korean immigrants as well as those from other colonized nations when they immigrated to Canada. Cho said that her experiences of racism were often indirect, but sexism could be overt and pointed. "Sexism is cruel," she said, "You wouldn't believe." Her own experience of sexism speaks to the kinds of challenges Anglo UCC members reported having in connecting to Korea Christians (see chapter 8). Gender dynamics were often a painful wedge that inserted themselves between people in the UCC and created problems for intercultural relationships.

Cho's experience also highlights the divisions that were sometimes felt within and between the ethnic ministry congregations and leaders in the UCC. In 1994, Cho was a member of a committee that reported to the General Council of the UCC and recommended the creation of an Ethnic Ministry Council which would have real power to address the needs of non-Anglo and non-White congregations in the UCC.[90] The theological preamble to the report included a reference to Minjung theology. Some observers worried, however, that the use of an Asian theology signaled the dominance of Asians within the new council and feared that less prominent ethnic communities would not be well represented.[91] But recognition of the distinct experience of Asian members was an essential factor in creating a safe environment. Michael Blair (see chapter 8) indicated that, in fact, the end of the EMC disproportionately impacted non-English speaking members such as Koreans and other East Asian communities who no longer had the language support which the EMC had provided within the UCC.[92] The balance was a delicate one.

Despite formidable barriers of racism and sexism, Cho persevered. A later congregation seemed to be more ready to embrace her and she was determined to share what she could of herself, including her Koreanness. Cho discovered congregation members in need of her special cultural resources. On one occasion, for example, a grieving widow came to see her, anxious and distraught that her family had been unable to find ways to share their grief or heal from the loss of her husband. Cho told her of the Korean practice of jesa (see chapter 1).[93] This was the annual gathering of a family to mark the death of a loved one and share a meal in their honour. Ironically, jesa had been banned by missionaries in Korea because of its association with ancestral spirits. But the woman found the suggestion helpful and later reported that she had tried it and that the family had greatly benefitted from it.[94]

Eventually Cho made connections with other racialized women in church leadership. One of these was Dr Wenh In Ng, a professor at Emmanuel College in Toronto. Together they came up with the idea of a gathering exclusively for racialized women in the UCC. It was the first of its kind and faced some opposition from White women, even missionaries, who felt they should be able to attend as well. But Cho and Ng were adamant. Racialized women needed their own space, they argued. It was a controversial stance, but both felt that racialized women had experiences that could only be safely shared with others who shared those same experiences. White people, even women, even missionary women, were likely to misunderstand. They tended to dominate conversations and to object to certain discussions about White privilege or prejudice. In addition, racialized women tended to be less vocal and needed more encouragement to speak out. The program was a great success and ran for almost twenty years starting in the early 1990s, the last one held in 2010. Its discontinuation was a source of pain for Cho.[95]

CONCLUSION

Starting in 1965 the relative influence that Koreans and Canadians had on one another and their respective nations shifted dramatically. Instead of Canadian missionaries travelling to Korea to convert new Christians and build new institutions, suddenly it was Koreans by the thousands who immigrated to Canada, established congregations, challenging UCC norms and transforming Canadian society and religion from within. Leaders of the Korean church such as Sang Chul Lee thought of this shift in terms of a reversal of the mission relationship. They were conscious of the fact that the Korean church and Korean Christians had something important to contribute to their new home and nation.

Koreans understood their new life in Canada in terms of pioneering efforts to break a path for the next generation. They knew their work would not be easy. Learning a new language and finding work in a society that did not recognize their credentials or experience was a challenge, as were the long hours of hard labour many had to endure to make a living. But confronting racism was a particularly difficult row to hoe and Korean Christians found they had to do this heart wrenching work within the UCC as much as any other place. As pioneers, part of what motivated them was the conviction that their faith was calling them to make a contribution to their society and not just to seek personal salvation in the life to come. In this sense, the mission of Korean Christians within the UCC continued in the tradition of the first Korean Christians who understood their faith as a vehicle to transform the political structure and address the injustices of colonialism in Korea.

The stories that Koreans told about their lives in Canada and the UCC not only challenged stories that White Anglo members of the Canadian church were telling themselves in the 1970s and 1980s, today they also reframe a historiography which has not adequately accounted for the influence of the non-Western Christianity on mainline Canadian Protestantism. The experiences of Korean Christians in Canada highlight the postcolonial realities and implications of migration, racism, and hybridity. Historical data discussed and interpreted from the Toronto Korean United Church and Korean Christian leadership within the UCC reveal that UCC policy and culture was slow to respond to these realities, a fact that would have greatly diminished its relevance in a multicultural Canadian society. This suggests that further research into the experiences of immigrant Christians within established Canadian churches would contribute to understanding the history of those churches in the postcolonial period. So too, would a study of the response of White congregations to the presence of racialized congregants and congregations within the church. To this subject we now turn our attention.

8

"Struggling to Understand Ourselves as 'Receivers,' as well as 'Givers'"

The United Church of Canada Responds to Korean Christians, 1976 to 1998

And finally, what has been our church's response to immigrant, and ethnic congregations? There have been exclamations about the "beautiful voices of the Korean choirs," and there have been invitations to share their music with other congregations. There have been exclamations about our "beautiful and colourful Korean costumes." There have been exclamations about how fast the Korean churches are growing. And yet, I wonder how much real "sharing" we do. Are we really sharing our faith and growing together, or are we going our separate ways?

Irene Chunghwa Lee[1]

Writing for the United Church of Canada's *Mission Magazine* in 1984, Irene Lee, the daughter Korean Christian immigrants, sought to educate the general Canadian population about Koreans, their migrant experience, and their life in the UCC. According to Lee, Canadians had not shown much enthusiasm for immigration despite the fact that there were few countries in the world that owed more to immigrants. Lee's experience as a 1.5-generation Korean Canadian, i.e., as a Korean who had immigrated to Canada as a child, gave her a unique vantage point on the older generation who had come directly from Korea to work in Canada and the second generation of children born to Korean migrant parents. She was shaped by the transition taking place as Koreans sought make a home for themselves in Canada and she was witness to the reception the Canadian church and society was extending to them. From her point of view, the challenge came down to a willingness to engage one another and to share cultural knowledge and perspective.

Even though the majority of Korean Christians found congregations outside the UCC, their impact on Canada's largest Protestant denomination was important. As the UCC absorbed Korean and other immigrant communities into itself, it was being transformed by the presence of new racial identities, languages, church practices, and spiritual experiences. How did UCC members understand the contribution Koreans were making to their church? If Koreans felt they were working hard to make a place for themselves, were established Canadians making a similar effort to welcome them? What was the impact of new Korean members, leaders, and congregations on UCC institutions and morale? If Koreans were now the new missionaries, how did Canadians experience this mission? The final chapter in our history of the relationship between the Korean-Canadian church will focus on these questions as it seeks to outline some of the major impacts of that relationship upon the Canadian church.

In this chapter a series of qualitative interviews with non-missionary UCC personnel and lay people will build on documentary evidence to describe some of the experiences of non-Korean UCC members when encountering their Korean co-religionists. These interviews provide significant data regarding the feelings, understandings, and changes that resulted from the encounter of Canadian Christians who, in most cases, had limited experiences with Koreans and unlike missionaries had not been formally educated or prepared for intercultural experiences. They also paint a picture of the post-missionary thinking about missions and inter-cultural encounters in the context of the church in Canada. The period for this chapter starts in 1976, the year Elsie Livingston acquired her Victory Shawl from Korea. For Livingston, the moment marked her first awareness of the Korean church and its struggle for political emancipation. It is likely that many were similarly awakened during the 1970s. What makes this a significant starting point is that the Victory Shall project was undertaken by Koreans in more or less direct contact with Canadian church women, sans missionary intermediary. This project therefore serves to symbolize a more immediate encounter between members of the UCC congregations and the Korean church and a decade in which social justice movements began to replace proselytization as the expression of the UCC mission in the minds of the church leadership. In 1981, the Rt Rev. Lois Wilson, as moderator of the UCC, traveled to Korea to participate firsthand in the Korean Democratization Movement. Changed by the experience, she made use of a church magazine and her prominent position in the church to communicate a vision for mission in which the Canadian church was as much a recipient of help from other churches as it was a giver. During the 1980s and 1990s, Mary Sanderson attended Bloor St United church, a congregation which shared its building with Toronto Korean United Church. Rev. Linda Butler was a minister of this same congregation in the 1990s. Both these women will help us to understand the ways Korean and Anglo congregation members and ministers interacted at the level of the local church in Canada. Patti Talbot and Michael Blair both currently serve in the UCC General Council with experience in the church that goes back decades. Interviews with these church leaders give a bird's eye view of the interactions of Koreans on the national church scene.

An important context of the different experiences reflected in the interviews is the state-to-state relationships developing between Canada and the two Koreas through this period. Both South Korea and Canada staged US nuclear weapons in the 70s and 80s. Cold War tensions were stoked when Russian fighters shot down Korean passenger flight 007. Pierre Elliott Trudeau negotiated the sale of Candu nuclear reactors with Chun Doo Hwan, the most vicious of South Korea's military dictators. North Korea bombed another South Korean airliner in the lead up the Seoul Olympics. South Korean electronics and cars began to appear on Canadian store shelves and in Canadian driveways. A second wave of South Korean immigration arrived in Canada in the 1990s following the first wave in late 60s and 70s. Though they are not mentioned in the interviews, all these experiences provided context for Canadians as they worked through their relationships with their Korean neighbours in the church pews. They underline how both societies fell within the sphere of American hegemony, a theme that is not much explored here but is important to remember as it shaped the range of things said and not recorded in documents and interviews.

ELSIE LIVINGSTON

On a Saturday morning in February 2020, I presented myself at St Paul's United Church in Saskatoon, Saskatchewan to deliver a presentation to a church group about the history of treaties in the province. After the presentation was over, a woman named Elsie Livingston approached to speak to me about my project to write about the history of the Korean-Canadian church relationship. Livingston has lived her whole life on the prairies and has been involved with the United Church from the time she was a young adult. She had heard me speak elsewhere about Korea and she wanted to let me know that she had a purple shawl that she had acquired many years ago that came from there. "I don't usually keep clothes for 40 years," she told me, "I have kept this. I think it is connected to what you were talking about." The shawl she had, it turned out, was a Victory Shawl (see chapter 6). I asked her if she would consent to an interview on the topic and she said she would.

Meeting over the phone because of the social distancing requirements of the COVID-19 outbreak, Livingston wanted to know how I had become interested in Korea. I told her that I had met my partner through an exchange program and Livingston shared that she had a Korean daughter-in-law. When I asked her to tell me the story of how she came to have the Victory Shawl she explained the United Church Women (UCW), an organization of lay women in the church with roots in the Woman's Missionary Society (WMS), had held an annual conference in Banff, Alberta every year for members in the western provinces of Canada. In the fall of 1976, she said, she got a chance to attend that conference. "That is where I learned about the project in South Korea," she said. Livingston could not remember many of the details of the story behind the shawl and was eager for me to tell her more when our formal interview ended but it nonetheless had a special significance for her: "It means something to me because I kept it," she said, "People always comment on it and I always make a point of saying it was made in South Korea."

Livingston's testimony that the shawl was imbued with a lasting significance is interesting. As discussed in chapter 6, the Victory Shawl project combined Western and Korean cultural elements. The colour and style of the garment are striking and memorable in their own right. Though the urgent plea for solidarity attached to its creation is no longer vividly recalled, there was enough of it still attached to the object that it evoked a memory when Livingston heard me speak about Korea. When pressed to remember more, Livingston shared that she knew it had something to do with a protest movement, and some concern with the governance of South Korea after the war and division of the peninsula. "I do remember somewhat hearing on the news at the time about the struggle for democratic government," she said, "I remember the name Park and also in my mind it was a young Kim Dae Jung." It was not so much the history of the shawl that was important, however: "The realization came to me, why did I keep this shawl for so many years. In 1976, when I went to the Banff women's conference, I was in my 40s. The shawl was an example of advocacy. People banding together. I kind of learned, if I was going to advocate for a certain cause, to be just and caring, to be effective you don't do that on your own. And also, it was such a creative idea for that advocacy."[2] The shawl, therefore, was connected to an important life lesson about justice work and creativity, one which Livingston said she has put into action on occasion. The learning attached to the shawl is something she cherishes and holds on to.

I asked Livingston if she could connect the shawl to missionaries. She shared that she had been raised an Anglican and that that church was proud of their missionary work. She had been asked to join the Woman's Missionary Society when she was twenty-five years old, around the time she married her husband, a United Church minister, and through the UCC had "learned a fair bit about the mission field." As a leader of Canadian Girls in Training (CGIT),[3] she recalled, "we always had a mission study." Livingston came away with the impression that "UCC missionaries were not so much proselytizing but digging wells and teaching and that sort of thing." This observation corroborates what we have already stated about the understanding of mission that the UCC leadership had been promoting since the 1960s and Wilna Thomas' visits to Korea (see chapter 3).

Livingston did not connect the story of the shawl to the work of missionaries in Korea, however. This makes sense. The Victory Shawl project was an initiative of women whose husbands were church leaders arrested because of a political action taken by their husbands. Lee Oo Chung, who was also detained as a result of her involvement in the March 1 Declaration for the Salvation of the Nation, was at the time also the chair of Korea Church Women United, a cross-denominational organization of Christian lay women. This organization had strong connections to similar organizations overseas and used these to promote awareness of these political prisoners.[4] Faye Moon, the American wife of one of the arrested Korean dissidents, for example, travelled to speak to the Women's National Assembly of the Presbyterian Church USA about the situation and share news about the shawls.[5] In Canada, the Victory Shawl project was relayed directly through the UCW.[6] This is what makes Livingstons' acquisition of the shawl an appropriate moment to begin to look at the impact on the Korean-Canadian church relationship on the church in Canada. It is an early sign of an unmediated connection. "The shawl, its significance, it was a symbol of advocacy," Livingston told me, "people standing together, a just and caring cause. To be effective you need support."[7] This was what she learned from the Victory Shawl.

Documentary evidence points to the fact that Livingston's was an early and rare experience of direct and effective connection between Anglo-UCC membership and members of the Korean church. In the 1970s, liberation theologies such as Minjung theology (see chapter 5) contributed to a strong focus in the UCC on issues of social well-being and justice. However, during this period, much of the justice work of the UCC was being carried out "at arm's length" from congregations through ecumenical coalitions and as a result, writes UCC historian Joan Wyatt, "the work that they did was largely unknown to the people in the pews."[8] There was not much interest at a grass roots level.[9] Indigenous leaders encountered this problem as they began to press the UCC to come to terms with structural racism suffered by First Nations within the church.[10] But the divide between aspects of the UCC's work meant that most congregants would not be impacted. Stan McKay, UCC minister from the *Koostakak* First Nation in Manitoba and later first Indigenous moderator of the United Church of Canada (1992–94), spoke of his frustrations in an interview with a church magazine in 1980. He complained that trying to talk to the UCC's Division of Mission in Canada (DMC) was one of his most "frustrating experiences" and that the the the church's understanding of racism was totally inadequate.[11] Livingston's experience, while not connected to the issue of racism, does represent a moment, contrary to the general experience of the church, when an effective connection was made with people working with the grassroots membership.

The UCC had understood it needed a new approach to overseas mission since at least the 1960s. In 1962, the Canadian denomination established the *Commission on World Mission*, whose mandate it was to look into the UCC's missionary past and come up with recommendations for the future direction of the church in that area of work. In their report, the commission acknowledged the undertone of colonialism in UCC missions and that interactions with people overseas had been presented in a way to make them "more acceptable" to the Canadian public, that is to cover up the injustices of colonialism.[12]

What the church needed now was a new vision in which people from different places and religions worked together as partners.[13] While it was easy to see *that* this must be done, it was not easy to see *how* it could be. Part of the answer, according to the commission, lay in an attitude of openness to the contributions of Christians from other lands. Its findings advised that Christians in the UCC should be ready to receive interpretations and practices of Christianity, which did not derive from their culture.[14] The task of preparing UCC members for this new approach was acknowledged to be "important, complex and difficult"[15] and that there was a need to guard against "slipping back inadvertently into outgrown ways of thinking."[16] The commission's final recommendation was "that constant, updated, systematic, well planned and challenging education be directed to the whole church from the pulpit and every other channel open to the church."[17] A plan to educate the average member of the UCC never materialized. In 1971, the Chair of the Board of World Mission (predecessor of the DWO) lamented that the UCC membership was "still generally living with a Nineteenth Century concept of mission" and that the communication gap was "colossal."[18] Stan McKay wondered if voices for change were being muzzled.[19] Livingston's encounter with the story of Korean church women and their struggle for justice was one of the first signs that things may be about to change. Five years later, a prominent member of the UCC would try to move the needle following a life-changing visit to Korea.

LOIS WILSON

In 1981, the Rt Rev. Lois Wilson, as newly elected moderator of the United Church, travelled to South Korea and had a direct encounter with the Korean church that spurred efforts to educate UCC congregants about the potential of cross-cultural relationships. Wilson is a well-known figure in the UCC. The first married woman to be ordained to the ministry and first woman to be elected moderator of the church, Wilson was the minister of the church where a young Floyd Axworthy, future Minister of External Affairs in the Liberal Government of Jean Chretien, was a member. Partly thanks to the connection with Axworthy, Wilson would play a role in Korean-Canadian relations for decades following her initial engagement with South Korea. I met Lois in the summer of 2019 at the General Council of the UCC in Oshawa, Ontario. Sitting together in a less-busy corner of the University of Ontario, Wilson shared with me the story of her trip to

South Korea and how it had been transformative for her. I have used documentary records to supplement her account.

In January 1981, Wilson was the only female member of a four-person team sent by the World Council of Churches to gather information on reports of Human Rights abuses by the authoritarian regime of Chun Doo Hwan. At the time, she was only vaguely aware of the missionary history of the UCC in that place.[20] Before she left Canada however, Wilson was briefed by Sang Chul Lee. Lee tried to give her a taste of the tensions she would have to navigate in the Korean church by sharing a little anecdote: The two main Presbyterian denominations on the peninsula each had a different reputation, he told her; members of the Presbyterian Church in Korea believed in Jesus and expected to go to heaven whereas the members of the Presbyterian Church in the Republic of Korea believed in Jesus and expected to go to prison. The reputation of the latter derived from its inclination to challenge the government on its human rights abuses. The PROK, he added, had a special history with the UCC. All this was new information for Wilson.[21]

Landing at Gimpo International Airport, the World Council of Churches team had been informed of their full, carefully crafted and officially sanctioned schedule by their Korean hosts. The serious tension in the Korean church, as Sang Chul Lee had suggested in his briefing to Wilson, was between those wishing to inform the outside world about the regime's abuses and others seeking to avoid negative attention from authorities in the high-surveillance state. The visitors' agenda, strongly influenced by those who did not wish to make political waves, limited their ability to find out what was really going on. Wilson had decided, perhaps with Sang Chul Lee's encouragement, to make time for visits outside the schedule with people connected with the PROK. An unofficial report documenting her engagements during the visit indicates that this is exactly what she did.[22]

During an unscheduled meeting with two women at a reception at the YWCA, Wilson heard reports of a massacre of civilians in the southeastern city of Gwangju and was urged to go and collect eyewitness accounts.[23] When she brought the idea to her WCC team leader, she met resistance. "You can't go," she was told, "we have all these church commitments. It's illegal. It's martial law!" But Wilson insisted, "I have to because these women asked me."[24] As chapter 6 has shown, the gendered space was critical for the Democratization Movement. In this case, too, the gendered space would have changed Wilson perhaps more than it did those she met.

Having decided to go down to Gwangju, Wilson turned to UCC missionary Walter Beecham to find a way.[25] In Gwangju they were met at the train station and taken to the YWCA in town. The director there was a woman named Cho A Ra.[26] Cho showed her the evidence of the violence, including bullet holes and blood stains running down the walls from the room above where dead bodies had been brought for safe keeping until family members could come and identify them. Wilson recalled: "The YWCA [in Gwangju] have left the bullet holes in windows and ceiling and walls as a reminder of what happened ... People were forbidden to enter the Y, as it was used as a morgue, and someone mentioned the blood seeping down the pipes from the floor above."[27] Cho also hosted a meeting between Wilson and a group of women and men who had heard of her visit to the YWCA and came to tell Wilson their stories in defiance of police threats. "I heard the most harrowing, harrowing story," recounts Wilson "You know," one mother told her, "I begged my son not to go downtown, but he said, no, this was critical." The woman never saw him alive again. It was "the hardest pastoral visit I have ever done in my life," said Wilson.[28]

Later, missionary Beecham would write to tell her what the visit had meant for many that she had met. "The Gwangju people were impressed with you and noted all the details of your visit – from your walking through the back alleys to whether you ate meat at the dinner to your willingness to talk at 5:30 AM any hour."[29] But though taking brave steps to meet with people, in her heart, Wilson had been scared. Partway through the trip she had been made aware of a KCIA agent tailing her.[30] When she returned to her hotel room in Seoul, she received calls from the front desk asking where she had been. She was worried the authorities might not let her leave Korea. The danger was real. Though she did not know it at the time, those she had met in Gwangju would suffer severe consequences for speaking with her.[31] Arriving at the airport, Wilson was filled with dread: "The last hurdle was to pass airport security when I left Seoul. In my shoe I had a list of political prisoners to give Amnesty International. In the pocket of my parka was the book listing the people I'd met illegally in the YWCA. If either of these were found, I would be detained without much thought for the niceties. When I finally reached my seat in the plane, I wept with relief."[32] Returning to Canada, Wilson responded to her experience by teaching UCC members about how they could reinterpret their relationship to missions. A special edition of the UCC's *Mission Magazine* was published under her direction later that year. Based on Wilson's first year as moderator of the UCC, it included stories of Christian involvement in political struggles around the globe. The largest allotment of space was dedicated to Korea.[33] In her editorial remarks, Wilson suggested that what she experienced with churches overseas was connected to an important shift driven by the leadership of non-Western churches: "We live today in an age in which we, as church, are struggling to understand ourselves as 'receivers,' as well as 'givers' in the world Christian Community. We are beginning to understand that our relationship to sister churches and agencies does not turn on the axis of money or personnel alone. There is a growing awareness, arising out of the debris and disappointments of our North American life-style, that we have critical need of the gospel insights and Christian faithfulness of our partners overseas." Wilson's comment reflects a personal transformation which she credits to the church in Korea.[34] As a non-missionary, her direct experience of Korean Christians in the Democratization Movement signalled a new kind of Korean-Canadian church interaction.

Wilson also used church channels to promote international peace. Working through the WCC, Wilson and other Canadians worked to bring a delegation of South and North Korean Christians together to discuss peace at a meeting convened in Tozanso, Japan in 1984. Wilson and Sang Chul Lee, along with former UCC missionary to China Rhea Whitehead and Canadian Mennonite Eric Weingartner, represented Canadian churches at that event. A meeting of South and North Koreans was later organized in Gilon, Switzerland in 1986. In 1988 a delegation of Canadian Christians representing the UCC, Anglican, Catholic, and Presbyterian denominations visited North Korea and then hosted a delegation of North Korean Christians to Canada in 1991.[35] Work to bring the two sides together succeeded in shifting the position of the Canadian government from isolation to engagement. In 1997, the Canadian government sent food aid to the North. In 2001, it opened diplomatic relationships with the DPRK.[36] Wilson, by this time, had been appointed by Prime Minister Jean Chretien to the senate where she sat as independent senator between 1998 and 2002. From the senate, Wilson was in a position to influence these changes. Later, together with Kay Cho (see chapter 7) and others, she helped to start the Canada-DPRK Association to promote the accurate sharing of information about North Korea in Canada.[37]

Three years after the first *Mission Magazine* was published, a second *Mission Magazine* was made available to members of the UCC. Although Wilson was no longer moderator at this time, it is likely she had encouraged the issue. The 1984 publication focussed uniquely on Korea and the Korean church. The issue featured articles about missionaries and interviews with political dissidents and sought to highlight the agency of Korean Christians and the work they were doing in Korea. But it also featured an article by Irene Chunghwa Lee. Lee had immigrated to Canada when her father, Rev. Sang Chul Lee, began his ministry at Stevenston United Church in British Columbia (see chapter 7). The purpose of the article was to lift up the efforts of Korean migrants as they worked to make a new home for themselves in Canada. But Lee also used her piece to reflect on the interactions of Koreans and non-Koreans within the UCC. One of the groups that was a source of both joy and concern was the new generation of children raised by Korean immigrants who sought a new place in the church somewhere between the Korean congregations of their parents and the Anglo congregations of the UCC, a place uniquely their own. This kind of congregation required a new kind of leadership but the UCC lacked people with the specialized skills and experience to do this work. Lee noted a lack of interest in immigrants and their families in the non-immigrant Canadian population at large, a shortcoming that was clearly evident in UCC congregations as well.[38]

Despite her own life-changing experience, Wilson has wondered if the connection she made in Korea and the efforts she made to change Canadians' understanding of mission had any impact on the wider UCC: "It influenced me. But I don't know that it impacted the church. So I tried to spread it abroad, but I don't know."[39] There is evidence that these personal transformations did indeed translate into opportunities for Canadians to learn about and participate in the struggle for democracy occurring in South Korea such as in exchanges between lay women's groups. Writing in 1995 one UCC member noted that the links between women of the PROK and UCC were "especially meaningful" and had resulted in a number of undertakings by UCC women: "There are many UCC women who wear fish pins [symbols of solidarity with the Democratization Movement], write letters in support of political prisoners, and have made solidarity shawls. Women did much of the education during a recent Korea mission study year. United Church Women are preparing prayer ribbons to contribute to the Jubilee year reunification effort. They have followed with interest and concern Korean women's research and action regarding women workers, prostitution, and nuclear energy. There is a sense in which many feel a special relationship with women in the PROK."[40]

But perhaps Wilson's concerns were not without reason. On an exchange in 1984, two Korean women, Kim Jee Song and Kim Kyung Ja, visited Canada and had the following to say when asked what had surprised them most about what they had seen of the UCC: "Most of all, we were surprised at the activity of women ... Here we found many women in headquarters and women elders and ministers ... People accept these women's ideas as much as the men's. Women participate in all programs and express themselves clearly. That surprised us."[41] However when it came time to hear what the Korean women had to say, the visitors found the UCC was less open. "When we came here, we had speeches prepared for the churches, and thought, 'this is a good opportunity to share.' But one lady stood up and said, 'Share? Then why did you come here? We want to teach you.' In two or three churches we had the same experience. This is an exchange program and so one party shouldn't do all the talking. At least in Christ there shouldn't be any discrimination."[42] Despite opportunities to learn directly from contexts and people outside of Canada and the UCC there was still a great deal of resistance to change in Canada. Wilson's misgivings about the degree to which UCC membership was open to new relationships with Koreans came from one of her visits to a UCC congregation which shared its building with a Korean congregation. She discovered that the UCC congregation had made no effort and seemed to show no interest in getting to know their Korean neighbours despite their close association through the building.[43]

MARY SANDERSON

Though there were many Anglo UCC congregations sharing their buildings with Korean immigrant congregations, both UCC and non-UCC, Bloor St United Church is a special case. Since 1969, the Bloor St building had been the home of the Toronto Korean United Church (TKUC) as well. The Bloor St congregation worshiped in the morning and the Korean congregation rented the space for worship in the afternoon. TKUC also rented office space for its staff through the week. With the strong leadership of Sang Chul Lee from 1969 to 1988 and Bloor St United Church's sense of itself as a leading congregation in the UCC, the two congregations sensed a special significance in their relationship and made efforts to get to know one another.

Mary Sanderson began to attend Bloor St United Church in 1984. Knowing of her through several shared acquaintances and through a brief personal interaction many years earlier, I contacted Sanderson to ask if she would be willing to share some of her thoughts on the UCC-Korean church relationship. She agreed and we met on the phone. Sanderson fondly recalls the interactions that took place between the two congregations: "They met right after Bloor St [worship service on Sunday]. We would be going, and they would be coming. There was a very good relationship between us all. We would recognize many of them and stop and say hello and 'How are you doing?' and stuff like that." In addition to the informal contact, the two congregations engaged one another on a variety of official levels. These yielded some important experiences that are worth reflecting on.

For Sanderson, one of the strongest and most vivid memories was serving on a TKUC committee charged with finding a new minister for the congregation. She recalls that her invitation from TKUC to serve on the committee was a "courtesy" to Bloor St United Church. The practice demonstrates a remarkable closeness between the congregations as it gave members of the Anglo congregation access to the inner workings of the Korean one. It also exposed them to some of the more difficult and painful aspects of congregational life at TKUC, such as congregational conflicts. Sanderson says she was delighted to be invited to sit in on the TKUC search committee but was not prepared for some of the heated discussions that took place. "The conversation was always in English unless there was a disagreement," she said, "When there was a disagreement, and this just blew my mind because I'd never seen this, the people would stand up and yell and scream at each other across the table. And I'd ask someone to translate for me and they never would (laughter). And I have a strong memory of that because it was something I had never seen before." Sanderson says that she attended about a dozen meetings of the search committee in the 1990s. She is able to laugh at the experience of intense open conflict, but it was clear she found it perplexing as well.

White Canadians, such as Sanderson, however, were not the only ones perplexed by outbursts of emotion. Koreans experienced similar outbursts from Anglo members of Bloor St United Church, and unlike in Mary's experience, sometimes those outbursts were aimed directly at them. Sanderson recalls another meeting of the members of both congregations to talk about the question of rent for the Bloor St facilities. She cannot remember the figures involved but was under the impression that the Anglo congregation had initially provided the use of its sanctuary to TKUC at a very reasonable rate out of a sense of "mission." But as the Korean congregation grew and Bloor St United Church began to experience financial pressures, the Anglo congregation decided they would try to renegotiate the rate. "The person who was chairing the meeting [for Bloor St United Church] was a big high-powered banker and strong businessman, and the Koreans of course were very reluctant to talk about money and were very diffident. But the chair of our committee was used to being very blunt. He pounded the table and said, 'We need more money!'" Sanderson, who was not present at the meeting says that the impression was that this outburst on the part of the Bloor St member "set back relations with the Koreans ten years." In retrospect, says Sanderson, the renegotiation of the rent was also part of the process of renegotiating the missionary relationship. Clearly there was awkwardness about the conversation, and one is reminded of the painful outbursts that were part of that renegotiation in Korea between the Korean church and the Canadian missionaries (see chapter 3 and 4).

For Sanderson, there were inspirational elements of the relationship as well. On the Sunday of the annual Toronto Santa Clause Parade the two congregations had a tradition of worshipping together, she says. This is because the parade, which passed in front of the church in the afternoon, would interrupt the TKUC worship service. So, the two groups would worship together and then watch the parade together as well. The two congregations were a good match for each other, Sanderson thinks, because theologically they were both liberal, whereas her impression is that other Korean congregations were generally more conservative. Sanderson recalls the laughter when the Bloor St minister would attempt to give the final blessing in Korean. But more profoundly, she says, "The experience of saying the Lord's prayer in both languages at the same time was powerful." Sanderson did not elaborate, but there was something in that experience of the melding of languages that was spiritually moving for her and represented a shared experience that transcended cultural differences. It is perhaps akin to the experience that moved Sang Chul Lee to become a Christian while living in Manchuria, a cacophony of prayer that sent "shivers up and down his spine."[44]

LINDA BUTLER

As the clergy responsible for the spiritual life of the Bloor St United Church from 1993 to 2006, Rev. Linda Butler has a slightly different experience of the relationship with TKUC than Sanderson, though their observations converge on a number of points. I knew Butler from my student days when she was a minister at Bloor St United Church and approached her about an interview aware of her history with the congregation and its relationship with TKUC. We met in person for the interview, on a deck outside of her home. Butler was a gracious host and offered honest reflections about aspects of the relationship between the members as well as between the staff of the two congregations.

It is clear that Butler, who had had no previous experience of Korean congregations before her time at Bloor St, felt the cultural and theological divide keenly as the minister of a congregation that prided itself on being "cutting edge" when it came to theological and social issues. As noted above, the Bloor St Congregation has a special place in the history and ethos of the United Church because it was the pulpit of the UCC's first moderator (see chapter 7). Once a strong supporter of the Missionary Enterprise, part of their new "cutting edge" identity came from the degree to which they distanced themselves for the missionary history of the church. "We knew that the missionary was bad, bad, bad!" said Butler of the Bloor St perspective.[45] Of course, Bloor St United Church was not the only congregation to feel that way in the 1990s. For many in Canadian society, Canada's missionary history was an embarrassment and something to be forgotten. Moon Chai Rin, who attended TKUC, was struck by this phenomenon in 1973 when he preached to St John's United Church in Toronto. The congregation he was addressing was the home church of A.H. Barker, a prominent Canadian missionary in Manchuria and someone whose heroic efforts to protect Koreans during the 3.1 uprising in 1919 was remembered with tremendous gratitude in Korea.[46] However, no one from the congregation remembered Barker and the congregation seemed collectively indifferent to the history, leaving Moon feeling very discouraged.[47] James Chong, a member of TKUC, was also quick to point out the help he had received from missionaries when he settled in Toronto and made his religious home in the United Church.[48] One wonders if the members of Bloor St United Church congregation had had an opportunity to hear some of the stories coming out of the Korean congregation about how missionaries were remembered. In Bloor St UC's case however, it was not merely indifference but active and conscious rejection of missionary history born of a sense that the church had to move beyond such forms of paternalism. Regardless of its progressive ideology, the congregation obviously still struggled with the intercultural relationship.

Like Sanderson, Butler also noted some friction around the sharing of a building. Coordinating times for meetings, social functions, and the use of the kitchen was sometimes difficult, and feathers got ruffled. But one particularly strong memory for Butler was, again, over the negotiation of rent. These discussions, she said, were preceded by other meetings that she understood were about developing trust and a common understanding of the nature of Christian relationships. She felt that all had come to a common understanding of that relationship defined by the theological concept of "covenant." Butler and others from the Bloor St congregation were then dismayed to discover that during the course of these conversations, TKUC had been looking for another place to worship. Butler was left with the question, "can we be real with each other?" Also like Sanderson, Butler was affected by the conflicts she witnessed in the Korean church. For her this was a very painful aspect of the relationship. Most of the conflict around TKUC, she said, took place within the congregation. "It's just hard, I found that very hard to understand why you split and have such battles with one another." Butler's close relationship with members of the congregation made seeing conflict at TKUC particularly painful.[49]

Where Butler found especially strong connection with the TKUC congregation was with their second-generation young people, those that had been raised in Canada by their immigrant parents. On occasion she was asked to preach for this group who worshipped in English in a different part of the church from their parents' congregation. Butler found conversations with this group very interesting as she could resonate with their struggles with the first generation. She remembers a movement towards creating a second-generation congregation for Korean, Japanese, and Chinese young people. Butler remembers the difficulties that the Korean young people had in negotiating the expectations and different cultural expectations of their first-generation parents.[50]

Irene Lee (quoted above), a younger English-speaking member of the congregation herself, described the unique position of the children of Korean immigrants in the religious life of the congregation. These young people she said, "are usually fluent in both Korean and English, and can be a bridge or mediator between the first and second generation [but] tend to shy away from becoming involved with only the Korean or only the Canadian community."[51] She noted a gathering of the North American Korean Students Conference in Toronto in 1983 where Korean-American and Korean-Canadian young people struggle with issues of culture, language, religion, and theology and how they could contribute to the society in which they found themselves. For many, the question of their place within the Korean and Canadian church was forefront of mind. A decade later, in the 1990s, Butler was involved with this group and found their presence helpful in interpreting some of the tensions experienced between the Bloor St United Church and TKUC.

Because of theological and cultural differences, Butler says that working with clergy counterparts from TKUC was not always easy. One of the ministers who succeeded Sang Chul Lee seemed to have an exceptionally low view of the role of women in the church, she said, and this made working with him very difficult. But the issue of the role of women in the church was not only a marker of difference between herself and the congregation on the issue of gender, said Butler, and neither did it always come across in a way that was interpreted as mean-spirited. One example she recalled was when a woman from TKUC approached her mother. The woman sought to comfort Butler's mother over the fact that Butler was not married and had no son. As a single female clergy, Butler found this attitude difficult but at the same time could see that it had been offered as way of supporting to her mother. It was an example of a woman from TKUC, for whom husbands and sons were an important marker of success, attempting to find common ground. The cultural divide was particularly noticeable for Butler among the women: "When the women of the two congregations got together the cultural divide was huge. Korean women introduced themselves as so and so's wife and so and so's mom. Canadian women talked about their professions." [52] On the hot issue of sexual orientation and gender identity, too, it was not easy to imagine any common ground. These experiences resonate with those of Kay Cho (see chapter 7) who experienced sexism as a major barrier to relationships between herself and Korean colleagues. They also harken back to Wilna Thomas' tenure as secretary for the Board of World Mission and questions regarding the kind of tensions that might have existed for her as she tried to navigate the Korean-Canadian church relationship as the first woman in that position (see chapter 3).

The perceived difficulty with the issue of LGBTQ Christians at TKUC existed regardless of the fact that Sang Chul Lee was its former minister. Lee had been the moderator of the UCC following the explosive

General Council of 1988 at which it was decided that sexual orientation would not be a barrier to serving as a minister of a UCC congregation. "The choice of Sang Chul Lee was spectacular," said Butler, because his gifts of wisdom and life experience helped the UCC negotiation some of the fallout from the controversy. But it is clear that subsequent ministers and her sense of the congregation in general created doubts in Butler's mind that they would be able to come to a shared acceptance of sexual diversity. While UCC members such as Butler perceived a wide chasm between themselves and Koreans in relation to gender and sexual diversity issues, it should be kept in mind that Canadian and South Korean societies were not too far apart all things considered. Women activists were under surveillance by the Canadian government until the mid-eighties[53] and women ministers were (and still are) paid less than their male colleagues in the UCC. At the same time, progress was being made on women's rights in Korea thanks to activists such as Lee Oo Chung (see chapter 6) while signs of a LGBT rights movement began to appear in Korea in the early 1990s, not long after it started to make headway in Canada.[54]

PATTI TALBOT

Patti Talbot was born in Japan to missionaries of the Presbyterian Church in Canada serving the Korean church in Japan. Before coming to work for the United Church as the Global Mission Personnel Secretary in September 1994, a role akin to that of Wilna Thomas in the 1960s (see chapter 3), Talbot also served for a three-year term with the Canadian Presbyterian church in Japan working for the Korean Christian Church of Japan. The period of her service was 1984 to 1987, the final years of the dictatorship before the return of democratic government to South Korea. During that time, she worked closely with UCC missionary Mary Collins and PROK minister Oh Jae Shik, both of whom had been forced to leave Korea by the military regime. So, she came to the interview with a lot of background knowledge of Korea, the Democratization Movement, and the involvement of the UCC.[55]

The focus of our conversation gravitated toward the election of Sang Chul Lee to the role of UCC moderator. At the time Talbot had just returned to Canada and had not yet begun to work for the UCC. But the election of a Korean as spiritual leader of the Canadian denomination was inspirational to her. As it was for Butler, it was significant for

Talbot that that election happened the day following the vote to remove barriers for gay and lesbian members to serve as ordained ministers. "I had great respect for that kind of witness," said Talbot, "The kinds of stereotypes people might have about the United Church or inclusion, everything was exploded there." For her, it meant that people could no longer assume that migrant communities were unable to accept sexual diversity in the church and simultaneously challenged racism.[56]

While Talbot was personally inspired by Lee and attracted to the UCC because of its choice of moderator, she admitted that she also heard some puzzlement in church circles about the election. Lee was different, he was non-White and spoke with an accent, people complained. Talbot was aware of certain stereotypes that were forming in Canada about the propensity for Korean congregations to split apart. She discerned an inability or unwillingness on the part of Anglo-churches to overcome linguistic barriers. In her work with the General Council of the UCC in the years since she has seen that there are forces at work that make it very hard for migrant ministers to work in the UCC. Although there has been a lot of work on the part of Korean and Filipino leaders to push the UCC to recognize the ministry credentials from their home churches, she says, progress has been slow. There is even a saying by migrant ministers that "the gate into the UCC is narrower than then gate to heaven."[57]

MICHAEL BLAIR

At the time of our interview, Michael Blair was the executive minister for the Church in Mission Unit. Currently serving as the first Black General Secretary of the UCC, the highest position of authority within the church, Blair was born in Jamaica and raised in the Baptist church. Ordained a Baptist, he was forced to leave the Baptist church in Canada when he came out as a gay man. He first started work for the UCC in 2002 as the executive director of the UCC Resource Centre in Regent Park, Toronto and was hired by the UCC General Council in 2008 to a position with oversight for the Ethnic Ministry Council. Though Blair's time with the church is more recent, his positions of responsibility required him to acquire an institutional memory of the UCC. His experience outside the UCC also provides him with an important perspective on past and current events within the church.

When Blair began to work for the UCC he learned of the denomination's decolonizing approach to mission, which, he understood, had been introduced and implemented in the 1950s and 1960s. But Blair also came to understand that there existed, still in the 2000s, a tension between the stated intentions and the lived reality of the UCC ideal of partnership in mission. "On paper it was about justice," he said, "in reality it was still charity." The problem lies, says Blair, in a "saviour complex." On principle, the UCC is committed to an approach that dictates that the partner in overseas church relationships is always right. This is important, says Blair, because it recognizes the unique perspectives and experiences of people on the ground in the places the UCC seeks to help. At the same time, he says, such an approach forecloses honest conversation and creates dependencies. When a partner asks for funding for a program, the response is to simply fund the program without any discussion of ways that program could be funded locally. In this way, Blair feels, the UCC hasn't lived out the depth of partnership. "In a true partnership," he says, "we change and the partners change because of the relationship."[58] Blair's observations reflect some of the contradictions that were in evidence when Wilna Thomas visited Korea in the 1960s (see chapter 3).

With responsibilities to oversee and encourage intercultural relationships within the UCC, Blair has had a particularly close view of the dynamics within and between ethnic congregations in the UCC. In his opinion one of the largest barriers for the participation of Koreans within the UCC is language and theology, a challenge that is shared with other East Asian congregations and ministers. With Sanderson and Butler, Blair says there is a perception in the UCC that Korean congregations are theologically conservative and often slower than Anglo congregations to accept sexual diversity. The language barrier, however, seems to be at least as significant, especially for Korean congregations who hire ministers who are not bilingual. In this case the congregation becomes like an island onto itself, said Blair. It is extremely hard to know how to overcome that barrier.[59]

For Korean ministers serving Anglo congregations the problem can also be serious. Blair notes that many Korean ministers are entering the UCC, more than any other ethnic/linguistic minority. The effort to adapt to the Korean-English accent of these new ministers is often a challenge for congregations. In the Toronto area, says Blair, there was talk among congregations to make language competence a requirement for admission into the order of ministry of the UCC. What it came down to, he said, was an issue of language accent and a struggle on the part of some to understand what their minister was saying. The language difference not only creates tension between ministers and congregations, but also creates barriers for Korean congregations in their attempts to interact with other congregations and church institutions. In Blair's experience, where there are language issues there is isolation. Currently, he says, there are few Koreans taking or making a place for themselves in the national structures of the church. This was an issue identified by Dong-Chun Seo in a report to the church in 1978 as well.[60] And Blair sees this as possibly the single biggest issue. "All need the freedom to function in the language of the heart," he said.[61]

The story of the EMC is an important one for understanding both the interactions of Korean congregations with the UCC in the 1990s and also for understanding Blair's perspective on experiences of Koreans within the UCC. The EMC was constituted in 1996[62] following the 1994 report of a task force that recommended the creation of a separate division within the national church structure for ethnic ministries.[63] The thinking behind the EMC signalled a shift from a perceived need to assimilate ethnic minority congregations to an affirmation and celebration of cultural and linguistic diversity as a strength of the church.[64] The EMC was designed to have a full-time staff of six and equal status within the national structure with other divisions such as the DWO and DMC. The EMC would thus bring issues related to the ethnic congregations out from under the purview of the DMC, a division that indigenous minister Stan McKay had criticized in 1980 for being deaf to issues of racism and colonialism.[65] Wenh In Ng argued that the establishment of the EMC was a significant move for the UCC because it tangibly empowered ethnic communities.[66]

The EMC was to be composed of thirty members representing the different ethnic groups (except indigenous and francophone groups) of the church. In addition it was to have eleven corresponding members. Those who supported the EMC argued that the UCC should put "the same amount of attention and resources to ethnic ministries as it does to other sectors of the church's mission."[67] The theological rational of the EMC was shaped by Minjung theology (see chapter 5). The ethnic peoples and congregations within the UCC were regarded as "minjung," i.e., a people with a common experience of "han."[68] It was further argued that this group had the potential to transform the UCC.[69] The special role of Minjung theology in the creation of the EMC points to the leadership of Koreans in its creation.

There were, however, concerns about the effectiveness of the new EMC. One such concern was that the new structure would permanently segregate ethnic congregations from the mainstream of the church.

A second was that it gave a considerable degree of power and allocated a considerable portion of the shrinking resources of the church to a group that consisted of less than 10 per cent of the UCC's total population.[70] Both these concerns were factors in the ultimate dissolution of the EMC ten years later, a decision for which Blair was largely responsible. Blair remarked to me that the structure of the EMC meant that Korean congregations, for example, met separately from other UCC bodies for the most part and only had interaction with other parts of the church when there was a crisis requiring oversight. In this case, there was not enough mutual understanding or trust between the different parts of the church to permit a satisfactory resolution of those crises. Blair feared the EMC was effectively isolating ethnic congregations. And budgetary pressures were also a big factor.[71]

Blair points out that in 1996 the General Council of the UCC had given the EMC a ten-year mandate and that that mandate had ended in 2006 with the commitment to become an "inter-cultural church," understood as an intentional engagement by the different cultural groups with one another. This new commitment, he felt, seemed to run counter to the idea of a separate Division of ethnic congregations. The decision in 2006 to disband the EMC was controversial. Blair wonders now whether the decision was made too quickly. Furthermore, the bringing of ethnic congregations back into direct relationship with non-ethnic congregations has meant the loss of a unique space in which common issues could come to the fore. Blair, therefore, still agonizes over whether the elimination of this unique division was the right move.[72]

The creation of the EMC in 1996, nearly a century since the beginning of Canadian Korea Mission, may represent the high-water mark for the influence of Koreans within the UCC. A generation has passed since then and the dynamics have changed. There are fewer Korean congregations in the UCC now compared to 1996 and fewer Koreans in positions of leadership within the UCC General Council. The interviews with Talbot and Blair have begun a reflection on what the years since have meant. But for the purpose of this study, the last years of the twentieth century are a good place to end.

CONCLUSION

The absence of Korean leadership within the national church structures since the end of the EMC points to the impact of that decision upon the Korean community. Blair laments that absence and wonders what it was that made it possible in the 1970s and 1980s for Sang Chul Lee to be so influential in the UCC. Blair never knew Lee personally but was aware of his impact. It seems to him there is need for someone to fill his shoes as a Korean leader within the UCC. "What is it about his history that led him to get involved?" Blair wonders.[73] This book may provide some of the answers, connecting Lee to the early ministry of Canadian missionaries in Kando and the northeast of Korea and to the emergence of the PROK following the Korean War. We now have an idea of the ways the early Korean Christian movement with its nationalist aspirations and the PROK with its activism in the face of neocolonial forces had shaped Lee and given him a progressive agenda to engage the people and structures around him.

Lee had a disarming way to get people to think about who belonged. "Canadians often ask why Koreans came to Canada," he wrote in a book published the year of his election as moderator of the UCC, "I suppose they want to hear about the plight of Korea, the North-South conflict, the economic situation, the unrest. But I prefer to make a point about what it means to be 'Canadian.'"[74] Lee would often remind people of a well-loved song whose verse ran, "This land is your land, this land is my land ... This land was made for you and me." When presented with the song, people would often laugh, perhaps surprised that Lee would know it and bring it up in the context of a discussion about Korean migration. So, Lee would put the question to them directly, "To whom do you refer when you sing 'you?'" [75]

In addition to an acknowledged debt on the part of the UCC to the leadership of Sang Chul Lee, this chapter has revealed some of the ways that non-Koreans in the UCC received the presence and participation of Koreans. It is clear that there were many aspects of the relationship that were perceived as positive. The impact of the Korean church overseas had a direct and transformative effect on Elsie Livingston and Lois Wilson. These women were inspired in their religious lives to continue and deepen their pursuit of justice and service. For Wilson, a different understanding of herself as a Christian from a Western church also resulted from her dramatic visit to Korea. Sang Chul Lee's election to moderator inspired Patti Talbot and Mary Sanderson. For Sanderson, the spiritual impact of worshipping together with a Korean congregation was also an important and formative experience.

At the same time, there were significant challenges. Non-Korean UCC members struggled with differences of language and culture, not to mention theology, in their relationships with Koreans. Seeing conflict in the Korean congregations while being unable to understand or respond appropriately was an important and painful experience for bother Butler and Sanderson, one that served both to underline the distance between Koreans and non-Koreans and the strength of the ties that had made the witness of those painful moments possible. Theological differences in the area of gender and sexual orientation, perceived and real, were another factor that contributed to a sense of distance for those interviewed. Furthermore, there prejudice seems to have been difficult to overcome. Talbot, for example, reflected on the "puzzlement" of White church members to the election of a Korean to moderator and Blair pointed out non-Korean members' reactionary response to different accents. Sanderson noted the clumsy and aggressive way members of the Anglo congregation approached Koreans over matters of money. Blair acknowledged himself, that decisions he had made on behalf of the Korean members of the UCC may have suffered from inadequate understanding of their circumstances.

In the mid-1960s when Canada changed its immigration laws and reached an immigration agreement with South Korea, Korean Christian leadership began to come to Canada even as the numbers of missionaries sent overseas from Canada continued to dwindle. At the very same moment, mainline Protestant churches began to shrink after more than a century of growth. Western church decline has been the subject of much debate among historians of religion since the 1980s. While the trajectory of religion was different, there were many ways in which Canada and Korea were moving in the same direction. Rising GDPs and growing manufacturing sectors, increased trade, military alignment with US foreign policy and development of nuclear power were all things that Canada and South Korea shared. While they were at different stages on the road, both countries saw progress on the rights of women and the first forays in the fight for the acceptance of sexual diversity. Canada also started to move towards re-engagement with North Korea.

This chapter has suggested that the impact of direct contact between Anglo and non-Anglo Christians within the UCC was ambiguous. Religious historian Lynne Marks has shown that the efforts of churches in British Columbia to absorb Asians into their fold at the turn of the twentieth century alienated some Whites and contributed to the low rates of church attendance and religious affiliation within the province.[76] While the above data does not show that a similar dynamic was at play in the UCC in the post-1960s, it does suggest that direct interaction with Koreans was work for Canadians, comparable in some ways to the work Koreans had to do when engaging their Canadian missionary guests in Korea. It was certainly a different kind of work than the traditional Western approach to missions had been, an approach that reinforced the positive self-image of Anglo Protestants and kept the average Canadian Christian a safe distance from the messy business of building cross-cultural relationship. The loss of the Missionary Enterprise as an animating force within the UCC has already been shown to have been a consequential development in the history of the church. But according to Blair, the traditional approach to mission lingers on. It is possible that the absence of a clear understanding of what true inter-cultural relationships are and an inadequate articulation of the positive aspects of such relationships may be contributing to the shrinking membership and resources or the UCC.

In 1984, Irene Chunghwa Lee wondered about the history of the Korean-Canadian church relationship. "Are we really sharing our faith and growing together, or are we going our separate ways?" she asked. Today, it is more than one hundred years since Korean Christians called on Canadian missionaries to come and join them in their land, to be a part of their lives, their communities, and their nation. In the postwar years, thousands of Korean Christians have migrated to Canada and made a place for themselves within the Canadian church. The relationship over the twentieth century depended on a renewal of the mutual commitment to do the hard work of engaging across cultural and historical differences. That engagement, though tenuous at times, has had and continues to have an impact on churches and societies in Korea and Canada.

Conclusion

The first death of a child of the mission was that of John Foote, who died in 1909 at the age of eight. Two children of Reverend and Mrs A.F. Robb died during this period: Marian, at the age of six in 1910, and Alexander, at the age of two in 1912.

...

In July 1941, Dr Scott and Dr Murray paid a visit to the newly acquired mission cemetery plot in Hamheung to which all graves from other mission stations had been transferred. As they bowed their heads in prayer in the last prayer of remembrance, the Japanese caretaker's wife reverently participated.

William Scott, in *Canadian Mission to Korea*, 1975[1]

In the process of preparing for retirement my wife and I took a day and went to the York Cemetery where we purchased a plot of land suitable for two graves. It was the first real estate transaction of our lives. I had conducted funerals for many church members with a sad heart. The thought of being buried beside them gave me a sense of gratitude and it seemed fitting. In my funeral sermons I had often preached, "As immigrants, when we bury our beloved in this strange ground with the pain of loss we are putting down roots." For a wanderer like me to find a place to be buried is something to be grateful for. How much more the thought that I am sending down a root among the many others that Korean immigrants have put down here.

Sang Chul Lee, in *God, Humanities' Hope*, 1989[2]

For both Canadian missionary and Korean immigrant, their final resting place and that of their family and friends were matters of great importance. William Scott did not omit a special mention in his history of the Canadian mission to Korea of the tragic death of missionary children or of heart wrenching farewell to missionary graves before being forcibly deported in 1942. Sang Chul Lee's reflection on the funerals he had done in Canada and of the future burial site for him and his life partner likewise evoked the heartache and struggles of Canadian immigrants in a "strange land." These poignant stories from both sides of the Pacific Ocean highlight the tensions that existed in the sense of belonging for Canadian missionary and Korean immigrant alike. Reaching down to touch the earth at these grave sites, one wonders to what degree it felt like home and to what degree it still felt foreign to Scott and to Lee. And staring down at their reflections in Dragon's Well, so to speak, to what degree did they see the reflection of a Korean or a Canadian looking back up at them? What could they not recognize? What did they feel affection for?

The stories of these graves convey a sense of attachment to a place at the very same time as they accentuate an opposite feeling of foreignness or "unhomeliness," a hallmark experience of the postcolonial era.[3] Whether Canadian missionary or Korean migrant, a sense of home was something that was always in the process of becoming; the feeling of already being at home existed side by side with the feeling of not yet being accepted or viewed as part of that place by others. The history of the relationship between the Korean church and the Canadian mission has likewise never been static or settled; its consequences are still being lived out on both sides of the Pacific. The historical transitions between colonial and postcolonial moments, between missionary enterprises and global migrations present an important context for understanding, among other things, the changes that have occurred in the Korean and Canadian national landscapes in general and in Korean and Canadian Protestantism in particular.

Canadian church historian Phyllis Airhart insightfully recognized that "the challenge of diversity – both religious and racial – sounded a knell for the aspirations that had energized those who founded the United Church."[4] In Canada, the history of the church relationship between Koreans and Canadians contributes to our knowledge of the effect that religious and racial diversity had for the UCC and its mission to Korea. From the beginnings of that relationship, Koreans clearly did not share the Anglo Canadian version of Protestant nationalism and in fact had their own version that challenged unexamined contradictions in the missionaries' approach to missions. The reality of a uniquely Korean Christianity with anti-colonial aspirations for an independent Korean nation was latent in the first Korean Protestant

Conclusion

converts. Later, a Korean Protestantism independent from missionary influence and free to think its own thoughts and develop its own way in theology and politics found one expression in the formation of the PROK. This event forced the Canadian church to consider its position vis-à-vis its colonial past and other Western missions. During the period of military dictatorship in South Korea, Korean Christians began to articulate their objections to the Canadian missionary attitudes and policies which had been entrenched since their arrival three generations earlier. As the South Korean Democratization Movement gathered steam, the PROK successfully forced the transformation of UCC missionary culture and the political economy of their relationship. At the same time, this transformation contributed to a new Korean theological approach that re-contextualized Christianity within the postcolonial era and deconstructed the authority of Western Christianity. UCC women, within the gendered third space, were also transformed by their experiences of political oppression and resistance. Later, as they arrived in Canada as immigrants, Koreans continued to challenge the UCC with a new vision for the Canadian church and nation in a way that was consistent with the critiques developed in Korea. Their presence in the Canadian church called into question its colonial foundations just as it helped contextualize its diminishing influence in postcolonial Canadian society.

The development of Korean Christianity had a significant impact on the UCC and the Canadian religious landscape. That impact cannot be fully understood outside the history of the Canadian Missionary Enterprise. Rather than empty vessels that allowed themselves to be filled with the water of Anglo Protestant ideas and culture, Koreans who came into contact with Canadian missionaries were pioneers who filled the furrows of their newly plowed fields with waters from their own wells of history, philosophy, religion and politics. Korean agency and the ways that Korean Christians adopted the Christian Protestant religion on their own terms are responsible for many of the changes that occurred in the Canadian mission in Korea and threw the church in Canada into postcolonial relief. Accounts of the beginning of Korean Christianity, for example, show that Korean Christians did not entirely let go of their past religious and cultural traditions. While Christianity provided a source of emotional and political support as well as a vehicle with which to transition into a modern society, it also became a vessel of precious Korean traditions, notably the Korean language and hangeul script which missionaries helped to resurrect, but also such traditions as jesa which were frowned on by Western missionaries. While many Koreans did abandon the jesa tradition after they converted, many did not. Kim Yakyeon, the leader of the Myeongdong community, is one example. Another example is the Rev. Kay Cho who three generations later introduced it to Anglo Canadian parishioners as a way of guiding them through their experiences of grief and loss. Thus, not only was the tradition kept alive in the Korean context and church, it was also passed on to the Canadian church and context through the channel of Korean Christian leadership. More generally with regard to the function of Christianity in preserving a distinct Korean culture, just as the early Korean congregations had done in Korea, Korean Christian communities in Canada used the church as a way to preserve and promote their culture and language in a strange land.

As the etymology of the word "mission" implies, the history of the Canadian mission in Korea is defined by the movement of people. The initial trickle of Canadian missionaries across geographical and national boundaries was only the beginning of a much larger movement. The conversion of Koreans to Christianity was connected to the migration of large numbers of Koreans flowing north across the boundary between Korea and China. The ascendency of communist forces in the same region led to a mass exodus as many thousands of those same Korean converts spilled across the 38th parallel to South Korea. Finally, globalization and neocolonial politics burst the Korean dam scattering a Korean diaspora across the Pacific and around the world. The initial trickle of missionaries created channels that contributed to the arrival of many in Canada and the settlement of a number of those in the UCC. The migration of Korean Christians to Canada turned out to be at least as significant to Canada and the Canadian church as the small envoy of Canadian missionaries had been to prewar Korea and its religious development.

In addition to a history of mutual influence, this study has shed light on the historic tension between religious and national commitments in relationships born of the Missionary Enterprise. Anglo nationalism was a core, if not always explicit, feature of Protestantism as it was presented to Koreans by Canadian missionaries. Canadians believed that their missionaries and the Anglo version of the Protestant religion they promoted were an important vehicle for "civilization," a code word for a society that resembled Anglo Protestant Canada under the influence of strong and stable (British imperial) government.

Canada's first prime minister had proclaimed "the best civilizers are our missionaries,"[5] and Canadian protestants believed it. They took for granted that a global population of Protestants, who shared their values, would help to unite the world in a new form of Christendom. However, Koreans detected the repugnant colonial assumptions hidden in this approach and did not passively receive what they were being offered; they countered with their own version of Protestant nationalism. For the first Korean Christians, both spiritual renewal and the impulse to resist Japanese colonialism flowed alike from the waters of their baptism. Eventually Korean Christians, struggling under a national government which had usurped the power of the people and aligned itself with American power, began to articulate their message of salvation in terms of a post-national concept, minjung. The minjung were a diverse group of people united by their culture of opposition against oppression. They were not a minjok, a population that identified uncritically with a nation-state fronted by those who looked and sounded like them.

The legacy of famous Canadian missionaries in Korea such as James Gale, Frank Schofield, and Oliver Avison has recently served Korea and Canada as a source of soft power for business and diplomatic engagements between the two countries. This speaks to the ongoing potential of Canada's missionary history to foster cooperation, particularly within the system of global American hegemony. Notwithstanding this connection and lingering memories of its colonial undertones, Canada's missionary past is celebrated in other parts of the world as well. Even in China, people still talk in positive terms of the Canadian "volunteers."[6] Beyond symbols of (potential) economic and political cooperation, however, it is important to reflect on the institutional engagement these missionaries represent and how the missionary engagement challenged Canada and its churches. With this self knowledge, Canadians have an opportunity to overcome colonial tendencies in their institutions, religious and otherwise, and further relationships with once-colonized peoples in more constructive ways than they have done in the past. The history of the Korean-Canadian church relationship, for example, has served in the past and could again serve as an important point of contact between the Canadian state and both North and South Korean states and an impetus for geo-political reconciliation and peace. Canadian missionaries buried in North Korea and remaining signs of their historic activity could still help to frame diplomatic relations with North

Korea. Korean-Canadians, such as Pastor Hyeon Soo Lim who was detained in North Korea in 2015 and spent two and a half years in prison, and Jeong Hak-pil who was interviewed for this book are examples of an ongoing connection between Canadians and North Korea. Lingering memories of a missionary past may be the reason Canada is still able to exert some influence on North Korea[7] in the same way that it continues to contribute to Canada's stature in China,[8] possibly allowing Canada to play an important mediating role in tensions in the region. And lessons learned from the missionary encounter might continue to help reframe Canadian foreign and domestic policy.

Nation-states and nationalisms, as defining features of the contemporary landscape, are challenged by mission histories such as this one. Missionaries who travelled and lived in Korea spent decades of their life there, buried family members there, and made some of their closest friends there. Rather than merely converting others, they were themselves transformed in many ways. As missionary Marion Current once said to me in conversation, "I'm an egg: white on the outside, but yellow on the inside." For her as for many others, Korea was home and she was, in some very real sense, Korean. Sang Chul Lee called four different nations home over the course of his life and sought to articulate for members of his congregation the reality that they could be Korean and Canadian at the same time without shame or contradiction. In Manchuria and northeastern Korea as well as in South Korea during the Democratization Movement, missionaries found that their empathy for the people they worked with compelled them to transgress their traditional national allegiances and sometimes, even, the law of the land. These stories of people on the move defy neat understandings of nations and nationalities and also question the viability of nation-states and nationalisms as they are currently conceived in the postcolonial world. As Wenh-In Ng humbly put it, "perhaps it is time for the church to be seeking as alternative interpretation of *national*."[9]

Finally, the challenge that Minjung theology has levelled at religious categories, including Christianity itself, resonates with many of the experiences connected to the Canadian Missionary Enterprise in Korea. In the same way that a nation cannot ultimately limit the political or ethical commitments of human beings, the history of the Korean-Canadian church relationship shows that Christians crossing national boundaries challenged Christian categories themselves. Interactions between Koreans and Canadian missionaries led to

Conclusion

challenges to Christianity's claims to be able to define and control the means of redemption and salvation. This constitutes a radical challenge to rigid Western definitions of religion and religious communities. Such a challenge has implications for Canadian society. A different understanding of religion would contribute to the truth and reconciliation process between Canadian churches and indigenous communities. It also promises to deepen conversations regarding systemic racism in Canadian society and institutions given that problem is often also connected to religious belief.

In short, the history of the Korean-Canadian church relationship underlines the changeable nature of human identities, particularly in the postcolonial era marked by an accelerated movement of people and blending of cultures. The identity of Korean Christians underwent tremendous change in the twentieth century. Each new context meant a reinvention of religious and national identities. Likewise, Canadian missionaries had to reinvent themselves and their institutions over the same period. Those transformations were visible in liminal moments reflected, as it were, on the water in Dragon's Well: on the contested Manchurian plains, inside a grand missionary house, in the gendered third space of the Democratization Movement, or in the shrinking Anglo congregations of the UCC. In each of these moments new identities emerged for Canadians as they transitioned from religious role models to friends, from models of moral uprightness to flawed human beings with a blemished past, from leaders to supporters, from landlords to tenants, from religious authorities to students of a new theology. While some of these new identities were fleeting, they all point to a new horizon of human possibility and a possible new chapter in Canadian Protestant history.

The graves of missionaries and Korean immigrants represent more than an ending. They also represent new beginnings. This was certainly the thinking of Sang Chul Lee when he purchased his grave plot in York Cemetery. His funeral plans, while a recognition of an ending, signified new roots, a new home, and a new history. Likewise, the passing of missionary children represented not only the death of young hopes and dreams, but the birth of an intercultural relationship that continues long after the missionary withdrawal from the northwestern provinces of the Korean peninsula and Kando, Manchuria. For some Canadian missionaries, it was important that their final resting place be Korea, so strong was their sense of connection to that place. Mainline Protestantism and the Missionary Enterprise that animated it are no longer the privileged organizations within the Canadian nation-state they once were. But the legacy of their existence, good and bad, is still very present in the Canadian postcolonial context and will likely shape our future. This is an ambiguous but ultimately hopeful reality. Gazing down Dragon's Well together, there is much to feel, much to identify with, and much to learn from.

Notes

INTRODUCTION

1 Yun Dongju, *Haneulgwa Baramgwa Byeolgwa Ssi* (Seoul: Mareubuk Geombani, 2017), 20. Translation by the author. Original text below:

자화상

산모퉁이를 돌아 논가 외딴 우물을 홀로 찾아가선 가만히 들여다봅니다. 우물 속에는 달이 밝고 구름이 흐르고 하늘이 펼치고 파아란 바람이 불고 가을이 있습니다.

그리고 한 사나이가 있습니다. 어쩐지 그 사나이가 미워져 돌아갑니다. 돌아가다 생각하니 그 사나이가 가엾어집니다. 도로 가 들여다보니 사나이는 그대로 있습니다.

다시 그 사나이가 미워져 돌아갑니다. 돌아가다 생각하니 그 사나이가 그리워집니다.

우물 속에는 달이 밝고 구름이 흐르고 하늘이 펼치고 파아란 바람이 불고 가을이 있고 추억처럼 사나이가 있습니다.

2 Hanguk Gidokgyo Jangnohoe, *Han Somang Anaeseo: Hanguk – Kanadagyohoe Seongyohyeopnyeok 100junyeon Ginyeommunjip* (Seoul: Hanguk Gidokgyo Jangnohoe Chulpan, 1998), 30.

3 용정 (룡정) - 龍井. Present day Longjing (龙井市); in Jilin Province, China. Variously inscribed as Lungchingtun, Ryong Jung, or Yung Jong by Canadian missionaries.

4 Young-Sik Yoo, "The impact of Canadian missionaries in Korea, a Historical Survey of Early Canadian Mission Work, 1888–1898" (PhD diss., University of Toronto, 1996), http://hdl.handle.net/1807/10655.

5 Alvyn Austin, *Saving China: Canadian Missionaries in the Middle Kingdom, 1888–1959* (Toronto: University of Toronto Press, 1986).

6 Moon Chai Rin and Kim Shin Mook, *Giringabiwa Gomannye-ui Kkum: Moon Chai Rin Kim Shin Mook Hoegorok* (Seoul: Samin Chulpansa, 2006).

7 William Scott, *A History of the Canadian Mission to Korea, 1898–1970s*, revised and expanded by J. Greig McMullin (Belleville, ON: Guardian Books, 2009).

8 Richard Rutt, *A Biography of James Scarth Gale and a New Edition of His History of the Korean People* (Seoul: Royal Asiatic Society, Korea Branch, 1972).

9 Lee Jang Nag, *I Shall Be Buried in Korea: A Biography of Dr Frank William Schofield*, trans. Choi Jin Young (self published, 1989); Kyu Hwan Sihn, "'The 34th National Representative,' Dr Frank Schofield (1889–1970)," *Yonsei Medical Journal* 60, no. 4 (April 2019): 315–18; Barbara Legault and John F. Prescott, "'The Arch Agitator': Dr Frank W. Schofield and the Korean Independence Movement," *Canadian Veterinary Journal* 50, no. 8 (August 2009): 865–72.

10 Allen D. Clark, *Avison of Korea: the Life of Oliver R. Avison, MD* (Seoul: Yonsei University Press, 1979); Jai Keun Choi, "Preeminent Medical Missionary in the 20th Century: Oliver R. Avison," *Yonsei Medical Journal* 59, no. 1 (January 2018): 1–3.

11 George *Patterson, Missionary Life among the Cannibals: Being the Life of the Rev. John Geddie, First Missionary to the New Hebrides, with a History of the Nova Scotia Presbyterian Mission on that Group (Toronto: James Campbell, 1882).*

12 Jean Tellier, *The North-West Is Our Mother: The Story of Louis Riel's People* (Toronto: Harper Collins, 2019).

13 "McDougall, George Millward," *Dictionary of Canadian Biography*, accessed 25 August 2020, http://www.biographi.ca/en/bio/mcdougall_george_millward_10E.html.

14 J.R. Miller, *Compact, Contract, Covenant: Aboriginal Treaty Making in Canada* (Toronto: University of Toronto Press, 2009).

15 John S. Milloy, *A National Crime: The Canadian Government and the Residential School System, 1879 to 1986* (Winnipeg: University of Manitoba Press, 2017).

16 Phyllis Airhart, *A Church with the Soul of a Nation: Making and Remaking the United Church of Canada* (Montreal and Kingston: McGill-Queen's University Press, 2014), 4.

17 Elizabeth A. McCully, *A Corn of Wheat: Or the Life of Rev. W.J. McKenzie of Korea* (London: Westminister Press, 1903).

Notes to pages 12–15

18 Robert A. Wright, *A World Mission: Canadian Protestantism and the Quest for a New International Order, 1918–1939* (Montreal and Kingston: McGill-Queen's University Press, 1991).

19 Alvyn Austin and Jamie Scott, introduction to *Canadian Missionaries, Indigenous Peoples: Representing Religion at Home and Abroad*, ed. Alvyn Austin and Jamie Scott (Toronto: University of Toronto Press, 2005).

20 John Webster Grant, *Moon of Wintertime: Missionaries and the Indians of Canada in Encounter since 1534* (Toronto: University of Toronto Press, 1984), 266.

21 Nancy Christie and Michael Gauvreau, "'Even the Hippies Were Only Very Slowly Going Secular': Dechristianization and the Culture of Individualism in North America and Western Europe," *The Sixties and Beyond: Dechristianization in North America and Europe, 1945–2000*, ed. Nancy Christie and Michael Gavreau (Toronto: University of Toronto Press, 2013), 4.

22 Brian Clarke and Stuart Macdonald, *Leaving Christianity: Changing Allegiances in Canada since 1945* (Montreal and Kingston: McGill-Queen's University Press 2017), 57, 197.

23 Airhart, *A Church with the Soul of a Nation*, 297.

24 Edward Said, *Orientalism* (New York: Random House, 1978), 122.

25 Edward Said, *Culture and Imperialism* (New York: Vintage Books, 1993).

26 Ruth Compton Brouwer, *Modern Women Modernizing Men: The Changing Missions of Three Professional Women in Asia and Africa, 1902–69* (Vancouver: UBC Press, 2002), 6.

27 Ruth C. Brouwer, "When Missions Became Development: Ironies of 'NGOization' in Mainstream Canadian Churches in the 1960s," *Canadian Historical Review* 91, no. 4 (2010): 661–93.

28 Ruth Compton Brouwer, "From Missionaries to NGOs," in *Canada and the Third World: Overlapping Histories*, ed. Karen Dubinsky, Sean Mills, and Scott Rutherford (Toronto: University of Toronto Press, 2016), 137.

29 Greer Anne Wenh-In Ng, "The United Church of Canada: A Church Fittingly National," in *Christianity and Ethnicity in Canada*, ed. Paul Bramadat and David Seljak (Toronto: University of Toronto Press, 2008), 208–9.

30 UCC Yearbook, 1988.

31 Loraine Mackenzie Shepherd, "From Colonization to Right Relations: The Evolution of United Church of Canada Missions within Aboriginal Communities," *International Review of Mission* 103, no. 1 (April 2014): 153–71.

Notes to pages 16–34

32 Homi K. Bhabha, *The Location of Culture* (New York: Routledge, 1994).

33 Mary Louise Pratt, *Imperial Eyes: Travel Writing and Transculturation* (London: Routledge Press, 1992).

34 Ruth Sanz Sabido, *Memories of the Spanish Civil War: Conflict and Community in Rural Spain* (New York: Rowman & Littlefield, 2016).

35 Sebastian C.H. Kim and Kirsteen Kim, eds., *A History of Korean Christianity* (Cambridge: Cambridge University Press, 2015), 6.

36 Sang Chul Lee and Eric Weingartner, *The Wanderer: The Autobiography of a United Church Moderator* (Winfield, BC: Woodlake Books, 1989).

37 Ibid, 86.

CHAPTER ONE

1 Gen. 1.1–2, New Revised Standard Version.

2 Kando of this period is roughly the same as present-day Jiandao Autonomous region otherwise known as the Yanbian Korean Autonomous Prefecture, located in Jilin province on the Chinese side of the border with North Korea. Kando is the spelling used by missionaries. Gando would be the proper spelling using the Revised Romanization system for the Korean language.

3 間島, the ideograms for Kando literally mean 間 – "in between" and 島 – "island." Canadian missionaries referred to it as the "In Between Place."

4 Prasenjit Duara, *Sovereignty and Authenticity: Manchukuo and the East Asian Modern* (Lanham, MD: Rowman and Littlefield, 2004), 44.

5 Norman Smith, introduction to *Empire and Environment in the Making of Manchuria*, ed. Norman Smith (Vancouver: UBC Press, 2017), 3.

6 Hyun Ok Park, *Two Dreams in One Bed: Empire, Social Life, and the Origins of the North Korean Revolution in Manchuria* (Duke, 2005), 43.

7 Ibid., 87.

8 Ibid., 156.

9 Mariko Asano Tamanoi, introduction to *Crossed Histories: Manchuria in the Age of Empire*, ed. Mariko Asano Tamanoi (Honolulu: Association for Asian Studies, 2005), 5.

10 Seonmin Kim, *Ginseng and Borderland: Territorial Boundaries and Political Relations between Qing China and Choson Korea 1636–1912* (Oakland, CA: University of California Press, 2017), 1ff.

11 Duara, *Sovereignty and Authenticity*, 41; Moon Chai Rin and Kim Shin Mook, *Giringabiwa Gomannye-ui Kkum: Moon Chai Rin Kim Shin Mook Hoegorok* (Seoul: Samin Chulpansa, 2006), 30.

12 James Reardon-Anderson, *Reluctant Pioneers: China's Expansion Northward, 1644–1937* (Stanford: Stanford University Press, 2005), 23.

Notes to pages 34–7

13 Moon and Kim, *Giringabiwa Gomannye-ui Kkum*, 38, 378.

14 Sang Chul Lee, *Vladivostok-eseo Toronto-kkaji: Yeollin Segyereul Gajin Nageune* (Korea: Hanguk Gidokgyo Jangrohoe Chulpansa, 2010), 23.

15 Moon and Kim, *Giringabiwa Gomannye-ui Kkum*, 80, 463.

16 Ibid., 155. Moon recalls that it was Koreans who designed their church in Yongjeong but Chinese labourers who did the hard work of building it.

17 Lee, *Vladivostok-eseo Toronto-kkaji*, 29.

18 Ibid., 34.

19 Florence Murray, *At the Foot of Dragon Hill: The Story of a Surgeon's Two Decades in Manchuria and Korea, and the Challenges She Faced as a Woman Doctor in a Culture So Primitive its Women Were Not Even Considered Worthy of Having Names* (New York: E.P. Dutton & Company, 1975), 29.

20 Norman Smith, *Intoxicating Manchuria: Alcohol, Opium, and Culture in China's Northeast* (Vancouver: UBC Press, 2012), 31.

21 Murray, *At the Foot of Dragon Hill*, 35.

22 Charles K. Armstrong, *The North Korean Revolution, 1945–1950* (Ithaca: Cornell University Press, 2003), 18.

23 義兵 – 의병, literally "righteous army," a term that was coined during the Japanese invasions of 1592 to identify bands of Korean freedom fighters operating independently of the national army.

24 Interview with Chun Sunyeong, 13 July 2019.

25 Andre Schmid, *Korea Between Empires 1895–1919* (New York: Columbia University Press, 2002), 252; Duara, *Sovereignty and Authenticity*. Duara argues that even after the creation of the puppet state of Manchukuo, the region had more latitude to guide their own development than is often realized.

26 William Scott, *A History of the Canadian Mission to Korea, 1898–1970s*, revised and expanded by J. Greig McMullin (Belleville, ON: Guardian Books, 2009), 527.

27 Armstrong, *The North Korean Revolution*, 9.

28 Ibid., 26.

29 Byung-Mu Ahn, *Stories of Minjung Theology: the Theological Journey of Ahn Byung-Mu in His Own Words*, trans. Hannah In and Wongi Park (Atlanta: SBL Press, 2018), 8.

30 Armstrong, *The North Korean Revolution*, 117.

31 Scott, *A History of the Canadian Mission to Korea*, 527.

32 Moon and Kim, *Giringabiwa Gomannye-ui Kkum*, 459.

33 Bruce Cumings, *The Korean War: A History* (New York: The Modern Library, 2010), 55.

34 Scott, *A History of the Canadian Mission to Korea*, 527.

246   Notes to pages 37–8

35 The "GOHEE" Committee for the Very Reverend Sang Chul Lee, eds., *The Path of a Wanderer His Vision and Dream* (Korea: Christian Literature Society of Korea, 1994), 36.

36 R.H. Hardie to Dr Grierson, 18 April 1909, file 3, box 1, accession 79.204C, UCC Archives, Toronto; Lee, *Vladivostok-eseo Toronto-kkaji*, 33.

37 R.H. Hardie to Dr Grierson, 18 April 1909, file 3, box 1, accession 79.204C, UCC Archives, Toronto; R. Grierson to R.P. MacKay, 11 January 1910, file 4, box 1, accession 79.204C, UCC Archives, Toronto.

38 A.H. Barker to A.E. Armstrong, 29 July 1911, file 5, box 1, accession 79.204C, UCC Archives, Toronto. Interestingly, I came across no reports of Buddhist activity in Kando.

39 Diana Lary, "Manchuria: History and Environment," in *Empire and Environment in the Making of Manchuria*, ed. Norman Smith (Vancouver: UBC Press, 2017), 28.

40 Moon and Kim, *Giringabiwa Gomannye-ui Kkum*, 206.

41 Ibid., 374–5.

42 Kyeongjae Kim, "Gajoksaui jipyeongeul neomeo," in *Giringabiwa Gomannye-ui Kkum*, ed. Moon Chai Rin Kim Shin Mook (Seoul: Samin Chulpansa, 2006), 627ff.

43 Letter from Moon Chai Rin to Lois Wilson re: book "Christianity and Korean Nationalism in Manchuria," dated 19 December 1980, file 8, box 1, accession 94.170C, UCC Archives, Toronto.

44 Moon and Kim, *Giringabiwa Gomannye-ui Kkum*.

45 Letter of Faye Moon to Ed, dated 23 January 1986, file 001682, box 48, U of T Special Collection on Democratization and Human Rights in Korea, Toronto.

46 Moon and Kim, *Giringabiwa Gomannye-ui Kkum*, 29, 374.

47 Scott, *A History of the Canadian Mission to Korea*, 419.

48 Moon and Kim, *Giringabiwa Gomannye-ui Kkum*, 33. The above is Moon's memory. Kim has a slightly different memory of the three points the Silhak leaders emphasized to encourage the community to move to Manchurcha: Moon and Kim, *Giringabiwa Gomannye-ui Kkum*, 375.

49 實學 – 실학, literally "practical learning" and often translated as the Realist School of Confucianism.

    It should be noted that Moon and Kim's description of Silhak scholars might be shaped by later developments and nationalist commitments. The term "silhak" was not used to refer to "practical learning" Confucianism until the 1920s and it is unlikely that Kim Yakyeon or any of the other scholars Moon and Kim speak about used that term to refer to themselves. For more information on the history of the Confucian school of Silhak

Notes to pages 39–41

please see Michael C. Kalton, "An Introduction to Silhak," *Korean Journal* 15, no. 5 (1975): 29–46.

50 Moon and Kim, *Giringabiwa Gomannye-ui Kkum*, 32.

51 Ibid., 380. 東學 – 동학 or "Eastern Learning."

52 The Donghak movement was rebranded the religion of Cheondokyo and survives to this day.

53 Moon and Kim, *Giringabiwa Gomannye-ui Kkum*, 378.

54 Ibid., 378ff.

55 Schmid, *Korea Between Empires 1895–1919*, 224–52; Stella Xu, *Reconstructing Ancient Korean History: Formation of Korean-ness in the Shadow of History* (Lanham: Lexington Press, 2016).

56 Moon and Kim, *Giringabiwa Gomannye-ui Kkum*, 54, 380.

57 Ibid., 41.

58 書堂 – 서당 literally "book place" sometimes translated as a "village school."

59 Moon and Kim, *Giringabiwa Gomannye-ui Kkum*, 41.

60 Ibid., 35.

61 明東 – 명동.

62 Moon and Kim, *Giringabiwa Gomannye-ui Kkum*, 402ff. (This is the village into which the famous resistance poet Yun Dongju, quoted in the introduction, was born.)

63 Ibid., 410.

64 Jeong was the father of David Chung, second minister of Toronto Korean United Church and later professor of Eastern Religions at Carlton University.

65 Moon and Kim, *Giringabiwa Gomannye-ui Kkum*, 44.

66 Lee, *Vladivostok-eseo Toronto-kkaji*, 33; Sang-Chul Lee and Eric Weingartner, *The Wanderer: The Autobiography of a United Church Moderator* (Winfield, BC: Woodlake Books, 1989), 32.

67 Moon and Kim, *Giringabiwa Gomannye-ui Kkum*, 375.

68 Ahn, *Stories of Minjung Theology*, 6.

69 Moon and Kim, *Giringabiwa Gomannye-ui Kkum*, 45.

70 Ahn, *Stories of Minjung Theology*, 6.

71 Ibid.

72 Ibid., 8.

73 Moon and Kim, *Giringabiwa Gomannye-ui Kkum*, 404. An was a Catholic and if Moon's recollection is true that he trained at a Protestant school this would be an example of the ways the nationalist commitment trumped denominational allegiances during this period.

74 Ibid., 450.

75 Ibid., 451.

76 Ibid., 83.

248 Notes to pages 42–4

77 Ibid., 413.

78 Seo Sangyun's brother, Seo Sangun, who was with him when he first met Ross, later moved to Sorae in northern Korea and was the one who, following William McKenzie's sudden death, wrote the letter to the Presbyterian church in the Maritimes asking that Canadian missionaries be sent to Korea.

79 Lak-Geoon George Paik, *The History of Protestant Missions in Korea 1832–1910*, 4th edition (Seoul: Yonsei University Press, 1987), 51; Sung-Deuk Oak, *The Making of Korean Christianity: Protestant Encounters with Korean Religions, 1876–1915* (Waco, TX: Baylor University Press, 2013), 50; Scott, *A History of the Canadian Mission to Korea*, 128.

80 Scott, *A History of the Canadian Mission to Korea*, 129; Paik, *The History of Protestant Missions in Korea*, 53–4.

81 한글.

82 Jahyun Kim Haboush, *The Great East Asian War and the Birth of the Korean Nation* (New York: Columbia University Press, 2016).

83 Kim Yong-bok, "Korean Christianity as a Messianic Movement of the People," in *Minjung Theology: People as the Subjects of History*, ed. Commission on Theological Concerns of the Christian Conference of Asia (Maryknoll, NY: Orbis Books, 1983), 84. Catholic Christianity had come to Korea a century earlier through the conversion in Beijing of a noble class Korean. He had brought with him Christian writings translated into the East Asian ideograms, which could only be read by the most educated of Korean society.

84 Suh Kwang-sun David, "A Biographical Sketch of an Asian Consultation," in *Minjung Theology: People as the Subjects of History*, ed. Commission on Theological Concerns of the Christian Conference of Asia (Maryknoll, NY: Orbis Books, 1983), 21–2.

85 Scott, *A History of the Canadian Mission to Korea*, 691.

86 Kim, "Korean Christianity as a Messianic Movement of the People," 84.

87 Ibid., 80.

88 Scott, *A History of the Canadian Mission to Korea*, 368.

89 Ahn, *Stories of Minjung Theology*, 6.

90 祭祀 – 제사.

91 Moon and Kim, *Giringabiwa Gomannye-ui Kkum*, 393.

92 Don Baker, "Unexpected Fruit: Catholicism and the Rise of Civil Society in Korea," preliminary version of a paper for a colloquium on Christianity in Korea (The Hahan Moo-sook Colloquium in the Korean Humanities), 21 October 2000, George Washington University; Donald N. Clark, "Christianity in Modern Korea" *About Asia* 11, no. 2 (Fall 2006): 35.

93 Moon and Kim, *Giringabiwa Gomannye-ui Kkum*, 426.

94 Ibid., 59.

95 Ibid., 76.

96 Scott, *A History of the Canadian Mission to Korea*, 407; R.H. Hardie to Dr Grierson, 18 April 1909, file 3, box 1, accession 79.204C, UCC Archives, Toronto; W.R. Foote to R.P. McKay, 11 August 1910, file 4, box 1, accession 79.204C, UCC Archives, Toronto.

97 Petition of Yongjeong Christians date 4 November 1912, file 8, box 1, accession 79.204C, UCC Archives, Toronto.

98 Interview with Chun Sunyeong, 13 July 2019; Interview with Kim Ikseon, 6 July 2019.

99 Timothy S. Lee, *Born Again: Evangelicalism in Korea* (Honolulu: University of Hawai'i Press, 2010), 34.

100 Commission on Theological Concerns of the Christian Conference of Asia, ed., *Minjung Theology: People as the Subjects of History* (Maryknoll, NY: Orbis Books, 1983), 18.

101 Ahn, *Stories of Minjung Theology*, 8.

102 Ibid., 10.

103 Young-sik Yoo, "The Impact of Canadian Missionaries in Korea: A Historical Survey of Early Canadian Mission Work, 1888–1898" (PhD diss., University of Toronto, 1996), 137ff.

104 In present-day Ryongyon County, South Hwanghae Province, North Korea.

105 Like McKenzie, MacKay was the founder of a Canadian mission. Until 1949, his was the only Protestant mission on the north part of the Island. Also like McKenzie, MacKay quickly acquired a following and made converts. Unlike McKenzie, however, his ministry lasted decades and his legacy has been embraced by the Taiwanese state and includes a large hospital in Taipei that was named in his honour. The mission he started remained with the Presbyterians after Church Union in 1925. With its parallel context of Japanese colonialism, this history offers an interesting comparison to the Korea Mission; Alvyn Austin, *Saving China: Canadian Missionaries in the Middle Kingdom, 1888–1959* (Toronto: University of Toronto Press, 1986), 34.

106 Paik, *The History of Protestant Missions in Korea*, 51; Yoo, "The Impact of Canadian Missionaries in Korea," 422.

107 The letter from the Koreans in Sorae was deliberately hidden by Canadian Presbyterian church officials anxious about taking on new mission expenses and then uncovered by an enthusiastic group of young adults connected to the Student Volunteer Movement. See Scott, *A History of the Canadian Mission to Korea*, 251ff.

250 Notes to pages 46–9

108 Hanguk Gidokgyo Jangnohoe, *Han Somang Anaeseo: Hanguk – Kanadagyohoe Seongyohyeopnyeok 100junyeon Ginyeommunjip* (Seoul: Hanguk Gidokgyo Jangnohoe Chulpan, 1998),160ff.

109 Paik, *The History of Protestant Missions in Korea*, 379.

110 Interview with Kim Ikseon, 6 July 2019.

111 Scott, *A History of the Canadian Mission to Korea*, 275. As mentioned above, Sorae was in the northwest, not the northeast, but was closer geographically and culturally to the Canadian mission field than the southeast which had been the alternative.

112 Ibid., 277.

113 Ibid.

114 Petition of Yongjeong Christians, dated 4 November 1912, file 8, box 1, accession 79.204C, UCC Archives, Toronto.

115 Scott, *A History of the Canadian Mission to Korea*, 407.

116 Ibid., 409.

117 Ibid., 419.

118 Ibid. The name means "dragon's well." 용정 (룡정) – 龍井.

119 Scott, *A History of the Canadian Mission to Korea,* 527.

120 Ibid., 432; Robert Kim, "The Forgotten American Missionaries of Pyongyang," *Atlas Obscura*, 25 April 2017, https://www.atlasobscura.com/articles/american-pyongyang-missionaries-north-korea.

121 T.D. Mansfield to A.E. Armstrong, 28 July 1911, file 5, box 1, accession 79.204C, UCC Archives, Toronto.

122 T.D. Mansfield to A.E. Armstrong, 28 November 1912, file 9, box 1, accession 79.204C, UCC Archives, Toronto.

123 Scott, *A History of the Canadian Mission to Korea*, 420.

124 Ibid., 442n87.

125 Lee, *The Wanderer,* 35; Interview with Kim Ikseon, 6 July 2019; Interview with Chun Sunyeong, 13 July 2019.

126 A.H. Barker to A.E. Armstrong, 29 July 1911, file 5, box 1, accession 79.204C, UCC Archives, Toronto.

127 J.M. Scott to R.P. MacKay, 20 November 1912, file 9, box 1, accession 79.204C, UCC Archives, Toronto.

128 R. Grierson to R.P. MacKay, 11 January 1910, file 4, box 1, accession 79.204C, UCC Archives, Toronto.

129 Jean Tellier, *The North-West is our Mother: The Story of Louis Riel's People, the Metis Nation* (Toronto: Harper Collins, 2019).

130 Catherine Macdonald, "James Robertson and the Presbyterian Church Extension in Manitoba and the North-West, 1866–1902," in *Prairie Spirit:*

Perspectives on the Heritage of the United Church of Canada in the West, ed. Dennis L. Butcher, Catherine Macdonald, Margaret E. McPherson, Raymond R. Smith, and A. McKibbin Watts (Winnipeg: University of Manitoba Press, 1985), 85.

131 Macdonald, "James Robertson and the Presbyterian Church Extension," 95.

132 Benjamin Smillie, "The Woodsworths: James and J.S. – Father and Son," in *Prairie Spirit: Perspectives on the Heritage of the United Church of Canada in the West,* ed. Dennis L. Butcher, Catherine Macdonald, Margaret E. McPherson, Raymond R. Smith, and A. McKibbin Watts (Winnipeg: University of Manitoba Press, 1985), 104.

133 Macdonald, "James Robertson and the Presbyterian Church Extension," 87.

134 Margaret E. McPherson, "Head, Heart and Purse: The Presbyterian Women's Missionary Society in Canada, 1876–1925," in *Prairie Spirit: Perspectives on the Heritage of the United Church of Canada in the West,* ed. Dennis L. Butcher, Catherine Macdonald, Margaret E. McPherson, Raymond R. Smith, and A. McKibbin Watts (Winnipeg: University of Manitoba Press, 1985).

135 Canada Council Laymen's Alex Sutherland Missionary Movement, *Canada's Missionary Congress* (Toronto: Canadian Council Laymen's Missionary Movement, 1909).

136 "Our Duty to the Asiatics in Canada," in *Canada's Missionary Congress,* ed. Canada Council Laymen's Missionary Movement (Toronto: Canadian Council Laymen's Missionary Movement, 1909), 110.

137 N.W. Rowell, "Canada's Opportunity at Home and Abroad," in *Canada's Missionary Congress,* ed. Canada Council Laymen's Missionary Movement (Toronto: Canadian Council Laymen's Missionary Movement, 1909), 39.

138 S.M. Zwemer, "The Impact of Christianity on Non-Christian Religions," in *Canada's Missionary Congress,* ed. Canada Council Laymen's Missionary Movement (Toronto: Canadian Council Laymen's Missionary Movement, 1909), 84.

139 Robert Grierson, "Episodes from a Long Long Trail," self-published memoir.

140 Mary Louise Pratt, *Imperial Eyes: Travel Writing and Transculturation* (London: Routledge Press, 1992), 6. Pratt's postcolonial theory about contact zones posits that in addition to the impact Europeans had on the societies they encountered abroad, their encounters also shaped Europe. This occurred often through the reports and descriptions Europeans would compose and send back to the metropole.

141 Elizabeth A. McCully, *A Corn of Wheat: The Life of Rev. W.J. McKenzie of Korea* (Toronto: The Westminster Co., 1904), vi.

142 Robert A. Wright, *A World Mission: Canadian Protestantism and the Quest for a New International Order, 1918–1939* (Montreal and Kingston: McGill-Queen's University Press, 1991), 53.

143 Ruth Compton Brouwer, *New Women for God: Canadian Presbyterian women and India Missions, 1876–1914* (Toronto: University of Toronto Press, 1990), 4.

144 Scott does not mention this in his history, perhaps out of a sense of modesty.

145 Interview with Kim Ikseon, 5 July 2019; Frederick J. Glover, "Friends, Foes and Partners: The Relationship between the Canadian Missionaries and the Korean Christians in North-eastern Korea and Manchuria from 1898 until 1927," *Studies in World Christianity: The Edinburgh Review of Theology and Religion* 23, no. 3 (2017): 194–217; Murray, *At the Foot of Dragon Hill*, 37; A. Hamish Ion, *The Cross and the Rising Sun: The Canadian Protestant Missionary Movement in the Japanese Empire, 1872–1931* (Waterloo: Wilfrid Laurier University Press, 1990), 192.

146 Ion, *The Cross and the Rising Sun*, 203.

147 Ibid.

148 Moon and Kim, *Giringabiwa Gomannye-ui Kkum*, 80: Murray, *At the Foot of Dragon Hill*, 29; Hanguk Gidokgyo Jangnohoe, *Han Somang Anaeseo*, 35.

149 Ion, *The Cross and the Rising Sun*, 206.

150 Scott, *A History of the Canadian Mission to Korea*, 591.

151 Glover, "Friends, Foes and Partners", 194.

152 Moon and Kim, *Giringabiwa Gomannye-ui Kkum*, 179.

153 Wright, *A World Mission*, 200.

154 Ibid., 202, 205.

155 Rowell, "Canada's Opportunity at Home and Abroad," 47.

156 Phyllis Airhart, *A Church with the Soul of a Nation: Making and Remaking the United Church of Canada* (Montreal and Kingston: McGill-Queen's University Press, 2014), 12.

157 C.T. McIntire, "Unity among Many: The Formation of the United Church of Canada, 1899–1930," in *A History of the United Church of Canada*, ed. Don Schweitzer (Waterloo, ON: Wilfred Laurier University Press, 2012), 14.

158 Greer Anne Wenh-In Ng, "The United Church of Canada: A Church Fittingly National," in *Christianity and Ethnicity in Canada*, ed. Paul Bramadat and David Seljak (Toronto: University of Toronto Press, 2008), 206ff.

159 Scott, *A History of the Canadian Mission to Korea*, 638–9, 726; Chung-shin Park, *Protestantism and Politics in Korea* (Seattle: University of Washington Press, 2003), 38–9.

160 Scott, *A History of the Canadian Mission to Korea*, 726.

CHAPTER TWO

1 Kim Chai Choon, "The Historical Significance of the PROK," *The Life and Theology of Changgong, Kim Chai Choon*, ed. Sung Kyu Hwang, trans. Yeong Mee Lee (Osan: Hansindaehakgyo Chulpanbu, 2005), 87; original Korean text in Kyeongjae Kim, ed., *JangGong Kim Jae-juneui Salmgwa Shinhak* (Osan: Hansindaehakgyo Chulpanbu, 2014), 346.

2 Kim Chai Choon, "The Historical Significance of the PROK", 87–8.

3 Ibid., 87.

4 The Northern Presbyterian Church or Presbyterian Church in the United States of America (PCUSA) was one of two American Presbyterian missions in Korea. The other was the Southern Presbyterian or Presbyterian Church in the United States (PCUS). This division was based on an historical division of the American Presbyterian church going back to the debate on the legitimacy of slavery.

5 Letter to Rev. McKay, 2 June 1909, file 3, box 1, accession 79.204C, UCC Archives, Toronto.

6 William Scott, *A History of the Canadian Mission to Korea, 1898–1970s*, revised and expanded by J. Greig McMullin (Belleville, ON: Guardian Books, 2009), 407.

7 Ibid., 367.

8 Ibid., 782.

9 Samuel Hugh Moffett, *A History of Christianity in Asia* VOLUME II: *1500 to 1900*, (Maryknoll, New York: Orbis Books, 2005), 524; Scott, *A History of the Canadian Mission to Korea*, 776n2.

10 Scott, *A History of the Canadian Mission to Korea*, 577.

11 Lak-Geoon George Paik, *The History of Protestant Missions in Korea 1832–1910*, 4th edition (Seoul: Yonsei University Press, 1987), 378ff.

12 Ibid., 215–16.

13 Ibid., 235.

14 Scott, *A History of the Canadian Mission to Korea*, 778.

15 Paik, *The History of Protestant Missions in Korea*, 216.

16 Ibid.

17 Ibid., 217.

18 Moon Chai Rin and Kim Shin Mook, *Giringabiwa Gomannye-ui Kkum: Moon Chai Rin Kim Shin Mook Hoegorok* (Seoul: Samin Chulpansa, 2006), 95.

19 Moon and Kim, *Giringabiwa Gomannye-ui Kkum*, 99.

20 Robert Grierson, "Episodes from a Long Long Trail," self-published memoir.

21 Scott, *A History of the Canadian Mission to Korea*, 782.

22 Moon and Kim, *Giringabiwa Gomannye-ui Kkum*, 110.

254 Notes to pages 62–6

23 Ibid., 109. Moon was the third to receive money from the Canadian church to travel abroad for theological study and the second to travel to Canada for a theological education. Chae Pil Kun received a bursary to study in Japan in 1919. Kim Kwan Shik traveled to Canada in 1922. Scott, *A History of the Canadian Mission*, 572.

24 Scott, *A History of the Canadian Mission to Korea*, 778.

25 Ibid., 582.

26 Moon and Kim, *Giringabiwa Gomannye-ui Kkum*, 110.

27 Frederick J. Glover, "Friends, Foes and Partners: The Relationship between the Canadian Missionaries and the Korean Christians in North-eastern Korea and Manchuria from 1898 until 1927," *Studies in World Christianity: The Edinburgh Review of Theology and Religion* 23, no. 3 (2017): 194–217.

28 Scott, *A History of Canadian Missions*, 581.

29 W.L. Swallen to Armstrong, June 1926, file 12, box 1, accession 83.006C, UCC Archives, Toronto.

30 William Scott to A.E. Armstrong, 9 August 1926, file 3 (Correspondence Dr Armstrong – Rev. Wm. Scott), box 1, accession 83.006C, UCC Archives, Toronto.

31 Scott, *A History of the Canadian Mission*, 593.

32 Kim Kyeong-jae, *Kim Chai Choon Pyeongjeon* (Seoul: Samin Chulpansa, 2001), 29.

33 Ibid., 32.

34 Ibid., 34–5.

35 Ibid., 43.

36 Ibid., 45–9.

37 Ibid., 59.

38 Ibid., 63, 67.

39 Ibid., 67.

40 Ibid., 69.

41 Scott, *A History of the Canadian Mission*, 821.

42 Kim, *Kim Chai Choon Pyeongjeon*, 75.

43 Ibid., 85.

44 Scott, *A History of the Canadian Mission*, 776.

45 Kim, *Kim Chai Choon Pyeongjeon*, 86.

46 Scott, *A History of the Canadian Mission*, 617.

47 Ibid., 620.

48 Ibid., 691.

49 Ibid., 637.

50 Ibid., 692.

Notes to pages 66–8

51 No missionaries spent time in jail or were executed over this issue that the author is aware of.

52 Scott, *A History of the Canadian Mission*, 691.

53 "Moffett, Samuel Austin (1864–1939)," accessed 17 July 2020, http://www.bu.edu/missiology/missionary-biography/l-m/moffett-samuel-austin-1864-1939.

54 Canadian mission schools in Kando were not officially within the Japanese Empire as the new nation Manchukuo was ostensibly an independent nation. They were therefore not subject to the same regulations regarding Shinto rituals.

55 Scott, *A History of the Canadian Mission*, 620.

56 Moon and Kim, *Giringabiwa Gomannye-ui Kkum*, 110.

57 Joseon (Usually spelled "Chosun" in English literature of the time. Hangeul조선, and hanja朝鮮, meaning "Morning Calm") was the name given to the country with the blessing of the Ming Emperor by the Yi Dynasty that governed Korea from 1392 to 1910. All Koreans (and Japanese as well) continued to use this name when referring to Korea throughout the Japanese occupation. Joseon seminary, therefore, could be translated Korea Seminary. The North Korean regime continued to use this moniker following the Korean war, perhaps in deference to their Chinese supporters. The South Korea regime, on the other hand, chose to rebrand its nation Hanguk (한국, 韩国, meaning "Country of the Han People") after the title given when, in an attempt to assert its sovereignty against imperial encroachments, the Yi dynasty renamed the country Empire of the Han.

58 Scott, *A History of the Canadian Mission*, 738; Kim Chai Choon, "An Open Letter, 1948," *The Life and Theology of Changgong, Kim Chai Choon*, ed. Sung Kyu Hwang, trans. Yeong Mee Lee (Osan: Hansindaehakgyo Chulpanbu, 2005), 52–3; original Korean text in Kyeongjae Kim, ed., *JangGong Kim Jae-juneui Salmgwa Shinhak* (Osan: Hansindaehakgyo Chulpanbu, 2014), 318.

59 Hanguk Gidokgyo Jangnohoe, *Han Somang Anaeseo: Hanguk – Kanadagyohoe Seongyohyeopnyeok 100junyeon Ginyeommunjip* (Seoul: Hanguk Gidokgyo Jangnohoe Chulpan, 1998), 53.

60 Ibid., 51; Yi MoonSuk, *Lee Oo Chung Pyeongjeon* (Seoul: Samin Chulpansa, 2012), 67–8.

61 Kim, "25 Years of Hanguk Theological Seminary History," 152; original Korean text in Kyeongjae Kim, ed., *JangGong Kim Jae-juneui Salmgwa Shinhak* (Osan: Hansindaehakgyo Chulpanbu, 2014), 407.

62 Kim, *Kim Chai Choon Pyeongjeon*, 152.

256 Notes to pages 68–72

63 Ibid., 117.
64 The stele reads, "學問과 敬虔" (scholarship and piety). Hanshin Daehakwon Sajinjip, *Yisoseongdae: Your Beginning Was Weak, but Your End Will Be Great* (Osan: Hansindaehakgyo Chulpanbu, 2015).
65 Hanguk Gidokgyo Jangnohoe, *Han Somang Anaeseo*, 52.
66 Ibid., 53.
67 Kim, *Kim Chai Choon Pyeongjeon*, 111.
68 Ibid., 294.
69 Ibid., 297.
70 Kim Chai Choon, "The Historical Significance of the PROK," 256; Kim, ed., *JangGong Kim Jae-juneui Salmgwa Shinhak*, 597.
71 Yi, *Lee Oo Chung Pyeongjeon*, 67.
72 Scott, *A History of the Canadian Mission*, 639.
73 Moon and Kim, *Giringabiwa Gomannye-ui Kkum*, 177.
74 Interview with Chun Sukyeong, 13 July 2019.
75 Moon and Kim, *Giringabiwa Gomannye-ui Kkum*, 177.
76 Ibid., 186.
77 Rob Pennington, "Minister Faced Prison Camp Death Three Times," *Toronto Star*, 2 May 1973.
78 Moon and Kim, *Giringabiwa Gomannye-ui Kkum*, 193.
79 Ibid., 196.
80 Ibid., 206.
81 Ibid., 213.
82 Yi, *Lee Oo Chung Pyeongjeon*, 65.
83 Kim, *Kim Chai Choon Pyeongjeon*, 119.
84 Kim, "25 Years of Hankuk Theological Seminary History," 157–8; Kim, ed., *JangGong Kim Jae-juneui Salmgwa Shinhak*, 416.
85 Kim, "25 Years of Hankuk Theological Seminary History," 163; Kim, ed., *JangGong Kim Jae-juneui Salmgwa Shinhak*, 421; Scott, *A History of the Canadian Mission*, 784; Yi, *Lee Oo Chung Pyeongjeon*, 65.
86 Yi, *Lee Oo Chung Pyeongjeon*, 66.
87 Moon and Kim, *Giringabiwa Gomannye-ui Kkum*, 221.
88 Scott, *A History of the Canadian Mission*, 801.
89 Hanguk Gidokgyo Jangnohoe, *Han Somang Anaeseo*, 54–5.
90 Scott, *A History of the Canadian Mission*, 823.
91 Hanguk Gidokgyo Jangnohoe, *Han Somang Anaeseo*, 55.
92 Scott, *A History of the Canadian Mission*, 823.
93 Moon and Kim, *Giringabiwa Gomannye-ui Kkum*, 229.
94 Kim, *Kim Chai Choon Pyeongjeon*, 152; Yi, *Lee Oo Chung Pyeongjeon*, 71.
95 Kim, *Kim Chai Choon Pyeongjeon*, 153.

Notes to pages 72–6

96 Kim, "25 Years of Hankuk Theological Seminary History," 163; Kim, ed., *JangGong Kim Jae-juneui Salmgwa Shinhak*, 422; Yi MoonSuk, *Lee Oo Chung*, 71.

97 Usually spelled "Hankuk" in the school's English literature.

98 Kim, *Kim Chai Choon Pyeongjeon*, 155.

99 Ibid., 154.

100 Scott, *A History of the Canadian Mission*, 789.

101 Kang In-cheol, "Protestant Church and Wolnamin: An Explanation of Protestant Conservatism in South Korea," *Korea Journal* 44, no. 4 (2004), 157–90.

102 Hanguk Gidokgyo Jangnohoe, *Han Somang Anaeseo*, 56.

103 Ibid., 57.

104 Ibid., 58.

105 Kang, "Protestant Church and Wolnamin," 157–90.

106 This is generally true although the dividing line was blurred and many Jesus Presbyterians would go on to be fierce and creative activists in the ensuing years of South Korean dictatorships.

107 Moon and Kim, *Giringabiwa Gomannye-ui Kkum*, 223.

108 Scott, *A History of the Canadian Mission*, 803.

109 Ibid., 801.

110 Ibid., 804.

111 Ibid., 805.

112 Ibid., 806.

113 Ibid., 813.

114 Ibid., 808.

115 Moon and Kim, *Giringabiwa Gomannye-ui Kkum*, 224.

116 Ibid.

117 Kim, *Kim Chai Choon Pyeongjeon*, 166; Hanguk Gidokgyo Jangnohoe, *Han Somang Anaeseo*, 61.

118 Hanguk Gidokgyo Jangnohoe, *Han Somang Anaeseo*, 31–3.

119 Ibid., 40; Moon and Kim, *Giringabiwa Gomannye-ui Kkum*, 110.

120 Moon and Kim, *Giringabiwa Gomannye-ui Kkum*, 224.

121 Phyllis Airhart, *A Church with the Soul of a Nation: Making and Remaking the United Church of Canada* (Montreal and Kingston: McGill-Queen's University Press, 2014), 150.

122 Ibid.

123 Robert A. Wright, *A World Mission: Canadian Protestantism and the Quest for a New International Order, 1918–1939* (Montreal and Kingston: McGill-Queen's University Press, 1991), 56.

124 Mary Rose Donnelly and Heather Dau, *Katharine Boehner Hockin: A Biography* (Winfield, BC: Wood Lake Books, 1992), 8.

258   Notes to pages 76–86

125 Stephen Endicott, *James G. Endicott: Rebel Out of China* (Toronto: University of Toronto Press, 1980).

126 Ruth Compton Brouwer, "From Missionaries to NGOs," in *Canada and the Third World: Overlapping Histories*, ed. Karen Dubinsky, Sean Mills, and Scott Rutherford (Toronto: University of Toronto Press, 2016), 133.

127 Ruth Compton Brouwer, *Canada's Global Villagers: CUSO in Development, 1961–86* (Vancouver: UBC Press, 2013).

128 Donnelly and Dau, *Katharine Boehner Hockin*, 164.

129 Wright, *A World Mission*, 257.

130 Laura Madokoro, *Elusive Refuge: Chinese Migrants in the Cold War* (Cambridge: Harvard University Press, 2016), 9.

131 Laura Madokoro, "'Belated Signing': Race Thinking and Canada's Approach to the 1951 Convention on the Status of Refugees," in *Dominion of Race: Rethinking Canada's International History*, ed. Laura Madokoro, Francine Mckenzie, David Meren (Vancouver: UBC Press, 2017), 17–18.

132 Reflection by Morley Hawley, 30 July 2018.

133 Kim, "The Historical Significance of the PROK," 87; Kim, ed., *JangGong Kim Jae-juneui Salmgwa Shinhak*, 346.

CHAPTER THREE

1 Report of the Commission on World Mission, UCC yearbook 1966, 322.

2 Ibid., 395.

3 *Gidokgyo Sasang* – 기독교 사상.

4 William Scott, *A History of the Canadian Mission to Korea, 1898–1970s*, revised and expanded by J. Greig McMullin (Belleville, ON: Guardian Books, 2009), 829.

5 Ibid., 811.

6 Ibid., 812.

7 Bruce Cumings, *The Origins of the Korean War*, vol. 1 (Princeton: Princeton University Press, 1981), 232.

8 Sebastian C.H. Kim and Kirsteen Kim, *A History of Korean Christianity* (Cambridge: Cambridge University Press, 2015), 157, 172; Chung-shin Park, *Protestantism and Politics in Korea* (Seattle: Washington University Press, 2003), 170. A significant segment of the population did support Rhee, but under the circumstances under which the vote took place it was not possible to know the true depth and breadth of that support. Furthermore, Rhee had been living in exile outside the country and his ability to organize support would have been limited.

9 Byung-Mu Ahn, *Stories of Minjung Theology: the Theological Journey of Ahn Byung-Mu in His Own Words*, trans. Hannah In and Wongi Park (Atlanta: SBL Press, 2018), 11.

10 Cumings, *The Origins of the Korean War*, vol. 1, 244ff, 259.

11 Brendan Wright, "Raising the Korean War Dead: Bereaved Family Associations and the Politics of 1960–1961 South Korea," *The Asia-Pacific Journal – Japan Focus* 13, issue 41, no. 2, 12 October 2015, https://apjjf.org/-Brendan-Wright/4387/article.pdf.

12 Letter of Romona Underwood to Mrs Taylor of the WMS, 2 June 1960, series 9, box 83, accession 83.058C, UCC Archives, Toronto.

13 Ibid.

14 Reflection by Morley Hawley, 30 July 2018.

15 Charles R. Kim, *Youth for Nation: Culture and Protest in Cold War South Korea* (Honolulu: University of Hawai'i Press, 2017), 173.

16 Reflection by Morley Hawley, 30 July 2018.

17 Letter of Romona Underwood to Mrs Taylor of the WMS, 2 June 1960, series 9, box 83, accession 83.058C, UCC Archives, Toronto.

18 Severance Hospital is associated with Yonsei University, which began as the Severance Union Medical College and was also started by Avison. Both have long been reputed to be among the best hospitals and universities in Korea. There is a pagoda on the campus of the University of Toronto, just north of the Emmanuel College building, that alumni of the Yonsei University College of Medicine sent from Korea in honour of Avison as well as Stanley Martin and Florence Murray who served the UCC mission in northeastern Korea and Manchuria.

19 Letter of Romona Underwood to Mrs Taylor of the WMS, 2 June 1960, series 9, box 83, accession 83.058C, UCC Archives, Toronto.

20 Kim, *Youth for Nation*, 179; Seungsook Moon, *Militarized Modernity and Gendered Citizenship in South Korea* (Durham: Duke University Press, 2005), 66.

21 Moon, *Militarized Modernity and Gendered Citizenship*.

22 Kim Kyeong-jae, *Kim Chai Choon Pyeongjeon* (Seoul: Samin Chulpansa, 2001), 184.

23 Report submitted by the Very Rev. Lee, Nam Kyoo to the mission work policy study committee, 20 February 1963, box 14, accession 83.011C, UCC Archives, Toronto.

24 Consultation between Leaders of Presbyterian Church ROK, Rev. E.F. Carey, and UCC missionaries, dated 23 November 1971, file A–232, box 10, accession 83.011C, UCC Archives, Toronto.

25 UCC Yearbook 1962, 187.

260   Notes to pages 88–91

26 Frederick J. Glover, "Friends, Foes and Partners: The Relationship between the Canadian Missionaries and the Korean Christians in North-eastern Korea and Manchuria from 1898 until 1927," *Studies in World Christianity: The Edinburgh Review of Theology and Religion* 23, no. 3 (2017): 194–217.

27 Ibid., 200.

28 Korea, Report of Board of Overseas Missions, UCC Yearbook, 1962, 187.

29 Ruth C. Brouwer, "When Missions Became Development: Ironies of 'NGOization' in Mainstream Canadian Churches in the 1960s," *Canadian Historical Review* 91, no. 4 (2010): 667; Sandra Beardshall, "'And Whether Pigs Have Wings': The United Church in the 1960s," in *The United Church of Canada: A History*, ed. Don Schweitzer (Waterloo: Wilfred Laurier University Press, 2012), 105.

30 Lee Young Min, "A Reflection on the History of Mission and Cooperation of the Churches in Canada and Korea," mission consultation between the UCC and the PROK, 16–18 August 1995, Academy House, Seoul, author's personal collection.

31 Jara Smith, *A Tree Planted by the Water: The Wilna Thomas Story* (Victoria, BC: The Estate of Wilna Thomas, 1993), 2.

32 Ibid., 4.

33 Ibid., 5.

34 Ibid., 14.

35 Wilna Thomas fonds, accession 94.053C, UCC Archives, Toronto.

36 Ruth Compton Brouwer, *New Women for God: Canadian Presbyterian women and India Missions, 1876–1914* (Toronto: University of Toronto Press, 1990), 57.

37 Ibid., 70; Marta Danylewyca, *Taking the Veil: An Alternative to Marriage, Motherhood, and Spinsterhood in Quebec, 1840–1920* (Toronto: McClelland & Stewart, 1987); Rosemary R. Gagan, *A Sensitive Independence: Canadian Methodist Women Missionaries in Canada and the Orient, 1881–1925* (Montreal and Kingston: McGill-Queen's University Press, 1992), x.

38 Brouwer, *New Women for God*, 52.

39 Report of the Commission on World Mission, appendix B, Yearbook 1966, UCC GC, 1966, 439.

40 Brouwer, *New Women for God*, 5.

41 Ibid., x.

42 Ibid., 84.

43 Smith, *A Tree Planted by the Water*, 35.

44 Ibid.

Notes to pages 92–4

45 Kang In-cheol, "Protestant Church and Wolnamin: An Explanation of Protestant Conservatism in South Korea," *Korea Journal* 44, no. 4 (2004), 157–90.

46 Scott, *A History of the Canadian Mission to Korea*, 810.

47 Robert A. Wright, *A World Mission: Canadian Protestantism and the Quest for a New International Order, 1918–1939* (Montreal and Kingston: McGill-Queen's University Press, 1991), 200; Moon Chai Rin and Kim Shin Mook, *Giringabiwa Gomannye-ui Kkum: Moon Chai Rin Kim Shin Mook Hoegorok* (Seoul: Samin Chulpansa, 2006), 179.

48 A. Hamish Ion, "Canadian Missionaries under the Japanese Empire" in *Canadian Missionaries, Indigenous Peoples: Representing Religion at Home and Abroad*, ed. Alvyn Austin and Jamie S. Scott (Toronto: University of Toronto Press, 2005), 180.

49 Ken C. Kawashima, *The Proletariat Gamble: Korean Workers in Interwar Japan* (Duke University Press: Durham and London, 2009), 18.

50 Smith, *A Tree Planted by the Water*, 37.

51 Ibid.

52 Notebook on Korea, circa 1961, Wilna Thomas fonds, Korea notes file 3, box 2, accession 94.053C, UCC Archives, Toronto.

53 Letter from Wilna Thomas to Mrs Taylor, 27 March 1961, Wilna Thomas fonds, Africa/India Correspondence notes, file 2-1, accession 94.053C, UCC Archives, Toronto.

54 Smith, *A Tree Planted by the Water*, 81.

55 Gagan, *A Sensitive Independence*, x–xi.

56 Ruth Compton Brouwer, *Modern Women Modernizing Men: The Changing Missions of Three Professional Women in Asia and Africa, 1902–69* (Vancouver: UBC Press, 2002), 25.

57 These records can be found in the Wilna Thomas fonds at the United Church Archives, Toronto.

58 Richard Allen, "Social Gospel," published online 7 February 2006, https://www.thecanadianencyclopedia.ca/en/article/social-gospel.

59 Brouwer, "When Missions Became Development," 665.

60 Phyllis Airhart, *A Church with the Soul of a Nation: Making and Remaking the United Church of Canada* (Montreal and Kingston: McGill-Queen's University Press, 2014), 243.

61 Ibid., 253.

62 Brouwer, "When Missions Became Development," 683.

63 Commission on Theological Concerns of the Christian Conference of Asia, ed., *Minjung Theology: People as the Subjects of History* (Maryknoll, NY: Orbis Books, 1983), 18.

262   Notes to pages 95–9

64 Hanguk Gidokgyo Jangnohoe, *Han Somang Anaeseo: Hanguk – Kanadagyohoe Seongyohyeopnyeok 100junyeon Ginyeommunjip* (Seoul: Hanguk Gidokgyo Jangnohoe Chulpan, 1998), 75.

65 Hong Kong/Korea notes 1963, Wilna Thomas, accession 94.053C, UCC Archives, Toronto.

66 Armstrong, *The North Korean Revolution*, 117.

67 Timothy S. Lee, *Born Again: Evangelicalism in Korea* (Honolulu: University of Hawai'i Press, 2010), 61; Sang-Chul Lee and Eric Weingartner, *The Wanderer: The Autobiography of a United Church Moderator* (Winfield, BC: Woodlake Books, 1989), 35.

68 Moon and Kim, *Giringabiwa Gomannye-ui Kkum*, 152.

69 Ibid., 229; Interview with Dong-Chun Suh, 21 November 2018.

70 Kang, "Protestant Church and Wolnamin," 157–90.

71 Hong Kong/Korea notes 1963, Wilna Thomas, accession 4.053C, UCC Archives, Toronto.

72 Ibid.

73 Ibid.

74 Ibid.

75 Hong Kong/Korea notes 1964, Wilna Thomas, accession 94.053C, UCC Archives, Toronto.

76 Galatians 3:28, Bible, New Revised Standard Version.

77 Allen Clark to Young People of Canada, 18 May 1931, file 47, box 2, Accession 83.006C, UCC Archives, Toronto.

78 Jeffrey Cox, *The British Missionary Enterprise since 1700* (New York: Routledge, 2008), 247.

79 Brouwer, "When Missions Became Development," 669.

80 Brouwer, *Modern Women Modernizing Men*, 7.

81 Report submitted by the Very Rev. Lee, Nam Kyoo to the mission work policy study committee 20 February 1963, box 14, accession 83.011C, UCC Archives, Toronto.

82 *Report of the Commission on World Mission*, UCC, Proceedings, GC22, 1966, 386.

83 Salary scale, 1969, file A–232, box 14, accession 83.019C, UCC Archives, Toronto.

84 Mission report by Joyce Sasse, dated 13 January 1971, file A–232, box 10, accession 83.011C, UCC Archives, Toronto.

85 Translation of the article on page 8 of the third issue of the Presbyterian News by Rev. Chung Yong Chul entitled "Having Read Mission Policy Report," box 14, accession 83.011C, UCC Archives, Toronto.

86 Ibid.

87 Ibid, emphasis added.

Notes to pages 99–104

88 Report submitted by the Very Rev. Lee, Nam Kyoo to the mission work policy study committee, 20 February 1963, box 14, accession 83.011C, UCC Archives, Toronto.

89 Andrew Walls provides this quote from a famous speech delivered fifty-three years earlier:
"Through all the ages to come the Indian church will rise up in gratitude to attest the heroism and self-denying labours of the missionary body. You have given your goods to feed the poor. You have given your bodies to be burned. We also ask for love. Give us FRIENDS!" Andrew F. Walls, *The Cross Cultural Process in Christian History* (Maryknoll, NY: Orbis Books, 2002), 70.

90 Notebook on Trinidad, 1960, Wilna Thomas fonds, Trinidad notes file 2–1, accession 94.053C, UCC Archives, Toronto. Trinidadian church leader Roy Neehall "admitted that there was not a real sense of fellowship between Trinidadians and Canadians. They do not enjoy each other – share their difficulties with each other."

91 Scott, *A History of the Canadian Mission*, 838.

92 Ibid., 838nn1–9.

93 Lee Young Min, "A Reflection on the History of Mission and Cooperation of the Churches in Canada and Korea," mission consultation between the UCC and the PROK, 16–18 August 1995, Academy House, Seoul, author's personal collection.

94 From a conversation the author had in Korea with a student who had been on Scott's soccer team.

95 Scott, *A History of the Canadian Mission*, 845.

96 Ibid., 820ff.

97 Interview with Kim Ikseon, July 2019.

98 Romona Underwood to M.D. Taylor, 21 August 1959, box 81–20, accession 83.058C, UCC Archives, Toronto.

99 Dana L. Robert, "Cross-Cultural Friendship in the Creation of Twentieth-Century World Christianity," *International Bulletin of Missionary Research* 35, no. 2 (April 2011): 105.

100 Ibid.

101 Accession 83.011C, box 9, file A–233, Presbyterian Church ROK – General Assembly, dated 1970. (This is an annual report by Morley Hammond enclosed in a mailing to Frank Carey with a letter dated 13 January 1970.)

CHAPTER FOUR

1 Margaret Atwood, *Survival: A Thematic Guide to Canadian Literature* (Toronto: Anansi Press, 1972), 35–8.

Notes to pages 105–9

2 Homi K. Bhabha, *The Location of Culture* (New York: Routledge, 1994), xi.

3 Martin Hart-Landsberg, *The Rush to Development: Economic Change and Political Struggle in South Korea* (New York: Monthly Review Press, 1993), 182.

4 Namhee Lee, *The Making of Minjung: Democracy and the Politics of Representation in South Korea* (Cornell University Press, 2007), 38.

5 Jang-jip Choi, *Democracy after Democratization: The Korean Experience* (Stanford: The Walter H. Shorenstein Asia Pacific Research Centre, 2012), 54.

6 Hart-Landberg, *The Rush to Development*, 26.

7 Ibid., 15.

8 Ibid., 16.

9 Ibid., 108.

10 Ibid.

11 Ibid., 147.

12 Ibid., 109.

13 Seungsook Moon, *Militarized Modernity and Gendered Citizenship in South Korea* (Durham: Duke University Press, 2005), 2.

14 Hart-Landberg, *The Rush to Development*, 174.

15 Bruce Cumings, *Parallax Visions: Making Sense of American East Asian Relations at the End of the Century* (Durham: Duke University Press, 1999).

16 "Economy," *The Canadian Encyclopedia*, accessed 11 February 2021, https://www.thecanadianencyclopedia.ca/en/article/economy.

17 Kang In-cheol, *Jeohang gwa Tuheang – Gunsajeonggwondeul gwa Jonggyo* (Osan: Hansindaehakgyo Chulpanbu, 2013), 267, 392.

18 Interview with Dong-Chun Seo, 12 November 2018.

19 Letter to Frank Carey from Young Min Lee, dated 28 September 1971, file A–2323, box 10, accession 83.011C, UCC Archives, Toronto.

20 UCC Yearbook 1971, vol. 2, 72.

21 Letter from Fred Bayliss of the Korea Mission UCC to Frank Carey, dated 4 January 1972, file A–232, box 11, accession 83.011C, UCC Archives, Toronto.

22 The breakdown of expenses is based on a later budget report: UCC Korea Mission 1978 Proposed Budget Summary, file Records of Asia Secretary, box 17, accession 83.019C, UCC Archives, Toronto.

23 Presbyterian Church ROK – General Assembly, dated 1970, file A–233, box 9, accession 83.011C, UCC Archives, Toronto.

24 UCC Yearbook 1971, vol. 2, 192ff.

25 Presbyterian Church ROK – Gen. Assemble, letter to Young Min Lee, dated 15 February 1971, file A–233, box 10, accession 83.011C, UCC Archives, Toronto.

Notes to pages 109–12

26 *Observer*, December 1974, 49. Minimum fulltime annual salary for UCC clergy in Canada was $5200 based on study of Yearbook 1971, vol. 1 – Statistics for 1970.

27 UCC Yearbook 1971, vol. 2, 192ff.

28 "Missionary Go Home someday, Not Yet," *Observer*, December 1974, 49.

29 DWO Executive March 1975, appendix G, a letter received from a missionary overseas, April 1975, XXIII, 367, Collection A676 United Church, Saskatchewan Archives, Saskatoon.

30 Salary scale, 1969, file A–232, box 14, accession 83.019C, UCC Archives, Toronto.

31 Ruth Compton Brouwer, *Modern Women Modernizing Men: The Changing Missions of Three Professional Women in Asia and Africa, 1902–69* (Vancouver: UBC Press, 2002), 24.

32 Letter from Morley Hammond to Frank Carey, dated 13 January 1970, box 9, accession 83.011C, UCC Archives, Toronto; mission report by Joyce Sasse, dated 13 January 1971, file A–232, box 10, accession 83.011C, UCC Archives, Toronto.

33 Translation of the article in the third issue of the *Presbyterian News* by Rev. Chung Yong Chul entitled "Having Read Mission Policy Report," box 14, accession 83.011C, UCC Archives, Toronto.

34 Letter from Frank Carey to Young Min Lee, dated 15 February 1971, file A–233, box 10, accession 83.011C, UCC Archives, Toronto.

35 Letter from Young Min Lee to Frank Carey, dated 28 October 1971, file A–233, box 10, accession 83.011C, UCC Archives, Toronto.

36 Letter from Frank Carey to Young Min Lee, dated 11 November 1971, file A–233, box 10, accession 83.011C, UCC Archives, Toronto.

37 Consultation between Leaders of Presbyterian Church ROK, Rev. E.F. Carey and UCC Missionaries, dated 23 November 1971, file A–233, box 10, accession 83.011C, UCC Archives, Toronto.

38 Ibid.

39 William Scott, *A History of the Canadian Mission to Korea, 1898–1970s,* revised and expanded by J. Greig McMullin (Belleville, ON: Guardian Books, 2009), 468.

40 Hanguk Gidokgyo Jangnohoe, *Han Somang Anaeseo: Hanguk – Kanadagyohoe Seongyohyeopnyeok 100junyeon Ginyeommunjip* (Seoul: Hanguk Gidokgyo Jangnohoe Chulpan, 1998), 163.

41 T.D. Mansfield to A.E. Armstrong, 21 November 1912, file 9, box 1, accession 79.204C, UCC Archives, Toronto.

42 For an idea of the size of the building a basic floor plan is provided on the following YouTube video: https://www.youtube.com/watch?v=uZLeZp2Cy8U.

266 Notes to pages 112–17

43 Memorandum dated 13 November 1979, Institute for Mission Education, file 1, box 21, UCLA Collection 358, Los Angeles.

44 Mission Committee – Korea – Minutes, letter from William Scott to Frank Carey, dated 21 December 1970, file A–232, box 9, accession 83.011C, UCC Archives, Toronto.

45 letter from E.J.O. Frazer to Frank Carey 13 January 1971, file A–231, box 10, accession 83.011C, UCC Archives, Toronto.

46 Consultation between Leaders of Presbyterian Church ROK, Rev. E.F. Carey and UCC Missionaries, dated 23 November 1971, file A–232, box 10, accession 83.011C, UCC Archives, Toronto.

47 Document on "The Future of Iri Hillside Farm," file DWO 1974, box 16, accession 83.011C, UCC Archives, Toronto.

48 Presbyterian Church ROK – General Assembly, letter to Frank Carey from Morley Hammond, dated 13 January 1970, file A–233, box 9, accession 83.011C, UCC Archives, Toronto.

49 Letter to Frank Carey from Morley Hammond, dated 13 January 1970, file A–233, box 9, accession 83.011C, UCC Archives, Toronto.

50 1970 Annual Report of the Iri Hillside Farm, file A–231, box 10, accession 83.011C, UCC Archives, Toronto.

51 Ibid.

52 More about this movement can be found at https://www.thecanadianency-clopedia.ca/en/article/antigonish-movement.

53 Korea Mission UCC Annual Meeting part III, dated 9–10 May 1970, Upper room Meeting Hall of Ewha University, box 9, accession 83,011C, UCC Archives, Toronto.

54 "The Future of Iri Hillside Farm," G. Clare Findlay folder, letter from Clare Findlay to Frank Carey, dated 30 April 1969, file DWO 1974, box 16, accession 83.011C, UCC Archives, Toronto.

55 Ibid.

56 Letter to Frank Carey from Young Min Lee, dated 17 June 1971, file A–232, box 10, accession 83.011C, UCC Archives, Toronto.

57 Letter from Young Min Lee to Russell Young copy for Frank Carey, dated 22 February 1972, file A–232, box 10, accession 83,011C, UCC Archives, Toronto.

58 Letter from Young Min Lee to Frank Carey, dated 2 December 1971, file A–232, box 10, accession 83.011C, UCC Archives, Toronto.

59 Iri Hillside Farm Board of Advisors, dated 24 November 1972, file A–232, box 10, accession 83.011C, UCC Archives, Toronto.

60 Letter to Frank Carey, dated 28 December 1973, file DWO 1974, box 16, accession 83.011C, UCC Archives, Toronto.

61 Ibid.

62 Letter from Carey to Findlay draft, dated 8 January 1974, file DWO 1974, box 16, accession 83.011C, UCC Archives, Toronto.

63 PROK General Assembly, no date, file A–233, Box 12, accession 83.011C, UCC Archives, Toronto.

64 Proposed Agenda for Discussion on Cooperative Work, no date, file A–233, box 12, accession 83.011C, UCC Archives, Toronto.

65 D.A. MacDonald to A.E. Armstrong, 23 November 1925, file 2, box 1, accession 83.006C, UCC Archives, Toronto.

66 Moon Chai Rin and Kim Shin Mook, *Giringabiwa Gomannye-ui Kkum: Moon Chai Rin Kim Shin Mook Hoegorok* (Seoul: Samin Chulpansa, 2006), 109.

67 Lak-Geoon George Paik, *The History of Protestant Missions in Korea 1832–1910*, 4th edition (Seoul: Yonsei University Press, 1987), 368.

68 Sang-Chul Lee and Eric Weingartner, *The Wanderer: The Autobiography of a United Church Moderator* (Winfield, BC: Woodlake Books, 1989).

69 Hanguk Gidokgyo Jangnohoe, *Han Somang Anaeseo*, 154.

70 Ibid., 82.

71 PROK General Assembly, Joint Statement of the Presbyterian Church in the Republic of Korea and the Division of world Outreach of the United Church of Canada, 1974, file A–233, box 12, accession 83.011C, UCC Archives, Toronto.

72 Hanguk Gidokgyo Jangnohoe, *Han Somang Anaeseo*, 80.

73 Interview with Kim Sang-geun, 5 July 2015.

74 Hanguk Gidokgyo Jangnohoe, *Han Somang Anaeseo*, 83.

75 Ibid.

76 DWO Executive minutes, dated 29 October 1973, 132, file 4, box 1, accession 92.109C, UCC Archives, Toronto.

77 DWO Executive minutes, dated 15 February 1973, 99, 73-49, file 4, box 1, accession 92.109C, UCC Archives, Toronto.

78 Lee, Young-Min, "A Reflection on the History of Mission and Cooperation of the Churches in Canada and Korea," mission consultation between the UCC and the PROK, 16–18 August 1995, Academy House, Seoul, author's personal collection.

79 Interview with Chung Suk Ja, 15 May 2015.

80 Hanguk Gidokgyo Jangnohoe, *Han Somang*, 83.

81 "Sending church" is a term used in church circles to denote those church organizations, traditionally in the West, who "sent" missionaries to other lands. "Receiving church" is the term used to denote those church denominations who accommodated and worked with the missionaries who were sent.

268   Notes to pages 123–33

82 Interview with Kim Sang-geun, 5 July 2015.

83 Kang, *Jeohang gwa Tuheang*, 159.

84 Hanguk Gidokgyo Jangnohoe, *Han Somang Anaeseo*, 80.

85 UCC Yearbook, 1976, 159, emphasis added.

86 Hanguk Gidokgyo Jangnohoe, *Han Somang Anaeseo*, 83.

87 Russell Young, "Food before Freedom," *Observer*, December 1974, 36–7.

88 Clifford Elliott sermon, dated 17 March 1974, file A–231, box 12, accession 83.011C, UCC Archives, Toronto.

89 Japan Property Transfer Agreement, Board of World Missions, file S II Minutes 1962–1964, box 29, accession 82.001C, UCC Archives, Toronto.

90 Hanguk Gidokgyo Jangnohoe, *Han Somang Anaeseo*, 82.

CHAPTER FIVE

1 Wi Jo Kang, *Christ and Caesar in Modern Korea: A History of Christianity and Politics* (Albany, NY: State University of New York Press, 1997), 103.

2 Ibid., 102.

3 Ibid., 101.

4 "Manifesto of Korean Christians," *New York Times*, 5 May 1974, file 3, box 79, UCLA Collection 358, Los Angeles.

5 Timothy S. Lee, *Born Again: Evangelicalism in Korea* (Honolulu: University of Hawai'i Press, 2010), 94.

6 Sherwood E. Wirt, "Korea: God's Loving Cup" *Decision*, August 1973, file 1, box 23, accession 83.019C, UCC Archives, Toronto.

7 Ibid.

8 Ibid.

9 Ibid.

10 Ibid.

11 Samuel Hugh Moffett, *Christians of Korea* (New York: Friendship Press, 1962), 54.

12 Lak-Geoon George Paik, *The History of Protestant Missions in Korea 1832–1910*, 4th edition (Seoul: Yonsei University Press, 1987), 374.

13 Lee, *Born Again*, 24.

14 Sang-Chul Lee and Eric Weingartner, *The Wanderer: The Autobiography of a United Church Moderator* (Winfield, BC: Woodlake Books, 1989), 39.

15 Yi Munsuk, *Lee Oo Chung Pyeongjeon* (Seoul: Samin Chulpansa, 2012), 181.

16 Paik, *History of Protestant Missions*, 375.

17 Quoted in Paik, *History of Protestant Missions*, 376.

18 Paik, *History of Protestant Missions*, 376.

19 Seok Choong Son, "Political Neutrality," *Third Day* 66 (September 1977): 11–17, file 46, box 26, UCLA Special Collection 358 Democracy and Unification in Korea, Los Angeles.

20 Eric O. Hansen, *Catholic Politics in China and Korea* (Maryknoll, NY: Orbis Books, 1980), 98.

21 Timothy S. Lee, "Born Again in Korea: The Rise and Character of Revivalism in (South) Korea, 1885–1988" (PhD diss., University of Chicago, 1996), 56, 136.

22 Lee, *Born Again*, 32.

23 Ibid., 122.

24 Dean Salter, "The PROK: Living the Hard Gospel in South Korea," *Mandate*, January/February 1984, file 000529, box 15, U of T Special Collection for Human Rights and Democratization in Korea, Toronto.

25 Sherwood E. Wirt, "Korea: God's Loving Cup" *Decision*, August 1975, file 1, box 23, accession 83.019C, UCC Archives, Toronto.

26 Kang In-cheol, *Jeohang gwa Tuheang – Gunsajeonggwondeul gwa Jonggyo* (Osan: Hansindaehakgyo Chulpanbu, 2013), 267. By contrast those denominations who sided with the PROK against Park made up about 6 per cent of South Korean Protestants. The largest number of Protestants remained neutral regarding the Park government.

27 Lee, *Born Again*, 33.

28 Ibid., 199.

29 Paul Y. Chang, *Protest Dialectics: State Repression and South Korea's Democratization Movement, 1970–1979* (Stanford: Stanford University Press, 2015), 106.

30 Dean Salter, "The PROK: Living the Hard Gospel in South Korea," *Mandate*, January/February 1984, file 000529, box 15, U of T Special Collection for Human Rights and Democratization in Korea, Toronto.

31 Willa Kernen, "It Was Impossible to Be Uninvolved," in *More Than Witnesses: How a Small Group of Missionaries Aided Korea's Democratic Revolution*, ed. Jim Stenzel (Seoul: Korea Democracy Foundation, 2006), 269.

32 NCCK Statement on recent pronouncements of Korean government leaders regarding Christianity, dated 18 November 1974, XXIII. 367, Collection A676 United Church, Saskatchewan Archives, Saskatoon; Foreign Missionaries Involvement in Politics DWO December 1974, XXIII. 367, Collection A676 United Church, Saskatchewan Archives, Saskatoon.

33 Rom. 13:1–5.

270 Notes to pages 136–8

34 William Scott, *A History of the Canadian Mission to Korea, 1898–1970s*, revised and expanded by J. Greig McMullin (Belleville, ON: Guardian Books, 2009), 516.

35 Statement of Position, dated 9 June 1975, file 1 DWO Human Rights, box 23, accession 83.019C, UCC Archives, Toronto.

36 Ibid.

37 Ibid.

38 Ibid.

39 Foreign Missionaries Involvement in Politics DWO, dated December 1974, XXIII. 367, Collection A676 United Church, Saskatchewan Archives, Saskatoon.

40 Marion Current, "A New Day Had Dawned," in *More Than Witnesses: How a Small Group of Missionaries Aided Korea's Democratic Revolution*, ed. Jim Stenzel (Seoul: Korea Democracy Foundation, 2006), 400.

41 Chang, *Protest Dialectics*, 106.

42 UCC Yearbook, 1976, 159.

43 Institute for Mission-Education of The Presbyterian Church in the Republic of Korea, June 1979, file 1, box 65, UCLA Collection 358, Los Angeles.

44 Volker Kuster, *A Protestant Theology of Passion: Korean Minjung Theology Revisited* (Leiden, Germany: Brill, 2010), 63.

45 Letter to Minister of Culture and Information Government of Korea form Frank Cary, dated 2 September 1976, file 10–2, box 2, accession 83.019C, UCC Archives, Toronto.

46 Transfer of property for the creation of the Mission and Education Centre, letter to Willa Kernen from Frank Carey, dated 20 February 1976, file 10, box 2, accession 83.019C, UCC Archives, Toronto.

47 Irwin Memoir, self published; Letter from Willa Kernen to Frank Carey, dated 31 January 1976, file 6, box 23, accession 83.019C, UCC Archives, Toronto.

48 See: https://www.youtube.com/watch?v=uZLeZp2Cy8U (accessed 13 September 2019).

49 Institute for Mission Education Memorandum, dated 13 November 1979, file 1, box 21, UCLA Collection 358, Los Angeles.

50 A theological description of this kind of action was given by German theologian Michael Welker, see *Touchstone: Theology Shaping Witness*, "Free Creative Self-Withdrawal," vol. 35, no.3 (October 2017).

51 UCC Yearbook, 1976, 159.

52 Hyeon-jun Yi, "The History of the Birth of the PROK Mission Education Centre aka. 'General Assembly Education Process for Students of a New

Era,'" in *Seodaemun Minjung Theological School Witness,* ed. Jin-gwan Gwon, Gwang-il Yi, and Hyeon-jun Yi (Seoul: Dongyeon Press, 2019), 44.

53 Interview with Seo Dong-Chun, 14 November 2018.

54 Institute for Mission Education Memorandum, dated 13 November 1979, file 1, box 21, UCLA Collection 358, Los Angeles.

55 Jin-gwan Gwon, "It Was a Special Happening, The Mission Education Centre Like Grace," in *Seodaemun Minjung Theological School Witness,* ed. Jin-gwan Gwon, Gwang-il Yi, and Hyeon-jun Yi (Seoul: Dongyeon Press, 2019), 9–11.

56 Gwang-il Yi, "'Seodaemun Minjung Theological School' Process of Establishment, Students and Professors," in *Seodaemun Minjung Theological School Witness,* ed. Jin-gwan Gwon, Gwang-il Yi, and Hyeon-jun Yi (Seoul: Dongyeon Press, 2019), 23–5.

57 Ibid..

58 Ibid.

59 Kuster, *A Protestant Theology of Passion,* 63

60 PROK News, no. 5, 25 April 1978, file 000079, box 2, U of T Collection Human Rights in South Korea, Toronto.

61 Letter from Willa Kernen to Newton Thurber, dated 19 June 1978, file 1, box 65, UCLA Collection 358 Human Rights and Unification in Korea, Los Angeles.

62 Yi, *Lee Oo Chung Pyeongjeon,* 139.

63 Letter from Willa Kernen to Newton Thurber, dated 19 June 1978, file 1, box 65, UCLA Collection 358 Human Rights and Unification in Korea, Los Angeles.

64 Kuster, *A Protestant Theology of Passion,* 63

65 民衆 – 민중.

66 Henry H. Em, *The Great Enterprise: Sovereignty and Historiography in Modern Korea* (Durham: Duke University Press, 2013), 111.

67 民族 – 민족.

68 Henry H. Em, "*Minjok* as a Modern and Democratic Construct: Sin Ch'eaho's Historiography," in *Colonial Modernity in Korea,* ed. Gi-Wook Shin and Michael Robinson (Harvard University Asia Center: Cambridge, 1999), 339.

69 Em, "*Minjok* as a Modern and Democratic Construct," 356.

70 Andre Schmid, *Korea Between Empires 1895–1919* (New York: Columbia University Press, 2002), 171.

71 Nancy Abelmann, *Echoes of the Past, Epics of Dissent: A South Korean Social Movement.* (Berkeley: University of California Press, 1996), 25.

72 國家 – 국가.

72 人民 – 인민.

74 Jang-jip Choi, *Democracy after Democratization: The Korean Experience* (Stanford: The Walter H. Shorenstein Asia Pacific Research Centre, 2012), 50.

75 General Outline of Activities in 1985, file 6, box 42, UCLA Special Collection 358 Democracy and Unification in Korea, Los Angeles.

76 Gi-Wook Shin, *Ethnic Nationalism in Korea: Genealogy, Politics, and Legacy* (Stanford: Stanford University Press, 2006), 171.

77 Chang, *Protest Dialectics*, 108; Abelmann, *Echoes of the Past, Epics of Dissent*, 23, 34, 37.

78 *Gidokgyo Sasang* – 기독교 사상.

79 Committee of Theological Study, NCCK, ed., *Minjung and Korean Theology* (Seoul: Korea Theological Institute, 1982). Most of this was translated and circulated widely two years later in an English publication: Commission on Theological Concerns of the Christian Conference of Asia, ed., *Minjung Theology: People as the Subject of History* (Maryknoll, NY: Orbis Books, 1983). This work was first published in 1981.

80 Sebastian C.H. Kim and Kirsteen Kim, eds., *A History of Korean Christianity* (Cambridge: Cambridge University Press, 2015), 239.

81 Suh Kwang-sun David, "A Biographical Sketch of an Asian Consultation," in *Minjung Theology: People as the Subjects of History*, ed. Commission on Theological Concerns of the Christian Conference of Asia (Maryknoll, NY: Orbis Books, 1983), 21.

82 This is not to say that Latin American liberation theology was anti-religious or anti-Christian. Though critics often accused them of being communists in disguise, Latin American liberation theologians borrowed from Marxist ideas to give expression to a political and religious agenda that was explicitly Christian. In criticizing the established church, many made use of Marxist theories such as fetishism that explain how religion is distorted so as to distract the people from the excesses and injustices of a capitalist system. Less is made of this critique in Minjung theology, which, despite the rise of state sponsored Evangelical Christianity, did not have an established religious institution with which to contend.

83 Suh Kwang-sun David, "Korean Theological Development in the 1970s," *Minjung Theology: People as the Subjects of History*, Commission on Theological Concerns of the Christian Conference of Asia, ed. (Maryknoll, NY: Orbis Books, 1983), 50.

84 R.S. Sugirtharajah, introduction in Byung-Mu Ahn, *Stories of Minjung Theology: The Theological Journey of Ahn Byung-Mu in His Own Words*, trans. Hannah In and Wongi Park (Atlanta: SBL Press, 2018), xiii.

85 Scott, *A History of the Canadian Mission to Korea*, 691.

Notes to pages 143–6

86 Suh, "A Biographical Sketch of an Asian Consultation," 20.
87 Kim Yong-bok, "Korean Christianity as a Messianic Movement of the People," in *Minjung Theology: People as the Subjects of History*, ed. Commission on Theological Concerns of the Christian Conference of Asia (Maryknoll, NY: Orbis Books, 1983), 84.
88 Kim, "Korean Christianity as a Messianic Movement of the People," 80–2; Ahn, *Stories of Minjung Theology*, 136.
89 Suh Nam Dong, "Theology as Story-Telling: A Counter-Theology," CTC *Bulletin* 5, nos. 3–6, no. 1 (December 1984–April 1985), 6–7.
90 Theology of Minjung by Prof. Suh Nam Dong, no date, file 1, box 68, UCLA Collection 358, Los Angeles.
91 恨 – 한.
92 Whether *han* is in fact a concept with a long tradition in Korean literature and thought is contested.
93 Suh Nam-dong, "Towards a Theology of Han," in *Minjung Theology: People as the Subjects of History*, ed. Commission on Theological Concerns of the Christian Conference of Asia (Maryknoll, NY: Orbis Books, 1983), 68.
94 Suh, "Theology as Story-Telling," 11.
95 Letter from Ahn Byung Mu distributed by ecumenical forum in Canada, dated 4 April 1977, file 001563, U of T Special Collection on Human Rights in South Korea, Toronto.
96 Paul Y. Chang, Gi-Wook Shin, Jung-eun Lee, and Sookyung Kim, "South Korea's Democracy Movement (1970–1993): Stanford Korea Democracy Project Report," Stanford University, 2007, 19, accessed 3 May 2016, https://fsi.stanford.edu/sites/default/files/KDP_Report_(final)-1.pdf.
97 *Yi Ddangae Pyeonghwareul, Kim Kwanseok Moksa kyohoeginyeom Munjipchulpanuiwonhoe* (Seongdeokinswesa: Seoul, 1991), 11. (Rev. Kim KwanSeok Church Anniversary Publications Committee, *Peace to This Land: The Human Rights Movement of the 1970s* [SeongDeok Publishers: Seoul, 1991], 11.)
98 Ahn, *Stories of Minjung Theology*, 10.
99 Accession 83.019C, box 23 of 24, file 7, letter from Willa, dated 16 May 1978, including translation from German of Ahn Byeong Mu's original thoughts regarding Minjung theology.
100 Ibid.
101 Ibid.
102 Choi, *Democracy after Democratization*, 74.
103 Sun-Chul Kim, *Democratization and Social Movements in South Korea: Defiant Institutionalization* (New York: Routledge, 2016).

274   Notes to pages 146–51

104 James H. Cone, preface in *Minjung Theology: People as the Subjects of History*, ed. Commission on Theological Concerns of the Christian Conference of Asia (Maryknoll, NY: Orbis Books, 1983), x.

105 Ibid., xiv.

106 Jürgen Moltmann, *Experiences in Theology: Ways and Forms of Christian Theology*, trans. Margaret Kohl (Minneapolis: Fortress Press, 2000), 258–9.

107 Sugirtharajah, introduction in *Stories of Minjung Theology*, xiii.

108 Kwok Pui-lan, *Postcolonial Imagination and Feminist Theology* (Louisville, KY: Westminster John Knox Press, 2005), 43.

109 "Suffering and Hope," an address to Hankuk theological seminary by Douglas Jay, dated 28 September 1978, file 002011, box 58, U of T Collection on Democratization and Human Rights in Korea, Toronto.

110 Current, "A New Day Has Dawned," 396.

111 Dean Salter, "The Church in Mission: A Canadian Looks at the Korean Church," *Mission Magazine* 8, no. 1, *South Korea: Challenge and Celebration* (pre–September): 1984.

112 Ibid.

113 Ibid.

114 "With the Minjung (People) of Korea: 100 Years of Mission Together," *Response-Ability* 21, Summer 1984, file 20, box 21, UCLA Special Collection 358 Democracy and Unification in Korea, Los Angeles.

115 *Canada Asia Currents* 1, no. 1, Winter 1979, file 000400, box 15, U of T Special Collection for Human Rights and Democratization in Korea, Toronto.

116 "Canadian Churches and the Trans-Pacific," *The History of Canadian-Asian Ecumenical Contacts: The Canada Asia Working Group and the Canada China Programme*, accessed 10 February 2021, http://transpacificchurches. blogspot.com/search/label/South%20Korea; these reports can also be found in file 000400, box 15, U of T Special Collection for Human Rights and Democratization in Korea, Toronto.

117 Chung-shin Park, *Protestantism and Politics in Korea* (Seattle: University of Washington Press, 2003), 69ff.

118 Joan Wyatt, "The 1970s: Voices from the Margins," in *The United Church of Canada: A History, ed.* Donald Schweitzer (Waterloo: Wilfrid Laurier University Press, 2012), 126–7.

119 Ibid., 128.

120 Ibid., 133.

121 Feasibility Task Group on Ethnic Ministries, Office of the General Council, *The Proposed Model for the Ethnic Ministries Council of The United Church of Canada*, presented to the 35th General Council in Fergus, ON,

Notes to pages 151–5

19–28 August 1994; EMC History dates 1994–1996, box 8–18, accession 2009.100C, United Church Archives, Toronto.

122 Kawuki Mukasa, "The New United Church Ethnic Ministry Council: Reflections on Origins and Prospects," *Touchstone* 13, no. 1 (January 1995): 13.

123 Sugirtharajah, introduction in *Stories of Minjung Theology*, xvi.

124 Ibid.

125 Letter to Frank Carey from Suh Nam Dong re: invitation to teach at Emmanuel College, 1983, file 6, accession 91.169C, UCC Archives, Toronto.

126 PROK News no. 14, dated 20 July 1981, file 000087, U of T Special Collection of Human Rights in South Korea, Toronto.

127 Ibid.

128 Yi, "Seodaemun Minjung Theological School," 24.

129 Jürgen Moltmann, *Minjung Theologies des Volkes Gottes in Sud-korea* (Neukirchen, 1984).

130 Theology of Minjung by Prof. Suh Nam Dong, no date, file 1, box 68, UCLA Collection 358 Human Rights and Unification in Korea, Los Angeles.

CHAPTER SIX

1 The *Sarang* was in fact a room that was the exclusive domain of the male head of the family. What Scott may have meant to refer to here is the *Anbang*, which was the women's room in a traditional Korean home. For more information on this room and its importance for the Missionary Enterprise in Korea please see the following: Lee-Ellen Strawn, "Korean Bible Women's Success: Using the Anbang Network and the Religious Authority of the Mudang," *Journal of Korean Religions* 3, no. 1 (April 2012).

2 William Scott, *A History of the Canadian Mission to Korea, 1898–1970s*, revised and expanded by J. Greig McMullin (Belleville, ON: Guardian Books, 2009), 498.

3 Murray was UCC mission doctor who served in northeastern Korea and Manchuria from 1921 to 1942 and returned to South Korea following the Pacific and Korean wars to continue her work until 1975.

4 Florence Murray, *At the Foot of Dragon Hill: The Story of a Surgeon's Two Decades in Manchuria and Korea, and the Challenges She Faced as a Woman Doctor in a Culture So Primitive its Women Were Not Even Considered Worthy of Having Names* (New York: E.P. Dutton & Company, 1975), 232.

276   Notes to pages 156–9

5 Ruth Compton Brouwer, *Modern Women Modernizing Men: The Changing Missions of Three Professional Women in Asia and Africa, 1902–69* (Vancouver: UBC Press, 2002), 25.

6 Homi K. Bhabha, *The Location of Culture* (New York: Routledge, 1994). 41.

7 Seung-Kyung Kim, *The Korean Women's Movement and the State: Bargaining for Change,* (London: Routledge, 2014), 30.

8 Kim, *The Korean Women's Movement and the State,* 30.

9 Yeoseong Nodong Haebangga (Women Worker Liberation Song), dated 1988, file 5, box 72, UCLA Archives Special Collection 358, Human Rights and Unification in Korea, Los Angeles.

10 Christian Conference of Asia – Urban Rural Mission, *From the Womb of Han: Stories of Korean Women Workers* (Hong Kong: CCA-URM, 1982).

11 Hanguk Gidokgyo Jangnohoe, *Han Somang Anaeseo: Hanguk – Kanadagyohoe Seongyohyeopnyeok 100junyeon Ginyeommunjip* (Seoul: Hanguk Gidokgyo Jangnohoe Chulpan, 1998), 77.

12 Letter from World Council of Churches Programme Unit on Faith and Witness to Participants in the Informal Consultation on Korea, dated 18 December 1975, file 23–1, box 23, accession 83.019C, UCC Archives, Toronto. Emphasis in original.

13 Andrew H. Malcolm, "Women Playing Important Role in Rights Struggle in South Korea," *New York Times,* 8 December 1976, file 000116, box 2, U of T Collection Human Rights in South Korea, Toronto.

14 Ibid.

15 Willa Kernen, "It Was Impossible to Be Uninvolved," in *More Than Witnesses: How a Small Group of Missionaries Aided Korea's Democratic Revolution,* ed. Jim Stenzel (Seoul: Korea Democracy Foundation, 2006), 292.

16 Handwritten note by Marion Pope, no date, file 003070, box 75, U of T Collection Human Rights in Korea, Toronto.

17 Marion Current, "A New Day Has Dawned," in *More Than Witnesses: How a Small Group of Missionaries Aided Korea's Democratic Revolution,* ed. Jim Stenzel (Seoul: Korea Democracy Foundation, 2006), 396.

18 Interview with Lois Wilson, 26 July 2018.

19 Interview with Elsie Livingston, 23 April 2020.

20 Margaret E. McPherson, "Head, Heart and Purse: The Presbyterian Women's Missionary Society in Canada, 1876–1925" in *Prairie Spirit: Perspectives on the Heritage of the United Church of Canada in the West,* eds. Dennis L. Butcher, Catherine Macdonald, Margaret E. McPherson, Raymond R. Smith, and A. McKibbin Watts (Winnipeg: University of Manitoba Press, 1985), 154.

Notes to pages 160–2

21 There are indeed histories written of the UIM by missionary George Ogle and UIM leader In Myung-jin, but there are more like blow-by-blow accounts of events than descriptions of the kinds of relationships that developed between the men who collaborated in the movement. See George Ogle and Dorothy Ogle, *Our Lives in Korea and Korea in Our Lives* (Bolton, ON: Xlibris, 2012); George Ogle, "Our Hearts Cry with You," in *More Than Witnesses: How a Small Group of Missionaries Aided Korea's Democratic Revolution*, ed. Jim Stenzel (Seoul: Korea Democracy Foundation, 2006); Myung-jin In, *The Story of Outside the Gate People the History of the Yong dong Po Urban Industrial Mission in the 1970s* (Republic of Korea: The Christian Literature Society of Korea and Korean Host Committee of for the WCC 10th Assembly, 2012).

22 Statement of Position, dated 9 June 1975, file 1 DWO Human Rights, box 23, accession 83.019C, UCC Archives, Toronto.

23 Hagen Koo, *Korean Workers: The Culture and Politics of Class Formation* (Ithaca: Cornell University Press, 2001), 95.

24 Ibid.

25 Marion Current, "A New Day Had Dawned," 405–6.

26 "Working Women of Korea," from *The Womb of Asia: Working Women of Korea*, file 1, box 75, UCLA Special Collection 358 Human Rights and Unification in Korea, Los Angeles.

27 Seungsook Moon, *Militarized Modernity and Gendered Citizenship in South Korea* (Durham: Duke University Press, 2005), 70.

28 "Working Women of Korea," from *The Womb of Asia: Working Women of Korea*, file 1, box 75, UCLA Special Collection 358 Human Rights and Unification in Korea, Los Angeles.

29 "Sarang-bang: An Example of Religious Freedom in the PROK," Fact Sheet #26, dated 1 March 1976, file 1, box 65, UCLA Special Collection 358 Democracy and Unification in Korea, Los Angeles. Fact Sheets were a tool used by concerned North American churches with missionaries in South Korea to disseminate information about the situation on the peninsula to their congregations and human rights organizations. Generally, they were composed by Fred Bayliss working from UCC HQ in Toronto. Bayliss was a onetime missionary to Korea, serving from 1962 to 1972. Upon returning to Canada, he worked for the Division of World Outreach but maintained an active interest in events in Korea. Most of the information for his "Fact Sheets" was gleaned from missionary reports. In this case, Fact Sheet #26, it is likely that all of the information came from Kernen, Pope, and Current.

30 Ibid.

31 Letter author and recipient unknown, dated December 1975, file 000597, box 18, U of T Special Collection Human Rights in South Korea, Toronto.

32 Hak-kyu Sohn, *Authoritarianism and Opposition in South Korea* (London: Routledge, 1989), 71.

33 Interviews with Lee Gwang-il, 29 April 2015.

34 Yi Munsuk, *Lee Oo Chung Pyeongjeon* (Seoul: Samin Chulpansa, 2012), 181.

35 Ibid.

36 Marion Current, "A New Day Had Dawned," 405.

37 Letter from Willa Kernen to Frank Carey, dated 31 January 1976, file 6, box 23, accession 83.019C, UCC Archives, Toronto.

38 Yi, *Lee Oo Chung Pyeongjeon*, 181.

39 Paul Y. Chang, *Protest Dialectics: State Repression and South Korea's Democratization Movement, 1970–1979* (Stanford: Stanford University Press, 2015), 108.

40 Letter from Willa Kernen to Frank Carey, dated 31 January 1976, file 6, box 23 of 24, accession 83.019C, UCC Archives, Toronto.

41 Current, "A New Day Had Dawned," 405–6. There is no record that Pope attended Sarangbang Church but it is very possible that she did.

42 Letter from Willa Kernen to Frank Carey, dated 31 January 1976, file 6, box 23 of 24, accession 83.019C, UCC Archives, Toronto.

43 Current, "A New Day Had Dawned," 405–6.

44 Ibid., 405.

45 U of T Special Collection Human Rights in Korea, box 44, file 001577, Galilee Church, dated 30 April 1976.

46 Current, "A New Day Had Dawned," 406.

47 Accession 83.019C, box 23 of 24, file 6, dated 31 January 1976.

48 UCLA Collection 358, box 65, file 1, Sarangbang Church fact sheet, Fred Bayliss, dated January 1976.

49 Current, "A New Day Had Dawned," 406.

50 Handwritten notes re: Sarang-Bang Church (by Marion Current, no name or date), file 003087, U of T collection, box 75, U of T collection of Democracy and Human Rights, Toronto; Current, "A New Day Had Dawned."

51 Moon Ik Hwan was a prominent dissident, Minjung theologian, teacher at the Mission Education Centre (MEC), and son of Moon Chai Rin and Kim Shin Mook, who attended Toronto Korean United Church and were associated with the UCC Mission in Yongjeong, Manchuria.

52 Current, "A New Day Had Dawned," 407.

53 This event will be discussed in detail below.

54 U of T collection, box 75, file 003087, handwritten notes re: Sarang-Bang Church (by Marion Current, no name or date).

55 UCLA Archives 358 Special Collection South Korean Democracy, box 14, file 2, handwritten account of Suh Nam Dong's trial.

56 Willa Kernen, "Timothy Moon: Poet and Prophet," *Mission Magazine* 8, no. 1 (1984), 8–11, file 000530, box 15, U of T Special Collection Human Rights in Korea, Toronto.

57 Willa Kernen to Frank Carey, dated 31 January 1976, file 6, box 23, accession 83.019C, UCC Archives, Toronto.

58 Letter from Willa Kernen to Walter and Lenore Beecham, dated 16 March 1975, file 23-3, box 23, accession 83.019C, UCC Archives, Toronto.

59 It is common for Koreans to speak of new apartment developments as "apartment forests."

60 Monday Night Group (MG), dated 23 August 2003, file 003070, box 75, U of T Collection Human Rights in Korea, Toronto.

61 Letter from Korea (author and recipient unknown), dated 1 March 1976, file 6, box 23 of 34, accession 83.019C, UCC Archives, Toronto. This was likely a letter from Willa Kernen to Frank Carey, the names of those involved have been deliberately excluded in case the document was intercepted by the authorities.

62 The record is not clear.

63 Kernen, "It Was Impossible to Be Uninvolved," 283.

64 Letter from Korea, dated 1 March 1976, file 6, box 23 of 34, accession 83.019C, UCC Archives, Toronto.

65 Yi, *Lee Oo Chung Pyeongjeon*, 215.

66 Ibid., 213.

67 Lee Jang Nag, *I Shall Be Buried in Korea: A Biography of Dr Frank William Schofield*, trans. Choi Jin Young (self published, 1989).

68 U of T Special Collection on Human Rights in South Korea, file 001563, Letter from Ahn Byung Mu distributed by ecumenical forum in Canada, dated 4 April 1977.

69 Chang, *Protest Dialectics*, 90.

70 Ibid., 108.

71 Letter from Ahn Byung Mu distributed by ecumenical forum in Canada, dated 4 April 1977, file 001563, U of T Special Collection on Human Rights in South Korea; Donald N. Clark, "Growth and Limitations of Minjung Christianity in South Korea," in *South Korean Minjung Movement*, ed. Kenneth M. Wells (Honolulu, University of Hawai'i Press, 1995), 89.

72 U of T Special Collection on Human Rights in South Korea, box 3, file 000118, Kim Dae Jung's final testimony in Seoul Court.

73 Human Rights Committee of the National Council of Churches in Korea, *1970 Democratization Movement*, vol. I (Seoul: National Council of Churches in Korea, 1986), 684–5.

74 Willa Kernen, "The Story of Lee Oo Chung," no date, file 1, box 75, UCLA Special Collection 358 Human Rights and Unification in Korea, Los Angeles.

75 Ibid.

76 "ROK Churchwoman Held in Seoul," New York (AP) *Japan Times*, 3 March 1976, file 6, box 23, accession 83.019C, UCC Archives, Toronto.

77 Yi, *Lee Oo Chung Pyeongjeon*, 214. An article dated 5 March 1976 was found in the *New York Times* archives (accessed 29 July 2020): https://www.nytimes.com/1976/03/05/archives/17-seoul-critics-said-to-be-held-signers-of-antipark-paper-are.html.

78 1 March fact sheet, dated 3 March 1976, file 2, box 14, UCLA Archives Special Collection 358 South Korean Democracy, Los Angeles.

79 Yi, *Lee Oo Chung Pyeongjeon*, 218.

80 Ibid., 223.

81 Willa Kernen, "The Story of Lee Oo Chung," no date, file 1, box 75, UCLA Special Collection 358 Human Rights and Unification in Korea, Los Angeles.

82 Yi, *Lee Oo Chung Pyeongjeon*, 230.

83 Wi Jo Kang, *Christ and Caesar in Modern Korea: A History of Christianity and Politics* (Albany, NY: State University of New York Press, 1997), 113.

84 Kenneth Wells, ed., *South Korean's Minjung Movement: The Culture and Politics of Dissidence* (Honolulu: University of Hawai'i Press, 1995), 89.

85 Human Rights Committee of the National Council of Churches in Korea, *1970 Democratization Movement*, vol. I (Seoul: National Council of Churches in Korea, 1986), 688; Sohn, *Authoritarianism and Opposition in South Korea*, 95; Gi-Wook Shin, Paul Y. Chang, Jung-eun Lee, Sookyung Kim, "South Korea's Democracy Movement (1970–1993): Stanford Korea Democracy Project Report" (Stanford University: December, 2007), 35, https://fsi-live.s3.us-west-1.amazonaws.com/s3fs-public/KDP_Report_%28 final%29-1.pdf; Chang, *Protest Dialectics*, 90, 152, 163, 206.

86 Chang, *Protest Dialectics*.

87 The Patriotic Declaration for Democracy, file 001979, U of T Special Collection Human Rights in Korea, Toronto.

88 Yi, *Lee Oo Chung Pyeongjeon*, 220.

89 Lee Oo Chung, Prayer for Salvation of the Nation, 27 August 1976, file 6, box 75, UCLA Special Collection 358 Human Rights and Unification in Korea, Los Angeles.

Notes to pages 172–81

90 Stanford Korea Democracy Project, 35.
91 Andrew H. Malcolm, "Women Playing Important Role in Rights Struggle in South Korea," *New York Times*, 8 December 1976, file 000116, box 2, U of T Collection Human Rights in South Korea, Toronto.
92 Faye Moon, "Hearts No Longer, and Some That Linger," in *More Than Witnesses: How a Small Group of Missionaries Aided Korea's Democratic Revolution*, ed. Jim Stenzel (Seoul: Korea Democracy Foundation, 2006), 174.
93 This is an unusual romanization of the Korean *minju hoebok* – 민주회복 (民主恢復).
94 The Story of the Victory Shawl, North American Coalition for Human Rights in Korea, October 1976, file 23–4, box 23, accession 83.019C, ucc Archives, Toronto.
95 Interview with Elsie Livingston, 23 April 2020.
96 Yi, *Lee Oo Chung Pyeongjeon*, 224.
97 Ibid., 208.
98 Willa Kernen, "The Story of Lee Oo Chung," no date, file 1, box 75, UCLA Special Collection 358 Human Rights and Unification in Korea, Los Angeles.

CHAPTER SEVEN

1 Sang Chul Lee, *Hananimi Inryueui huimang* (Toronto: Grover Printing, 1989), 210.
2 Wilbur Howard, a Black man, was elected moderator in 1974.
3 Hugh McCallum, "Lee's Church: Celebrate, Not Retreat," *Observer*, September 1988, New Series 52, no. 3, 8.
4 Interview with Patti Talbot, 29 May 2020
5 *Report of the Commission on World Mission*, ucc, Proceedings, GC22, 1966, 402.
6 Sang-Chul Lee and Eric Weingartner, *The Wanderer: The Autobiography of a United Church Moderator* (Winfield, BC: Woodlake Books, 1989), 90.
7 Ibid., 93.
8 Ibid., 95.
9 Irene Chungwha Lee, "Koreans in Canada" in *Mission Magazine* 8, no. 1, *South Korea: Challenge and Celebration* (1984), file 000530, U of T Collection Human Rights in Korea, Toronto, 45; Nancy E. Hardy, "A Challenge," *Mission Magazine* 8, no. 1 (1984); K. Seang, "Life That Starts Again," *Seonguja – People Restarting* 4 (April 1971); H.P.O., "Life That Starts Again," *Seonguja – People Restarting* 4 (April 1971); W.H.S., "Life that Starts Again," *Seonguja – People Restarting* 4 (April 1971);

282 Notes to pages 182–6

Cho Seong-jun, "Life that Starts Again," *Seonguja – People Restarting* 4 (April 1971); interview with Jeong Hakpil, 18 November 2018.

10 Interview with Richard Choe, 14 November 2018.

11 Interview with Songsuk and James Chong, 16 November 2018.

12 Cecil Foster, *They Call Me George: The Untold Story of Black Train Porters and the Birth of Modern Canada* (Windsor, ON: Biblioasis, 2019).

13 Reg Whitaker, *Canadian Immigration Policy since Confederation* (Toronto: Department of Political Science York University, 1991), 18–19. Despite being hailed as an enlightened policy that eliminated the injustice of racial discrimination in Canada's immigration policy, the change can also be seen as a fundamentally self-interested move in support of an expansionary economy in which more immigration was needed to fill skilled labour, technical, and professional jobs.

14 History of the Fifteen Years of the Toronto Korean United Church Editorial Committee, *History of the Fifteen Years of the Toronto Korean United Church* (Toronto: Sseon Printers, 1982), 11.

15 Interview with Jeong Hakpil, 18 November 2018.

16 Greer Anne Wenh-In Ng, "The United Church of Canada: A Church Fittingly National," in *Christianity and Ethnicity in Canada*, ed. Paul Bramadat and David Seljak (Toronto: University of Toronto Press, 2008), 211.

17 Interview with Jeong Hakpil, 18 November 2018.

18 *History of the Fifteen Years of the Toronto Korean United Church*, 13.

19 Interview with Richard Choe, 14 November 2018.

20 Ibid.

21 Moon Chai Rin and Kim Shin Mook, *Giringabiwa Gomannye-ui Kkum: Moon Chai Rin Kim Shin Mook Hoegorok* (Seoul: Samin Chulpansa, 2006), 273.

22 *History of the Fifteen Years of the Toronto Korean United Church*, 20.

23 Moon and Kim, *Giringabiwa Gomannye-ui Kkum*, 276.

24 Ibid., 275.

25 Ibid., 276.

26 *History of the Fifteen Years of the Toronto Korean United Church*, 13.

27 Ibid., 16.

28 Ibid., 21.

29 Luis Liang and Ben C.H. Kuo, "A Brief History of the Taiwanese Immigrant Church in Canada," in *People of Faith, People of Jeong (Qing): The Asian Canadian Churches of Today for Tomorrow*, ed. Nam Soon Song, Ben C.H. Kuo, Dong-Ha Kim, and In Kee Kim (Eugene, OR: Wipf & Stock Publishers, 2020), 20ff.

30 Lee, *Hananimi Inryueui huimang*, 14.

31 Ibid., 21.

32 Interview with James and Seong-suk Chong, 16 November 2018.

33 Sang Chul Lee, "Editor's Note," *Seonguja – First Publication* 1 (April 1970).

34 先驅者 – 선구자.

35 Lee and his community were aware of and sensitivity to Indigenous issues stemming from their unfair treatment in the history of Canada and its expansion westward. It does not occur to him here, however, to qualify this analogy in light of these issues.

36 Sang Chul Lee, "Details of the Life of a Pioneer," *Seonguja* 1, *First Publication* (April 1970).

37 Ibid.

38 Jin-shil, "How Must We Live in This Land?," *Seonguja* 2, *Seeking a Korean-Canadian Identity* (October 1970), 20.

39 Sang Chul Lee, "Editor's Note," *Seonguja* 2, *Seeking a Korean-Canadian Identity* (October 1970); John Porter, *The Vertical Mosaic: An Analysis of Social Class and Power in Canada* (Toronto: University of Toronto Press, 1965).

40 Lee, "Editor's Note."

41 W.A. Burbidge, "Our Expectations for Korean Canadians," *Seonguja* 2, *Seeking a Korean-Canadian Identity* (October 1970).

42 Ibid.

43 Hwan Jim-mu is not a Japanese name. It might be a Korean reading of the Chinese characters for what would in Japanese have more than three syllables.

44 Hwan Jim-mu, "A Japanese Minister in Canada," trans. Han Kang-yeon, *Seonguja* 2, *Seeking a Korean-Canadian Identity* (October 1970).

45 W.H.S., "Life That Starts Again," *Seonguja – People Restarting*, no. 4, April 1971.

46 Pak Eun-myeong, "Impression after Having Participated in Heritage Ontario," *Seonguja* 8, *Complex Cultural Society and the Race Problem* (October 1972).

47 Ibid.

48 Jeon Chung-lim, "Pessimism about the Canadian Government's Multiculturalism Policy," *Seonguja* 8, *Complex Cultural Society and the Race Problem* (October 1972).

49 Ibid.

50 Ibid.

51 Letter to Member Churches from the World Council of Churches, dated 12–23 August 1968, GC mins, exec and sub-exec 1968–70, file 1, box 32, accession 82.001C, UCC Archives, Toronto; The Program to Combat Racism, The Executive [of General Council], dated 20–23 November

284 Notes to pages 191–8

1972, file SII Minutes 1971–1974, box 33, accession 82.001C, UCC Archives, Toronto; Report of the Sessional Committee on the Program to Combat Racism, The Executive [of General Council], dated 20–3 November 1978, file SII Minutes 1974–1984, box 34, accession 82.001C, UCC Archives, Toronto.

52 Information packet, 43rd *General Council*, 24 October 2020.

53 Jo Seongjun, "The Problem of Racism: Report from an Educational Conference," *Seonguja* 8, *Complex Culture Society and the Race Problem* (October 1972).

54 Ibid.

55 Oh Yeong-ju, "Planting a Woman's Dream in a New Land," *Seonguja* 5, *Women and Life in the New Land* (July 1971).

56 Lee Sang Chul, "Editor's Preface," *Seonguja* 8, *Complex Cultural Society and the Race Problem* (October 1972).

57 Sang Chul Lee, *Hananimi Inryueui huimang* (Toronto: Grover Printing, 1989), 210.

58 Interview with Richard Choe, 14 November 2018.

59 Moon and Kim, *Giringabiwa Gomannye-ui Kkum*, 301.

60 Yi, *Lee Oo Chung Pyeongjeon*, 223.

61 Moon and Kim, *Giringabiwa Gomannye-ui Kkum*, 301; Poster, "The Recently Quelled Rebellion in Kwangju," file DWO Human Rights, box 23 of 34, accession 83.019C, UCC Archives, Toronto.

62 Interview with Richard Choe, 14 November 2018.

63 Kim Heung-su, "Hanguk minjuhwa gidokja dongjihoe-ui gyeolseonggwa hwaldong," *Hangukgidokgyowa yeoksa* 9 (September 2009).

64 Ng, "The United Church of Canada: A Church Fittingly National," 227–8.

65 Sang Chul Lee fonds, UCC Archives, Toronto.

66 Lee and Weingartner, *The Wanderer*, 52.

67 Ibid., 96.

68 "Histoire des franco-protestants," *Aujourd'hui Crédo: la revue franco-phone et œcuménique de l'Église Unie*, Janvier–Février 2014, https:// egliseunie.ca/wp-content/uploads/2015/03/Aujourdhui_Credo_2014_ Histoire-des-franco-protestants.pdf.

69 J.R. Miller, *Residential Schools and Reconciliation: Canada Confronts Its History* (Toronto: University of Toronto Press, 2017), 3, 246.

70 Lee, *The Wanderer*, 86.

71 Lee, *Hananimi Inryueui huimang*, 91–2.

72 17th Annual Meeting of the Association of Korean Christian Scholars in North America "Minjung Theology and Korean Immigrants," 26–7 May 1983, file 32, box 26, UCLA Special Collection 358 Democracy and Unification in Korea, Los Angeles.

Notes to pages 199–206

73 Interview with Richard Choe, 14 November 2018.

74 Interview with Dong-Chun Seo, 12 November 2018.

75 Ibid.

76 Generally speaking this term was used to denote any congregation that was non-White and/or did not use English in worship.

77 Interview with Dong-Chun Seo, 12 November 2018.

78 Dong-Chun Seo, *A Research Study of Ethnic Ministries: Toronto Area*, dated February 1978, file 10, box 5, accession 2009.014C, UCC Archives, Toronto.

79 Phyllis Airhart, *A Church with the Soul of a Nation: Making and Remaking the United Church of Canada* (Montreal and Kingston: McGill-Queen's University Press, 2014), 12; Brian Clarke, "English Speaking Canada from 1854," *A Concise History of Christianity in Canada*, ed. Terrence Murphy and Roberto Perin (Toronto: Oxford University Press, 1996), 357; Ng, "The United Church of Canada," 204.

80 Interview with Dong-Chun Seo, 12 November 2018.

81 Interview with Kay Cho, 21 November 2018

82 Interview with Kay Cho, conducted by HyeRan Kim-Cragg for McGeachy Project (2011–13).

83 Interview with Kay Cho, 21 November 2018.

84 Ibid.

85 Ibid.

86 Ibid.

87 Interview with Kay Cho, conducted by HyeRan Kim-Cragg for McGeachy Project (2011–13).

88 Interview with Kay Cho, 21 November 2018.

89 Lee Oo Chung and Yi Hyeon-suk, *Hanguk Gidokgyo Jangnohoe Yeoshindohoe 60nyeonsa* (Seoul: Hanguk Gidokgyo Jangnohoe Yeoshindohoe Jeonkuk Yeonhaphoe, 1989), 216.

90 Feasibility Task Group on Ethnic Ministries, Office of the General Council, *The Proposed Model for the Ethnic Ministries Council of the United Church of Canada*, presented to the 35th General Council in Fergus, ON, 19–28 August 1994; EMC History dates 1994–1996, box 8–18, accession 2009.100C, United Church Archives, Toronto.

91 Kawuki Mukasa, "The New United Church Ethnic Ministry Council: Reflections on Origins and Prospects," in *Touchstone* 13, no. 1 (January 1995): 13.

92 Interview with Michael Blair, 18 August 2020.

93 祭祀 – 제사.

94 Interview with Kay Cho, 21 November 2018.

95 Ibid.

CHAPTER EIGHT

1 Irene Chunghwa Lee, "Koreans in Canada," *Mission Magazine* 8, no. 1, *South Korea: Challenge and Celebration* (1984), 44–7, file 000530, U of T Collection Human Rights in Korea, Toronto.

2 Interview with Elsie Livingston, 23 April 2020.

3 CGIT is a program for young girls that sprang out of the Canadian Protestant church and was traditionally strongly supported by the UCC.

4 Yi MoonSuk, *Lee Oo Chung Pyeongjeon* (Seoul: Samin Chulpansa, 2012), 224.

5 Young Mee Moon, *To Korea with Love* (Singapore: Stallion Press, 2014), 195.

6 Willa Kernen, "It Was Impossible to Be Uninvolved," in *More Than Witnesses: How a Small Group of Missionaries Aided Korea's Democratic Revolution*, ed. Jim Stenzel (Seoul: Korea Democracy Foundation, 2006), 287.

7 Interview with Elsie Livingston, 23 April 2020.

8 Joan Wyatt, "The 1970s: Voices from the Margins," in *The United Church of Canada: A History, ed.* Donald Schweitzer (Waterloo: Wilfrid Laurier University Press, 2012), 128.

9 Ibid., 126–7.

10 Ibid., 133.

11 "Sharp Criticism for UCC," *Observer*, September 1980, vol. 151, no. 3, 7.

12 *Report of the Commission on World Mission*, UCC, Proceedings, GC22, 1966, 312.

13 Ibid., 336.

14 Ibid., 426.

15 Ibid., 431–2.

16 Ibid., 433.

17 Ibid., 435.

18 Ruth Compton Brouwer, "From Missionaries to NGOs," in *Canada and the Third World: Overlapping Histories*, ed. Karen Dubinsky, Sean Mills, and Scott Rutherford (Toronto: University of Toronto Press, 2016), 137.

19 "Sharp Criticism for UCC," *Observer*, September 1980, vol. 151, no. 3, 7.

20 Interview with Lois Wilson, 26 July 2018. She could think of only one missionary, a woman by the name of Beulah Bourns who, she remembered hearing, had run an orphanage somewhere.

21 Lois Wilson, *Turning the World Upside Down: A Memoir* (Toronto: Doubleday Canada, 1989), 82.

22 Memorandum from Ted S—t to Lois Wilson, dated 2 February 1981, file 8, box 1, accession 94.170C, UCC Archives, Toronto.

Notes to pages 215–22

23 Interview with Lois Wilson, 26 July 2018.
24 Ibid.
25 Ibid.
26 Jo A-ra (조아라). Memorandum from Ted S—t to Lois Wilson, dated 2 February 1981, file 8, box 1, accession 94.170C, UCC Archives, Toronto.
27 Memorandum from Ted S—t to Lois Wilson, dated 2 February 1981, file 8, box 1, accession 94.170C, UCC Archives, Toronto.
28 Interview with Lois Wilson, 26 July 2018.
29 Letter from Walter Beecham to Lois Wilson, dated 26 January 1981, file 8, box 1, accession 94.170C, UCC Archives, Toronto.
30 Interview with Lois Wilson, 26 July 2018.
31 One man who met Wilson in Kwangju and told her about the death of his son spent two years in prison as a result.
32 Wilson, *Turning the World Upside Down*, 88.
33 "Faith and Justice: The Moderator's Message," *Mission Magazine* 5, no. 3 (1981), file 6, box 1, accession 94.170C, UCC Archives, Toronto.
34 Interview with Lois Wilson, 26 July 2018.
35 "DPRK: A Resource for Education and Engagement," Canada-DPR Korea Association, no date, URL no longer in operation, www.canada-dprk.org.
36 Due to ongoing tensions connected to the DPRK's nuclear program embassies were never established and relations were suspended in 2010.
37 "DPRK: A Resource for Education and Engagement," Canada-DPR Korea Association, no date, URL no longer in operation, www.canada-dprk.org.
38 Irene Chunghwa Lee, "Koreans in Canada," *Mission Magazine* 8, no. 1, *South Korea: Challenge and Celebration* (1984), 44–7, file 000530, U of T Collection Human Rights in Korea, Toronto.
39 Interview with Lois Wilson, August 2018.
40 Fred Bayliss, "United Church of Canada – Presbyterian Church in the Republic of Korea: from Past to Future," Mission consultation between the UCC and the PROK, 16–18 August 1995, Academy House, Seoul, file 000748, box 50, U of T Special Collection Human Rights in Korea, Toronto.
41 Pat Wells, "Two Koreans Look at the Canadian Church," *Mission Magazine* 8, no. 1, *South Korea: Challenge and Celebration* (1984), 42, file 000530, U of T Collection Human Rights in Korea, Toronto.
42 Ibid.
43 Interview with Lois Wilson, August 2018.
44 Sang-Chul Lee and Eric Weingartner, *The Wanderer: The Autobiography of a United Church Moderator* (Winfield, BC: Woodlake Books, 1989), 39.
45 Interview with Linda Butler, 3 May 2020.

46 Hanguk Gidokgyo Jangnohoe, *Han Somang Anaeseo: Hanguk – Kanadagyohoe Seongyohyeopnyeok 100junyeon Ginyeommunjip* (Seoul: Hanguk Gidokgyo Jangnohoe Chulpan, 1998), 163.

47 Moon Chai Rin and Kim Shin Mook, *Giringabiwa Gomannye-ui Kkum: Moon Chai Rin Kim Shin Mook Hoegorok* (Seoul: Samin Chulpansa, 2006), 119.

48 Interview with Songsuk and James Chong, 16 November 2018.

49 Interview with Linda Butler, 3 May 2020.

50 Ibid.

51 Lee, "Koreans in Canada," 46 (found in file 000530, U of T Collection Human Rights in Korea, Toronto).

52 Interview with Linda Butler, 3 May 2020.

53 Christabelle Sethna and Steve Hewit, *Just Watch Us: RCMP Surveillance of the Women's Liberation Movement in Cold War Canada* (Montreal and Kingston: McGill-Queen's University Press, 2018).

54 Kim, Hyun-young Kwon, and John Cho, "The Korean Gay and Lesbian Movement 1993–2008," in *South Korean Social Movements: From Democracy to Civil Society*, ed. Gi-Wook Shin and Paul Y. Chang (New York: Routledge, 2011).

55 Interview with Patti Talbot, 29 July 2020.

56 Ibid.

57 Ibid.

58 Interview with Michael Blair, 18 August 2020.

59 Ibid.

60 Dong-Chun Seo, A Research Study of Ethnic Ministries: Toronto Area, dated February 1978, file 10, box 5, accession 2009.014C, UCC Archives, Toronto.

61 Interview with Michael Blair, 18 August 2020.

62 Greer Anne Wenh-In Ng, "The United Church of Canada: A Church Fittingly National," in *Christianity and Ethnicity in Canada*, ed. Paul Bramadat and David Seljak (Toronto: University of Toronto Press, 2008), 210.

63 Kawuki Mukasa, "The New United Church Ethnic Ministry Council: Reflections on Origins and Prospects," in *Touchstone* 13, no. 1 (January 1995): 4.

64 Mukasa, "The New United Church Ethnic Ministry Council," 8.

65 "Sharp Criticism for UCC," *Observer*, September 1980, vol. 151, no. 3, 7.

66 Ng, "The United Church of Canada," 210.

67 Mukasa, "The New United Church Ethnic Ministry Council," 9.

68 Feasibility Task Group on Ethnic Ministries, Office of the General Council, *The Proposed Model for the Ethnic Ministries Council of The United*

Church of Canada, presented to the 35th General Council in Fergus, ON, 19–28 August 1994; EMC History dates 1994–1996, box 8–18, accession 2009.100C, UCC Archives, Toronto.

69 Mukasa, "The New United Church Ethnic Ministry Council," 10.

70 Ibid.

71 Interview with Michael Blair, 18 August 2020.

72 Ibid.

73 Ibid.

74 Lee and Weingartner, *The Wanderer,* 115.

75 Ibid.

76 Lynne Marks, *Infidels and the Damn Churches: Irreligion and Religion in Settler British* Columbia (Vancouver: UBC Press, 2017), 161ff.

CONCLUSION

1 William Scott, *A History of the Canadian Mission to Korea, 1898–1970s,* revised and expanded by J. Greig McMullin (Belleville, ON: Guardian Books, 2009), 469, 641.

2 Sang Chul Lee, *Hananimi Inryueui huimang* (Toronto: Grover Printing, 1989), 12.

3 Cynthia Sugars, ed., *The Unhomely State: Theorizing English-Canadian Postcolonialism* (Peterborough, ON: Broadview Press, 2004).

4 Phyllis Airhart, *A Church with the Soul of a Nation: Making and Remaking the United Church of Canada* (Montreal and Kingston: McGill-Queen's University Press, 2014), 152.

5 Quoted in John S. Moir, *Enduring Witness* (Burlington, ON: Eagle Press Printers, 1987), xi.

6 Nathan VanderKlippe, "China's History with Missionaries Forms Modern Canada Relations," *Globe and Mail,* 14 April 2017, https://www.theglobeandmail.com/news/world/chinas-history-with-missionaries-forms-modern-canada-relations/article34714775.

7 Tina Park, "The U.S. has failed in its handling of North Korea – creating an opportunity for Canada to prove it is 'back' on the world stage," *Maclean's,* 14 August 2017, https://www.macleans.ca/opinion/as-the-north-korean-crisis-escalates-canada-must-step-up.

8 VanderKlippe, "China's History with Missionaries."

9 Greer Anne Wenh-In Ng, "The United Church of Canada: A Church Fittingly National," in *Christianity and Ethnicity in Canada,* ed. Paul Bramadat and David Seljak (Toronto: University of Toronto Press, 2008), 237.

Index

1 March (3.1) Independence Movement, xxi, 6, 64, 168–9, 222

1.5-generation Korean immigrants, 208

19 April (4.19) uprising, 20, 86, 87, 89

Abington Bible Commentary, 61, 65, 73

Ahn Byung Mu, 22, 41, 45, 65, 86, 137–40, 142, 144–5

Airhart, Phyllis, 12, 13, 53, 76, 94, 201, 234

American Presbyterian Mission, 46, 62, 71, 253n4; Northern Presbyterian Church USA, 58–9, 67, 71, 79

American missionaries, 19, 55, 60, 73, 75

Anglo UCC, 7, 8, 9, 10, 12, 18, 44, 51, 53, 107, 129, 181, 187, 200–1, 203, 204, 206, 210, 213, 218, 219–21, 226, 227, 231–2, 234–5, 236, 239

Anglo-Protestantism, 8, 12, 51, 180

Avison, Oliver R., 6, 237, 259n18

Bayliss, Fred, 24, 277n29

Beecham, Walter, 110, 160, 216

Bhabha, Homi, 16, 105, 156

biblical interpretation, 12, 59, 69

Billy Graham Crusade, 21, 130–1, 133–5, 142

Black Canadians, 182, 190, 191, 192–3, 203, 226

Black Christians, 142, 148, 191, 192–3, 203, 226

Blair, Michael, 205, 210, 226–32

Board of Overseas Missions (BOM), 75, 89

Board of World Mission (BWM), 89, 91, 109–10, 114, 117, 214, 224

Brouwer, Ruth Compton, 14, 50, 76, 89, 91–4, 97, 109, 156, 214

Brown, George, 7

Buddhism, 134, 169

Burbidge, W.A., 185, 189

Butler, Linda, 210, 221–5, 227, 231

Canadian Asian Working Group (CAWG), 149

Carey, Frank, 109–10, 112, 114–19, 122, 127, 152

Catholic Church, 7, 8, 37, 39, 43–4, 107, 136, 144, 147, 162, 167, 169, 172, 217, 247n73, 248n83

Chang, Paul Y., 144, 163, 172

Cheondogyo, 169

Cho, Kay (Kyung Ja), 202–6, 217, 224, 236

Choe, Richard, 183–4

Choi, Jang Jip, 41, 105

Chong, James and Songsuk, xxix, 182, 187, 222

Christian Democratization Movement, xxvii, xxviii, 10, 15, 20, 24, 45, 72, 76, 123, 124, 125, 133, 135–6, 155, 157, 158, 161, 165, 169, 171–2, 195, 217, 218, 225, 238

Christian Thought (journal), 84, 142

Christianity, 96, 170, 238; Canadian, 23, 27, 94, 148, 189, 190, 198, 206, 214, 235–6; and communism, 36, 95; Korean, xvi, xxvii, 8, 17–18, 21, 27, 41–5, 54–5, 57–8, 60, 63, 69, 72, 75, 94, 131–4, 169, 172, 198, 234–6; missionary, 32, 37, 48–54; post-colonial, 78, 146

Chung, David, 70, 184–5

Chun Doo Hwan, 149, 158, 210, 215

Chun Sunyeong, 35, 44

Chung Suk Ja, 123

Church Union, 19, 52–4, 59, 62–3, 94, 112, 119, 129, 186, 197, 249n105

colonialism, 9, 16, 33, 34–5, 42; American, 105; British, 190; Canadian, 10, 14, 18, 19, 23, 27,

51, 83, 92, 105, 115, 127, 147, 150, 154, 190, 234; Japanese, 19, 48, 51, 52–4, 57, 65, 70, 92, 105, 128, 168; Missionary, 8, 19, 20, 51, 58, 85, 92, 96, 101, 105, 115, 133

Commission on World Mission. See *Report of the Commission on World Mission*

Communism, 13, 35–6, 52, 70, 95, 134, 141, 236

compounds, missionary, xxi, 3, 34, 47–8, 51, 109, 111, 116, 122, 166

Cone, James, 142, 146, 148

Confucianism/Confucius, 37, 38, 39, 40, 42–4, 64, 69, 139, 140, 204, 246n49

contact zone, 16–17, 251n140

Current, Marion, xxviii, 77, 110, 147–8, 150, 159, 163–8, 173–4, 238, 277n29

"the Decision," 20, 88–9, 98, 102

Declaration for National Salvation (1976), 22, 155, 158, 165, 166–75, 196, 212

Democratization Movement: missionaries supporting/impacted by, xxvii, 10–11, 21, 24, 136, 147–8, 165, 195, 210, 238

devolution, 62, 88

Division of Mission in Canada (DMC), 193, 213, 228

Division of World Outreach (DWO), 117–23, 125, 191, 195, 196, 214, 228

Dominion of Canada, 19, 48–9, 51, 53, 54

Donghak, 39, 169

Index

ecumenism, 45, 69, 74, 75, 91, 94, 102, 144, 147, 150, 163, 169–70, 196, 213

education, 19, 39–41, 54, 60–1, 62, 64, 66, 68, 70–3, 79, 93, 106, 115, 119, 139–40, 152, 154, 157, 203, 214; theological, 19, 60, 64, 68, 71, 73, 79, 139–40, 152, 254n23

Emergency Measures #9, 167, 169

Endicott, James, 76, 169

Eunjin Mission School, xvi, xx, xxii, xxiii, 65

Ethnic Ministries Council EMC, 151, 205, 228–9

feminism, xxviii, 139, 146, 156, 174

Findlay, Clair, 113, 114–18, 125

Foote, William Rufus, 59, 233

French Canadians, 7, 8, 53, 147, 190, 197

friendship, 20, 99–101, 103, 156, 160

Gale, James Scarth, 6, 100, 237

gender issues, 91, 106, 156, 204, 224, 225, 231; gendered third space, *see* third space

General Assembly, pre-war Korean Presbyterian church, 73

General Assembly, post-war PCK, 73, 75

General Assembly, PROK, 56, 73, 74, 75, 78, 88, 98, 108–9, 116, 117, 119, 121, 137

General Council, UCC, 83, 89, 124, 191, 192–3, 196, 204, 210, 214, 225, 226, 229

Grierson, Robert, 48–50, 52, 59, 61

Hamkyeong Province, 35, 38, 46, 64, 157, 199

Hammond, Morley, 102, 114

han, 143, 151, 157, 228, 273n92

hangeul, 42–3, 235

Hanguk Seminary, xxv, 10, 68, 72–3, 75, 84, 108, 118, 137, 147, 182, 255n57. *See also* Joseon Seminary; Hanshin University

Hanshin University, 10

Hawley, Morley, 78–9, 86

Heritage Ontario, 190–1

Heungnam exodus, 199

historical criticism. *See* biblical interpretation

Hockin, Katharine, 76–7

immigration: and Canada, 9, 15, 23, 77, 106, 129, 182–3, 197, 208, 231, 282n13; and Koreans, 22, 24, 120, 179–81, 210; and Japanese, 189; and Manchuria, 32–3

imperialism, 14, 52, 63, 77, 97, 104, 128, 140, 146

Imun Dong, 22, 155, 161–5

Independence movement (Korean), xvi, xvii, xix, xxi, xxii, 6, 18, 35, 38, 40–2, 44, 51–2, 64, 75, 134, 168, 170

Indigenous history in Canada, 5, 7, 8, 9, 12, 13, 48, 49, 52, 53, 190, 191, 192–3, 197, 213, 228, 239

Iri farm, 111–19, 121, 125

Irwin, Milton Macdonald and Alice, 112

Jay, Douglas, 147

Jeon Taek-bo, 183

Jeong Byeong-tae, 40–1, 43, 71, 184, 247n64

Index

Jeong Hak-pil, 183, 238
Jesa, 43–4, 205, 236
Joint Board, 85, 88, 95
Joseon Seminary, xx, 10, 19, 67–75, 182, 255n57. *See also* Hanguk Seminary; Hanshin University

Kando, xxii, xxiii, 31–2, 34–42, 45–52, 54–5, 58, 65, 68, 70, 72, 85, 144–5, 184, 230, 239, 244n2, 246n38, 255n54
Kang In-cheol, 73, 74, 92, 95, 107, 123, 134–5
Kang, Wi Jo, 130, 172
Kang Won Yong, 72, 110
Kernen, Willa, xiii, xxvii, xxviii, 77, 110, 112, 123, 159, 163–7, 170, 173–4, 277n29, 279n61
Kidogkyo Sasang. See *Christian Thought* (journal)
Kim Chai Choon, xx, xxii, xxv, 19, 56–7, 63–5, 67–74, 78, 84, 88, 100, 105, 130, 133, 160, 171, 181, 196
Kim, Charles, 86
Kim Chi Ha, 167
Kim Dae Jung, 10, 169, 173, 196, 212, 279n72
Kim Ikseon, 44, 100,
Kim Sang-geun, 121, 123
Kim Shin Mook, xvii, xix, 4, 37–8, 41, 43, 65, 137, 184
Kim Sun-Chul, 146
Kim Yakyeon, xviii, xix, xx, xxiii, 40, 44, 139, 236, 246n49
Koo, Hagen, 160–1
Korea Mission (UCC), xx, xxxii, 7, 10, 17, 21, 26, 56, 58, 72, 75–6, 79, 83–5, 87–92, 96, 99, 101, 103, 104, 107–14, 118, 121,
124, 126, 128–9, 166, 183, 185, 195, 229, 249n105
Korean Central Intelligence Agency (KCIA), 164, 167, 171, 196, 200, 216
Korean Presbyterian Church, xxiv, 19, 56, 58–9, 63–4, 66, 71, 74, 75–6, 78, 88
Korean War, xxvi, 9, 13, 18, 26, 72, 76, 78, 111–12, 182, 199, 202, 255n57
Kwok Pui Lan, 146

Lee, Irene (Chunghwa), 27, 114, 208, 218, 223, 232
Lee Nam Kyoo, 98–100
Lee Oo Chung, xxviii, 72, 132, 137, 139, 144, 156, 158, 163, 167–8, 170–3, 196, 212, 225
Lee, Sang Chul, xxii, xxix, xxxii, 17, 26–7, 40, 132, 179, 181, 183–4, 186–7, 189, 193, 194, 195–9, 201, 206, 215, 217–19, 221, 224–5. 230, 233, 234, 238–9
Lee, Timothy, 44, 95, 130, 133
Lee Young Min, 89, 109–10, 116–18, 121–2, 127
LGBTQ Christians, 224–5
liberation theology, 142, 146, 147, 150, 213, 272n82
Livingston, Elsie, xiii, xxxi, 159, 209, 210–14
Lungtsingchun/Lungchingtun. *See* Yongjeong

McKenzie, William, 45–6, 249n105
Mackay, Stan, 193, 213–14, 228
Manchuria, xvi, xvii, xxii, xxiii, 3, 5, 6, 18, 26–8, 38–52, 65, 70 85, 100, 108, 111–12, 118, 138,

145, 181, 183–5, 188, 197, 199,
   202, 221–2, 238–9, 259n18,
   275n3, 278n51
Mansfield, J.D., xxvii, 47,
   111–12, 120
Martin, Stanley, 51, 112, 259n18
marxism, 141, 142, 146, 272n82
minjok, 140–2, 237
minjung, 140–1, 142, 145–6, 151,
   228, 237
Minjung Movement, 142, 147,
   150, 172
Minjung theologians, xxii, 42, 142–
   6, 147, 152, 157, 164, 278n51
Minjung theology, 21, 45, 120,
   127, 128–9, 133, 142–53, 164,
   198, 205, 213, 228, 238, 272n82
Mission and Education Centre
   (MEC), 120, 137–40, 141, 144,
   147, 152–3, 166, 278n51
Missionary Congress (Canada), 49,
   50, 53, 60
Mission Magazine (United Church
   of Canada), 208, 210, 216–17
missionaries: American, 19, 24, 56,
   60, 61, 63, 67–9, 72–3, 119;
   Catholic, 43; Methodist, 40, 46,
   59, 71, 136; as model citizens,
   87; paternalism, 20, 62, 84,
   93–4, 101, 118, 133, 180, 223;
   Presbyterian, 19, 47, 73; pro-
   Japanese, 51, 52, 66, 92, 135;
   protection against Japanese
   oppression, xxi, 8, 48, 51, 222;
   women, xxviii, 20, 21, 22, 90,
   154–9, 161, 165
Moltmann, Jürgen, 146, 153
Moon Chai Rin, xvii, xix, 4, 37–40,
   43–4, 52, 62–3, 65, 70, 75, 119,
   137, 171, 184–5, 222, 278n51

Moon Dong Hwan, xxii, 65, 71,
   137, 196
Moon Ik Hwan, xvi, xvii, xix, xxii,
   65, 71, 137, 165, 167, 278n51
mosaic society, 189
multiculturalism, 13, 190–1, 194,
   197, 207
mutuality, the missiology of, 20, 83,
   93, 110–11
Myeongdong (Manchuria): church,
   xix; school, 40–1, 70, 184; village, xix, 40–1, 44, 184, 236
Myeongdong Cathedral (Seoul),
   167, 169–70

nationalism, 26, 27, 38, 42–5,
   50–4, 65, 140, 142, 145, 189,
   234, 236–8
Nevius method, 59
New York Times, 130, 158, 170,
   172
Ng, Wenh In, 15, 53, 183, 205,
   228, 238
non-Korean UCC members, 22,
   209, 218, 230–1
North Korea, xxxii, 108, 112, 124,
   134, 162, 183, 184, 210, 217,
   231, 237–8, 244n2, 249n104

Observer (United Church of
   Canada magazine), 179, 109,
   125, 179, 213, 214, 228
Orange Lodge, 7, 48

Pacific War, xxvi, 7, 8, 19, 26, 70–1,
   85, 112, 137
Paik Lak-Geoon, 42, 46, 59, 60,
   119, 132–3
Park Chung Hee, 20, 21, 36, 87,
   104–6, 120, 125, 129–30, 133,

134, 146, 149, 151, 158, 167, 172, 182, 200

Park Hyung Gyu, 130

partnership, missiology of, 7, 20, 83, 96–8, 101, 103, 227

People's Army (North Korean military), 72, 112

People's Revolutionary Party PRP, 15, 162, 196

Pope, Marion, viii, 28, 77, 112, 117, 163, 165–8, 173, 174, 277n29

Porter, John, 189

postcolonialism, 13–14, 16, 105, 128–9, 142, 146, 147, 150, 155–6, 234

Pratt, Mary Louis, 16, 244, 251n140

Presbyterian Church in Canada (PCC), 48, 49, 186, 225

Presbyterian Church in Korea PCK, 15, 19, 56, 73, 74, 75, 84, 108, 160, 185, 215

Presbyterian Church in the Republic of Korea PROK, 11, 10, 15, 20–2, 25, 27, 10, 19, 20, 55–8, 73–6, 78, 79, 84, 85, 88, 89, 91, 92, 94–8, 101, 102, 103–5, 107, 108–11, 114–29, 135, 137, 139, 157, 166, 180, 182, 185, 195, 204, 215, 218, 225, 230, 235

Pyeongyang Seminary, 19, 58, 59, 61, 62, 65, 66, 68, 71

Qing dynasty, 31, 33

racialized people, 151, 183, 193, 205, 207

racism, 9, 11, 23, 50, 77, 101, 150, 180, 187, 189, 190–192, 194, 195, 203–7, 213, 226, 228, 239

Report of the Commission on World Mission, 83, 89, 129, 147, 213–14

residential schools, 8, 13, 52, 129, 193, 194, 197

revivalism, 130–5; 1907 Revival, 132–3

reunification, 10, 87, 156, 172, 218

Reynolds, W.D., 59, 60

Rhee Syng Man, 20, 85–6, 258n8

Robb, Alec F., 59

Robb, Ian, 87, 136, 160

Roberts, Dana, 101

Ross, John, 42,

Russia, 26, 33, 34, 35, 36, 47, 70, 85, 95, 210

Salter, Dean, 148, 269, 274

Sanderson, Mary, 210, 219–21, 223, 227, 230–1

Sarangbang Church, 161, 164, 165, 167, 174, 278

Schofield, Frank, 168, 237, 242, 263–6, 279

Scott, William, xviii, 4, 45, 46, 51, 60–3, 65–7, 71, 73, 74, 84, 99, 154, 160, 233, 242, 245, 252n144, 263n94, 275n1

Second generation Korean immigrants, 208, 223

Seo Dong-Chun, 271, 199–202

Seo Sang-yun, 42

Severance Hospital, 6, 87, 111, 168, 259n18

Seungjin, 64, 65, 112

Shepherd, Loraine Mackenzie, 15

Index

Shinto obeyance, 19, 64, 65–7, 68, 75, 79, 255n54
Silhak, 17, 38, 39, 40, 43, 44, 139, 246n48, 246–7n49
sin, the charge of, 88, 93, 143
Social Gospel, 94
socialism, 52, 141
Song Chang-geun, 61, 64, 68, 72
Sorae, 45, 46, 248n78, 249n107, 250n111
Speer, Robert E., 50, 60
Steveston United Church, 180, 197
Sugirtharajah, R.S., 142, 151, 272, 274, 275
Suh Nam Dong, 137, 142, 143, 148, 152, 164, 165, 196, 273, 275, 279
Swallen, W.L., 61–3, 254

Talbot, Patti, 179, 210, 225–6, 230, 281, 288
"Theological Declaration of Korean Christians," 130
theology: conservative, 45, 63, 68, 74, 91, 149, 204, 221, 227; liberal, 12, 623, 68, 74, 91, 94, 132, 143, 213, 221; liberation, 142, 146, 147, 150, 213, 272n82; Minjung, 21, 45, 120, 127, 128–9, 133, 142–53, 164, 198, 205, 213, 228, 238, 272n82
Third Day, 133
third space, xii, 16, 21, 154–9, 161, 165, 170, 174, 175, 235, 239
Thomas, Wilna, xxvi, 20, 89–97, 99, 102, 115, 212, 224–5, 227
Thursday Prayer Meeting, 162–4
Toronto Korean United Church (TKUC), 15, 22, 23, 107, 171,

179, 182–8, 190–1, 195–6, 199–200, 203, 207, 210, 219–24

United Church Women (UCW), 187, 211, 213, 218, 281n95
United Nations, 78, 149, 182
Urban Industrial Mission (UIM), 95, 160, 276n21
United States Army Military Government in Korea (USAMGIK), 15, 85–6, 107

Victory Shawl, xiii, xxxi, 159, 172–4, 209, 211–13, 281n94

Wells, Kenneth, 172, 279n71, 280n84
White people, 77, 179, 190, 205
Wilson, Lois, 23, 90, 159, 209, 214–19, 230, 246n43, 276n18, 287n20, 287n34, 287n39, 287n43
World Council of Churches (WCC), 75, 94, 158, 168, 171, 191, 196, 202, 215, 217
Women's Missionary Society (WMS), 86, 89, 90, 211
Women's National Assembly of the Presbyterian Church USA, 212
Wright, Robert, 12, 50, 52, 76, 77, 92

Yang Jeong-shin, 204
Yi dynasty, 38, 42, 128, 255n57
Yi Gwang-il, 120
Yongjeong, xxi, xxii, 4, 18, 35, 41, 44, 47, 65, 70, 71, 112, 137, 139, 184, 185, 245n16, 249n97, 250n114, 278n51

Yonsei University, 6, 199, 259n18, 267n67, 268n12

Young, Russell, 114–16, 125, 266n57, 268n87

Young Women's Christian Association (YWCA), 215–16

Yun Dongju, xvi, xxii, 3–4, 28, 241n1, 247n62

Yushin Constitution, 129, 163, 200